NEW VIEWS: A MOSAIC SERIES IN LITERATURE
No. 14

New Views of
THE
EUROPEAN NOVEL

Edited

by

R. G. Collins

and

Kenneth McRobbie

University of Manitoba Press
Winnipeg 19, Canada
1972

MOSAIC

A Journal for the Comparative Study of Literature and Ideas

V/3 SPRING, 1972

Editors

R. G. Collins   Kenneth McRobbie

Review Editor
Ralph T. Berry

Associate Editor
Robert E. Finnegan

Editorial Board
C. A. E. Jensen (*Chairman*), Ralph T. Berry, H. Bessason, R. G. Collins, W. J. Condo, P. M. Daly, Robert E. Finnegan, André Joubert, Alan A. Klass, Kenneth McRobbie, R. P. O'Kell, G. Swinton.

Advisory Board
William Arrowsmith, *Middlebury, Vermont*
Geoffrey Durrant, *University of British Columbia*
George Ford, *University of Rochester*
Northrop Frye, *Victoria College, University of Toronto*
Maurice Lebel, *Université Laval*
József Lengyel, *Budapest*
Frederic Samson, *Royal College of Art, London*
Antoni Słonimski, *Warsaw*
George Whalley, *Queen's University, Kingston*
E. Mary Wilkinson, *University College, London*

Administrative Assistant
Elizabeth Kischuk

Editorial Assistant
Terry Fitzgerald

Articles on subjects in the general area of literature and ideas as well as on the themes selected for specific issues should be addressed to The Editor, MOSAIC, Box 2 Administration Building, The University of Manitoba, Winnipeg, R3T 2N2, Canada.

Articles printed in English and French (the two official languages of Canada); all others in translation.

Review articles by invitation only.

Second class mail registration number 1461.

Subscriptions: $6.00 one year (4 issues), $11.00 two years (8 issues), single copies, $1.75 (Cheques payable to The University of Manitoba should be addressed to the Business Manager, MOSAIC). Special issues hard bound $4.95.

MOSAIC is subsidized in part by a grant from The Canada Council.

All articles that appear in MOSAIC are listed under the PMLA Abstract System.

U.S. distribution through: B. DeBoer, 188 High Street, Nutley, New Jersey 07110.

Printed by Hignell Printing Ltd., Winnipeg, Manitoba, Canada.

All illustrations in this collection are from the series "Squares and Streets in the City," by Professor V. J. Kostka, (Head of the Department of City Planning at the University of Manitoba) from whom the originals are available.

CONTENTS

New Views of The European Novel

PREFACE

*The present collection of "New Views of the European Novel" was con-
ceived as a companion group to the selection entitled "New Views of the
English and American Novel," published by MOSAIC last spring. From the
beginning, however, (as certain basic differences in the two channels revealed
themselves), it became apparent that the intended parallelism could not be
achieved. The "European Novel," as here covered, is not comprehensive in
any sense, of course; on the contrary, all of the essays deal with either French,
German, Italian or—in one solitary instance—Scandinavian writers. A collection, "New Views of the Eastern European Imagination in Literature,"
now in preparation under the hand of Kenneth McRobbie and due to appear
next year, will cover some of the gaps. Nonetheless, however wide the sweep,
it is clear that there is no possible way that a measured view of the European
Novel as such can be offered. To start with, the novel in Europe in the
twentieth century has a far more intellectual function on the whole than its
counterpart in English. From the beginning, the novel in France and Germany
has unabashedly subjected its readers to the rigours of complex thought.
While the borderlines of the recent English novel merge with those of poetry,
as has often of late been pointed out, the distinctions between the essay as
genre, philosophy as a mental discipline, and fantasy as narrative had as early
as the eighteenth century disappeared within the capacious folds of the
European novel. If the European novel has been entertainment, it has been
far more complex and demanding than diversionary in nature. Heir of early
novelistic traditions from the picaresque to the* Bildungsroman, *the novel
in Europe has regarded itself with high seriousness and does so even today.
When one compares the great novelists of the English tradition—Fielding,
Dickens, Conrad, D. H. Lawrence, to select at random and with Joyce
obviously omitted—with Goethe, Balzac, Flaubert, Mann, Sartre, the differences leap forth: the attitude towards the fictional matter, or story, the
consciousness of the artist as creator, the ordering of events to yield philosophical or social relationships far in excess of the narrative requirements.
The novel, to a greater extent on the Continent, has achieved artistic greatness while retaining its tie to biography, to the exemplum, and to the dis-
quisition, at the same time that it has been capable of a bold aesthetic
conviction beside which the English novel seems cautious and conservative.*

*The task of paralleling the English and American novel on one hand, and
the European novel, on the other, is difficult, then, because the continental
novel fills territory that the English novel leaves largely unoccupied. Moreover, criticism of the continental novel is itself apt to approximate creative
expression, since the boundaries of the genre are so expanded. Particularly
in recent years, the mental cosmography of the artist has been seen as parallel
to the universe that must be explored—Proust and Gide (and here we must
also acknowledge Joyce) see the aesthetic consciousness of the artist as the
key to discovery of that harmony for which all separate and imperfect things
search. But before them, Goethe and Flaubert look in different corners for
what may be very much the same thing; while a dialectical conception of*

harmony sees opposites—a rigorous consciousness of death as redemptive, for instance—as creating a tension whereby life endures and even flowers. Mann and Nietzsche may differ, but they meet to do so. It is both a retreat and an advance to move on to Sartre and Robbe-Grillet and Pinget who seek in their separate ways to validate a point of observation, using question as progress towards answer.

The European novel is complicated, then, in ways perhaps no more artistic than the English novel but certainly more diversified. The ten essays on French literature presented here range from the high romanticism of Rousseau to the high "post-classicism" of Flaubert, the stylized art of Zola, the homely craft of Vallès, the delicate artifice of Cocteau, the questions of Sartre, down to the oscillating surfaces of Pinget, all the way down to Claude Mauriac viewing himself and his own art, writing in his Paris home especially for this collection as recently as only a few weeks before it goes to press. Of the eight articles on German literature, two return to Goethe and see the eighteenth century as anticipating both the concerns and the techniques of the twentieth, while Jack Zipes' survey of the novels of the divided Germanies today raises significant questions for the decades ahead. The masters of the first half of the twentieth century are well represented—Mann, Hesse, Lagerkvist, Sartre— while interest in the nineteenth-century novel obviously continues unabated as attested by other essays here. In brief, while a wide swath is cut by this issue of MOSAIC, its success is to light up its own limitations, to show the incredible richness and diversity of the Continental novel, and to reveal how much more remains unaccounted for.

In preparing this issue I am indebted particularly to Professor André Joubert of the University of Manitoba for his skill in editing and preparing the articles in French, as well as for acting as liaison with some of the authors. This is the largest collection of essays yet to appear at one time under the MOSAIC imprint. For various reasons, many other excellent critical studies had to be omitted. I regret that necessity, but offer the consoling thought that it proves the flourishing state of critical scholarship in the area of the European novel.

April, 1972   R G C

Growing Pains in the Contemporary German Novel— East and West

By JACK D. ZIPES

A hump-backed dwarf who drums up his past adventures in an insane asylum, a hung-up clown who turns beggar, an art thief who steals paintings to protect them from his father, a poor rich boy who cannot come to grips with himself in postwar Germany, a homecoming veteran who still clings to harmful illusions at the end of World War II, a disturbed journalist who questions the development of East German socialism, a young woman whose social vigor is sapped away by a socialist disease, all alienated, all struggling to find roots in the new societies of Germany—these are the "heroes" of the German novel since 1945. They are undeveloped and underdeveloped protagonists whose growing pains reflect the growing pains of the societies around them. German novelists have purposely chosen such "stunted" people as the subjects of their works in order to portray as realistically as possible the enormous developmental problems that have confronted Germans from the postwar reconstruction period to the present. In particular, they have all experimented in one way or another with the *Entwicklungsroman* (the novel of development) to demonstrate why the traditional initiation process no longer works in East or West Germany: whereas the bourgeois initiation ritual and humanistic ideals were at the center of the classic *Entwicklungsroman* from the late eighteenth century up through Thomas Mann's *The Magic Mountain* (1924) and Hermann Hesse's *The Glass Bead Game* (1943), negation of bourgeois society, scepticism of socialist society, and alienation are the main themes of the contemporary *Entwicklungsroman*.

Although various studies of the contemporary German novel have noted changes in the *Entwicklungsroman*,[1] there have been few studies that have compared the novel of development in East and West Germany. In fact, there have been very few books in English dealing with East German literature alone,[2] and this is unfortunate since it leads to a distorted view of German literature as a whole. The tendency among English-speaking scholars has been to slight East German literature as well as Austrian and Swiss literature, which are usually considered part of the greater West German cultural empire. However, the literature of these countries demands that sociological distinctions be made if the literary tradition and trends are to be fully understood. The changes in the *Entwicklungsroman* since 1945 prove this point, and I should like to discuss these changes with regard to problems of alienation in East and West Germany, using several novels to demonstrate why the *Entwicklungsroman* has become parodied and reutilized. But before dealing specifically with the novels, it is necessary to make a few remarks about the tradition of the German novel of development.

German critics have used such terms as *Entwicklungsroman, Bildungsroman*, and *Erziehungsroman* to define the novel of development, and their definitions generally depend on their concepts of development, education, and upbringing.[3] Often the differences are semantic. No matter what term is used, they all refer to the same literary tradition, which includes Karl Philipp Moritz's *Anton Reiser* (1785-90), Wieland's *Agathon* (1766, 1773, 1794), Goethe's *Wilhelm Meister's Apprenticeship* (1795-6), Karl Immermann's *Epigonen* (1836), Gottfried Keller's *Green Heinrich* (1854, 1880), Adalbert Stifter's *Nachsommer* (1857), Wilhelm Raabe's *Der Hungerpastor* (1864),

---

[1](For clarity's sake I have used the English titles of the German novels that have been translated and are fairly well known. In all other cases I use the German title and supply a translation in parenthesis. All translations in the text are my own unless otherwise indicated). There are numerous short essays on particular novels. For the two best general studies, see Hans Mayer, "Deutsche Literatur seit Thomas Mann," *Zur deutschen Literatur der Zeit* (Reinbek bei Hamburg, 1967), pp. 261-393, and Frank Trommler, "Der zögernde Nachwuchs: Entwicklungsprobleme der Nachkriegsliteratur in Ost und West," *Tendenzen der deutschen Literatur seit 1945*, ed. Thomas Koebner (Stuttgart, 1971), pp. 1-116.

[2]There are three which are all uneven in their approach: Peter Demetz, *Postwar German Literature* (New York, 1970); John Flores, *Poetry in East Germany: Adjustments, Visions, and Provocations 1945-1970* (New Haven, 1971); Theodore Huebener, *The Literature of East Germany* (New York, 1970).

[3]Lothar Köhn gives the most thorough account about the problem of definition in "Entwicklungs- und Bildungsroman. Ein Forschungsbericht," *Deutsche Vierteljahrsschrift*, 42 (1968), pp. 427-473, 590-632.

Thomas Mann's *The Magic Mountain* (1924), and Hermann Hesse's *The Glass Bead Game* (1943) among the more outstanding examples. Though the list may vary, most German critics would agree with Roy Pascal, who states that

> the 'Bildungsroman' is the representation of an arduous journey out of inwardness into social activity, out of subjectivity into objectivity, and for this reason it is 'the German species of the modern novel.' The theme is not absent from the literature of other peoples, but it is central and predominant only in the German novel. The 'Bildungsroman' is peculiarly German, too, in that it deals essentially only with the weaning of heroes from their inwardness, with their spiritual preparation for social life, and stops or falters when they actually enter upon it.[4]

Strictly speaking, the German novel of development, as a product of the eighteenth-century Enlightenment, is a bourgeois art form: the prosaic epic structure has evolved so as to reflect the difficulties encountered by bourgeois heroes (from childhood to early adulthood) who struggle to fulfill an inner calling within a society that appears at first to be hostile to that calling. Almost all of the German *Entwicklungsromane* evince a similar pattern. During adolescence the bourgeois protagonist feels compelled to rebel against his parents and upbringing in order to gain a sense of his inner mission, and sometimes he is even forced to leave his original habitat. He wanders and has numerous adventures which bring out his best qualities. During maturation he becomes more confident of his abilities and of the role he can play within the social establishment. Finally, he decides to re-enter bourgeois society with a clear understanding of the social demands and of his ideals and capabilities.

Often the development of the protagonist is organic, as in *Wilhelm Meister*. The hero unfolds like a sensitive plant when acted upon by outside forces. Or the protagonist himself is the catalytic agent, struggles against outside forces, makes numerous mistakes, and learns from his errors. No matter how, the hero grows—and he always grows morally, spiritually, and idealistically. The assumption is made that he is *free* to grow once he recognizes his innate talents and cultivates them in harmony with the highest humanitarian precepts of the bourgeoisie. Growth is linked to a bourgeois concept of freedom and humanitarianism, which is at odds with that of the aristocracy. Important here is the stress on individualism in relation to the entrepreneurism of early capitalism and on the growing acceptance of the bourgeois principles of life tied to the Protestant ethic. On the one hand, the protagonist of the *Entwicklungsroman* celebrates bourgeois industriousness, moral decency, liberalism, and inventiveness. On the other, he is critical of crass utilitarianism, philistinism, and exploitation of oppressed classes. The process of his own cultivation suggests means by which all members of society can be cultivated. His return into the fold of bourgeois society is predicated on his belief that he can further his own growth and contribute to the growth of broad humanitarian values in a bourgeois society.

As Pascal has noted, the hero stands at the threshold of a new life at

---

[4]*The German Novel*, (Manchester, 1956), p. 299.

the end of the novel. The ending of a German *Entwicklungsroman* is both the final step of an initiation process and the beginning of active social participation which will affirm the highest ideological principles of bourgeois liberalism. This was characteristic of the *Entwicklungsroman* up through 1945. Even during the Nazi period, both in fascist Germany and in the emigration, German novelists wrote *Entwicklungsromane*, which were, of course, diametrically opposed in their political and philosophical views concerning the development of their protagonists,[5] but they all emphasized initiation and integration: the culmination of the hero's development is revealed through his final awareness that he must play an active role in society in conformity with higher ideals esteemed by the more cultivated leaders of that society.

This emphasis on initiation is abandoned in the postwar period. Most fittingly, it is Thomas Mann who sounded the death knell of the traditional *Entwicklungsroman*. His last great novel, *The Confessions of Felix Krull* (1954), though generally considered to be a picaresque novel,[6] is very much within the tradition of the German *Entwicklungsroman*. In fact, it relies on the classical pattern of the *Entwicklungsroman* to illustrate the anachronism of the forms and ideas of bourgeois society; through parody the *Entwicklungsroman* is turned in against itself. Though Mann actually began the novel before World War I and though it deals with that early epoch, it is significant that he felt drawn to the material once more in the early 1950's and that he never finished the novel. Mann saw that the problematic quality of his material was related to the contemporary situation of the two Germanies, and he had no answer for solving that situation. Felix Krull "develops" into a con artist and stands outside bourgeois society with no intention or real desire to become a member in good standing. He is fully alienated from the mores and customs of bourgeois society, and at most Krull can play superficially and trick people who cherish him as an art figure[7] and cling to their decadence like a prized possession. At times it appears as though most of the ultra-typical aristocratic and bourgeois characters have been lobotomized so that Felix Krull can appear ultra-human. But the truth of the matter is that Krull is just as much a victim of the bourgeois conditioning process as they are. He is not a genuine artist—he is a con artist, and the only difference between him and the other characters of the novel is that he is simply more aware of his alienation.

In essence, Krull cannot grow. His artistic talents are drained and warped by people and conditions around him. His play is juvenile and auto-erotic, and he becomes a caricature of the commercial artist who sells himself to the highest bidder and gains no real sense of pleasure through his work. As con artist, his situation anticipates that of the bourgeois artist-heroes in the post-

---

[5]See Lionel Richard, *Nazisme et littérature* (Paris, 1971); Heinz D. Osterle, "The Other Germany: Resistance to the Third Reich in German Literature," *German Quarterly*, XLI (1968), pp. 1-22.

[6]Many of the novels of development could be considered picaresque novels. See Norbert Schöll, "Der pikarische Held: Wiederaufleben einer literarischen Tradition nach 1945," *Tendenzen der deutschen Literatur seit 1945*, ed. Thomas Koebner, (Stuttgart, 1971), pp. 302-321.

[7]For a discussion of the art figure, see Hans Mayer, "Günter Grass and Thomas Mann: Aspects of the Novel," *Steppenwolf and Everyman*, trans. Jack D. Zipes, (New York, 1971), pp. 181-199.

war *Entwicklungsromane* written by the West German novelists Günter Grass, Heinrich Böll, Martin Walser, Siegfried Lenz, and others. Though less characteristic of the novels of development in East Germany, *Felix Krull* does, however, introduce the same element of problem that has become the predominant concern of East and West German writers—alienation.

Some of the conditions between 1933-1945 which fostered alienation, such as fascism, exile, war, enslavement, and imprisonment, are apparent. However, the restructuring of the two Germanies has brought about new modes of manipulation and exploitation that lead to the encapsulation and fragmentation of the individual. In order to expose these modes, East and West German novelists address themselves to the peculiar difficulties of social and political reorganization within their societies, and the *Entwicklungsroman* has been regarded as the most appropriate "Germanic" genre for reflecting upon and criticizing conditions which have stifled human freedom and growth in different socio-political systems. The prose styles and patterns of the contemporary novels of development reveal how closely the aesthetics of the works are bound to the authors' concern with alienation. The story-lines are generally fragmented. Flashbacks and anecdotes suggest an uneven development. The tone is often documentary—stand-offish, cold, objective. It is as if the author were purposely separating himself from his product by creating a grotesque mask or an anonymous reporter. In this way the very activity of writing the novel is alienated activity, corresponding to the alienated activity of the story. The dry, ironic atmosphere is not a tone conducive to growth and sympathy. However, it does tend toward a critical appraisal of society: the alienation is paradoxically intended to contribute to the growth of the reader. In other words, the alienation within the story and the alienation of the narrator from his work and from the reader are meant to provoke the reader to think about means to deal with and overcome alienation.

Generally speaking, the contemporary German *Entwicklungsroman* is an episodic, realistic representation of a protagonist's growing alienation and his refusal to comply with the socio-economic pressures that lead to one type of reification or another. The traditional novel of development undergoes either parody (in the West) or reutilization[8] (in the East). The protagonist's awareness of his alienation becomes a measure of his humanity; and his resistance to it, a guideline for establishing standards for real growth.

Before turning to contemporary novels of development, I want to be more explicit about my conception of the term alienation. As Bertell Ollman has pointed out in his book *Alienation: Marx's Conception of Man in Capitalist Society*, alienation has always existed in one form or another, but it is necessary to distinguish the forms as they evolve in different systems. In capitalism, alienation stems from the fact that

> labor is still productive activity performed in the service of someone else, a response to external pressures rather than the fulfillment of a need. The product is still one from which the worker is cut off, and whose misunderstood needs he must seek to satisfy. The resulting relations

---

[8]In East Germany the term *Umfunktionierung* (reutilization) has become a standard expression. It is employed in a socialist sense: to take and use the best of bourgeois and capitalist developments and turn them around so that they function for socialism.

between people in the same class and between classes are still dominated by competition after jobs, goods and money.

Evidence of these alienated relations can be found throughout capitalist society. In every area of life, man remains an object of manipulation by others and by his own products. As a producer, he is told when, where and how to work. As a consumer, he is told what to buy and how to use it.[9]

In countries where the state controls the means of production, there is a qualitative difference to the alienation, but essentially all relations remain alienated because "labor is still productive activity in the service of someone else." Here it is the state which is controlled by elite groups, and the state as an apparatus is separate and alien to the people; it has acquired a life and movement of its own which cannot be subject to man's will.

Alienation in the affluent society of capitalist West Germany and alienation in the planned socio-economic system of socialist East Germany take various shapes and form different relations in all spheres of life. The German novels of development mirror these alienated shapes and relations, and I want to begin by studying the types of alienation in the West German novels, since they are more directly connected to the example of *Felix Krull*. Here, three works are more characteristic of the general trend: Günter Grass's *The Tin Drum* (1959), Heinrich Böll's *The Clown* (1963), and Siegfried Lenz's *The German Lesson* (1968). After examining these works, the following East German novels will be analyzed: Dieter Noll's *Die Abenteuer des Werner Holt* (*The Adventures of Werner Holt,* 1960, 1963), Max Walter Schulz's *Wir sind nicht Staub im Wind* (*We're Not Dust in the Wind,* 1962), Hermann Kant's *Die Aula* (*The Auditorium,* 1965), and Christa Wolf's *The Quest for Christa T.* (1968).

At one point in his long, droll narrative, Oskar Matzerath, the thirty-year-old hunch-backed dwarf, who is locked in an insane asylum for allegedly killing a nurse, makes the following remark:

I remained the three-year-old, the gnome, the Tom Thumb, the pigmy, the Lilliputian, the midget, whom no one could persuade to grow.... I remained the precocious three-year-old, towered over by grown-ups but superior to all grown-ups, who refused to measure his shadow with theirs, who was complete both inside and outside, while they, to the very brink of the grave, were condemned to worry their heads about 'development,' who had only to confirm what they were compelled to gain by hard and often painful experience, and who had no need to change his shoe and trouser size year after year just to prove that something was growing.[10]

Obviously, Grass and his little Oskar are toying with us. Like Felix Krull, Oskar is a con artist and an art figure, not to be trusted. Yet, his perspective is the only one we have, and we must accept and understand it for what it is—the voice of the alienated artist, who has become dysfunctional and worries most about survival. Consequently, Oskar's precocious and creative talents

---

[9]Ollman, *Alienation* (Cambridge, England, 1971), pp. 244-5.
[10]*The Tin Drum*, trans. Ralph Manheim, (New York, 1962), pp. 53-4.

are used as weapons to fend people off, to manipulate, destroy, exploit, maneuver, and irritate. As an artist, Oskar is largely negative, and yet, because he negates, we gain a thorough understanding of the warped times and the conditions which bring about warped attitudes.

Parodying the typical *Entwicklungsroman*, Oskar narrates the history of his ancestors and then takes us to Danzig of the 1930's. He reveals that he stopped growing because he did not want to become a grocer like his father. Instead he developed his artistic powers: his drumming captivates people; his voice can destroy objects because of its high pitch. These powers enable him to extricate himself from dangerous encounters with the Nazis. Once the city becomes occupied by the Germans, Oskar goes on tour of the western front with a troupe of acrobats to entertain the German troops, and he is almost trapped during the invasion of Normandy. At this point he decides to return to Danzig, and he becomes the leader of a gang of hoodlums who pull off many robberies in the city. After the death of his father, which coincides with the downfall of the Nazis, Oskar begins to grow, and he is taken to a hospital in Düsseldorf by his step-mother Maria. In postwar West Germany he involves himself in black market activities, takes a job as a model, plays the drum in a jazz group, and finally, until his imprisonment, becomes a solo performer earning a great deal of money by drumming up the past.

Throughout his adventures, Oskar witnesses and causes death without remorse. He pursues women (especially his step-mother Maria), runs away from the black witch Death, and competes with his rival the Christ Child. All in all, he is really not much different from his fellow citizens. Oskar's amorality, his manipulation of other people, his treating them as objects, his competitive urge—all these activities are alienated activities. His imprisonment in a mental sanitorium is symbolically the highest stage of development he can reach in West German society. It is there that he grows a little more by playing with his drum. In other words, in a state of auto-eroticism Oskar derives pleasure merely from his fantasies and wish-fulfillments. There is no meaningful social intercourse. There are no real prospects that he will be able to nurture his creative gifts so that he can truly develop and gain a sense of himself *in* society. Oskar remains a symbol of the economic miracle in postwar capitalist West Germany—a mutation.

The situation of Hans Schnier in Heinrich's Böll's *The Clown* is not much better. The main difference is that Schnier has more candor and is more honest. Otherwise, he, too, is as twisted and deformed as Oskar. He, too, pursues a Marie, and his Virgin Mary complex is related to his problems with the Catholic Church.[11] Though a Protestant, Hans is an extremely moral and religious person. His first person narrative (like *The Tin Drum*) can be read as the confession of a holy sinner. Ironically the total count of his sins adds up to an accusation against the Church and the operations of capitalists in West Germany.

Böll's narrative technique in *The Clown* is reminiscent of J. D. Salinger's *The Catcher in the Rye*. This is no coincidence: Böll helped his wife in the translation of Salinger's novel about the same time he wrote *The Clown*. Like

---

[11]Both Böll and Grass are Catholic and have endeavored to come to terms with their Catholicism in their works.

Holden Caulfield, Hans Schnier is the son of rich parents with whom he cannot communicate. He has been sent off to private schools, never finishes his education, constantly tries to recall the saintly memory of his dead sister Henrietta (with Holden it is a brother), is forthright in his fight against phoniness and prostitution, and desperately seeks human contact and sympathy through telephone conversations—the case in both Salinger's *Catcher in the Rye* and *Franny and Zooey.*

Both Salinger and Böll comment on the hopeless situation of a poor rich boy who becomes aware of the emptiness and hypocrisy of his family and social class and does not know how to combat the moral turpitude around him. Salinger leads Caulfield to a mental sanitorium. Böll leads Schnier to the Bonn railroad station where he begs. In both instances, there is very little hope that they will overcome their despair and develop within their respective societies.

More parallels could be drawn between *The Catcher in the Rye* and *The Clown,* but most significant is the fact that Böll, like other West German novelists, is drawn to an American literary tradition of adolescent novels that dates back to *Huckleberry Finn* and that stresses alienation, not initiation. Though twenty-seven years old, Schnier is essentially an adolescent (as is Oskar), and his growth is limited by social conditions which maim him and will continue to do so.

The break with the traditional German *Entwicklungsroman* is apparent. Böll employs the flashback and telephone conversation to allow Schnier to tell us his past history. His career as clown is threatened because he drinks and does not keep in shape. His long relationship with Marie Derkum is at an end because of her greater dedication of Catholicism. Both art and love are impossible for him, and the reasons for this are connected to the rise of affluence in West Germany during the 1950's. Using Bonn, capital of the German Federal Republic as symbolical center, Böll has Schnier trace the continuity between the fascist social order and the reconstructed capitalist system in West Germany by recounting the behavior of his own family and friends. "If our era deserves a name," he says, "it would have to be called the era of prostitution. People are becoming accustomed to the vocabulary of whores."[12] As an artist, Schnier has trained his eye to observe the little things, for he believes that the little things are what make for the terror. He witnesses —and we witness—how people seek to manipulate him for their benefit and pleasure, and how their religious activity, which is largely employed in maintaining the Catholic Church as an institution, is turned against them so that they are forced to negate their best *natural* qualities in the service of nonsense and the clerical hierarchy. Schnier refuses to play their game. This refusal is typical of protagonists in other West German novels of development. It is a sign of the artist's integrity. But, in the end, Schnier gains nothing from this: he has an empty look in his eyes; his face is painted, the "face of a corpse."[13]

The ending of Siegfried Lenz's *The German Lesson* allows for more optimism than Böll's novel, but not much. Siggi Jepsen, a twenty-one-year-old thief who is serving a sentence in a progressive penal institution for stealing

---

[12]*The Clown*, trans. Leila Vennewitz, (New York, 1965), p. 242.
[13]*Ibid.*, p. 224.

paintings, is asked to write an essay on the joys of duty. He needs more than the hour permitted by his German instructor to write the essay. In fact, he needs several months, for the theme demands that he recall his entire past history, which also will explain why he became an art thief. The director of the institution, which is located on an island near Hamburg, complies with Siggi's wishes; and, like Oskar Matzerath, Siggi is kept under lock and key and watched over by a guard, while he writes about the joys of duty and how he "developed" into a thief.

Siggi is actually not much interested in the joyful aspect of fulfilling one's duty, but considerably more concerned with the Eichmann-like aspect of doing one's duty with unswerving loyalty to the state, whether the state be corrupt, exploitative, or whatever.[14] In order to grasp the Eichmann mentality, he brings us back to his hometown, Rugbrüll, in the northernmost part of Germany, during 1943, when his father, the district patrolman, receives the order to put a stop to the painting of his good friend Max Ludwig Nansen, because the Nazis consider his work decadent. Nansen refuses to stop painting, and for the next two years, and even after the war, a battle ensues between the two sly old men. Siggi's father holds to the letter of the law (as though he were its legislator) and confiscates Nansen's paintings whenever he can. He is so dedicated to duty and the state that he sacrifices his human feelings and his family to an abstraction he does not even comprehend. As a consequence, Siggi is drawn more and more to the humanity of Nansen. In order to safeguard Nansen's paintings, he begins to steal them; and even when the war ends and Nansen receives international recognition, Siggi continues to steal until he is finally caught and sent to the penal institution.

Needless to say, Siggi is no ordinary art thief. Like Oskar and Schnier, he is an artist. He has been taught by Nansen to appreciate tone and colors, has done some painting himself, and is an extraordinary writer. His essay or book about "the joys of duty" is basically a vivid, colorful picture of small-town life under fascism and, also, later, of destroyed lives in postwar Hamburg. Siggi has learned from Nansen that seeing means exposing in such a way that one cannot be deceived by illusions; seeing means inventing whatever is needed. His narrative is a necessary invention, a necessary coming to terms with the past, and Siggi sees that he, like many others of his generation, is being punished for the mad patriotism and criminality of his parents. This realization sets him free, and in fact, he is to be released from the institution at the end of the novel. This freedom is a mixed blessing: Siggi is alone and is not prepared to adapt himself to the alienating conditions of West German society. Like Oskar and Schnier, he has only his art and strong social awareness, and he will undoubtedly have to use all his strength (as he did in the past) to keep himself together and contend against the alienating forces which will summon him to rejoice in duty to the state.

---

[14]Ollman sums up the main theme of *The German Lesson* when he states: "To be patriotic is to recognize one's duties not to real living people, but to the abstract community, to the very links of alienation which bind the social whole after the human ties have been cut. ... Other human beings are recognizable only as fellow patriots, only as beings which share the same degrading relations to scraps of paper, a hat, a piece of cloth, a song, a mace. These relations are degrading because they do not exist for the satisfaction of human needs but for the satisfaction of the community which arises out of the destruction of such needs," *Alienation*, pp. 217-18.

In contrast, East German novelists are not so much concerned with the artist as the central protagonist in their novels of development. Nor do they rely as much on first person narrative as they do on third person reportage and stream-of-consciousness. This difference can be seen clearly in Dieter Noll's two volumes of *Die Abenteuer des Werner Holt*. Noll's story begins in 1943 and centers on the tortuous journey that the sixteen-year-old Werner Holt must take to develop a social consciousness that will enable him to free himself from a proclivity toward decadent living. This proclivity has its origins in a bad family life and naturally, as the author presents it, in his declining social class. Werner's parents are divorced because his mother, daughter of a wealthy industrialist, cannot abide the fact that her husband, a chemical scientist, will not put his mind to good use for the Nazi cause. Holt lives alone in a boarding house in a small city of central Germany where he attends the gymnasium. He is estranged from both his mother and father, and he can only gain a sense of himself through his comradeship with his schoolmates and love affairs with different girls and women. In particular, he forms a close relationship to Wolzow, an officer's son, whose life becomes dedicated to militarism and violence. In 1944, Holt, Wolzow, and their friends are commanded to report to an anti-aircraft unit. Later they are sent to Czechoslovakia, where exposure to the brutality of the SS and the senselessness of the war stirs Holt to break with Wolzow and abandon the fascist cause. At the end of the first volume of his adventures, Holt is captured by American troops.

The second volume is concerned largely with Holt's attempt to regain footing in one of the two German societies. First he joins his father in East Germany and tries to re-establish a relationship with Gundel, a young woman whom he had helped during the war. However, Holt becomes jealous of Gundel's new interest in the Communist youth group and her friendship with the youth leader, Schneidereit. In addition, he cannot adjust to the routine of school. Therefore, he decides to leave for Hamburg where his mother is living. No sooner arrived, he finds himself repulsed by the superficiality and coarseness of the upper classes. He seeks escape in the Black Forest of Swabia with a former girl friend who has become a bitter recluse. However, he cannot communicate with her and returns once again to East Germany where he completes high school and makes an endeavor to understand the importance of re-education under socialism. Despite his endeavor, Holt continues to have numerous problems: he looks down upon the organizational work done by Schneidereit; he has little trust in members of the older generation including his father; he betrays the friendship of a young woman involved in an unhappy marriage; he seduces a young girl at the gymnasium. The novel ends with Holt full of guilt and remorse, with the desire to fight against his decadent ways but not entirely confident that he can win, even though he has the aid of both friends and socialist innovations.

Holt does not feel committed to either East or West Germany. The only thing he feels is, paradoxically, his own alienation. Noll's narrative records Holt's struggle to grasp the forces which alienate him, and he gradually comes to understand that these forces emanate from the class nature of society and the destructive nature of capitalism. However, he declares to Gundel: "I read Marx and I understand him more and more. I learn, learn, learn, like Lenin demands, and so gradually, very slowly and imperceptibly, I think a little differently today than the way I thought yesterday, and tomorrow I'll again think a little more differently than I did today. Yes, Gundel, to become a new person . . . But not by a majority decision! To become a new person, that's really a long-term program."[15]

Holt resists party decisions and doctrine, and in this respect he is a negative hero. At the end of the novel of development, Holt still stands outside the growing East German society, and neither the understanding shown by his friends, nor the socialist programs have succeeded in bringing about initiation. Though not stated expressly, Noll appears to insist that the younger generation —actually the generation which has now assumed most of the responsible functions in the German Democratic Republic—will not become socialists until they are led to comprehend the past and experience genuine socialist policy *in practice*, not just in proclamations. This means that the bourgeois reactionary past cannot simply be dismissed, but that socialism involves the mastering of those alienating forces which degrade mankind. Holt symbolizes this past in all its manifold aspects, and the success of East German socialism will be measured to a large extent on its ability to convert him as a negative hero to a new way of life which offsets the alienation that was dominant under capitalism and fascism. In *Die Abenteuer des Werner Holt* integration in the socialist system is still problematic.

The problem is also treated by Max Walter Schulz in *Wir sind nicht Staub im Wind*. Like Noll, Schulz uses a journalistic style; however, he favors the multiple perspective and employs a great deal more stream of consciousness and narrative commentary. His hero, too, is a victim of fascism, and he strives to discover the driving force in life (the wind is used metaphorically throughout the novel to symbolize various forces acting upon the characters). The setting is Germany, 1945. Rudi Hagedorn, twenty-four years old, narrowly escapes a firing squad by deserting his anti-aircraft unit. As the war comes to an end, he manages to return to his home town in the Russian zone with a young woman, Hilde, whom he intends to marry. However, upon his return, he learns that Lea Füssler, a young Jewish woman, with whom he had been infatuated during his youth, has been saved from the concentration camp, and he passionately desires to see her and be with her. Lea is equated with the Diotima of Hölderlin's *Hyperion*; she symbolizes the dream of an idealistic bourgeois culture that had always attracted Rudi, a sanitation worker's son. This infatuation will prove harmful to him as it did in the past, for it ties Rudi to an ideology that has outlived its purposes and makes things unreal for him.

Rudi cannot see this and does not want to break his connection to Lea. It is her cynicism which eventually drives him away; in confusion, Rudi wants to flee his home. The situation becomes even more complicated when Hilde, who is pregnant, decides to leave him. Rudi follows her out of guilt, is almost killed in a train accident, and at the end of the novel, comes to his senses: he hopes to begin teaching at an elementary school and work out his relationship with Hilde. This ending is told in the future tense, and it is not clear whether everything will go as smoothly as predicted. The novel of develop-

---

[15]*Die Abenteuer des Werner Holt*, II, (Berlin, 1964), p. 367.

ment up to this point—as in Noll's work—has depicted how Rudi was victimized by the Nazis and misled by bourgeois aspirations. Just as Werner Holt was not fully capable of mastering his class background, so Rudi is incapable of breaking with the petit bourgeois mode of thinking, which prevents him from committing himself to the new socialist cause. In both cases the heroes are plagued by bad consciences. They see the necessity to break with fascism and bourgeois ideology; yet, they are suspicious of a new socialist order which appears manipulative. The result of the conflict between a need for change and the fear of manipulation is hesitation and scepticism. Rudi wants to be more in touch with himself and his friends, but this good intention to overcome estrangement is the end of part one of an *Entwicklungsroman* which has yet to see the continuation promised by the author.

Significantly, Schulz and Noll have not written the promised sequels to their novels of development, which would have to deal more with the contemporary problems in East Germany and of necessity portray the integration of their protagonists. Otherwise the books would be banned by the state cultural authorities. This is not to say that there can be no criticism of the state. Indeed, one of the more interesting *Entwicklungsromane*, *Die Aula* by Hermann Kant, contains a good deal of criticism of the state, in dealing with the themes of education and alienation. Robert Iswall, a journalist, is asked to deliver a speech in 1961 at the formal closing of one of the Workers and Farmers Colleges (Arbeiter-und-Bauern-Fakultät), which had been temporarily established right after the war to help deprived young men and women of the proletariat to obtain their high school diplomas and then study at the university. Iswall, who had at one time been an electrician, begins to reflect upon the past, and the more he does, the more he is uncertain about what he wants to say about the school, his development, and that of his friends. As Iswall goes through his daily activities, his present thoughts are interwoven with memories of the past, and they center on his four closest friends, Karl-Heinz Riek, Gerd Trullesand, Jakob Filter, and Vera Bilfert, who attended school at Greifswald with him. Actually he is most concerned about the first two, since he knows that Vera and Jakob are settled and relatively happy: Vera is his wife, a practising physician, and Jakob is a leading functionary in the department of forestry.

In Trullesand's case, Iswall has strong guilt feelings because he managed to have Trullesand sent to China for seven years so that he would not be able to compete for Vera's hand. Riek, at that time a mathematician deeply committed to communism, left East Germany after passing his examinations and set up a bar in Hamburg. For Iswall to give the commemoration speech at the school, he must grasp the actions of the past. He meets Trullesand in Jena after ten years and comes to a new understanding with him, although he learns that Trullesand is not entirely happy with his situation. As for Riek, Iswall had met him in Hamburg while covering a story on the flood catastrophes, and he still puzzles over the reasons for Riek having left East Germany. Iswall believes that these reasons must be understood objectively, if East Germany itself is to grow and help its people to develop.

These reasons are never explored in the speech Iswall was to give, for he receives a telegram from the party functionary Meibaum informing him that the commemoration plans have been changed. This telegram hints at the reasons why Riek may have left. Certainly it is symbolic of why growth is hindered in the German Democratic Republic. It is an alienating incident in Iswall's life: the arbitrary manner in which the telegram was sent, and the actions of Meibaum and other party officials, can only create distrust. Meibaum, in particular, represents doctrinaire thinking and narrow-minded pedagogy, which are satirized throughout the novel. As Jost Hermand has noted,[16] Kant attacks the plastic bureaucrats and technocrats who are part of a new elite class. To be sure, Kant's novel is not a devastating critique of these privileged people and the educational process in East Germany, it is more on the order of an essay. Iswall, the central protagonist, who functions in the present, endeavors to cope with the problems of the past in order to improve the future. The dialectics of the narrative structure are related to the theme. Iswall, though alienated, is not completely cut off from his society, and there⹀ fore, he writes about the *dangers* of alienation. While in the third person, the narrative is told entirely from his perspective, and Iswall is not so much hostile as concerned with the possibilities of realizing one's full individual potential within a socialist system. Individuation is contrasted with the general policies and practices of the state, and Iswall seeks to gauge the amount of freedom and the alternatives for individual growth within the East German framework. His own growth and critical consciousness are to be understood as a result of the same conditions which produced the estrangement of his friends Trullesand and Riek. It is because of his knowledge of past mistakes in a transitional social system and of the present dangers of alienation in a bureaucratic socialist system that Iswall is able to continue working in East Germany toward a better future.

The theme of alienation in contemporary East German novels is most pronounced in Christa Wolf's *The Quest for Christa T*. Here, a young woman, as narrator, tries to piece together the life of her friend Christa T., who died of leukemia at the age of thirty-five. We learn that Christa T. experienced the chaos of the Nazi years, fled from her hometown, resettled in East Germany, completed her high school education, studied German literature at the University of Leipzig, became a teacher, left her job because of a clash with bureaucratic regulations, married a veterinarian, and moved to the countryside in Mecklenburg where she had three children and did some writing. Though devoted to her husband, her marriage was not a happy one, and she fell in love with a hunter. Nothing ever developed out of that affair, and nothing ever developed out of Christa T.'s life, which was cut short by cancer.

In outline form, the story seems trivial. There is nothing outstanding or remarkable about Christa T. But, that is exactly the point. Christa Wolf writes about an average woman in East Germany, and she wants to understand why this woman is "drained" of her exuberance for life. In this respect, a disease, leukemia, is used metaphorically, as Solzhenitsyn uses it in *Cancer Ward*: Christa T. is suffering from a social sickness, which emanates from pathological conditions in her society. The narrator of the story feels compelled to analyze this sickness because she, too, may become "infected," and hence, seeks a cure.

As in Kant's *Die Aula*, there is a dialectical relationship established between

---

[16]"Hermann Kant: Die Aula," *Unbequeme Literatur* (Heidelberg, 1971), pp. 176-192.

the narrator and her material. The past life and development of Christa T. are critically examined in the present so that the future may be changed. Using notes and diaries bequeathed her by Christa T., the narrator reconstructs the picture of a woman who had great hopes about contributing as a teacher to socialist development in the German Democratic Republic. However, these hopes were dampened by the hypocrisy and rigidity of petty bureaucrats. As a woman, she felt manipulated, and the result is that Christa T. withdrew into herself, reluctantly, in order to escape being reified by the social system. However, Christa T. never gives up hope for the socialist revolution, as one of her last dreams reveals. She is only overcome by the "disease," and the cure for this disease is partially suggested in the telling of Christa's story:

> One day people will want to know who she was and who it is that's been forgotten. They'll want to see her, and that's only natural. They'll wonder if that other figure was really there, the one we obstinately insist on when we mourn. Then people will have to produce her, create her, for once. So that the doubts may be silenced, so that she may be seen.
> When, if not now?[17]

This refrain, "when, if not now?" occurs throughout the novel, and it becomes clear that the narrator has written about Christa's growing alienation in order to question the conditions which led to her withdrawal and death. This life of an average young woman in East Germany must be made known *now*, because the narrator, as a woman and citizen of the German Democratic Republic, shares the alienation of Christa T. and conveys it continually in her narrative. In this respect the narrative is more of a struggle than a quest, a struggle against the insidious disease which cuts man off from both himself and the rest of mankind.

Both East and West German novelists fight against "disease," and social illness of alienation. The similarities in their novels of development stem from the fact that they are from the same generation and have shared unforgettable experiences during fascist rule, the Second World War, and the chaotic postwar period. Consequently, they all write their *Entwicklungsromane* in order to confront and overcome this past. Overcoming the past also means overcoming a sense of alienation which was closely bound to the socio-economic conditions of the past. It means exploring and exposing each alienating factor which contributed to the fragmentation and encapsulation of the individual in the past and then tracing these factors as they still function in the present. This is where the similarity of these novels of development ends—in the present.

West German novelists are apparently more alienated from their society than are the East Germans, largely due to the continuation of capitalism in their society. The West German novelists reflect this alienation in different ways. They write their books in the first person, and the fragmented episodic style mirrors the breakdown rather than the development of the individual. In almost all their novels, which tend to be picaresque parodies of the *Entwick-*

---

[17]*The Quest for Christa T.*, trans. Christopher Middleton, (New York, 1970), p. 185.

lungsroman, the hero ends up outside society with little hope of pulling himself together and becoming active within the social framework. The emphasis is on the *breakdown* of the individual, on decadence, on distortion, on cynicism, and on competition—it is the individual against society and his fellow men. There is no hope of communication, since all people and all institutions in capitalist societies are part of the mode of production that engenders alienation. The narrators of the novels of development are even unsure of their audiences: they cry out as though into the night, they cry out for help. Their art is turned in against themselves, and the result is unrelieved negation.

The *Entwicklungsroman* in West Germany is deliberate parody of a bourgeois genre which no longer serves a useful purpose, and its basic thematic concern is the impossibility of genuine development in a capitalist society. This literary evolution is explained by Marx: "History is thorough and goes through many phases when it buries an old form. The last phase of a world historical form is its comedy."[18] In West Germany, the *Entwicklungsroman* has become comic. The novelists seek to make society appear ridiculous and grotesque by illustrating the manner in which people are made into commodities, into prostitutes, and the manner in which people act like commodities and prostitutes. Neither the individual nor society is real, in the sense of being natural, and this makes it even more difficult for novelists to cope with reality in their works. They resort to parody in order to negate the plasticity and the alienated forms in society. In this way, the traditional bourgeois *Entwicklungsroman* is being buried in West Germany. No new form has risen yet.

A new form may arise in East Germany, although this, too, seems highly unlikely.[19] The literary trend in the German Democratic Republic is controlled carefully by cultural supervisors. Great stress is placed on social realism, accurate representation of typical persons and events, tendentiousness, and the reutilization of the bourgeois culture for socialist purposes. It is possible, then, to speak of the bourgeois *Entwicklungsroman* in East Germany as a reutilized, socialist, form. Most of the East German novels of development follow the classical pattern of the traditional *Entwicklungsroman* but place greater emphasis on the class struggle and realistic documentation. With few exceptions, e.g. *The Quest for Christa T.*, the novels are written in the third person, and the protagonists develop their social awareness to the point that they recognize the need for a new social order to help them overcome their alienation. These narratives follow a prescribed form dictated by party cultural policy, and it is here that they reflect and deal with problems of alienation which are different from those in West Germany.

Unlike the situation in West Germany, where novelists react to a free market economy that they see dominated by monopolistic groups that exploit the lower classes, the situation in East Germany is defined by the SED-Party which controls the means of production and legislates strict socio-economic plans, leaving little room for individual freedom. This strict planning de-

---

[18]Karl Marx und Friedrich Engels, *Werke*, vol. 1 (Berlin, 1957), p. 382.

[19]For a most interesting discussion of the *Entwicklungsroman* in East Germany, see Frank Trommler, "Von Stalin zu Hölderlin: Über den Entwicklungsroman in der DDR," *Basis*, 2 (1971), pp. 141-190.

termined by an elite group within the party covers all spheres of life, including the cultural. Hence, the East German *Entwicklungsroman* must necessarily be more uniform than the West German, and the development of the protagonist is not against and *cannot* be against the socialist society, since the socialist society does its best to further individual development. At least, this is the official point of view.

Unofficially—and this is implied in many of the East German novels—the party controls too much, and the society has yet to achieve real socialism, which means that there are grave contradictions within the East German framework. The most apparent one is the new class system where classes are referred to as "levels" (*Schichten*) which allows an elite to profit from the labor of lower social groups. The dominant social "level" consists of bureaucrats and technocrats, all party functionaries, and both Kant and Wolf are direct in their criticism of these types. Schulz and Noller *imply* criticism; and as has been mentioned before, they leave their novels unfinished, with their heroes still outside socialist society.

Like the West German novels, alienation is the main theme of the East German *Entwicklungsromane*, but it is qualitatively different. There is a stronger human element in the alienated activities of the East German characters, and this is due to the fact that socialist innovations have, in truth, improved the quality of life of the masses. Secondly, greater concern is shown by the state for each and every individual, since the state has a greater investment in the productive capacity of each individual. This also accounts for the greater repression and manipulation of the state, and this is what the East German novelists criticize most. Interestingly, East German novelists do not allow their protagonists (none of whom are artists) to become resigned at the end of their novels. They struggle with hope and with the belief that people and governments can be changed. The fact that their heroes are not allowed to resign according to the cultural tenets of the party is naturally an alienating sign, but still, the struggle of the protagonists does indicate the authors' sincere commitment to the socialist cause which may easily be distinguished from commitment to a repressive state.

Whether committed to East or West Germany, German novelists have had great difficulties in writing about the development of young men and women in the two German societies which have evolved since World War II. The difficulty has been best portrayed in Uwe Johnson's *The Third Book about Achim* (1961) centering on the West German journalist Karsch, who wants to write about the development of Achim, the bicycle champion of East Germany. An anonymous narrator tells us why Karsch was unable to write the book, while at the same time giving us an account of Achim's life and Karsch's difficulties in collecting and assembling his material. This book, written by a novelist who has moved from East Germany and now resides in the West while still committed to socialism, is an interesting comment on the state of the German *Entwicklungsroman* today. Johnson parodies the bourgeois *Entwicklungsroman* and also reutilizes bourgeois elements to stress the need for social changes.

Of course, evolutionary changes are being made constantly by the governments in East and West Germany. Whether they are for the best and whether they will help to eliminate the sense of displacement and alienation, these are disturbing questions which have yet to be answered, and which continue to be asked by German novelists in both the East and the West.

New York University
New York

Uwe Johnson's Anti-Liberalism

By W. G. CUNLIFFE

Uwe Johnson has an assured place in the history of modern German literature as the novelist of divided Germany. When *Mutmassungen über Jakob*
(*Speculations about Jacob*) appeared in 1959, commentators were quick to
appreciate that Johnson's was the first serious treatment of a strangely
neglected theme,[1] and *Das dritte Buch über Achim* (*The Third Book about
Achim*) of 1961 confirmed Johnson's position as the writer of the two
Germanies.[2] All such comments are true enough, but need qualifying, for,
as the reader soon notices, Johnson's theme is not so much the two German
states themselves, as the fact of their separation. In other words, he does not

---

[1] e.g. Herbert Ahl, *Literarische Porträts* (Munich and Vienna, 1962), p. 7.
[2] Günter Blöcker, *Kritisches Lesebuch* (Hamburg, 1962), p. 196, calls Johnson
"Dichter der beiden Deutschland."

compare the two systems nor does he discuss or evaluate their differences, but rather points insistently to the gap separating them. It is, he claims, an unbridgable gap. The concluding note to *Achim* hints cryptically at this overriding interest:

> Die Personen sind erfunden. Die Ereignisse beziehen sich nicht auf ähnliche sondern auf die Grenze: den Unterschied: die Entfernung und den Versuch, sie zu beschreiben. (The characters are invented. The events refer, not to similar ones but to the border: the difference: the distance and the attempt to describe them.)[3]

Commentators have observed the absence of discussion and explanation in Johnson's novels. One of them, Diller, attributes this inhibition to a distrust of intellectual explanations, while another, Horst, writes of Johnson's distrust of both objective and subjective approaches.[4] Analyses along these lines, however, overlook Johnson's pervasive anti-liberalism. It is plainly not Johnson's aim in his novels to promote discussion, to present an issue or attack abuses. Rather he is interested in the clash of opposites that denies the possibility of reconciliation or compromise. In other words, his approach to the German question, as reflected in his novels, can fairly be described as anti-liberal, as this analysis will try to show.

Above all, then, Johnson's novels dwell on the differences that separate East from West. The theme of separation runs constantly through all the novels. In the first novel, *Jakob*, however, this separation is but one aspect of a prevailing lack of comprehension that separates man from man and makes truth inaccessible. Human motives are shrouded in fog, and the novel demonstrates this fact in its structure, for it proceeds by a series of conjectures and suppositions, so that it is often uncertain whose thoughts or words are being recorded. All the minor conjectures that go to make up the novel are finally gathered into the conjecture as to the ultimate cause of Jakob's death, when crossing the railroad tracks in a fog. The death may well be a case of suicide, motivated by Jakob's secret despair at his position, torn between East and West, but this is deliberately left uncertain.

The subsequent novels are far more vehement in pointing to the gap separating the two Germanies and far less inclined to stress the isolation of the individual. In *Achim* the separation is no longer shrouded in fog, but concretely represented in a central symbol, the inability of the Western journalist, Karsch, to write the biography of the East German bicycle racer, Achim. The separation is here quite plainly a matter of opposing ideologies. Achim's achievements as an athlete increase the prestige of the East German state, and any book about him must support this overriding purpose. An East German official, Herr Fleisg, explains to Karsch what his book must be about —the construction of a new economy, and a new contentment in life, and the spectators waving flags at the edge of the race-track.[5]

---

[3]Uwe Johnson, *Das dritte Buch über Achim* (Frankfurt, 1961), p. 337. My translation.

[4]Edward Diller, "Uwe Johnson's Karsch: Language as a Reflection of the two Germanies," *Monatshefte*, LX (1968), 36, and K. A. Horst, *Kritischer Führer durch die deutsche Literatur der Gegenwart* (Munich, 1962), p. 137.

[5]*Des dritte Buch über Achim*, p. 59.

Herr Fleisg's views of the function of literature are never discussed, but the reader is still, so to speak, invited to comment. In his next two books, Johnson seems to be more irascible and uncompromising. The story "Eine Reise wegwohin 1960" in the volume *Karsch und andere Prosa* (1964), for example, takes up the theme of *Achim*. Again Karsch sets out for a few days' stay in East Germany, but remains considerably longer to write the memoirs of a popular bicycle racer. Again he fails, but now the Western journalist is an unhappy neurotic, tortured by sleeplessness and peevishly dissatisfied with East German hotel services and consumer goods. In *Zwei Ansichten* (*Two Views*) of 1965, East and West never meet but are handled in alternating chapters concerning a man, B, from the West and a woman, D, from the East. The principle of separation is embodied in the very structure of the novel, so that even the possibility of discussion between the parties is removed.

Yet even the first novel, *Jakob*, for all its undogmatic speculativeness, is far from taking a liberal, detached view of the two Germanies. It is misleading to assume that Johnson is taking some independent stance, attacking tyranny impartially in the tradition of the Western man of letters. Johnson is not an heir to this tradition, although commentators on *Jakob* are sometimes inclined to believe that he is.[6] Johnson shows the readers where his preferences lie by showing the allegiance of Jacob, the wholly admirable hero, to the East German cause. Thus he serves the State with patience and fortitude, undeterred even when his mother, feeling harassed by Rohlfs and his agents from the counter-espionage department, abruptly departs for the West. In fact, it is not until he is in Western Germany visiting his mother that Jakob finally loses his temper, when somebody plays the Badenweiler March on the jukebox. He is enraged that Hitler's favorite march should be played in public, to him an inadmissible liberty, but he apparently is not concerned that Hitler's favorite methods of control should be used in the East, where the secret police are shown to be active even in a little seaside town and where telephone-tapping is almost routine.

To analyse the situation in neutral terms—a thing which Johnson carefully avoids doing—Jakob prefers purposiveness to freedom, and it is his voice that dominates the novel. This preference emerges in the figure of Rohlfs, the East German counter espionage agent, a remarkable portrait. In the course of the conversations and monologues that make up the novel *Jakob*, the reader learns his past history—he deserted to the Russians in World War II —and of his determination to uphold the authority of the new state. To the reader brought up in the liberal tradition, Rohlfs at his most authoritative is indefensible. For example, in one monologue Rohlfs fulminates against the intellectual Jonas Blach, a young university assistant who has been guilty of attending illegal political meetings. Rohlfs' feelings for Blach and his kind are summed up in contempt for the lack of power of the kind available to the state—"Als hätten sie ein Ministerium und einen operativen Stab." ("As if they had a ministry and an operative staff.")[7] This pampered intellectual is going to have a fine birthday present, Rohlfs promises himself with relish. In liberal eyes, then, Rohlfs is a disgusting worshipper of power of the sort

---

[6]Gerhard Haas, "Das essayistische Gestaltungsprinzip," *Deutschunterricht*, III (1967), 70, compares Johnson to Molière.

[7]Uwe Johnson, *Mutmassungen über Jakob* (Frankfurt, 1959), p. 119.

often portrayed with satirical loathing as, for example, O'Brien in George Orwell's *1984*. In Johnson's novel, Rohlfs is regarded with understanding. His views on Jonas Blach are, after all, conventional Marxism, somewhat provocatively expressed. Blach's refusal to conform could not, of course, be accepted by the Marxist as truly revolutionary. He would reject it as lacking the true consensus of popular support. Unorganized, the revolt can be written of as amateur and romantic—thus Günter Grass's Brecht condemned the Berlin uprising of 1953 in *The Plebeians Rehearse the Uprising*.

It is important to note that the admirable Jakob, far from being repelled by Rohlfs, seems to agree with him, if one can speak of agreement where there is no discussion. Rohlfs says as much when he is putting the handcuffs on Blach: "Dass er mit Jakob sich hätte verständigen können."[8] Jakob, too, is scornful when the young academician speaks of freedom, although he, unlike Rohlfs, tries to advise Blach in a kindly fashion. Essentially, both Jakob and Rohlfs believe that freedom in the Western liberal sense is an illusion. Jakob, for example, does not believe in his own freedom to take up any employment that pleases him and Rohlfs deplores the freedom of movement between East and West (which was removed when the East Germans built the Berlin Wall in 1961). Their attitude can best be summed up in Engel's famous dictum, quoted in the novel by Jonas and encountered as a slogan in East Germany, to the effect that "Freedom is the Realization of Necessity"—"Freiheit ist die Einsicht in die Notwendigkeit."[9] It is a view of freedom that is satirized from the liberal point of view in *1984*. There the Party slogan inscribed on coins and stamps reads: "Freedom is slavery."

In Johnson's novel the liberal cause has no such robust representative. On the contrary, with a conspicuous absence of liberal fairplay, the liberal opposition is characterized by the feebleness of its representative, Jonas Blach, who is unable even to muster enough decisiveness to move to the West. He has been guilty of attending illicit meetings at which the liberalization of the East German regime was discussed. Throughout the novel the reader watches Rohlfs pursue him, while he thrashes about in despair. In a conversation with Cresspahl he describes himself self-deprecatingly as "incorrigible" (the epithet for enemies of the Communist regime) and yet "devoted" (the word used to describe the unwaveringly loyal Party member)—UNBELEHRBAR ERGEBEN.[10]

With such a creature, enfeebled by consciousness of thoughtcrime, there can be no question of discussion. Indeed, the absence of discussion accords with Rohlfs' own opinion of its undesirability. The final conclusion he arrives at toward the end of the novel, just before he arrests Jonas, is that conversation, discussion, is a mistake—"Gespräch ist ein Fehler."[11] Here is the unrelenting insistence on keeping distant which Pongs points to as an example of Marxist dialectic deliberately destroying dialogue.[12] It is on this principle that Matti, in Brecht's play *Mr. Puntila and his Hired Man Matti*, rejects the approaches of his employer in a genial mood. Johnson's novel, then, presents

---

[8]*Jakob*, p. 308.
[9]*Jakob*, p. 123.
[10]*Jakob*, p. 171.
[11]*Jakob*, p. 293.
[12]Hermann Pongs, *Dichtung im gespaltenen Deutschland* (Stuttgart, 1966), p. 29.

such an anti-liberal, Marxist front that one critic was able to compare it with novels of the "social realist" school, in which there is a popular hero and a weak and wavering intellectual.[13] Yet the whole is overshadowed by a question-mark, and veiled in the mists of speculative uncertainty. Is the hero as fully in accord with the regime as he appears to be on the surface, or is his death a case of suicide based on despair? The pervasive doubts give Johnson's first published novel an air of undogmatic liberalism.

The next novel, *Das dritte Buch über Achim*, shows a distinct movement away from this suggestion of liberalism. *Achim* again employs the contrast between a hardworking, technically skilled East German and a dilettante West German. The former, the bicycle racer Achim, places his hardness and technical mastery at the service of the regime. At one point in the narrative he tells the West German, Karsch, of a snub administered to a government which failed to pay tribute to his team's victory by playing the East German national anthem. Neither Karsch nor the author have any comment to make on this piece of jingoism, or on the use of sporting prowess to bolster up a regime. Moreover, even though Johnson has chosen to make the hero of his novel a Communist athlete, the highly relevant question of professionalism in sport is never raised, nor, more particularly, the well-known bicycle race from Warsaw to Prague by way of East Berlin, organized by the East German government for "amateurs."[14]

The incident of the photograph provides an example of Karsch's helpless silence in the face of illiberal practice and theory. Karsch receives one day a photograph revealing that Achim, now a pillar of the regime, had taken part in the Berlin rising of 1953. Karsch taxes him with this, wishing to include it in the biography, but Achim calmly denies that the photo shows what it does show, namely, his taking part in the revolt. After all, from the East German point of view the striving for truth that serves no useful purpose is perverse, mere bourgeois dilettantism.

It is this way of regarding facts which Orwell has satirized from the liberal point of view in 1984. Here, too, there is an incident involving a photograph, inconvenient to the authorities, which O'Brien places in a memory-hole, declaring that it never existed. His victim, Winston Smith, however, incorrigibly bourgeois, has difficulty in mustering the necessary double-think until he has been tortured. In Johnson's novel, the Westerner gives way easily to the East German's hard certainties. "Mir fällt nichts mehr ein" is Karsch's final confession of helplessness before departing for the West, the book about Achim for ever unwritten.

Even though nobody in *Achim* speaks up for the West, Karsch's helpless neutrality invites the reader to discuss and argue on his behalf. In the story "Eine Reise wegwohin 1960", Karsch ceases to be neutral and turns neurotic and querulous. Moreover, the story describes, as the novel does not, Karsch's return to the West, and this develops into an attack on the West. Karsch, we read, plans a series of articles advocating the recognition of East Germany by the West German government. Not only does his own newspaper refuse to print them, but Karsch finds it impossible to get them accepted anywhere.

[13]Marcel Reich-Ranicki, *Deutsche Literatur in West und Ost* (Munich, 1963), p. 233.
[14]For a brief description of this race see *Die Zeit* 18 May 1971, p. 21.

Moreover, after a television debate in which Karsch defends the recognition of the East German state, his room is searched by the police. At first sight, it looks as if Johnson is aiming at some balanced presentation of oppression. Karsch cannot publish his life of Achim in the East, nor his defence of the East in the West. In fact, however, the West is being burdened not only with its own faults—selfishness, lack of moral fiber and of honest convictions— but also with the illiberalism and downright chicanery of the East, about which Johnson is always frank. This is highly unfavorable to the West, because their oppression is conducted without the convictions that sustain even the spy Rohlfs. In fact, Johnson's argument is "unfair" because there were, as Reich-Ranicki points out, even in 1960, West German publishing houses that would have published Karsch's material, providing a further example of illusory bourgeois freedom.[15]

Zwei Ansichten takes to extremes not only the separation between East and West, but also the contrast. The hospital nurse D from the East is pleasant, conscientious, honest, a little naïve but nobody's fool. The counter-figure B from the West is a freelance photographer, indifferent at bottom to everything except fast cars. The very nature of B's work suggests flunkeyish lack of principle as he bends and bows to make snapshots: "Brauchbar und tüchtig ging er in die Knie, bog sich in die Hüfte und im Kreuz, legte sich auf Bauch und Rücken, hockte, kauerte, kniete, hielt die Kamera seitlich und übern Kopf und nahm auf."[16]

In a vague way, B believes he ought to help D, a former girlfriend, to flee to the West after the building of the Berlin wall. He goes to Berlin, where his exotic foreign sports car is stolen. After this he takes to drinking heavily. Thus, by a kind of oblique logic, even the Berlin wall redounds to the credit of East Germany, for D has something more real to occupy herself than B's stolen luxury car.

The wall, is, in fact, an occasion for East German patriotism, a sentiment which seems permissible in Johnson's novels. When it is built, we are told, D is disappointed rather than angry, for the voluntary nature of her choice of East Berlin is denied her.[17] Even when D does finally flee to the West, after uttering further patriotic sentiments, it is not through B's initiative but through the automatic functioning of an escape organization which B has set in motion during a drunken stupor. To cap it all, when D presents her forged passport, she finds that B has forgotten the color of her eyes.

Enzensberger praised Johnson's first novel for its neutrality.[18] The novelist's detachment from his characters and use of ambiguity justified this description. The increasingly palpable partisanship for the Eastern cause in the later novels makes the term less readily applicable. But it is not merely Johnson's praise of the Soviet technician or indulgence in the matter of East German patriotic manifestations that give his novels an anti-liberal tone. Even more important is the refusal to treat the difference as a matter for discussion, indeed, the aggressive urge to exacerbate the difference. This kind of intractability accords with an often-quoted passage from Engels' *Die Entwicklung des Sozialismus*

[15]Marcel Reich-Ranicki, *Literatur der kleinen Schritte* (Munich, 1967), p. 53.
[16]Uwe Johnson, *Zwei Ansichten* (Frankfurt, 1965), p. 7f.
[17]*Zwei Ansichten*, p. 47.
[18]H. M. Enzensberger, *Einzelheiten* (Frankfurt, 1962), p. 236.

von der Utopie zur Wisenschaft in which he contemptuously dismisses "eclectic Socialism" (i.e., liberalism) as a mish-mash which is the more easily brewed as the definite sharp edges of the individual constituents are rubbed down in the stream of debate like rounded pebbles in a brook—"eine Mischung, die sich um so leichter bewerkstelligt, je mehr die einzelnen Bestandteile im Strom der Debatte den scharfen Ecken der Bestimmtheit abgeschliffen sind wie runden Kieseln im Bach."[19] It is perhaps disconcerting that the first and, so far, best novels about the two Germanies should be written by an author who, by and large, seems to approve of the division. The Western, liberal tradition, after all, is to disapprove of all boundaries. Johnson's rejection of this tradition can perhaps be seen as a sign of the times. Johnson seems to combine rejection of the West with a keen interest in the American scene, evinced in his latest novel *Jahrestage*, which has an American setting. This combination of rejection and interest is strongly widespread among German intellectuals of Johnson's and younger generations.

University of Wisconsin
Madison

---

[19]Karl Marx, Friedrich Engels, *Werke* (Berlin, 1962), 19, 201.

Friedrich Dürrenmatt, Escape Artist: A Look at the Novels

By RENATE USMIANI

When Jacques Barzun proclaimed some 25 years ago that a "Bovary-ectomy" seemed indicated in the case of the contemporary novel, then as now on the critical list, he could scarcely have anticipated how fully his prescription would be carried out. The novel subsequently cut itself off, deliberately and thoroughly, from all the roots connecting it to the tradition which had given birth to Emma, and Charles Bovary and their contemporaries. While critics proclaimed the death of the novel, there emerged a new phenomenon, free of the conventional trappings of character, plot or even consciousness: the contemporary anti-novel. Hailed by the supporters of the avant-garde as the take-off point for a new era in fiction, the anti-novel has been viewed with alarm by more conservative critics and novelists. Thus, Heinrich Böll sees the anti-novel heading rapidly towards a literary cataclysm, an ultimate "automatic novel" which would register only "the death throes of humanity" before the final extinction. A frightening prospect—but still to be averted, if only writers become more conscious of their responsibility:

> "Anyone who still recognizes responsibility of any kind, as a Christian, as a Socialist, even as an ill-defined Liberal who believes in some sort of humanism, will not let go that grain of humor . . . which alone makes it possible for him to go on living on this earth."

Thus, Böll traces the suicidal bent of contemporary literature to its basic lack of humor; that humor:

> "Always goes beyond the mere physical, cannot be without at least a trace of the transcendent . . . I dare to call it sublime."[1]

He is no doubt correct in establishing this correlation between a lack of humor in the novel and the absence of humanistic attitudes in both the novelists and in the current Zeitgeist.

On this point, Friedrich Dürrenmatt fully concurs with Böll. His grotesque satires represent one undaunted individual's attempt to come to terms with the absurdities of life in the 20th century. He himself has pointed out that his work can be understood only from the point of view of "humor taken seriously."[2] Emphasizing its particular significance in the twentieth century, he points out that:

> "The language of freedom in our time is humor, even if it has to be black humor."[3]

Humor means many things to Dürrenmatt. On the simplest level, it means a love for clever invention ("Einfall"), surprise effect, and laughable incongruities. The general pattern of his work regularly shows the collapse of an orderly world through the sudden intrusion of an unexpected, mostly accidental element. One ought not to take too lightly his acknowledgment of Aristophanes and Nestroy as his masters (rumor even has it that admittance into Dürrenmatt's circle of friends can be gained only by those who own a critical edition of the great Viennese playwright!) However, Dürrenmatt's type of humor goes deeper than the spirited gaiety of Nestroy, and is more pessimistic than the satire of Aristophanes. There is in it a touch of the Pirandellian "*umorismo*," with its emphasis on the accidental character of all the so-called "great" events which determine the life of man and the course of his history; with its fierce dedication to the task of tearing masks off faces and façades off ideologies; and its acceptance of the relativity of all concepts and values. Like Pirandello, Dürrenmatt would present to us the emperor in his nightgown, rather than wearing imperial purple—and the result is both ludicrous and pathetic. His strong point is the grotesque, applied

---

[1]Heinrich Böll, "Uber den Roman," in *Erzählungen, Hörspiele, Aufsätze,* (Köln, Berlin, 1961), p. 426. My translation.

[2]Interview, quoted in Horst Bienek, *Werkstattgespräche mit Schriftstellern,* (München, 1962), p. 102.

[3]Friedrich Dürrenmatt, *Theaterschriften und Reden,* (Zürich, 1966), p. 72.

to social satire. The use of grotesque techniques in no wise represents a purely negative attitude. On the contrary. Like all great writers of comedy, Dürrenmatt considers himself a moralist—an admission which in itself constitutes no small act of courage in the twentieth century:

> "The grotesque . . . is not the art form of the nihilist, but much rather of the moralist, not decay, but salt . . . it is unpleasant, but necessary."[4]

His effective use of satire and grotesque alienation in the stage plays is well known. Less known is the fact that he has applied the same technique with perhaps even greater success, to some of the minor genres—radio drama,[5] short story and light novel. I will deal here in particular with *Once a Greek* (*Grieche sucht Griechin*), a satire on the lending-library type novel (it even includes a charming, tongue-in-cheek "ending for lending libraries"), and, briefly, his thrillers, *The Promise* (*Das Versprechen*), *The Quarry* (*Der Verdacht*), and *The Judge and his Hangman*, (*Der Richter und sein Henker*).

Dürrenmatt's little-known radio plays are definitely superior to most of his serious drama; and as for producing a "serious" novel, he has never even tried, preferring to restrict himself to the minor genres in his fiction. It is tantalizing to speculate upon the reasons for Dürrenmatt's obvious preference for these minor genres—"*Trivialgattungen*," as they are called, even more derogatorily, in German. Aside from the very realistic fact that these works represent for the artist valuable "*Brotarbeit*," that is, a source of income, I think they could be interpreted as a threefold escape: escape from the critics; escape from the pressures of the avant-garde; and escape from nihilism and the philosophy of the absurd. He could, then, be defined as an artist who escapes into escape Literature.

Dürrenmatt is notoriously suspicious of the proponents of literary criticism, whom he reproaches not only with their obtuseness and lack of sensitivity, but most of all for their tendency to take themselves too seriously. To avoid being subjected to "learned" analysis, he takes refuge in those genres least likely to attract the attention of the academic critic—and most likely to secure a broad public. So far, he has been eminently successful in his little manoeuver, a fact which undoubtedly fills him with great satisfaction. His novels, widely available in cheap paperback editions, have failed to command the interest of the literary scholars, while providing continued delight to suspense story aficionados. In the game of cat-and-mouse which he has all along been playing with the critics, Dürrenmatt still remains one step ahead of us.

It is also safe to assume that Dürrenmatt has gone underground into the minor genres, which still allow at least outwardly, for a conventional approach because of a deep distrust of the extreme avant-garde. His one venture into a technically contemporary, what might be called a Beckett-type work, *Play Strindberg* (Arche, 1969) represents, in my opinion, a dismal failure (although it does bring out quite successfully the monstrous marriage theme). Dürrenmatt is too much of a humorist and too much of an individualist to fall into a pattern of any sort. Rather than join an avant-garde, he prefers to retain

---

[4]*Ibid.*, p. 137.

[5]Cf. Renate Usmiani, "Masterpieces in Disguise: The Radio Plays of Friedrich Dürrenmatt," *Seminar*, VII, 1, March 1971.

conventional trappings, reserving to himself the privilege of revealing their absurdity through grotesque alienation.

Finally, and most important, I suggest that Dürrenmatt's light novels represent an escape from the nihilism and the philosophy of the absurd which permeate all "serious" contemporary literature. In spite of his Calvinistic background and a youthful bout with nihilism, Dürrenmatt essentially remains an optimist. No doubt he meant it when he once exclaimed:

> "I don't really believe in the end of the world, except while I'm reading the newspapers."

This in no wise invalidates the writer's serious concern with, and full awareness of, the metaphysical anguish of modern man; it means only that he refuses to give himself up to total despair. It may not be unrealistic to draw a parallel between his *Weltanschauung* and his way of coping with the central problem of his private life, the fact that he is a diabetic. He has come to face the world the way he must face the disease: as something which, although inexplicable, meaningless, and impossible to overcome, must yet be lived through, somehow. "*Die Welt bestehen*" is one of his key phrases. To live through the ordeal of an absurd sickness does not call for heroic grandeur; instead, it requires unglamorous daily discipline, the somewhat grotesque routine of the hypodermic needle, and a dash of humor. The same applies when facing an absurd universe. The Jew Gulliver, in *Der Verdacht* (*The Quarry*) sums up Dürrenmatt's attitude when he tells Inspector Barlach:

> "... So sollen wir die Welt nicht zu retten suchen, sondern zu bestehen, das einzige wahrhafte Abenteuer, das uns in dieser späten Zeit noch bleibt."
> ("...and so we should no longer seek to save the world, but to live through it—the only true adventure that remains to us at this late hour.")

The heroism which Dürrenmatt advocates (he himself prefers the term "courage") resembles that advocated by Camus in *Le Mythe de Sisyphe*, a heroic resignation and acceptance of life in spite of its absurdity. In fact, Dürrenmatt was at one time considered another "romancier de l'absurde" in France.[6] He himself, however, quickly disclaimed any such categorization. Beyond the realization of the absurd, he wishes to show the paradox in human life, and the quixotic quality to which our age has reduced any attempt at heroism.

In his early works, he alternates between Promethean rebellion and the facile consolations of religion. A despairing nihilism breathes in the expressionistic fragments of his early prose, such as *Weihnacht* (*Christmas*), *Der Folterknecht* (*The Torturer*) or *Die Falle* (*The Trap*)—the latter originally entitled *Der Nihilist*.[7] In the epilogue to the collection, written several years after the stories themselves, Dürrenmatt mentions that these fragments represent an attempt: "To fight a battle which can be meaningful only if it is

---

[6]Cf. Marcel Schneider, "Friedrich Dürrenmatt, le Fils Prodique de l'Occident," *Revue de Paris*, August, 1961.
[7]Friedrich Dürrenmatt, *Die Stadt. Frühe Prosa*. (Zürich, 1952).

lost." He did not remain a nihilist long. His involvement with the Christian religion was a more deep-seated one,[8] and for a time brought him peace and respite from despair: "Immer noch hat der Engel recht, immer noch ist die Erde das Wunder," he says in his notes to *Ein Engel Kam Nach Babylon*:

> "Der Engel mag uns weltfremd scheinen, ich glaube jedoch, dass jene weltfremder sind, welche die Welt nur als Verzweiflung sehen. Die Erde hängt nicht im Nichts, sie ist ein Teil der Schöpfung. Das ist ein Unterschied."
> ("Still the angel is right, still the world constitutes THE miracle. The angel may appear to us unrealistic, but I believe that those who see the world only as despair are even more unrealistic. The world is not suspended in a void, it is a part of creation. That makes a difference.")

Such statements, as well as the religious themes of his early plays and his general preoccupation with the problems of evil and guilt have led to the mistaken assumption that Dürrenmatt is essentially a religious writer.[9] The bulk of his mature work, as well as his own pronouncements, speak against such a view. Neither absurdist, nor religious writer, nor *engagé* in any way, Dürrenmatt remains entirely *sui generis*, a paradox among contemporary authors, an artist capable of turning the most tragic truths into grotesque farces. Besides the concept of *"bestehen,"* another key term provides a glimpse into his way of thinking: the expression *"noch möglich"* (still possible), which constantly recurs in his writings. Rather than feeling totally hemmed in, Dürrenmatt believes that a limited number of artistic modes of expression remain open to the artist in the twentieth century, foremost among them the possibility of dealing with serious facts in a flippant manner. Courage remains a possible quality in the world of Dürrenmatt because he tempers it with a tinge of the ridiculous: his slightly absurd Count Ubelohe, Emperor Romulus, and Archilochos, the idealistic bookkeeper, make perfect sense in an absurd universe.

To examine Dürrenmatt's use of grotesque alienation as a means for social satire, one must first establish his views on the contemporary socio-political scene. It is an easy task, for he himself recently elaborated these views in his *"Monstervortrag über Gerechtigkeit und Recht"* (*"Monstrous Lecture on Justice and Right."* The German term *"Recht"* includes the concept of "law" as well as that of "right"), given before the general assembly, the *studium generale*, of the Johannes Gutenberg University in Mainz. The lecture itself is vintage Dürrenmatt, spiced with a number of witty fables and ending up with a parable which paradoxically invalidates the whole concept of justice. It also reveals a mature outlook, tinged with paradox, but free from nihilism, as well as from Christian piety. A few key statements are enough to reveal his basic thinking on justice and social order:

> "Ich bin mit Sokrates der Meinung, die Grösse eines Menschen liege darin, das Unrecht, das ihm widerfährt, ertragen zu könen, es braucht jedoch soviel Grösse dazu, dass ich es für meine politische Pflicht halte,

---

[8]Cf. his autobiographical "Dokument," in *Theaterschriften und Reden*, p. 30 ff.
[9]Cf. especially Hans Bänziger, *Frisch und Dürrenmatt*, (München, 1960).

alles zu versuchen, was einen Menschen hindert, in die Lage zu kommen,
die Grösse aufzubringen, ein solches Unrecht ertragen zu müssen . . ."
("With Socrates I am of the opinion that the greatness of a human being
is revealed in his ability to withstand the injustice which he must suffer;
however, there is so much greatness needed here that I consider it my
political duty to try everything to prevent the human being from getting
into a situation where he must show the greatness with which to withstand such injustice.") [10]

Quiet irony and a casual mode of expression here work together to produce
a most effective understatement. Dürrenmatt sees the injustice of any social
order as inherent in the paradox of social organization as such:

"Es gibt keine gerechte Gesellschaftsordnung, weil der Mensch, sucht
er Gerechtigkeit, mit Recht jede Gesellschaftsordnung als ungerecht,
und sucht er Freiheit, mit Recht jede Gesellschaftsordnung als unfrei
empfinden muss."
("There is no such thing as a just social order, because a man who looks
for justice must consider any social order as unjust; a man who looks
for freedom, any social order as a restriction of his freedom.")

There is no way out of the dilemma: Man craves both justice and freedom,
but the two terms are mutually exclusive. Any social order, whether it be
the capitalistic "wolf game" or the socialist "sheep game" represents a compromise solution which must remain unsatisfactory. This does not mean a
total rejection of either system on Dürrenmatt's part, but rather a cautious
detachment and, above all, categorical refusal to posit absolute ideologies:

"Ich habe nichts gegen Gesellschaftsordnungen, die partiell vernünftig
sind, ich weigere mich nur, sie heilig zu sprechen und den gewaltigen
Rest ihrer Unvernunft und Tabus als gottgegeben hinzunehmen. Ich
halte halbwegs vernünftige Gesellschaftsordnungen für verbesserungs-
würdig."
("I have nothing against social orders which are partially reasonable;
I only refuse to canonize them and to accept their enormous share of
irrationality and taboos as god-given. I consider halfway reasonable
social orders as worthy of improvement.")

His ideas on how to effect the proposed improvements, however, remain vague,
although he includes a strong warning against the emotional force of ideologies, "the cosmetics of power politics." He suggests that in politics, as in
literature, it may be beneficial to look at reality with critical imagination,
rather than ideologically:

"Es könnte dazu führen, die Ideologien als blosse Arbeitshypothesen zu
begreifen, die leichter durch andere Arbeitshypothesen zu ersetzen
wären, erwiese es sich als notwendig; eine nur kleine Sprachkorrektur,
gewiss, doch einer Arbeitshypothese zuliebe wären die Gefangnisse und
Zwangslager weniger bevölkert als einer Ideologie zuliebe. Ebenso wäre
das Wort Vaterland durch das Wort Verwaltung zu ersetzen: Wer hielte

---

[10]Friedrich Dürrenmatt, *Gerechtigkeit und Recht*, (Zürich, 1969).

es schon fur süss, fur eine Verwaltung zu sterben!
("This could lead to an understanding of ideologies as pure working hypotheses, which could easily be replaced by a different set of working hypotheses if it should prove necessary; a small semantic change, only, true, but nevertheless the prisons and concentration camps would be less filled for the sake of a working hypothesis than for the sake of an ideology. In the same way, the word "fatherland" should be replaced by the term "administration;" what man would find it sweet to die for an administration!")

Dürrenmatt holds out hope for a rational solution to man's dilemma, but he is not free of the pessimism of the age. Like Böll, he sees an unchecked continuation of current trends leading to the disaster of a fully automatic machine age, an age where computers and other complex hardware would turn the world back from civilization into a barbaric jungle, with an elite of technicians and scientists functioning as the medicine men of the space-age savages. It is this threat of imminent barbarism which most concerns him in his fiction; already, he sees us living in a state where a technological accident can set off a cosmic cataclysm and where man has lost all of his grandeur and most of his dignity. His laughable, pathetic and grotesque heroes are the last upholders of a civilization on the decline, his escape into a "still possible" humanism.

Such a "hero" is Arnolphe Archilochos, hot-milk-and-Perrier-sipping central character of the satirical little novel *Griece Sucht Griechin* (Once a Greek).[11] Under the guise of light entertainment literature, Dürrenmatt here presents us with a scathing satire on political, social and moral orders, bringing out their paradoxical quality. At the same time, he uses grotesque alienation techniques in a brilliantly successful attempt to turn the True-Romance-type love story into a caricature of itself. The story concerns itself with the fate of Arnolphe Archilochos, idealist. Monsieur Arnolphe, as the shabby, but respectable-looking little man is known to his friends, has spent the forty-five years of his life in strict devotion to duty. Most of the meager income he earns as a bottom-echelon bookkeeper in the enormous Piett-Paysan Works (atomic guns and surgical forceps) goes for the support of his good-for-nothing brother Bibi and his brood, so that Archilochos himself is reduced to living in a miserable garret. He takes his meals in a cheap little café run by motherly Madame Bieler, who has kindly agreed to hang the portraits of some of his heroes up on the wall in the corner where he eats, for Monsieur Arnolphe's life rests on the solid foundation of an "ethical universe," made up of eight key figures in society whom he has chosen as his models. A strict order of priorities governs this ethical universe. Numbers one and two, the President of State and the bishop of Arnolphe's sect, hang in Madame Bieler's café, as well as number eight, Fahrcks, the revolutionary, included by Archilochos as the necessary negative principle, and adopted by Madame Bieler for reasons of prudence ("you can never tell in politics," as she wisely observes). Numbers three to seven adorn the walls of Archilochos' bedroom.

The perfect routine of Monsieur Arnolphe's life is broken when he allows Madame Bieler to persuade him to advertise for a wife in the matrimonial

---

[11]Friedrich Dürrenmatt, *Griece sucht Griechin*, (Zürich, 1955).

column of the local newspaper: "Greek seeks Greek wife," as he insists the ad must be run, although his Greek ancestry lies many generations back. On the appointed day he waits nervously in the café, a glass of hot milk on the table before him, when in floats a breathtaking vision of youth, beauty and charm, who identifies herself as his correspondent. All of a sudden, his life is transformed. As he walks through the streets on the arm of Mademoiselle Chloé, dignitaries of all sorts smile and wave. The next morning, having become officially engaged to the fair lady (who tells him she works as a maid), he is called into the general manager's office and promoted to the post of director; that same afternoon, his bishop elevates him to the dignity of World Church Councillor. In the evening, still dazed from all the unexpected strokes of fortune, he comes to visit his fiancée at her home—a most magnificent estate—and out of nowhere, there appears a lawyer who makes the estate over to him, "as a little wedding gift from Mlle. Chloé's employers." In spite of his growing confusion, he dares not question Chloé and goes along with the preparations for the wedding, to be held next day. The ceremony takes place amidst untold splendor, with all the notables of church, state and industry in attendance. The naïve Archilochos is radiant with happiness. It is only at the end of the ceremony that the truth suddenly dawns upon him: "I have married a courtesan," he exclaims, as he rushes out in despair. Pursued by a howling mob, he finally reaches his garret and decides to commit suicide. But just as he is ready to slip his head into the noose, Fahrcks, the communist revolutionary, puts in an unexpected appearance. He easily persuades Archilochos to combine suicide with a useful act of revenge upon the system, which has so shamefully duped him, by assassinating the President of State. However, Archilochos fails miserably in his attempt at violence, and at dawn he resignedly returns to his villa, ready to forgive Chloé. Chloé, however, has disappeared; instead of her, Bibi and his clan fill the house with their noise and debauchery. In a sudden fit of fury, Archilochos throws himself upon his brother and proceeds to single-handedly beat to a pulp Bibi and every one of his gang. The end of the book finds a lonely and melancholy Archilochos surveying the ruins of his property.

This sad state of affairs is somewhat remedied in the subsequent "ending for lending libraries," where Dürrenmatt engineers a reunion of the lovers in their ancestral homeland and an eventual return. However, even this happy ending is tinged with melancholy. The government now really is overthrown, and Fahrcks, the revolutionary, takes over the power. But nothing really changes. Arnolphe's ethical universe has collapsed, but the conversion of brother Bibi (as a result of Arnolphe's energetic measures) somehow does not make up for its loss. And finally, the melancholy shadow of boredom and futility looms over the idyl of Arnolphe and Chloé restored to a bourgeois way of life.

This ending also serves to bring out, delightfully, the "working hypothesis" character of political ideologies, as we witness the changeover from "wolf-game" to "sheep-game" and back again:

> "Der Staat krachte zusammen. Fahrcks mit dem Kreml-Orden unter
> dem Doppelkinn kam ans Ruder, rot färbte sich der Nachthimmel.
> Überall Fahnen . . . Riesenbilder Lenins und des gerade nicht gestürzten

russischen Ministerpräsidenten. Doch der Kreml war fern, der Dollar notwendig, die eigene Macht verlockend. Fahrcks zog ins westliche Lager, liess den Chef der Geheimpolizei aufknüpfen und residierte aufs würdigste im Staatspalais am Quai de l'Etat, ven der gleichen Leibwache mit den goldenen Helmen und den weissen Federbüschen wie sein Vorgänger beschützt ... Er milderte sein Regiment, seine Weltanschauung verblich, und eines schönen Ostersonntags besuchte er die Sankt Lukas-Kathedrale."

("The state collapsed. Fahrcks with the Order of the Kremlin under his double chin took over the power, red covered the evening sky. . . . Everywhere flags . . . gigantic portraits of Lenin and of the not-yet-over-thrown Russian Premier. But the Kremlin was far away, the dollar a necessity, the acquisition of power, a temptation. Fahrcks moved into the Western camp, had the head of the secret police hanged and took up residence in a most dignified manner in the Palace of State on the Quai de l'Etat, protected by the same guards with the gold helmets and white plumes as his predecessor. . . . He tempered his rule, his ideology paled, and one fine Easter Sunday, he attended services at the Saint Lucas Cathedral.")[12]

In a similar way, the novel brings out the interchangeability of social and moral value systems. At the outset of the book, the line of distinction is clearly drawn; the social and moral establishment is represented by the eight pillars of society, who together form Archilochos' "ethical universe," while the anti-establishment invades the story in the form of brother Bibi and his clan. As the book proceeds, the towering personages of Archilochos' ethical universe begin to totter, revealing all the weaknesses of ordinary mortals. Meanwhile, brother Bibi and his good-for-nothing family have become converted into hardworking, law-abiding, church-going citizens. As he visits his brother in the latter's newly acquired plant nursery, and as he watches the once-formidable mother knitting placidly away, while her sea captain-lover calmly puffs on his pipe, Archilochos cannot escape the uncomfortable feeling that somehow things have cancelled each other out, that nothing much was accomplished after all. And this realization fills him with melancholy—a melancholy which can be cured only, as the author points out in an ironic digression into Hollywood *Kitsch*, by the ever-present power of "Love."

However, the main interest of the book rests with Archilochos himself and the monstrous story of his venture into matrimony. There are traits of both Candide and Parzifal in Dürrenmatt's hero. Candide in reverse, he is catapulted from misery into what appears to be the best of all possible worlds; but his strokes of good luck turn out to be as disastrous for him as the original Candide's bouts with misfortune. There are strong echoes of "*cultivons notre jardin*" in Dürrenmatt's ambiguous final idyl of Chloé and Arnolphe, running a small, family-type *pension* in their beautiful villa. Again, Archilochos strikes one as a latter-day Parzival: a middle-aged, slightly overweight Parzival, to be sure, forever cleaning his thick-lensed glasses, a grotesque travesty of the original, but a Parzival figure, none the less, in his absolute purity and innocence. Archilochos, indeed, is the "pure fool" of the legend, like Parzival too shy to ask the necessary questions when he encounters mysteries beyond his

---

[12]*Ibid.*, p. 197.

ken. True to his calling, he emerges a conqueror—though in keeping with the cynicism of our age, he wins the town courtesan, rather than the Holy Grail, an achievement which, as Dürrenmatt would be quick to point out, has the advantage of remaining in the range of what is "still possible."

But the use of the grotesque goes far beyond the characterization of Archilochos himself. Dürrenmatt achieves some outstanding effects by clever plot manipulation, which involves alienation in two directions: an originally harmless event is alienated into a finale of horror, and, in contrast, a monstrous happening is turned into the most innocuous affair. The result in both cases is grotesque and tinged with ambiguous humor. As Kayser has pointed out,[13] the difference between grotesque humor and the merely comical, lies in the reader's reaction: while the comical presupposes distance and detachment, grotesque humor involves the reader's emotions. In spite of the fairytale quality of much of the book, Dürrenmatt's grotesque developments are sufficiently rooted in reality, both psychological and social, to make it impossible for the reader to achieve a safe distance and with it, emotional detachment. The wedding scene provides an excellent example of displacement, from perfect happiness to utter horror. The author lovingly describes the setting for the ceremony, a chapel flooded with candle light and filled with elegant wedding guests:

> "(die Kapelle) strahlte auf, wurde freundlich und warm, das Glitzern der Geschmeide und Perlenketten füllte den Raum, Schultern und Brüste leuchteten auf, und Wolken besten Parfüms stiegen in die Höhe. . . . Bischof Moser bestieg die Kanzel, würdig in seiner schwarzen Amtsrobe. Er legte die Bibel mit ihrem leuchtenden Goldschnitt auf das spriessige Kanzelpult, faltete die Hände und sah hinunter. . . . Gerade unter ihm sass das Brautpaar, Chloé mit grossen, schwarzen, gläubigen Augen, strahlend vor Freude, in einer barten Schleierwolke, in der ein Sonnenstrahl zitterte, und Archilochos steif daneben, nun auch verlegen, im Frack. . . ."
>
> "(the chapel) lit up, turned warm and friendly, the glittering of jewels and pearl necklaces filled the room, shoulders and breasts shone, and clouds of the best perfume rose up. . . . Bishop Moser stepped up to the pulpit, full of dignity in his black robe of office. He put the Bible with its bright gold edge on the rough lectern, folded his hands and looked down. . . . The bridal pair sat directly beneath him, Chloé radiant with joy, her big, black eyes full of faith, all wrapped up in a delicate, veil-like cloud in which there shimmered a sunbeam; Archilochos stiffly next to her, now also embarrassed, in his tail coat. . . .)[14]

A truly touching scene of impending bliss, with only the slighest touches of irony to indicate the coming turn of events. For, no sooner is the ceremony terminated and the new bridegroom prepared to leave the chapel on the arm of the lovely Chloé, to the tune of Mendelssohn's wedding march, than he is overcome by a sudden flash of insight. He cries out like a mortally wounded animal and escapes from the scene of his shame—out into the street where he is greeted by a howling mob, who pursue him with insults and stones. He

---

[13]Wolfgang Kayser, *Das Groteske*, (Oldenburg, 1957), p. 128.
[14]*Grieche sucht Griechin*, p. 152.

finally finds refuge in a dark corner under the staircase of a tenement building, where he cowers until the crowd has tired of the pursuit. Thus ends the wedding ceremony. Dürrenmatt generally tends to take a dim view of marriage, and the light tone of this particular book is not enough to conceal this basic pessimism. What more eloquent condemnation of "holy matrimony" could be imagined than this monstrous marriage, which turns the innocent Archilochos into a grotesque caricature.

Dürrenmatt is equally effective when he applies the alienation technique in reverse; a potentially horrible situation gently turns into its opposite. A charming example is provided by the episode of Archilochos' pitiful assassination attempt upon the President of State. Bomb in pocket, he scales the wall of the palace, intent upon his act of revenge upon society. When he eventually does confront his victim, however, events take a somewhat unexpected turn:

> "Er eilte über den weichen Teppich, doch stand, als er die Türe aufriss, die Hand mit der Granate erhoben, der Staatspräsident vor ihm, im Schlafrock, so überraschend, dass Archilochos eben noch die Bombe in seiner Manteltasche verbergen konnte. "Entschuldigen Sie," stammelte der Attentäter."[15]
> ("He walked rapidly across the soft carpet, but as he threw open the door, his hand with the grenade lifted high, the President of State stood before him in his dressing gown, so unexpectedly that Archilochos was barely able to hide the bomb in his coat pocket. "Pardon me," stammered the would-be assassin.")

The introduction of one unexpected and incongruous element—the President's dressing gown—here becomes the pivot upon which the situation turns into its opposite. Would-be murderer and intended victim end up enjoying a candlelit, midnight snack of cold chicken and champagne together. The satire here is of a gentler nature than in the ferocious wedding scene. Rather than selecting one victim for ridicule, the author throws a benignly satirical light on all the participants—the absurd revolutionary, the ineffectual assassin, and the picture-book *Staatspräsident*. The author emerges as a man who is able to smile at the absurdities of the world he depicts.

Another element in the book serves to temper its pessimism: the author's occasional digressions into Hollywood-style fantasies. These are particularly apparent in some of the descriptions, descriptions which clearly reveal the fact that their author has worked on film scenarios more than once. These excursions into the never-never lands of *Kitsch* and soap opera stand in stark contrast to the feeling of futility expressed at the end of the book, and take away much of its impact—an escape into escape literature. Perhaps the most interesting example of this type of description occurs on the occasion of Archilochos' first visit to his bride's home. Dürrenmatt, who normally uses great restraint when it comes to erotic fantasies (food fantasies are more along his line) here indulges himself in a full flight of fancy. The result is the kind of sequence typical of the movies of the 40s and 50s, where sex is discreetly hinted at by luxurious settings and carefully selected props. So Archilochos, having entered Chloé's magnificent villa, is led along a trail of colorful paper

---

[15]*Ibid.*, pp. 173-174.

cut-outs in the shape of stars and comets on an intricate treasure hunt, which leads him past a cozy little boudoir, through a resplendent green and black bathroom, perfumed water steaming in the recessed tub, into the inner sanctum of Chloé's own bedroom. The Bower of Bliss, rediscovered. A similar concession to the public's love of luxury is made in the description of the upper regions of the Petit-Paysan office tower where Archilochos works. This top floor is a fantasy world of space, warmth and light, with baskets of flowers everywhere, soft music replacing the clatter of office machines, and delicate period furniture, lending a cultured air to the premises. It is a tongue-in-cheek description of the executive suite, to be sure. The incongruity reaches its peak, as Petit-Paysan, himself, emerges from his office, a volume of Hölderlin's esoteric poems in his hand. Nevertheless, descriptions of this sort represent temporary escapes from the ultimate conclusion of the novel, which is anything but gay.

The detective novels represent another form of Dürrenmatt's escape into escape literature. They contain less social satire than *Once a Greek*, and the grotesque element in them leans more heavily towards the monstrous. First and foremost, they testify to the author's love of story-telling. But they all contain the basic features typical of Dürrenmatt's work and Weltanschauung: ambiguous treatment of the hero, ambiguous treatment of the genre, and heavy use of the grotesque. The stories all center around a quixotic hero, a detective *sans peur et sans reproche*, who brings the full force of his intellectual acumen and moral conviction into an absurd and lonely battle for justice. Barlach in *The Quarry* and *The Judge and his Hangman*, Matthäi in *The Promise*, all have left the police force for the sake of pursuing a single-minded obsession. Like Archilochos, they are successful in their quest; like Archilochos, they are doomed to an ultimately absurd fate. Matthäi ends in an alcoholic stupor, Barlach in one novel falls into the trap he himself has set, and in the other, is made to realize the final futility of all his efforts as his recurring pain reminds him that death is imminent. A courageous man may still assert himself in the face of a hostile and callous world—in fact, Dürrenmatt posits such assertion as a moral imperative:

> "Ich weiss, wie fragwürdig wir dastehen, wie wenig wir vermögen, wie leicht wir uns irren, aber auch, dass wir eben trotzdem handeln müssen . . ."
> ("I know how questionable is our position, how little we are capable of, how easily we make mistakes, but I also know that just because of this, we must act.")

says his spokesman, Dr. H., in *The Promise*.[16]

Nevertheless, the ultimate absurdity remains, equally shocking whether it is caused by the transcendent fact of death or simply by one of the unfortunate and accidental combinations of circumstances which determine the life of man. With the help of cleverly constructed mystery plots, however, Dürrenmatt manages to temper the pessimistic impact of his novels.

Although conventional at first glance, Dürrenmatt's detective stories subvert the basic principle of the classical mystery, namely, that events must be

---

[16]Friedrich Dürrenmatt, *Das Versprechen*, (Zürich, 1952), p. 19.

developed by the rules of logic, as in a chess game. In so doing, the author again turns the genre into a satire of itself, a dead-end street, as he was well aware when he subtitled *The Promise* a "requiem to the detective novel." Arbitrary, accidental occurrences, rather than logical developments, become the pivots which determine the development of his plots. The narrator of *The Promise*, Dr. H., serves as the author's mouthpiece when he gives a vigorous critique of the conventional detective story and its lack of concern for the realities of life:

> "... ich ärgere mich über die Handlung in Euren Romanen. Hier wird der Schwindel zu toll und zu unverschämt. Ihr baut Eure Handlungen logisch auf; wie bei einem Schachspiel geht es zu. . . . Diese Fiktion macht mich wütend. Der Wirklichkeit ist mit Logik nur teilweise beizukommen. . . . auch spielt das Zufällige, Unberechenbare, Unkommensurable eine zu grosse Rolle."
>
> ("I am annoyed about the plot in your novels. Here the deception becomes too boldly outrageous. You build up your plots in a logical manner; things happen as if it were a chess game. . . . This kind of fiction makes me furious. Reality can be tackled only partially by logic. . . . the accidental, unaccountable, unexpected elements play too large a part.") [17]

Dr. H. equally reflects the author's views when he exhorts writers humbly to acknowledge the presence of the absurd element in the world, and include it in their calculations. The principle is effectively illustrated in the story line of *The Promise*. Inspector Matthäi really is a genius whose superb tactics prove fully successful—but a stupid accident prevents him from cashing in on the success of the manoeuver to which he has sacrificed his career. When the truth finally does come out, and Matthäi appears fully vindicated, he is too far gone in absinthe even to register the news.

Finally, there appears in the detective novels Dürrenmatt's usual love of the grotesque element, which deflects the tragic potential of his narrative into ambiguous humor. Again, the most brilliant example of grotesque alienation can be found in *The Promise*. An originally routine situation is here shifted into a finale of absolute horror, while glaring incongruities as well as dramatic irony provide multiple levels of ambiguity. It is one of Dürrenmatt's most successful single scenes. The setting is in a hospital, where Dr. H. has been summoned at the request of a little old lady on her death bed. He goes grudgingly, since it is Sunday, and he expects nothing more than a routine donation to the policemen's fund. The incongruity of the physical situation foreshadows the explosive divergence between the story he is about to hear and the manner of its presentation. It is difficult at first for Dr. H. to grasp that the old woman really is dying, so lively is the expression on her finely wrinkled, delicate face, so full of charm is her tone of voice. Eventually, however, he notices the gruesome tubes which protrude from under her blankets, like tentacles of some monstrous animal, connecting her to mysterious, evil-looking apparatus. As she begins to speak, in the rambling manner of the very old, it soon appears that this gentle-looking nonagenarian is kept alive

---

[17] *Ibid.*, p. 16.

only by the one supreme passion of her life, her hatred towards her even older sister. The story she tells the police commissioner, upon the insistence of her confessor, appears quite without particular relevance to her—and so the dying old woman reveals a series of frightful murders in a totally casual and unconcerned way. It turns out that the multiple sexual assaults and killings, which Matthäi has been trying to track down all his life, were performed by her dearly beloved, late husband, "*Albertchen selig*," as she calls him. The monstrous character of the man is totally ignored by Frau Schrott, who eagerly babbles on about how she decided to marry poor little Albert, (a strapping 23-year old), because he would have been lost in the world outside, being somewhat mentally retarded; how he never gave her any trouble, performed his handyman's chores faithfully and treated her with full respect, even to addressing her as "mother." But one fine day, as he returned from a bicycle excursion, she finds blood on his shirt and discovers he has killed a little girl. She scolds him severely; but unfortunately the incident repeats itself, little Albert has brought back the Buick full of blood. "Have you been killing a little girl again, Albert, dear, I said and I was very strict with him . . . he wasn't allowed to use the Buick for a week."[18] Eventually we find out that Albert dear was killed in a freak accident, just as he set out for his third kill—the trap Matthäi had set for him, unsuccessfully. The old lady neglects to notify the authorities of Albert's misbehavior, because such revelations would have been a source of triumph and spite to her sister. It is obvious that she herself attaches little importance to the incidents.

The horror of the situation is here brought out in threefold relief: by the ambiguous way the story is told; by the irony contained in the fact that the clues to Matthäi's life-long search have been found, but too late; and by the monstrousness of the "little Albert" who emerges from the old lady's description. The characters involved reflect two of Dürrenmatt's favorite grotesque themes: the monstrous nature of extreme old age, and the monstrous meal. Only in *Die Panne* has Dürrenmatt created monsters of senility that compare with the hateful and futile Frau Schrott. The monstrous meal is a common motif in the work of the author. Not surprising for a diabetic, Dürrenmatt tends to link together surfeit of food and impending judgment and catastrophe. The monstrousness of "*Albertchen selig*" is thus brought out in contrast to his seemingly innocent passion for food—in fact, his wife declares his weakness for chocolates to be his only shortcoming. A typically Dürrenmatt "monstrous meal" situation arises when he is found out a second time. He is sitting at breakfast, gulping down his eggs, four at a time, together with innumerable pieces of bread and jam and pickled cucumbers, when Frau Schrott warns him never to kill a little girl again: " 'Alright, Ma,' he said, fixed himself another piece of bread and jam, and went out into the yard." The discrepancy between the contents of the narrative and the flippantly casual manner of narration is explosive; the grotesqueness of the situation underscores its total futility. Justice stands no chance in this sort of a world; and Matthäi's heroic efforts are doomed from the beginning.

It is perfectly clear that Dürrenmatt is a writer who thrives on paradox at all levels. A great believer in the power of art, he goes underground into

---

[18]*Ibid.*, p. 202.

genres which normally escape this classification. A profound pessimist, he makes us laugh; an unalterable optimist, he points out to us the absurdity of our universe. A cynic, he insists on creating images of courageous men; a humanist, he reduces his heroes to caricatures. He, himself, is fully aware of his own paradoxical nature. We find a typical confession to this effect in one of his lectures:[19]

"In dieser Zeit Schriftsteller sein zu wollen, heisst mit dem Kopf durch die Wand rennen. Mein Damen und Herren, das tue ich leidenschaftlich gern, und ich bin der Meinung, dass Wände geradezu dazu erfunden sind...."

("To wish to be a writer in this day and age means to go with your head through the wall. Ladies and gentlemen, I am passionately fond of doing just that, and I rather think that walls have been invented for that specific purpose.")

Mount Saint Vincent University
Halifax, Nova Scotia

---

[19]"Fingerübungen zur Gegenwart," in *Theaterschriften und Reden,* p. 44.

The Death of Language in *Death in Venice*

By Graham Good

George Steiner, in his recent essay "The Language Animal,"[1] states that "there occurred in the first quarter of this century a crisis of language and a re-examination of language in the light of that crisis."[2] Among the works he cites in this connection are "Hofmannsthal's *Lord Chandos Letter*, which, as early as 1902, poses the problem of the deepening gap between language and meaning, between the poet's addiction to personal truth and the eroded mendacities of his idiom . . . the language-polemics of Karl Kraus . . . Wittgenstein's *Tractatus* and the linguistic-logical exercises of the Vienna Circle." Other reflections of the crisis are to be found in Kafka ("No writer has ever made of the resistance of language to truth, of the impossibility of adequate

---

[1] *Encounter*, 33, No. 2 (August 1969), 7-24.
[2] This, and subsequent quotations from Steiner, are on pp. 12-13.

human communication, a more honest or more eloquent statement"), in Hermann Broch's *The Death of Vergil* ("In it the poet comes to recognize in the act of poetry, in a commitment to language, a blasphemy against life and the needs of man"), and in Elias Canetti's *Auto-da-fé* ("the representative fable of speech-civilisation going to violent ruin"). Steiner includes "new uses of silence in the music of Schönberg and Webern" among further expressions of this "Central European school of silence" whose forebears are Hölderlin, Rimbaud and Mallarmé. It is tempting to add to Steiner's list such items as Heidegger's habit of taking Greek and German words back to their origins, or Rilke's attempt in the *Sonnets to Orpheus* to treat words less as references to things than as higher and more real substitutes for them: "Gesang ist Dasein."[3] And of course one could pursue the list beyond Steiner's frame of reference to include such works as Sartre's *La Nausée* or Beckett's *L'Innommable*.

This crisis, which Steiner takes as the concentration of a wider "malady of civilisation," may be stated as the opposition between a societal language felt as untrustworthy or meaningless, and various attempts at founding a "pure" language, whether purely logical, purely self-referring, or pure in the sense of "original, uncorrupted." These attempts may end in the ultimate purity of silence. (A second answer is the critique of impure language; in literature this often takes the form of parody, the attempt to raise a structure of implied meaning through the arrangement of outdated or corrupted styles.) But this kind of linguistic purism is very precarious; by retreating, by refining itself so drastically, it comes to lack the cultural vitality it needs to affect the general use of language. Although all artistic and philosophical language is in some degree a heightened or purified version of ordinary language, the distance between the two is now felt as almost unbridgeable. On one hand the "pure" languages develop into closed, autonomous systems demanding initiates rather than common readers, while societal language is rejected or parodied on the other.

Thomas Mann's *Death in Venice* (1912) fits squarely into Steiner's framework (Central Europe, 1900-1925), and may usefully be read in terms of the "crisis of language." Although both the themes (most obviously the conflict between 'art' and 'life') and the language[4] of the story have been thoroughly analysed, the thematic role of language *within* the story has been relatively neglected. The conflict between Aschenbach and Venice is not only a battle between art and life, but also an opposition of two modes of language: the "pure" writing style of Aschenbach and the "impure," vague, and suggestive speech patterns of Venice.

Of course Aschenbach cannot be taken as a representative of all the different linguistic "purists," yet the austere and fastidious character of his art clearly associates him with this trend. Among the qualities central to his mature work are "adelige Reinheit, Einfachheit und Ebenmässigkeit der

---

[3]"Song is Being," *Sonette an Orpheus*, I, 5.

[4]Notable among stylistic studies are Frederic Amory, "The Classical Style of *Der Tod in Venedig*," *Modern Language Review*, 59 (1964), 399-409; Fritz Martini, "*Der Tod in Venedig*," in *Das Wagnis der Sprache: Interpretationen deutscher Prosa von Nietzsche bis Benn* (Stuttgart: Ernst Klett, 1954), 176-224; and William H. McClain, "Wagnerian Overtones in *Der Tod in Venedig*," *Modern Language Notes*, 79 (1964), 481-495.

Formgebung," "Meisterlichkeit und Klassizität."[5] But at the point where the story opens, Aschenbach's language is showing signs of *rigor mortis*: "er wandelte sich ins Mustergültig-Feststehende, Geschliffen-Herkömmliche, Erhaltende, Formelle, selbst Formelhafte . . ."[6] His straining for a cold purity of language is starving his art to death. Yet instead of dying in the solitude of the study, it dies in Venice. Aschenbach abandons the solitary work of refining language into written art and becomes captivated by language as sound, echoing and fading in the open. The active writer, exhausted, becomes the passive listener, seduced by the disintegration of language in the public spaces of Venice (the canals and squares, the hotel and beach) into a multilingual buzz, into repeated lies and echoed servilities, into whispers and mutterings and mumbled confessions, into music and meaningless sound.

This linguistic and aesthetic transition is linked to an ethical one. Aschenbach's classicistic style defies his period's predominant use of language to suggest, vaguely and impressionistically, more than it states, and this is linked to his moral sternness in defying that period's apparent sympathy and intellectual complicity with ethical weakness.[7] In Venice he comes to welcome both of these tendencies that he had previously defied. Steiner speaks of "Kraus' maniacal conviction that clarity and purity of syntax are the ultimate test of a society," and Mann's Venice fails on both counts: its moral degradation is expressed in its degradation of language. Thus between isolated purity and public corruption, whether linguistic or ethical, there is no longer any continuity, no longer any middle possibility of honest and straightforward relationships. The most striking thing about Aschenbach is that he is unsociable, a writer who cannot or will not speak. His love affair is predicated on the absence of normal social relations, in fact, on the absence of speech altogether. Between the solitary perfection of literary art and the corruption of social speech, the sane and vital middle ground of language has disappeared. In the gap which it leaves, Aschenbach's quite normal fatherly admiration for Tadzio—Mann hints, "Einen Sohn hatte er nie besessen"[8]—is left *unspoken*, and because of this it slowly becomes *unspeakable* in the sense of tabu.

Aschenbach does not plan his holiday with a view to making friends. The spoken word, the vehicle of normal social life, does not attract him. Resting from writing, he does not want to talk, but to enjoy in his accustomed solitude a release from the bonds of words. He wants to hear languages that he cannot understand, and he is attracted to the Adriatic island partly by the prospect

---

[5]"A discriminating purity, simplicity and evenness of attack," "mastery and classicism." Thomas Mann, *Sämtliche Erzählungen* (Frankfurt a.M.: S. Fischer, 1963), p. 362. English versions of the quotations are from *Death in Venice*, A revised edition of the authorized translation by Kenneth Burke, with a critical essay by Erich Heller (New York: Random House Modern Library College Editions, 1970). Future references will give: first, a page reference to the German edition cited; second, the English translation; and third, a parenthetic page reference to the English edition (in this case, p. 17). Where there is no direct quotation, the German page reference is followed simply by the English one in parenthesis.

[6]362. "He inclined toward the fixed and standardized, the conventionally elegant, the conservative, the formal, the formulated, nearly" (18).

[7]This period is presumably around the turn of the century, when Naturalism, Symbolism, Impressionism and Aestheticism were sometimes considered together, as in Max Nordau's famous polemic *Entartung* (1893), under the general heading of "Decadence."

[8]363. "He had never had a son" (18).

of its "in wildfremden Lauten redenden Landvolk," but the relief is baulked
by what he finds in the hotel: "eine kleinweltliche, geschlossen österreichische
Hotelgesellschaft."[9] The last thing he wants is a linguistically closed circle,
particularly a German-speaking one. The island is far from the "Allerwelts-
ferienplatz"[10] which he initially planned for himself, and which he finds in
Venice.

Here, like the elements of sea, land and sky, the languages of the world
erode their dividing lines and flow into one another. In the Lido hotel
Aschenbach finds, instead of German alone, a mixture of many tongues:
"Gedämpft vermischten sich die Laute der grossen Sprachen."[11] The Babel
of the hotel is echoed on the beach by Tadzio's friends, who chatter in Polish,
French and several Balkan languages.[12] On Aschenbach's first evening, dinner
is announced in English, while Tadzio's mother speaks to the governess in
French. After Aschenbach's abortive departure the Swiss liftboy says to the
German writer, "Pas de chance, monsieur."[13] The latter's arrival in Venice
is accompanied by the jeering French phrases of the old dandy. French, as
Joel A. Hunt has noted, is often used by Mann in contexts of charlatanry or
eroticism; it appears as the specious "*lingua franca* of the international set,"[14]
the language into which the Russian Clavdia Chauchat lures the German Hans
Castorp, and in which the swindler Felix Krull is so fluent. It is the linguistic
medium of the international hotel and sanatorium, both melting pots of the
separate identities of nations and individuals.

The situation of the two protagonists, a German writer and a Polish boy
in a cosmopolitan Italian resort, is almost maximally polyglot. Indeed, one of
the contributory factors of Aschenbach's infatuation is Tadzio's linguistic
remoteness. A comparable affair with a German boy in Munich is unthinkable.
For the writer, the incomprehensibility of the boy's "weich verschwommenen
Sprache"[15] gives it the musical seductiveness of sound without sense: "Aschenbach verstand nicht ein Wort von dem, was er sagte, und mochte es das
Alltäglichste sein, es war verschwommener Wohllaut in seinem Ohr. So erhob
Fremdheit des Knaben Rede zur Musik . . .[16]

The counterpoint to this seduction of Aschenbach by the music of uncom-
prehended language is the falling silent of his own tongue. As Venice breeds
lies to conceal the plague, German is the first language to be hushed. German
is the voice of truth for Aschenbach, the voice of his past literary life, but now
he is left alone among the exotic sounds which he had originally sought merely
for refreshment. Suddenly it seems to him "als ob die deutsche Sprache um ihn
her versiege und verstumme, so dass bei Tisch und am Strand endlich nur

---

[9]364. "Natives who . . . made strange sounds when they spoke;" "a provincial and
exclusively Austrian patronage at the hotel" (20).

[10]357. "Popular resort" (10; literally, "a vacation spot for all the world").

[11]373. "Sounds of all the principal languages formed a subdued murmur" (33).

[12]379 (43).

[13]386 (52).

[14]"The Stylistics of a Foreign Language: Thomas Mann's Use of French," *Germanic
Review*, 33 (1957), p. 10.

[15]373. "Soft vague tongue" (38).

[16]388-389. "Aschenbach did not understand a word of what he said, and though
it might have been the most ordinary thing in the world, it was a vague harmony in his
ear. So the foreignness of the boy's speech turned it into music . . ." (57).

noch fremde Laute sein Ohr trafen."¹⁷ Searching for the truth about the
epidemic in the newspapers, he found nothing in the foreign-language ones;¹⁸
only those in his own language, owing to the death of an Austrian tourist
shortly after returning from Venice, are at all aware of the gravity of the
situation; and printed German, like spoken German, soon vanishes from his
hotel. This language thus becomes the symbol of the order that Aschenbach
has abandoned.

The few conversations Aschenbach has in Venice are all with social
inferiors, with those in a position to serve him in some capacity. From the
beginning these dialogues are absurd, pointless or perfunctory, and they are
the only verbal contacts he makes. Their governing characteristic is repetition.
He often receives a fawning echo of his own words instead of a real reply.
The ticket clerk on the steamer faces Aschenbach like a grotesque double,
mocking the act of writing with his unnecessarily elaborate script and his
mannered manipulations of paper, ink and sand. His spoken words too are a
mere unctuous echo: " 'Nach Venedig!' wiederholte er Aschenbachs Ansuchen
. . . 'Nach Venedig erster Klasse!' "¹⁹ This servile manner is parodied by the
drunken old dandy, who endlessly reiterates his compliments to Aschenbach's
"Liebchen."²⁰

Communication also breaks down with the unlicensed gondolier who rows
Aschenbach to the Lido, and whose rhythmic and incomprehensible mutter-
ing to himself is a leitmotif of the encounter. Aschenbach repeats his orders
ineffectually: " 'Zur Dampferstation also,' sagte er . . . 'Zur Dampferstation
also,' wiederholte er . . ."²¹ The gondolier's words "Ich fahre Sie gut" are
echoed twice in the mind of the now submissive Aschenbach, along with the
words of his admission of their truth: "Das ist wahr . . ."²² Mostly, however,
Aschenbach meets subservience; more typical of those who serve him is the
obsequious gondolier whom he employs to follow the Polish family's boat, and
who takes up his customer's tone with lewd complicity and repetitious flatteries,
assuring Aschenbach "in demselben Tone . . . dass er bedient, dass er gewissen-
haft bedient werden solle."²³

Now Aschenbach's tone in this case is "hastig und gedämpft,"²⁴ just as
later he speaks to the street singer "gedämpft und fast mechanisch."²⁵ In
imprecision and repetitiveness he begins to imitate the corrupted Venetian
speech patterns that surround him, and on both sides this corruption
spreads with the plague. Even when he is privately sure of the truth,
Aschenbach takes a perverse delight in hearing repetitions of the same

¹⁷396. "German . . . seemed to be dropping away, so that finally he heard nothing
but foreign sounds at table and on the beach" (68).
¹⁸397 (70).
¹⁹364. " 'To Venice!' He repeated Aschenbach's request . . . 'To Venice, first class!' "
(20).
²⁰368 (27).
²¹369. " 'But it's to the steamer dock,' he said . . . 'To the steamer dock!' he
repeated" (28).
²²371. "I am rowing you well;" "That is so" (30).
²³399. "In the same tone that his wishes would be carried out, carried out faithfully"
(72).
²⁴399. "A hurried undertone" (72).
²⁵404. "In an undertone, almost mechanically" (80).

false answer to the same false question, desiring to be soothed again and again by the Venetians' musical lies. He enquires about the disinfectant successively of the shopkeeper, the hotel manager and the street singer. The replies he gets constitute between them a desperately false-sounding series of variations on the same themes and words, and a mocking use of the leitmotif technique: "eine vorbeugende Massregel . . . eine Massnahme der Polizei . . . eine vorbeugende Massregel . . . eine Verfügung der Polizei . . . eine polizeiliche Anordnung."[26] One of the most frequently recurring words ironically picks up Aschenbach's original idea of his holiday as "eine hygienische Massregel;"[27] both of these measures end in failure. Repetition approaches hysteria when he utters to the singer the fatal word "Übel" and gets this as a reply: "Ein Übel? Aber was für ein Übel? Ist der Scirocco ein Übel? Ist vielleicht unsere Polizei ein Übel? Sie belieben zu scherzen! Ein Übel!"[28] Speech here degenerates into a cheap and hollow quasi-musicality.

Even the English travel clerk at first takes up familiar phrases about preventive measures, but then he tells Aschenbach the truth "in seiner redlichen und bequemen Sprache,"[29] English forming a sufficient contrast to the sounds of the "spitzbübisch behenden Süden"[30] to be a vehicle of the truth without shocking Aschenbach by a revival of his own silent and forsaken language. This conversation with the Englishman is the only exchange of important true information in the story, and yet even this is ineffectual since its aim is to get Aschenbach to leave at once. Not only does he ignore this advice himself, he also fails to communicate it to others, even though he actually phrases his warning to Tadzio's mother.[31] Thus the truth fails to break through the predominating use of language to deceive, flatter and reassure, to produce acquiescence rather than action. Words are uttered and then evaporate without effect; heedless of words the gondolier goes on rowing to the Lido, the plague goes on spreading, Aschenbach stays on in Venice.

Besides the mixture of languages and the ineffectuality of the dialogues he is involved in personally, Aschenbach is surrounded by many instances of actual physical erosion of speech, where the words go beyond uselessness to imperceptibility. If his own conversations dissolve into quasi-musical repetition and variation, it is a pattern he hears all around him. Speech and its close counterpoint of gesture become indistinct and incomprehensible. This process is already prefigured on the steamer to Venice as Aschenbach, reclining half asleep on the deck, is troubled by shadowy figures who pass him "mit unbestimmten Gebärden, mit verwirrten Traumworten."[32] When the gondoliers gather round to pick up the ship's passengers, their dialect is even further removed from understanding by the very atmosphere of the city: "Die Ruderer zankten immer noch; rauh, unverständlich, mit drohenden Gebärden. Aber

---

[26]397, 401, 404. "A matter of precaution . . . a police regulation . . . a precautionary measure . . . a police regulation . . . a regulation of the police" (70, 76, 80).

[27]355. "A hygienic precaution" (7).

[28]404. "A plague? What kind of plague? Is the Sirocco a plague? Perhaps our police are a plague? You like to joke! A plague!" (80; I have supplied the translation of the third sentence, omitted by Burke).

[29]407. "In his forthright, easy-going English" (83).

[30]406. "Tricky, nimble-witted South" (83).

[31]409 (87).

[32]366. "With vague gestures, muddled dream words" (24).

die besondere Stille der Wasserstadt schien ihre Stimmen sanft aufzunehmen, zu entkörpern, über der Flut zu zerstreuen."[33] The very acoustics of Venice thus seem to exert a disembodying and destructive effect on words while giving them a haunting, almost Wagnerian beauty.

On the beach, too, words float unheeded in the air: the Russian parents are always calling the names of their heedlessly playing children[34] and soon the ritual calling of Tadzio's name, whether by his friends[35] or by his all-female family party,[36] becomes a leitmotif. Charmed by it, Aschenbach manages to ascertain "dass 'Tadzio' gemeint sein müsse, die Abkürzung von 'Tadeusz' und im Anrufe 'Tadziu' lautend."[37] This orderly piece of deduction costs him a considerable exertion because he is already beginning to accept speech as pure non-referential sound or music; he is already "abgelenkt von den Stimmen der Jugend."[38] Even when he has worked out the boy's name, his only use for it is a private relishing of its music: "Er freute sich des Klanges, er fand ihn in seinem Wohllaut dem Gegenstande angemessen, wiederholte ihn im stillen . . ."[39] Aschenbach makes no audible contribution to Tadzio's aureole of sound, but only listens with closed eyes to "diesen in seinem Innern antönenden Gesang."[40]

Just as speech tends to disintegrate into music, so music itself is an important accompaniment to the disintegration of order. Except for Tadzio's friends, each of those noisy, gesticulating groups which prefigure the Bacchic rout of Aschenbach's final dream has an actual musical accompaniment. The sound of military horns excites the gang of clerks and draws them up on to the deck of the steamer as it lies in the lagoon. The singers who entertain Aschenbach on his way to the Lido have mandolins and guitars. In the Mass at San Marco, he stands among the murmuring congregation listening to the singing of the priest.[41] To Aschenbach himself, Venice is historically a city "welche den Musikern Klänge eingab, die wiegen und buhlerisch einlullen."[42]

The scenes of the street singing and of Aschenbach's dream bring to a climax the dissolving of rational speech into chaotic sound. The leader of the singers is "fast ohne Stimme,"[43] his song is "lediglich albern dem Wortlaute nach,"[44] and the final encore is "ein dreister Schlager in unverständlichem Dialekt."[45] Even these worthless words, even the musical accompaniment, vanish in the laughing chorus, and the mouth is abandoned to pure noise.

---

[33]369. "The rowers were wrangling, harshly, incomprehensibly, with threatening gestures. But the strange silence of this canal city seemed to soften their voices, to disembody them, and dissipate them over the water" (28).

[34]377 (40).

[35]379 (43); 416 (97).

[36]380 (43-44).

[37]380. "That it must be 'Tadzio,' the shortened form of 'Tadeusz,' and sounding in the vocative like 'Tadziu' " (43).

[38]379. "Diverted by the childish voices" (42).

[39]379. "He was pleased with the resonance of this; he found it adequate to the subject. He repeated it silently" (42).

[40]380. "This song ringing within him" (44).

[41]398 (71).

[42]399. "Suggested to composers seductive notes which cradle and lull" (73).

[43]402. "With not much of a voice" (77).

[44]403. "Stupid enough so far as the words went" (78).

[45]405. "A 'big number' in incomprehensible dialect" (81).

This development culminates soon afterwards in the orgiastic sounds of the dream: "Rasseln, Schmettern und dumpfes Donnern, schrilles Jauchzen dazu und ein bestimmtes Geheul im Gezogenen u-Laut,—alles durchsetzt und grauenhaft süss übertönt von tief girrendem, ruchlos beharrlichem Flötenspiel, welches auf schamlos zudringende Art die Eingeweide bezauberte."[46] All that remains of words is an isolated phrase, not linked to other words to make sense, but left to gain a terrible obscurity through its detachment from discourse: "Aber er wusste ein Wort, dunkel, doch das benennend, was kam: *'Der fremde Gott!'* "[47]

The converse of the disintegration of outward communication is the increase of introspection. Feeling, undisciplined by clear expression, grows beyond bounds. Words which would be unutterable to another are turned inwards and privately savoured. Tadzio, that name he dare not call out, he repeats instead to himself on the beach,[48] and as he falls asleep alone by the open window in the dawn, his lips slowly form a name.[49] It is made clear that talking to himself is not one of Aschenbach's previous habits, but something that overtakes him in Venice. About to leave for the station, he thinks he is seeing Tadzio for the last time, "und indem er gegen seine Gewohnheit das Gedachte wirklich mit den Lippen ausbildete und vor sich hinsprach, fügte er hinzu: 'Sei gesegnet!' "[50] Normally, Aschenbach keeps speech, thought and writing apart and orderly; but here he succumbs to half-utterance, his lips forming the words but no ear catching them. Near the end we see the famous writer sitting in the deserted square: "seine schlaffen Lippen, kosmetisch aufgehöht, bildeten einzelne Worte aus von dem, was sein halb schlummerndes Hirn an seltsamer Traumlogik hervorbrachte."[51] The words which he has refused to utter have rotted inside him and lost all order and sense. They are neither wholly suppressed nor properly uttered, but merely bubble to the surface and agitate the lips to no purpose.

In the midst of all this corruption of the spoken word, the love of Aschenbach and Tadzio is eloquent by its very silence. Aschenbach's verbal declarations of affection and love are made unheard and in solitude. It is to himself, alone in the darkness of the park, that Aschenbach whispers the universal formula of longing, "Ich liebe dich!"[52] Tadzio knows his secret and guards it by silence. "Er sah ihn, und verriet ihn nicht."[53] Theirs is the language of looks, the adoration of the "Einsam-Stummen"[54] for one who epitomizes "das

---

[46]410. "Clanking, blaring, and a dull thunder, with shrill shouts and a definite whine in a long-drawn-out u-sound—all this was sweetly, ominously interspersed with and dominated by the deep cooing of wickedly persistent flutes which charmed the bowels in a shamelessly intrusive manner" (88).

[47]410. "But he knew one phrase; it was veiled, and yet would name what was approaching: 'The strange god!' " (88).

[48]379 (42).

[49]394 (64).

[50]383. "He did what was unusual with him, really formed the words on his lips and spoke them to himself; then he added: 'God bless you!' " (49).

[51]414. "His loose lips, set off by the cosmetics, formed isolated words of the strange dream logic created by his half-slumbering brain" (95).

[52]396. "I love you!" (68).

[53]413. "He saw him, and did not betray him" (93).

[54]372. "A man who lives alone and in silence" (32).

Göttlich-Nichtssagende."[55] Fritz Martini's formula for this affair is a just one: "eine wortlose Liebe aus reinem Gefühl."[56] There is a strong correlation between the wordlessness and the love: feeling, released from the restraints of communication, is intensified beyond all reason, beyond all limits.

Silence is the ultimate fate of language on either side of the gap which has opened up within it. It must die either of its own aloofness from social life or of its own degradation by that life. The story of Aschenbach demonstrates this. The moral and artistic purity of his writing makes it more and more arid and lifeless; as a silenced writer, he falls silent as a social, moral and emotional being. He displays successive and interrelated failures to speak: first, he does not open normal friendly relations with Tadzio and his family; second, he does not warn them about the plague; and third, he does not declare his love to Tadzio. Instead of speaking to others he either talks to himself or listens to others, and this listening passes from an aesthetic music-appreciation into an immoral acquiescence in the face of lies. Aptly enough, Aschenbach's avowal of support to the Venetians' effort to "hush up" the plague is itself yet another of those repetitive whispers that go unheard. " 'Man soll schweigen!' flüsterte er heftig. Und: 'Ich werde schweigen.' "[57] The moral impurity of this silence makes it the opposite of Wittgenstein's "Wovon man nicht sprechen kann, darüber muss man schweigen."[58] Aschenbach refuses to tell the truth, Wittgenstein refuses to tell untruths. And yet, after all, silences sound very much alike. How is one to tell the pure silence of the artist or philosopher who refuses to risk flattery and lies from the impure silence of those who fail to speak out against flattery and lies of others?

At the beginning of the story the plight of Aschenbach's writing is its loss of emotional persuasiveness: "es schien ihm, als ob ermangle sein Werk jene Merkmale feurig spielender Laune, die, ein Erzeugnis der Freude, mehr als irgendein innerer Gehalt, ein gewichtiger Vorzug, die Freude der geniessenden Welt bildeten."[59] Language as austere truth-content will earn respect, but will seem impoverished without the excitement of sensuality and feeling. Aschenbach abandons the one only to be swamped by the other. This is his language crisis: that veracity and persuasiveness, the sense and the music of language, have parted company, leaving a choice between lifeless truth, flattering lies, and silence.

There is, however, one example in the story of how language can regain its wholeness and reunite its estranged capabilities. It is, of course, the essay that Aschenbach writes as he sits on the beach watching Tadzio, "die Musik seiner Stimme im Ohr."[60] From this inspiration come the qualities of "Lauterkeit, Adel und schwingende Gefühlsspannung"[61] which distinguish the piece from

---

[55]378. "The divinely arbitrary" (41). Literally the phrase is "godly nothing-saying;" "divine incommunicativeness" is my suggestion.

[56]   "A wordless love out of pure feeling" (*Das Wagnis der Sprache*, p. 202).

[57]409. " 'It must be kept quiet!' he whispered fiercely. And: 'I will keep quiet' " (87).

[58]   "Whereof one cannot speak, thereof one must be silent." *Tractatus Logico-Philosophicus* (London: Routledge & Kegan Paul, 1922), p. 189.

[59]357. "It seemed to him that his work lacked those marks of fiery, sportive emotionalism which, themselves the fruits of joy, and more direct in their appeal than any depth of content, set the conditions for the delight of an appreciative public" (9).

[60]391. "Listening to the music of his voice" (61).

[61]391. "Clarity, . . . poise, and . . . vibrant emotional tension" (61).

the stiff correctness of his recent work. It is not, as one might have imagined, some last frenzied and poetic outpouring, but a very social piece of writing, a "kleine Abhandlung"[62] composed in response to a topical cultural controversy. The striking incongruity between this intellectual product and its erotic and musical inspiration shows how far their respective qualities have drawn apart. Yet, despite its tantalizing slightness, the essay hints at a possible reunion between meaning and music, clarity and feeling, truth and persuasion. By this time it is too late for Aschenbach to realise this possibility in any substantial work. But Mann, in *Death in Venice* as a whole, makes good Aschenbach's failure in his triumphant description of it, a description whose intellectual reach and musical-emotional richness make it a major step in overcoming the crisis of language.

University of British Columbia.

---

[62]391. "Little tract" (61).

Technique and Function of Time in Hesse's *Morgenlandfahrt:* A Culmination

J. Kotka

By Karen O. Crenshaw and Richard H. Lawson

Die Morgenlandfahrt (The Journey to the East, 1932) represents the culmination of the innovative use of time by Hermann Hesse. *Demian* (1919) though showing occasional signs of the disintegration of chronological time, is still rooted in a narrative continuity. *Der Steppenwolf* (1927) lacks a strong narrative framework against which to measure time; time no longer serves primarily as a framework, but rather as a cyclic subconscious force, a subjective indicator of the tides of personality and emotion. And after *Die Morgenlandfahrt*, in *Das Glasperlenspiel* (1943) Hesse goes back to the psychological novel, making use of heavily stylized, though occasionally distorted, chronological time.

Die Morgenlandfahrt, since it is written in the form of a fairy tale, is exempt from the necessity of continuous narration, from many of the conventions of cause and effect, and from the consequences of time. Hesse has freed himself from the restraint of having, in effect, to defend the technique of time distortion within a realistic or psychological novel. Time, forming a commentary on what is expected versus what is actual in a fairy-tale world, functions as a distancing device, and this tale, as fairy tales do, becomes abstract and cerebral.

There is nothing *ad hoc* in our designation of *Die Morgenlandfahrt* as a fairy tale. Critics of a quarter century ago, while Hesse was still writing— and long before his cisatlantic popularity among the disaffected young—des-ignated it as a fairy tale,[1] despite its obvious deviations from the norm of that genre, as represented by, say, the Grimm fairy tales (*Kinder- und Hausmärchen*). (Length would be the most prominent of such deviations; the correlate of length, narrative complexity, another.) Although Hesse himself —or the first-person protagonist, H. H.—does not precisely designate *Die Morgenlandfahrt* as a fairy tale, there are ample first-level indicators. The journey itself is said to be a journey not only to the East, but also into the realm of the fairy tale, "ins Märchenreich."[2] H. H. describes his profession as "Violinspieler und Märchenleser"—violin player and reader of fairy tales —and even reiterates the self-designation "Märchenleser" (pp. 29, 99). In brief, despite the role of the mystical—which becomes predominant toward the end—in limiting the effectiveness of the fairy-tale elements, we can accept *Die Morgenlandfahrt* as essentially a fairy tale.

The fairy-tale form is especially conducive to changes and permutations of time. If by being set in a mythical or vague locale, the fairy tale achieves a kind of universality, then this universality is reinforced by a parallel vagueness of time: "einmal," "once upon a time." Such formulas do not eliminate time; rather, they allow enough temporal detail to effect a balance between alienation and understanding on the part of the listener or the reader.

The transcending of chronological time and the compromising—if not ignor-ing—of logic may well be a more successful technique for describing existence than is the use of logical consequence. It would, accordingly, seem well adapted to the subtle and effective expression of a philosophy. Hesse's fairy-tale stage, foreshadowed—at least so far as the important category of time-treatment goes—in *Demian* and *Der Steppenwolf*, and represented precisely by *Die Morgenlandfahrt*, embraces his most successful expression of a philosophy.

As actual and fictitious places are mixed in *Die Morgenlandfahrt*, for example, on the one hand, Famagusta, and on the other, Morbio Inferiore, so the time element is neither unreal nor real; it draws from both categories. The actual journey to the East took place shortly after World War I. We infer the nonsequential nature of time from the simultaneity, or at any rate non-chronological juxtaposition of familiar historical data, for example, the im-plied simultaneity of post-World War I and the Hohenstaufen conquest of Sicily. Already one step further removed, and consonant with the narrative

---

[1]For example: Richard B. Matzig, *Hermann Hesse in Montagnola* (Basel: Amerbach, 1947), p. 94: "*Die Morgenlandfahrt* (1932) ist ein symbolisches Märchen...."

[2]Hermann Hesse, *Die Morgenlandfahrt* (Frankfurt: Suhrkamp, 1969), p. 7. Subse-quent page references in our text are to this edition. Translations are our own.

intermixture of history and fiction, is the juxtaposition of historical time, again, say, post-World War I, and a literary figure from a different era, thus Don Quijote. Such instances are plentiful, but we need not depend entirely on their evidence. Hesse clearly indicates his concept, first, of time as flowing, undemarcated, a stream: "Es strömte dieser Zug der Gläubigen und sich Hingebenden nach dem Osten, nach der Heimat des Lichts, unaufhörlich und ewig, er war immerdar durch alle Jahrhunderte unterwegs...."[3] And, second, each component of this diachronic procession, whether an individual or a group, "war nur eine Welle im ewigen Strom der Seelen, im ewigen Heimwärtsstreben der Geister..." (p. 17).[4]

Once the world of marked and counted time is overcome—"eine von Geld, Zahl und Zeit betörte Welt" (p. 18) and its appurtenances like railroads and timepieces—once all this is overcome, then the way is open for diachronic experience. Narration—telling, a function of time measurement—becomes difficult: "Schwierig wird das Erzählen ferner dadurch, dass wir ja nicht nur durch Räume wanderten, sondern ganz ebenso durch Zeiten" (p. 31).[5] And, now with the blending of the spatial and the temporal, it is but one step from the diachronic to the synchronic: "... unser Morgenland war ja nicht nur ein Land und etwas Geographisches, sondern es war die Heimat und Jugend der Seele, es war das Uberall und Nirgends, war das Einswerden aller Zeiten" (p. 31).[6] With the conversion of all times into one, H. H. is quite free of the tyranny of chronological time and of the latter's corollary: cause and effect. A so-called future event, or even a fictional event, may bring about a present result: "... so riefen wir das Gewesene, das Zukünftige, das Erdichtete schöpferisch in den gegenwärtigen Augenblick" (p. 33).[7]

Magic, that familiar fairy-tale component, bears a primary relationship to nonsequential time, for it can bypass sequential time, and space as well. The use of magic as a description or metaphor of psychological states is limited only by the limits of the mind. Hesse uses this kind of fairy-tale description in *Die Morgenlandfahrt* to emphasize the weaknesses of man's normal, that is, chronological perceptions of time. The musician and fairy-tale reader, H. H., having lost his perception of timelessness, or inner time, sees life in terms of a sequence of logical events which have happened since his break with the Brotherhood. These events, comprising the latter half of the tale, are at such paradoxical variance with the timeless prospectus of the first half that they produce a remarkable structural tension and, correspondingly, a growing uneasiness, a desire for resolution, on the part of the reader. That H. H., even as he resolves "niemals zu rechnen ... stets den Glauben stärker

---

[3]"This procession of the faithful and the submissive streamed toward the East, toward the home of light, incessantly and eternally—throughout the centuries it was ever under way...."

[4]"...was only a wave in the eternal stream of souls, in the eternal homeward urge of the spirits...."

[5]"Narration is also made difficult by the fact that we moved not only through areas, but also through eras."

[6]"...our East was not only a country and something geographical, but it was also the home and youth of the soul—it was the everywhere and nowhere, it was the unification of all eras."

[7]"...thus we creatively summoned into the present moment the past, the future, and the fictional."

zu wissen als die sogenannte Wirklichkeit" (p. 55),[8] nonetheless believes that these events can be set down in a history, is, of course, the crowning indication of his compartmentalization and of his separation from actual, that is, from synchronic time.

H. H. realizes that time was indeed transcended by the Brotherhood, but now that he is outside of the Brotherhood, he can no longer see how it was done, nor even the essential contradiction—the source of the reader's disquiet—in his own relationship to time. He struggles unwittingly with this contradiction but he is quite unable to formulate it: how can he express timelessness, the *Einswerden* of time, in terms of a history, a chronology of events in a cause-and-effect chain?

His renewed contact with the Brotherhood after a time-lapse is a measure of his sensed but unformulated need. The preliminary and external sign of this need is his "fixe Idee," his constant adverting to Leo, the capable, ever-present servant on the journey to the East, the Leo with whose disappearance at Morbio Inferiore H. H.'s connection with the journey dissolved: "Sie [H. H.] kommen immer und immer wieder auf die Episode mit jenem Diener Leo zurück. . . ." (p. 62). H. H.'s need has become so great that he is again receptive to the Brotherhood. Its timeless world has continued to exist all around H. H. ever since he had left it for the chronological world.

H. H.'s reunion with the Brotherhood, effected by the rediscovered Leo, takes place in a faceless building, among millions of well-catalogued archives, under the scrutiny of a vague and shifting company of characters. His reunion with timelessness is a reunion with a mystical—perhaps Jungian—higher personality. The characters whom he had tried to describe and record as separate personalities became the different manifestations of the united Brotherhood when he himself could again perceive them in the state of time-lessness. That a reunion with timelessness is to occur, that time will dissolve, that chronological time will cease to hold sway over H. H. is foretold even as Leo leads him by a much-detoured, zigzag route to the headquarters of the Brotherhood. Once more the familiar alignment of spatial multiplicity and temporal reduction to oneness, the latter process in the case of H. H. not yet quite complete: "Man hätte den Weg, der uns den ganzen Vormittag kostete, recht wohl in einer Viertelstunde zurücklegen können" (p. 88).[9]

The final demonstration of the fallacy of chronological sequence, and of cause and effect, is almost anti-climactic, almost trivial, as, with H. H. in the archives, the fairy-tale thread weakens, and the mystical dominates. H. H. is permitted to see three presumed histories of the journey to the East and the affair at Morbio Inferiore—his own account and those of two other would-be historians. Needless to say, the accounts do not agree, and were there ten rather than three, H. H. now realizes, "sie hätten vermutlich alle zehn einander widersprochen. . . . Nein, es war nichts mit unsern historischen Bemühungen. . . ." (p. 119).[10] As the separately described personalities be-came a variety of manifestations of the Brotherhood when H. H. perceived

---

[8]"never to count . . . always to know faith to be stronger than so-called reality."

[9]"The distance, which cost us the whole morning, could have been traversed very easily in a quarter of an hour."

[10]"all ten would probably have contradicted one another . . . No, our historical endeavors had come to nought. . . ."

them in timelessness, so the chronology of separate events which he had tried to analyze and order is now seen as a merely momentary, temporal manifestation of timelessness.

The highly developed function of time in *Die Morgenlandfahrt*, as both a way and an obstacle to timelessness, the latter state achieved with the final dissolution of the personality into the greater unity, has its inchoate antecedents in *Demian*. To be sure, the earlier novel is arranged on a conventional narrative framework. Events happen one after another; previous events have logical consequences. The plot can be told, and the clear sequence of events requires a reliance on time as an absolute.

But within this chronological framework in *Demian*, we can detect a pulsing—a lengthening and shortening of given periods of time. Sinclair's painting, for example, is a nonsequential description of time with lengthened pulse. The alternation of the light world and the dark world in Sinclair's childhood is a description of an otherwise undefined passage of time, which is comprised of smaller units of similar chronological uncertainty. The appearances and disappearances of Demian constitute a similar indicator of inner time for Sinclair. Each swing of the pendulum of his relationship with Demian marks an inner period, undefinable against the standard of chronological time, but definite by contrast with the different states which preceded and followed it. Toward the end of the novel, Demian appears in Sinclair's life less and less consequentially, that is, with less narrative motivation. Sinclair can now call Demian, or Demian's mother, without regard to time and space. Once Sinclair has internalized Frau Eva on the battlefield, he has internalized the eternal and achieved timelessness. Thus his final parting from Demian is not a parting in time, regardless of whether or not Demian has died, because Sinclair and Demian are now two elements in a continuing relationship, quite outside of time.

In *Der Steppenwolf* the narrative sequence is still further weakened, as Hesse increasingly subjectifies time. Chronological time is no longer a reliable framework. Of the several techniques used in *Der Steppenwolf* to subjectify time, one of the most effective is the box-within-a-box-within-a-box position of the original events. An observer begins the "story" by explaining how he came to possess the Steppenwolf manuscript. The events he describes occurred some time in the past and lasted a few months. The manuscript itself contains no indication of the quantitative passage of time. Within this timeless narrative in which minutes are powerful and weeks may be passed over without a word, we have the "Traktat vom Steppenwolf." The time described therein may be any time. The distinction of today, tomorrow, and yesterday, and any clear sequence of events, are completely lost. Time periods—with the significant exception of Harry Haller's reluctant visit to his former friend, the bourgeois professor, who measures his life by conventional time—are defined by inner monologues or by alternation of mood and subject.

In his conversations with Goethe and Mozart, Harry can already perform acrobatics with time. It does not matter whether the explanation is hallucination or the supernatural. The point is that time constitutes a continuum through which certain existences can move, if they are not trapped by the illusion of the reality of an hour. In his own small present, Harry can experience the minds of the past; he has learned to bring eternity into the present. When he learns to dance, he equates his feeling of eternity with the timelessness and self-forgetfulness of the experience. As subsequently in the Magic Theater, Harry finds that his personality and the problems attendant on it are manifestations of conventional, of chronological time. As he approaches timelessness, he becomes aware that both his personality and his problems are dissolving before him. What Pablo calls the prison of personality can no longer restrain; its giving way is equated precisely with "Uberwindung der Zeit," the conquest of time.[11]

Clearly Hesse's development of timelessness as the alternative to chronological time, and above all as the solvent for time-bound personality in its quest toward a higher unity, has, with *Der Steppenwolf*, reached the point where it is pushing through and around the confines of the realistic or psychological novel. Further development will require a more congenial genre, one better adapted to transcending chronological time. That, as we have seen, is the fairy tale, and with *Die Morgenlandfahrt* Hesse's innovative time technique attains a parity with his innovative time function.

Hesse's arrival at a parity, a harmony, between time technique and time function—as well as his subsequent abandonment thereof in *Das Glasperlenspiel*—bears comparison with a similar development, arrival, and abandonment on the part of Virginia Woolf. Like *Demian*, *The Voyage Out* is still essentially a narrative novel, but it too shows signs of the emergence of a different technique. Passage of time is slightly obscured, exact durations are vague and incalculable. Time begins to be described as the extension of a mental state rather than as an absolute measure. With *To the Lighthouse*, time becomes a cyclic subconscious force, much as in *Der Steppenwolf*, vague, subjective, prone to distortion by the personality of the characters, visible in constant change. *Orlando*, like *Die Morgenlandfahrt* a fairy tale, contains a freely moving time, which, effortlessly spanning centuries, marks the power, or the restlessness of the mind. And with *The Waves*, time no longer expresses a variable, pulsing inner continuum—perfectly realized in *Orlando*—but instead expresses an inner chaos. Difficult to read, as is *Das Glasperlenspiel*, *The Waves* suffers from an incoherence resulting from a chaotic and essentially threatening view of time.[12]

As far as concerns time technique and function, *Das Glasperlenspiel* amounts to a regression, or perhaps a reversion. Not only has Hesse returned to the psychological novel, but in it he displays a virtuosity of logical technique. Descriptions of time are conventional, indeed stylized. Time, far from expressing meaning, seems to serve as a "tangler" of meaning. Those earlier works of Hesse which we have considered were characterized by the striving of an individual after an integrated state, a striving which involved—

---

[11] Hermann Hesse, *Gesammelte Schriften* (Zürich: Suhrkamp, 1968), IV, 370.

[12] Despite similar progression and reversion in development of technique and function of time, Hesse and Woolf have, at bottom, very different ideas of time. Hesse shows human perception of conventional time to be an illusion, and human personality to be a result of that illusion. Through the resolution of *apparent* opposites in the categories of time and personality, man can pass beyond time and personality into timelessness and unity. Woolf, on the other hand, entertaining no hopes of unity, sees time as the enemy. A frail human personality is all one has with which to fight against this enemy. She would ideally achieve timelessness by means of personality; Hesse would achieve it by transcending personality.

required—the resolution of all temporal opposites and contradictions into a unity without time distinctions. In *Das Glasperlenspiel*, Josef Knecht is also striving after integration. But he shows no sign of being close to resolving the multiplicities of time, and his author gives no indication that the achievement of timelessness is even possible. Knecht's progress, or rather movement, on his quest is not marked by fewer and fewer time distinctions and a gradual approach to timelessness, but rather by one blind exploration after another of one temporal illusion after another.

Only in the short biographies which Hesse ultimately decided to place at the end of the novel does one find a sense of simultaneity. But while Knecht's life told from several points of view does produce something of the effect of many events happening at one time, timelessness is not so much emphasized as are the irreconcilable opposites which exist within the limits of time. This isn't to say that the germ from which timelessness in Hesse springs, that is, narrative time distortion, is not present, either in the concluding biographies or in the novel proper. But instead of giving the reader a sense of Knecht's inner perception of time, time distortion here succeeds only in distorting Knecht's personality itself—and with no indication that this will be followed by a dissolution of personality, to the end that he may attain a higher unity. If somewhat in *Demian*, increasingly in *Der Steppenwolf*, above all in *Die Morgenlandfahrt*, time distortion expressed an irregularly paced inner continuum, in *Das Glasperlenspiel* it expresses an inner chaos. Knecht, overwhelmed by the disorder of time, can find no resolution to his conflict; his drowning is inevitable—a drowning in chaos.

San Diego State College

Goethe's *Wanderjahre* as an Experimental Novel

J. Kostka

By EHRHARD BAHR

> IN WANDERJAHRE *the foundations*
> *. . . of the modern novel were laid.*
> Hermann Broch, "James Joyce and the Present."

"Every novel is an experiment," it has rightly been observed. Goethe's last novel *Wilhelm Meisters Wanderjahre oder die Entsagenden* (*Wilhelm Meister's Journeyman Years or the Renunciants*) is perhaps even more of an experiment than most other novels in world literature in view of the author's experimental attitude towards life and especially literature, as well as the *avant-garde* nature of his late works.[1] Though one can hardly claim that

---

[1] I am obliged to R. G. Collins' essay "Divagations on the Novel as Experiment," *Mosaic*, IV, 3 (1971), 1-11, for providing a stimulus as well as the introductory citation

Goethe's *Wanderjahre* directly influenced the form of the modern novel, excepting perhaps the works of Hermann Broch, the final shape of his work is surprisingly similar to the forms of the modern and contemporary novel.

Wilhelm Meisters Wanderjahre is probably the least read of Goethe's novels in Germany and abroad. The first part, *Wilhelm Meisters Lehrjahre* (*Wilhelm Meister's Apprenticeship*), though not as successful as the earlier narrative work, *Die Leiden des jungen Werther* (*The Sufferings of Young Werther*), a literary sensation, nevertheless had quite an impact on the history of the novel. It provided world literature with a new genre, the *Bildungsroman*, while in German literature *Lehrjahre* created a model for the nineteenth and twentieth century novel, from Gottfried Keller to Hermann Hesse, Thomas Mann, and Günther Grass. Thomas Carlyle's translation of this novel was relatively successful in the English-speaking world, giving rise to Wilhelm Meister's "English kinsmen" from Charles Dickens to Samuel Butler. Within the last few years, such English and American authors as Doris Lessing in *The Four-Gated City*, and Mary McCarthy in *Birds of America* have made use of the form of the *Bildungsroman*. (In a final note of comment on her novel, Doris Lessing writes: "This book is what the Germans call a *Bildungsroman*. This kind of novel has been out of fashion for some time: which does not mean that there is anything wrong with this kind of novel.")[2]

The second part of Goethe's novel, *Wanderjahre*, has only recently been discovered by critics who are interested in the form of the experimental novel. Interestingly enough, they have found Goethe to be a more radical experimenter with the form of the novel than such modern writers as Alfred Döblin, Hermann Broch, Robert Musil, and even Samuel Beckett. Formerly, *Wanderjahre* was either rejected as evidence of Goethe's artistic decline and senility, or it was treated with benevolent neglect as a curiosity, as a re-

for this article. My discussion of *Wanderjahre* is based to a large extent on Erich Trunz' commentary to *Goethes Werke*, vol. 8 (Hamburg, 1950), and on Hans Reiss' *Goethe's Novels* (London, Toronto, 1969), the latter bringing Goethe's complete narrative works to the attention of the English reading public. I am also in debt to those of my colleagues and friends in Goethe scholarship who have concentrated their attention on Goethe's last novel, among them Claude David, "Goethes Wanderjahre als symbolische Dichtung," *Sinn und Form*, 8 (1956), 113-128; Katharina Mommsen, *Goethe und 1001 Nacht* (Berlin, 1960), pp. 57-68; 118-152; Arthur Henkel, *Entsagung: Eine Studie zu Goethes Altersroman*, Hermaea, N.S. vol. 3, 2nd ed. (Tübingen, 1964); Bernd Peschken, *Entsagung in Wilhelm Meisters Wanderjahren* (Bonn, 1968); and Heidi Gidion, *Zur Darstellungsweise von Goethes Wilhelm Meisters Wanderjahren*, Palaestra, vol. 256 (Göttingen, 1969).

In the comparison of *Wanderjahre* to the *nouveau roman*, I base myself entirely on Klaus Netzer, *Der Leser des Nouveau Roman* (Frankfurt, 1970). For the concluding part of the article I am indebted to Karl Löwith, *From Hegel to Nietzsche: The Revolution in Nineteenth-Century Thought* (Garden City, N.Y., 1967). For the relationship of Goethe to Hegel, see Löwith, *ibid.*, pp. 2-28; Georg Lukacs, *Goethe und seine Zeit* (Bern, 1947), pp. 142-176; Hans Mayer, "Goethe und Hegel," *Von Lessing bis Thomas Mann: Wandlungen der bürgerlichen Literatur in Deutschland* (Pfullingen, 1959), pp. 180-197; Ernst Bloch, "Das Faustmotiv der Phänomenologie des Geistes," *Hegel-Studien*, 1 (1961), 155-171.

I have changed the literal translation of the title *Wilhelm Meister's Wandering* [or: *Travelling*] *Years*, which distorts the original meaning, to *Wilhelm Meister's Journeyman Years*. The text of *Wanderjahre* is cited according to book and chapter.

[2]*The Four-Gated City* (London, 1969), p. 711.

ceptacle of his old-age wisdom. In English translation the novel never had much of an audience. Carlyle translated only the first fragmentary edition of *Wanderjahre* of 1821, and it was not until 1890 that a complete translation of the second edition of the work of 1829 finally became available to the English reader.

Goethe's general attitude towards life tended to be experimental; as a matter of fact, experience (*Erfahrung*) was one of the key words of his thought and in his writing. In his autobiography he stressed the importance of experience for his own intellectual growth (*Poetry and Truth*, II, 7); and in his play *Die natürliche Tochter* (*The Natural Daughter*) he expressed the idea that experience is the master of life. Goethe believed that everything in life depended on so-called "primary experiments" (*Urversuche*); theories based on these "primary experiments" were to be considered safe and sound (*Maxims and Reflections*, 613). To him experience was infinite; the entire universe was open to experience in all directions (*Maxims and Reflections*, 308). "The further one progresses," he went on to say, "the closer one comes to the unexplorable," that is, the divine (*Maxims and Reflections*, 706). Appropriately, also, the history of science was regarded by him as a conflict between the individual on the one hand and direct experience and tradition on the other. In his *Theory of Colours* he recorded the history of experimental science, while at the same time conducting and minutely describing a great number of experiments in the field of optics. Moreover, his writings include an essay on the nature of experiments as intermediaries between subject and object. Philosophically, then, experiment to Goethe was a most basic need, acquainting man with his environment and establishing a relationship between man and his world ("The Experiment as Mediator between Object and Subject," 1792).

This experimental attitude also dominated Goethe's approach to his writing. His method was not that of the writer turned scientist, as outlined in Zola's famous treatise entitled *Le Roman expérimental*, but rather the artist's method of trial and error. Three versions of *Iphigenie auf Tauris* came into existence before the final form of the blank verse drama in 1787. Similarly, the *Lehrjahre* of 1795-96 was preceded by an earlier fragmentary version dating back to 1777. And, of course, it took Goethe more than sixty years to complete *Faust*. Only a few of his books were finished in one uninterrupted flow of work, as was *Die Leiden des jungen Werther*. The characteristic pattern of Goethe's literary work consists of a number of relatively brief creative periods that were staggered throughout his life. Whenever he was unable to finish a piece of writing in one creative streak, he put it aside to rest for a while. Later, he would resume work again, for a second and even a third time, writing from a somewhat different perspective until the project would reach its final form in what might be regarded as an evolutionary process of organic growth.

Work on *Wanderjahre* underwent three such creative periods; the first in 1807, when Goethe wrote a number of novellas that were to be included in the novel, with one of the novellas developing into a novel of its own, *Die Wahlverwandtschaften* (*The Elective Affinities*), published in 1809. The second period, in 1820, preceded the publication of the fragmentary version of 1821, with the final period following in the years 1825 to 1828, when

Goethe wrote the last and definitive version for print in 1829. The great differences between the two versions bear witness to the degree of experimentation that took place between the years of 1821 to 1829.

As early as 1807, when Goethe began to work on the continuation of *Lehrjahre*, he looked at a great number of narratives of the kind that consists of a series of tales held together by a frame story, such as *The Canterbury Tales*. Indeed, in one respect it is not difficult to compare *Wanderjahre* to Chaucer's stories, since seven of the eight novellas in Goethe's novel may be regarded as belonging to the "Marriage Group," that is, dealing with problems of marriage. However, Goethe did not read Chaucer's *Canterbury Tales* at that time; he did read Boccaccio's *Decameron*, Margaret of Navarre's *Heptameron*, Antoine de la Sale's *Cent Nouvelles nouvelles*, and *Thousand and One Night*. In arranging his narrative material, Goethe was looking for a guiding principle. Experimenting with various forms of narrative art, he spent more than twenty years in completing the final version of *Wanderjahre*.[3]

Since the text of 1821 is so different from the second and last version that critics have been insisting "it is almost impossible to speak of two different novels,"[4] it becomes evident that much experimenting was still going on in the years 1825 to 1828. The final version clearly shows that Goethe was no longer interested in simply telling a story, but in reflecting the totality of life. In this respect Goethe's endeavors were closely related to those of Hegel who tried to establish a relationship between man and his world, and between human action and natural events, all being parts of a total process. While their methods and media were different, the goal common to both Goethe and Hegel was recognition and experience of the totality of life. For his vast influence on the next centuries Hegel is indebted to Karl Marx, who, as one of the most forceful interpreters of Hegelian philosophy, preserved, though in a dialectical fashion, the modernity of Hegel's thought. Goethe fared less well at the hands of his critics. Traditional German Goethe scholarship has largely denied him the reputation of a modernist.

The *Wanderjahre* of 1829 consists of three books, including eight novellas, as well as numerous letters, a diary and archival documents. In addition, the novel contains two comprehensive collections of almost two hundred aphorisms each, "Betrachtungen im Sinne der Wanderer" ("Reflections in the Spirit of the Wanderer"), and "Aus Makariens Archiv" ("From Makarie's Archive"), as well as two philosophical poems "Vermächtnis" ("Testament") and "Im ernsten Beinhaus" ("In the Burial Chamber"), also called "Gedicht auf Schillers Schädel" ("Poem on Schiller's Skull"). Neither the aphorisms nor the poems show any clear relationship to the narrative, but they contribute to the multitude of literary forms assembled in this novel, not to mention the great variety of styles.

The protagonist Wilhelm Meister is as an individual no longer the center of attention as in *Lehrjahre*, but he becomes a novelistic device connecting a number of small, self-contained worlds which are independent of one another though affecting each other. There is no clearly defined linear plot structure. Wilhelm travels with his son Felix from one place to another, from one world to another, as the direct or indirect witness of various modes of life. His

---

[3]See Katharina Mommsen, *Goethe und 1001 Nacht* (Berlin, 1960), pp. 57-68.
[4]Hans Reiss, *Goethe's Novels* (London, Toronto, 1969), p. 225.

travels, his conversations, readings and writings become the connecting links between the various independent worlds. Goethe used the same type of technique in *Faust, Part II*; in a conversation with Eckermann, he agreed with the latter's statement that he used "the fable of a well-known hero only as a sort of string winding its way through the entire story in order to tie onto it whatever he fancied."[5] These views of *Faust* equally apply to *Wanderjahre*, despite the great differences of genre and type of protagonist in the two works.

Wanderjahre is not a novel of individual development, or *Bildung*, but a novel about people functioning in groups. Individual biography which, according to George Lukács, is the traditional theme and structure of the novel, is replaced by human social behaviour in general.[6] Marriage and family as basic units of social life play a major role and form the main theme of the interpolated novellas. However, not only the more intimate forms of social behaviour, such as love and friendship, are depicted, but also the more public forms of human association, such as educational, philanthropic, professional, economic, political and religious groups. They form the major part of the action in the frame story. The most important groups include the Pedagogic Province, a kind of educational utopia, the secret Society of the Tower, which in its teachings and practices resembles the Masonic order, the League of Emigrants whose members are to found and maintain a new state in America, and the League of Immigrants who, while staying behind in another part of Europe, also plan a new type of society. Finally, there is the circle around Makarie, a saint's figure, who participates not only in human life on earth but also in the life of the universe. One of Goethe's most daring creations, Makarie is part of the solar system and center of the family of man depicted in the novel; she represents cosmic love regulating human actions and affairs. All these societies are experiments in new forms of communal life, thereby turning the novel into a Utopia. *Wanderjahre* deals with the emergence of a new type of man who, together with other likeminded men and women, is to build a new society. This collective aspect of the novel's theme is reflected in the structure of its individual parts. In an aesthetic sense, the "separate but equal" societal entities correspond to the "separate but equal" narrative entities. Goethe was very conscious of the experimental and collective character of *Wanderjahre* and, with ironic understatement, he characterized the novel as "a collective undertaking, so to speak, ... only put together for the purpose of linking disparate entities,"[7] "a mere aggregate,"[8] "a mélange."[9] Yet, the novel does not lack unity.

Its unity is one of a higher level. Corresponding to the character of the novel, it is a utopian unity, a unity that has to be established by the reader himself. The text of the novel, completed in 1829, has externally little in the way of a unified aspect. The unity of the work must be recreated with each new reading. As Goethe wrote to a reader of the first version in 1821:

[5]*Conversations with Eckermann*, 13 February 1831.
[6]*Die Theorie des Romans: Ein geschichtsphilosophischer Versuch über die Formen der grossen Epik*, 3rd ed. (Neuwied, 1965), pp. 79-82.
[7]Letter to Johann Friedrich Rochlitz, 28 July 1829 (quoted from H. Reiss, p. 222).
[8]Conversation with Friedrich von Müller, 18 February 1830 (quoted from H. Reiss, p. 222).
[9]Letter to Karl Friedrich Zelter, 5 June 1829 (quoted from H. Reiss, p. 222).

Coherence, aim and purpose lie within the book itself. If it is not of One piece, it is of One meaning, and this was precisely the task: to bring strange external events together so that the reader may feel that they belong together.[10]

And in a letter of 1829, following the same idea, Goethe wrote: "The intelligent reader will discover the serious and careful efforts with which I conducted and executed this second experiment (*Versuch*) to unite such disparate elements."[11] Such an experiment requires the highest degree of co-operation between narrator and reader. Goethe himself gave a demonstration of his experiment within the text of the novel.

In a letter to his wife Natalie, Wilhelm Meister tells the story of his friendship with the fisherman's son who drowned. The loss of this friend and the memory of his own helplessness are the basis for Wilhelm's later decision to become a surgeon. In the last chapter of the novel, Wilhelm is able to save his own son from the same kind of danger, namely, death by drowning. At first, when Wilhelm wants to tell his story, he realizes the difficulties of deciding where to begin. He is aware of the fact that as narrator he has complete freedom in arranging his material. But "there are so many things to tell," he says. He is less concerned with the various elements of the plot than with the projection of the *One* meaning he wants his reader, Natalie, to understand. The *One* meaning, however, cannot be found in the successive events of the plot, but only in the arrangement of the two separate and independent events, the death of his friend and his decision to become a surgeon, events which, on the surface, are unrelated to each other. Yet later, they stand revealed as having deep subliminal inter-relationships.

Wilhelm is fully aware of his own decision in choosing the element of the story to be told first, yet at the same time, he is bound to the succession of words in time. He complains "that the intermediate and auxiliary members of our thoughts which are reciprocally developed and interwoven as swiftly as lightning, cannot be reproduced and expressed in momentary connection and association" (II, 12). Therefore, he begins his story in a state of resignation, recommending the same to his reader Natalie:

You must resign yourself to patience and read on and on, for, in the end, there will suddenly dawn upon you, and seen quite naturally, that which spoken in *One* word would have struck you as exceedingly strange, and in fact to such a degree, that you would hardly have cared afterwards to give a moment to these introductions in the form of explanations (II, 12).

The *One* meaning cannot be expressed "in *One* word." Wilhelm recommends continued reading until suddenly *One* meaning becomes clearly established in the mind of the reader. Since the narrator cannot present momentary but only successive "connections and associations" of events, he invites the active co-operation of the reader. Natalie herself must supply the meaning of Wilhelm's childhood experience and its connection with his new profession of surgeon.

The direction to the reader that he is to "supply" (*supplieren*) the meaning

---

[10]Letter to Joseph Stanislaus Zauper, 7 September 1821.
[11]Letter to Sulpiz Boisserée, 2 September 1829.

himself, becomes a standard exhortation by Goethe to his readers concerning his last works, especially *Faust, Part II*. This example, demonstrating the complex possibility of story-telling, clearly indicates that Goethe's indifference to conventional narrative techniques should not be regarded as a sign of artistic decline or failure, but rather as evidence of the experimental and *avant-garde* nature of his late works.

The active participation on the part of the reader, required by *Wanderjahre*, sheds a revealing light on the modernity of this novel, especially when compared to the *nouveau roman*, as represented by Michel Butor, Alain Robbe-Grillet, and Nathalie Saraute. Many of the observations recently made by Klaus Netzer about the characteristics of the *nouveau roman* apply equally to Goethe's *Wanderjahre*, especially when Netzer stresses the importance of the role assigned to the reader. As in Goethe's novel, the active participation of the reader in the *nouveau roman* is an essential element of the work.[12] The process of reading, in Sartre's words, represents a "synthese de la perception et de la creation."[13] In brief, a narrative work of art consists not only of communication, but also of construction. The reader is an integral part of this construct, contributing his own important part to the novel as a whole.[14]

Furthermore, Goethe's indifference to traditional forms of the novel and its unity has its counterpart in the term *"anti-roman"* which is applied by the French novelists to describe their own negative attitude to the conventional novel. And to both *Wanderjahre* and the *nouveau roman*, the motif of the quest is a basic narrative feature, especially in its enigmatic character. The symbol of the book within a book, also, plays an important role in *Wanderjahre* as well as in several of the *nouveaux romans*. The protagonists read books, or manuscripts of books, or novellas, which lend a significant multiple perspective to the novel.[15]

Other common elements include the destruction of conventional narrative illusion and the absence of a linear plot structure which has given way to an enigmatic structure. A fragmentary mode of narration prevails, while the chronological order of time has been abandoned. Technical descriptions of objects and processes are numerous. Both Goethe's novel and novels of the *nouveau roman* make use of the technique of mirror reflections.[16] Finally, *Wanderjahre* as well as the *nouveau roman* are intended to change and transform present society, contributing to the founding of a new society not only by the novels' characters but also through the changing perception of their actively participating readers.[17]

While techniques are surprisingly similar, thematic problems naturally differ. Yet, even in this respect, Goethe's novel proves to be astonishingly modern, anticipating major problems of the nineteenth century, as does Hegel's philosophy, including such problems of modern bourgeois society,

---

[12]*Der Leser des Nouveau Roman* (Frankfurt, 1970), pp. 7-16; 23-28; 82-85.
[13]*Qu'est-ce que la Littérature* (Paris, 1948), p. 55 (cited from K. Netzer, p. 12).
[14]Netzer, pp. 12-13.
[15]*Ibid.*, pp. 15; 17-22; 28-30.
[16]*Ibid.*, pp. 31-35; 41-45; 50-58; 66-68.
[17]*Ibid.*, pp. 106-108; H. Reiss, p. 238.

as those of education and labor, and such general questions as those of religion and man's confronting of his own existence.

The main topic of *Wanderjahre* is indicated by its subtitle: "Or the Renunciants." Renunciation became a major theme in bourgeois literature of the nineteenth century. As George Lukács so accurately observed: "The aged Goethe was one of the first to strike this note of resignation. It was the symptom of a new period in the evolution of the bourgeoisie." Balzac, with his utopian novels, followed in Goethe's footsteps.[18] One might add that, in German literature, Gottfried Keller and Theodor Fontane are the most important writers in this tradition.

In *Wanderjahre* renunciation is seen not only in negative but also in positive terms. To be sure, the characters of the novel must resign themselves to relinquishing certain things in life, but their renunciation is neither stoic nor ascetic, neither surrender nor abandonment. It means continuation of the process of living on a different level; in fact, renunciation leads to a more mature affirmation of life. Self-denial is transformed into greater self-assurance.

The most obvious kind of renunciation is encountered in the relationship of love and marriage. The reader is introduced to a great number of different forms of resignation in love, not only in the interpolated novellas which function as *exempla* of renunciation, but also in the main plot. The protagonist Wilhelm Meister must leave his newly wedded wife Natalie in order to embark on his journeyman travels, together with his son Felix. As the Society of the Tower rather harshly stipulates, on these travels he may never stay more than three nights under the same roof. This rule is designed to turn his journeying into an exercise of renunciation, with Wilhelm always meeting new people but not becoming part of their lives, being only marginally involved in the fate of others, though sometimes quite painfully so, until in the end he joins the group of emigrants to America. For the time being, Wilhelm has to give up happiness and fulfilment in his private life, as husband and lover, in order to pursue an unselfish social career as a surgeon, thus preparing himself for his future as "a useful and necessary member of society" (II, 11). At the end of the novel, Wilhelm is rewarded for his renunciation when he is able to save his own son through his skill as a surgeon, a skill acquired for the general benefit of society. This final scene, in which individual and societal goals blend harmoniously, represents the climax of the novel.

This plot situation clearly shows one of the problems Goethe had in mind when he wrote *Wanderjahre*, namely, the relationship between man as a private individual and man as a member of society. This dualistic aspect of man has been the "fundamental problem of all modern theories of the state and society," as Karl Löwith has pointed out:[19] for Rousseau this relationship was incongruous, true harmony between the private individual (*homme*) and the citizen (*citoyen*) being impossible. Goethe, on the other hand, tried to overcome this incompatibility in *Wanderjahre* through renunciation, thus establishing a harmonious balance between the two basic aspects of human

---

[18]*Studies in European Realism*, intro. Alfred Kazin (New York, 1964), p. 52.

[19]*From Hegel to Nietzsche: The Revolution in Nineteenth-Century Thought* (Garden City, N.Y., 1967), p. 232.

existence in modern society. The function of society in *Wanderjahre* is "to maintain conformity in the main things and, in things permissible, to grant everyone his will" (III, 11). Goethe's train of thought parallels that of Hegel who, in his *Philosophy of Right*, similarly tried to reconcile the principles of individuality and generality in his design of the modern European state. Certainly, some aspects of Hegel's ideas smack of absolutism, especially when he envisaged his ideal of the modern state of the future being established in the contemporary state of Prussia. But then, Goethe's utopia, too, bore some traits of a police state. His American utopia in *Wanderjahre* is described as consisting of people who "do not think about justice, but police. . . . Whoever makes himself a nuisance is being removed" (III, 11). Despite these authoritarian features, which perhaps are characteristic of all utopias, both Goethe and Hegel recognized and attempted to solve, in theory or fiction, one of the fundamental problems of modern society. Karl Marx's answer to the problem, of course, was the classless society and the abolition of private property.[20]

Other problems treated in *Wanderjahre* concerned work and education. Both, according to Karl Löwith, "become the substance of the life of bourgeois society" in the nineteenth century.[21] Goethe describes the dangers of industrialization and the threat of unemployment. As one character in the novels explains:

> What, however, suppresses me is an economic problem; though not for the moment, but for the whole of the future. Industrialization (*Maschinenwesen*), which is getting the upper hand, torments and frightens me; it comes rolling on like a thunderstorm, slowly, slowly, but it has taken a definite direction. It will come and strike. . . . People think of it, speak of it and neither thinking nor speaking can help. And who would like to imagine such terrors!" (III, 13)

The experimental alternatives to industrialization offered in *Wanderjahre* are emigration and the new utopia. In a speech to the emigrants, their leader Lenardo explains that people are convinced "of the high value of private property (*Grundbesitz*), and that one is forced to look upon it as the first, the best thing that can be man's." It becomes evident that society here is based on the concept of private property. However, this concept is replaced by the idea of work and achievement when Lenardo adds: "If what man possesses is of great value, then a still greater value must be ascribed to what he does and achieves" (III, 9).

These ideas come very close to the philosophy of Hegel and also that of Marx. Hegel, too, saw the essence of man in work: man only exists insofar as he produces. He also realized the dangers of industrialization and of the resulting poverty, and he, too, offered emigration to America as an alternative. Marx followed in Hegel's footsteps, acknowledging the latter's achievements in understanding and defining the nature of work as a process of "man's self-generation." But he was critical of the fact that Hegel saw only the positive and not the negative aspects of work, such as man's self-alienation.[22]

---

[20]*Ibid.*, pp. 233-244.
[21]*Ibid.*, p. 260.
[22]*Ibid.*, pp. 262-267; 270-279.

Education in *Wanderjahre* is related to work. Man is urged to acquire a useful skill which can be applied for the common good. As Wilhelm Meister is told: "Now is the time for specialization; happy he, who comprehends this, and who works for himself and others in this spirit. . . . To limit oneself to a craft is the best" (I, 4). Therefore, Wilhelm becomes a surgeon, a profession which at that time was still considered a craft, almost on a par with the work of a barber. The time for the universal education of man had passed. Wilhelm has to renounce his Renaissance ideal of education, the privilege of only a few members of the nobility. In *Wanderjahre* man's goal in education is to mould himself into "the most necessary link of . . . [the] chain" of society (II, 7). Universal education of the individual is renounced in favour of specialization of the individual who, together with others like him, make up a universally educated society, thus leading to harmony of the individual within the group as well as within himself. Goethe's idea of specialization in education for life foreshadows the division of labor in industrial production, which was to become one of the basic principles of modern industry.

Hegel was similarly opposed to an élitist educational individualism, favoring a type of education which would enable man to contribute to society. Marx went one step further in criticizing the class character of education, conscious of the fact that education for some was a class privilege, with the rest of society tied to the drudgery of labor.[23]

Furthermore, the beginnings of nineteenth century criticism of religion, specifically of Christianity, are reflected in *Wanderjahre*. Religion is transformed into a kind of "secular piety" (*Weltfrömmigkeit*), as it is called (II, 7). In the Pedagogic Province, attitudes of "reverence" (*Ehrfurcht*) are taught. Three types of religion are acknowledged: an ethical kind of religion based on reverence for that which is above us; a philosophical religion, which is based on reverence for what is equal to us; and the Christian religion, which is founded on reverence of that which is below us (II, 1). However, the specific nature of the Christian religion and its central component, Christ's sufferings and death, are withheld from the sight of the students of the Pedagogic Province, being hidden behind a veil. In the tradition of eighteenth century enlightenment, Christ "appears as a true philosopher . . . as a sage in the highest sense" (II, 2). Thus Christianity becomes secularized and transformed into an ethical philosophy.

Religion is transcended by philosophy in similar fashion in Hegel's writings, where religion, in fact, becomes the highest form of philosophy. The more radical Marx regarded religion as an indispensable aid in man's struggle to survive the miseries of human existence. While for Hegel and Goethe, religion is an ethical, humane attitude and practice, of help to the whole of mankind, for Marx it is the wish-dream of an oppressed humanity, who only need to be liberated in order to see the dream come true on earth. Religion itself would then become obsolete.[24]

The image of man in *Wanderjahre* is determined by the humanistic idea of mankind. But Goethe also projects a more spiritual and cosmic point of

---

[23]*Ibid.*, pp. 286-291; 260.
[24]*Ibid.*, pp. 323-329; 347-351.

view. This standpoint is represented by Makarie, who occupies the central physical as well as metaphysical position in the life of man and in the universe. She symbolizes cosmic love, as well as man's monadic relationship to the absolute, that is, the divine. Makarie's function in the novel corresponds to Hegel's ideas of the absolute spirit as the universal essence of man. It is not enough for man to be engaged in useful activities for mankind. Both Goethe and Hegel wanted to emancipate man, leading him towards a universal and absolute existence. Marx, on the other hand, wanted to liberate individual man so as to become generic man (*Gattungsmensch*); he turned to the proletariat where he expected to find the type of people necessary for bringing about his ideal of universal and absolute man. The fundamental difference between Goethe and Hegel on the one hand, and Marx on the other, are evident, especially in their discussions of man in general. Goethe's and Hegel's worlds were bourgeois in the best sense of the word, while Marx's world was not.[25]

These problems, raised and discussed at length in *Wanderjahre*, show not only the realistic and prophetic nature of Goethe's novel, but also its experimental and modern features. The projects of the different societies, while realistically described, are never implemented in the novel but remain always on the purely experimental level. Experimental, too, is the central figure of Makarie. A fairy-tale character, not quite authentic as a person, her story is told as a parable of the ideal existence of man. At the same time, her lofty sidereal traits are made ironic by the narrator in his description of Makarie as the family aunt, as well as by his denial of all responsibility for the incomprehensible, fantastic accounts of her solar existence. Projected as an ideal image of all that is most lovable in man, Makarie is the very essence of a novel which is totally experimental not only in its individual features, but also in its form and structure as a whole. *Wanderjahre* thus becomes Goethe's symbol for the valuable and desirable aspects of man's existence— a vision which is quite imperfect and far from complete, but which nevertheless serves as a premonitory hint of the totality of life, and as a model of inspiration to be followed and sought after by generations of future readers.

University of California, Los Angeles

---

[25]*Ibid.*, pp. 304-307; 309-313.

J. Kostka.

Werther Revisited: Two Hundred Years of a Masterpiece

By MENO SPANN

Goethe's short epistolary novel, *The Sorrows of Young Werther*, written and published in 1774, was much more often translated and reprinted in the 18th century than those other two famous love stories, *Julie ou La Nouvelle Héloise* by Rousseau and Bernardin de Saint Pierre's *Paul et Virginie*. Ever since the fifties of our century, new translations and reprints have appeared for the growing number of readers both inside and outside the universities and colleges of the English speaking world. If one were to believe the repeated judgments of the standard histories of German literature, he would see in *Werther* only a typical work of the preromantic period, by which it was inspired (and to which it contributed more than it took from it). But certainly to a modern reader, this novel is considerably more than that. The sorrows of Werther go far beyond those feelings with which the young men and women of the sentimental period had been infected during the declining age of reason. They are today the sorrows of the West, "our sufferings," a closer though clumsier translation of *"Die Leiden,"* the German word used in the original title. This modernity and the true literary excellence of the work explain its recent revival. The modern reader forgets or forgives the purely sentimental passages and the frequent lachrymose outbursts of the hero, two-hundred-year old vestiges of the novel's time of origin.

The story is told in only 112 pages, of which 81 contain letters written by Werther to his best friend William. A fictitious editor tells the events during the last days of the hero's life.

From the letters and the information supplied by the editor evolves the simple plot: Werther, at odds with his widowed mother, has left her to spend some time in the solitude of a little town in the Lahn valley. At first he believes himself to be fully content, enjoying the beautiful landscape around him, although he is somewhat restless and seems unfulfilled. At a country dance he meets his ideal woman, Lotte, falls deeply in love with her, although he knows that she is engaged to another man; from now on he lives only for visiting her, even after the arrival of her fiancé, Albert. The two men become friends, but Werther cannot endure this situation too long. Tearing himself away from Lotte and Albert, on the advice of his mother and his friend William, he accepts a secretarial position at the court of a German prince. Less than five months later, requested to leave a party because some influential aristocrats did not desire the presence of the commoner Werther at such an occasion, he asks to be relieved of his post.

Hurt, and sick with longing for Lotte's company, Werther returns to her. Since, in the meantime, she has become Albert's wife, the old friendship of the three cannot be revived. Albert does not like to see his wife's admirer too often at his home; however, without having been invited either by Albert or Lotte, Werther pays her a desperate visit. To distract him she asks him to read to her from his translation of some Ossian poems. Both are overcome by the desolate mood of the poetry and the hopelessness of the situation. Werther, beside himself, kisses her passionately, but Lotte, wavering between love and anger, sends him away. At midnight of the same day Werther does what he had been thinking of even before he met Lotte; he shoots himself.

This shot, as is widely known, reverberated all over Europe. Several young readers, suffering from the Werther fever which broke out after the publication of the book, followed the hero all the way. One of these, a young girl of noble birth, drowned herself in the wintry Ilm, near Goethe's garden house.

More than by these tragic consequences, the clergy was angered by the defense of suicide in the book and the disrespect shown the official Christian churches by a former apprentice lawyer at the Supreme Court in Wetzlar, who obviously knew nothing about God's laws! The Bishop of Milan had his clergy buy up the entire edition of the newly translated work; the city council of Leipzig was induced to punish the sale or distribution of the book with 10 Talers for each offense. Lord Bristol, Bishop of Derry, visited Weimar in 1797 and told Goethe to his face: "Der *Werther* ist ein ganz unmoralisches, verdammungswürdiges Buch."[1] Goethe found himself in the strange situation

---

[1]The Goethe texts used throughout are those of the *Gedenkausgabe der Werke, Briefe und Gespräche,* edited by Ernst Beutler (Zürich and Stuttgart, 1949 ff.). The translations are the author's. Vol. 24 N. 741.

of being forced to preface the second part of the second printing with a warning quatrain, which ended "Sei ein Mann, und folge mir nicht nach."[2]

The critics of the older generation were aroused to anger or contempt. Even the great Lessing asked the silly question of whether a Greek or Roman youth would have ever taken his life for such a reason or under similar circumstances and called for a parody—the more cynical the better. Parodies did appear, in great numbers, but at the same time there were new printings of the novel. By the end of the century Werther could be read in translation wherever interest in literature existed. Before 1810 Werther had been published six times in the United States and an English imitation: *The Letters of Charlotte, during her Connexion with Werter* [sic] had three American reprints. Eight Werther poems (all sentimental drivel) appeared in the newspapers during the same period.[3] The hostile critics, the raving eulogists, the witless parodists—including Thackeray—had all forgotten that the title read "Sorrows," not "Sorrow," that the book consequently contained something more than a love story.

Goethe remained for 58 more years, to the end of his life, "the author of *Werther*." Only after his death and the appearance of "Faust," part II, both in 1832, did he acquire the metonym "The author of Faust." He did not complain about being "the author of Werther," particularly since he esteemed the book all his life, but "Werther's shadow" followed him for decades to come. Between 1782 and 1786 Goethe revised the novel for the first edition of his collected works. Kestner, the life model for Lotte's husband, had felt compromised by the way he appeared in the first version and Goethe, as the admirer of Lotte, consequently had to ennoble the character of her husband.

In the spring of 1790 the poet was yearning not for an unattainable love but because he, the passionate lover, had to endure several months of separation from his passionate mistress. Among the many angry distichs of the *Venetianische Epigramme* are three which refer to the love story, world famous by then.

> Hat mich Europa gelobt, washat mir Europa gegeben?
> Nichts! iche habe, wie schwer! meine Gedichte bezahlt
>
> Deutschland ahmte mich nach, und Frankreich mochte mich lesen
> England! freundlich empfingst du den zerrütteten Gast.
>
> Doch was fördert es mich, dass auch sogar der Chinese
> Malet, mit ängstlicher Hand, Werthern und Lotten auf Glas?[4]

---

[2]Vol. 2 N. 164. (Be a man and do not follow me).

[3]E. D. Davis, *Translations of German Poetry in American Magazines 1741-1810* (Philadelphia: Americana Germanica Press, 1905) *passim*.

[4]Vol. 1, p. 221.

> Europe praised me indeed but what did it give me?
> Nothing! I paid and dearly! for my poems
>
> Germany imitated me and France liked to read me
> England! Thou didst give the heartbroken guest a friendly reception.
>
> But what good is it to me that even the Chinese
> Paint with a careful hand Lotte and Werther on glass?

In 1808 Goethe discussed his little novel with an unsuccessful author of a love story, with Napoleon himself. In that year, the Emperor had invited Alexander I of Russia, four kings and thirty-four German princes to attend the Congress of Erfurt. On the second day he wanted an interview with *Monsieur Göt*, the author of *Werther*, who had come from nearby Weimar. Napoleon told the poet that he had read *Werther* seven times, and that the book had accompanied him during his Egyptian campaign. He criticized the double motive for the suicide: unrequited love and hurt ambition. Goethe agreed politely, though not from conviction, not knowing that Napoleon himself in 1785 had written an autobiographical love story *Clisson et Eugénie*, at the time when he was engaged to Désirée Eugénie Clary and still had literary ambitions. He subsequently rewrote the text four times and even took the manuscript with him to St. Helena.[5]

In 1816 Goethe wrote to his friend, the composer Zelter: "Vor einigen Tagen kam mir zufälligerweise die erste Ausgabe meine, 'Werthers' in die Hände, und dieses bei mir längst verschollene Lied fing wieder an zu klingen. Da begreift man denn nun nicht, wie es ein Mensch noch vierzig Jahre in einer Welt hat aushalten können, die ihm in früher Jugend schon so absurd vorkam."[6] Goethe was sixty-seven when he wrote that letter. He was almost seventy-five when he repeated the idea of the questionability of existence, this time in a poem. The publishers of the first edition of *Werther* wanted to bring out a memorial edition in 1824, half a century after the first edition, and asked the author for a prologue. He obliged with the poem "An Werther." The first stanza begins:

> Noch einmal wagst du, vielbeweinter Schatten,
> Hervor dich an das Tageslicht.
> . . . .

and ends:

> Zum Bleiben ich, zum Scheiden du erkoren
> Gingst du voran—und hast nicht viel verloren.[7]

This poem also introduces the *Trilogie der Leidenschaft* whose main piece is entitled *Elegie*, often quoted as *Marienbader Elegie*. During his repeated visits to Marienbad Goethe had met in 1821 a young girl of seventeen, with whose family he had been acquainted for years. He met her again the next year, and in 1823 the seventy-four-year-old author of *Werther* asked, through

---

[5]Herbert Koch, ed. and trans. a bilingual edition of Napoleon Bonaparte, *Clisson und Eugenie* (Munich: Winkler Verlag, 1969).

[6]Vol. 21, p. 147.
"Several days ago I came accidentally upon the first edition of my "Werther," and this old forgotten song began to ring out again. Then one wonders how a man could bear forty more years in a world which had struck him in early youth as quite absurd."

[7]Vol. 1, p. 473.
> Once more, much bewailed shadow thou darest
> to come forward into the light of day
> . . . .
> I chose to stay, you to depart
> Thou didst precede me—and didst not lose much.

his friend, the Prince of Weimar, for her hand. There was a gentle rejection, but Goethe suffered deeply. He felt as if the last hope had gone out of his life, he knew a woman's love was never again to inspire him, and so it was almost necessary for him that the much bewailed spirit of *Werther* should appear for the last time in his poetry.

He still discussed the novel occasionally with his faithful admirer Eckermann, who reports about his conversations in "*Gespräche mit Goethe.*" However, one need not quote further to illustrate the often forgotten fact that Goethe himself took his *Werther* very seriously.

"The long forgotten song" rings out again today, and it sounds clearer to us today than ever. Experiences of the last two decades, and living in a declining era of history help us to understand young Werther who, likewise, lived at a time of crumbling values.

The very beginning is an example of this new understanding our time makes possible for us. As far as can be ascertained, none of the commentators in the past have realized that Werther did not leave home in the way that one would expect of a man in his twenties, but that he had, literally, run away from his widowed mother. In fact, he communicates with her only about business matters and money; he does not notify her about the important events in his life, e.g., the acceptance of a position at court and his resignation half a year later. He does not even leave a last note for her before his suicide, but includes the few words: "*Liebe Mutter, verzeiht mir!*[8] in the last note to his friend.

The generation gap between son and mother is that between the dying roccoco and the evolving romantic period. In Werther's eyes, his mother adores the spurious values of a society he despises and which causes him some of his most painful experiences. As soon as his father died she had taken her son, still a child, away from the little town he calls *lieb und vertraulich*, in order to lock herself up in her city which to Werther is *unerträglich*.[9] Young readers today will understand, for certainly many of them have tried to flee from parents and unbearable cities. But, as ever, the lovely and intimate towns in beautiful valleys to which the young flee are few and far away, and the people there wary of the dissenting young strangers in their protest uniforms. Werther too shows his protest in his attire: a simple blue coat, a yellow waistcoat, breeches and riding boots. This more comfortable and masculine outfit imitated English fashion. Worn by young Goethe, it was aped by so many of the readers of the novel, that contemporaries talked about a Werther-fashion.

The greatest difference between mother and son, as well as the greatest difference between Goethe and his time, is signaled in the first letter, the overture of the novel. Mrs. Werther claims a share of a legacy an aunt is holding back, and wants her son to talk to this woman during his journey. The matter is easily settled, since the aunt is not the evil woman they make of her at home; she is lively, hot tempered but at the same time very kindhearted. The successful interlocutor observes:

---

[8]Vol. 4, p. 507. (Dear mother, forgive me!)
[9]Vol. 4, p. 453. (lovely and intimate—unbearable).

> Und ich habe, mein Lieber, wieder bei diesem kleinen Geschäft gefunden, dass Missverständnisse und Trägheit vielleicht mehr Irrungen in der Welt machen als List und Bosheit.[10]

"Perhaps"—the little aperçu is cautiously expressed; its author is young, but he is wary of dogmatic statements in this time which worshipped dogma in religion, philosophy, political science, education, poetics, diet, and so forth. But Werther's observation is not a little aperçu at all; it sets the tone for the entire novel, the outstanding feature of which is to be deeply concerned with ethical values. And yet Goethe's love story has little to do with the traditional Christian dualism: good and evil have nothing to do with its popular interpretation of abstinence and concupiscence. The eighteenth century authors of love stories developed these concepts with a finesse never reached again. They also discovered that even the most virtuous man can be outdone by a woman.

A few passages from Rousseau's *Nouvelle Héloise* and Saint Pierre's *Paul et Virginie* would reinforce the point, but space forbids detailed treatment. (Rousseau's work appeared just 13 years before Goethe's and Saint Pierre's 11 years after). Nonetheless, the romantic hero of the eighteenth century clearly suffered from feminine virtue. Julie, Rousseau's heroine, preaches in almost every letter about *honneur* (chastity) and *vertu* of which she has immeasurable quantities. On her death bed she confesses in her last letter to her lover Saint-Preux that she had always loved only him, rather than her husband, and that her death was not untimely because she might have yielded to temptation. Patiently suffering Saint-Preux is her husband's friend and a member of the family. She closes with the remark that *vertu* kept her separated from her lover but would unite them in the beyond. What kind of consolation prize her likewise virtuous and loving husband will receive she does not say, but then: *le mari a toujours tort.*

Rousseau's disciple Bernardin de Saint Pierre surpassed his master in portraying a virtuous woman. His love story *Paul et Virginie* shows two children of tropical nature growing up together and chastely falling in love with each other. Virginie must leave Paul to spend several years in Paris, where an evil aunt tries to make a lady *à la mode* of her. Overcome by her love for Paul, and by homesickness, she escapes from corrupt Paris and flees back to paradise. Just before landing her ship is wrecked within shouting distance of the shore and begins to sink. Many passengers swim ashore, but Virginie, the ladylike child of nature, cannot swim. A sailor begs her permission to save her but insists that she shed her outer garments, which would pull them both to death. Virginie steadfastly refuses and achieved a memorable place in literary history; lifting her radiant face to the blue tropical sky, where the God of her deistic faith dwells, she goes down with the ship before the eyes of her fainting but inwardly agreeing fiancé. *L'enfant de la nature* has preferred death to a few moments of "immodesty." Her last prayer is answered; Paul joins her in the tropical skies two months later.

Admittedly, the same mocking tone would not be out of place if a critic were to discuss certain religious passages in *Werther*. Why this is never done

---

[10]"And again, my dear, I observed through this little transaction, that misunderstandings and indolence [of the heart] cause perhaps more confusions in the world than cunning and meanness."

is hard to say. Respect for even the most naïve manifestations of Christian faith or even the less admirable passages in a work by Goethe, or both, may have prevented criticism. Werther is not a church-going Christian; he even refuses to accept the consolation of religion which his epistolary friend suggests: "Ich ehre die Religion, das weisst du, ich fühle dass sie . . . manchem Verschmachtenden Erquickung ist. Nur—kann sie denn, muss sie denn das einem jeden sein?"[11] Nevertheless, Werther sometimes speaks the naïve jargon of that deism which the believers in a picture-book God used in his day. Almost all of these dubious passages deal with faith in an eternal life, where the situations of the day will be continued in the beyond forever, since age, differences caused by different death-dates, and the changeability of human emotions, are never admitted. Werther ends his life with the same certainty as that of Rousseau's Julie—that heaven prefers lovers; the husbands can go to—another part of the infinite place.

> Und was ist das, dass Albert dein Mann ist? Mann! Das wäre denn für diese Welt. . . . Du bist von diesem Augenblicke mein! mein, O Lotte! Ich gehe voran! gehe zu meinem Vater, zu deinem Vater. Dem will ichs klagen, und er wird mich trösten, bis du kommst, und ich fliege dir entgegen und fasse dich und bleibe bei dir vor dem Angesichte des Unendlichen in ewigen Umarmungen.[12]

Such is the style of the literature of religious entertainment of the 18th century, unusual as it is in the work of the great author. Various explanations in *Werther* commentaries have been given; none of them are very convincing. Perhaps Goethe realized how shocking his work would otherwise be to the devoted Christians among his friends, such as F. H. Jacobi, a religious author, and J. C. Lavater, a Swiss pastor and famous physiognomist, as well as for that grand old man of literature, Klopstock (who was not Goethe's friend, and was offended later, anyway, by the pagan novel); Goethe may have thought to pacify these men with a little pious talk. Since almost all these passages occur in the second part, they may well have been an afterthought of the author. In the beginning of the book, he speaks in beautiful and entirely different language about the Eternal. In pantheistic prose hymns, he apostrophizes the Supreme Power with expressions like: *Der ewig Schaffende, das Wesen, das alles in sich und durch sich hervorbringt*,[13] and so forth.

Another passage of this sort deserves mention. At the end of the first part Werther has decided to leave Lotte and take up his secretarial position at court. He meets his unsuspecting friends for the last time, as he thinks, and is perturbed when the conversation turns toward resurrection after death. He is deeply touched when Lotte, who is convinced of eternal life, showers him with

---

[11]Vol. 4, p. 468. "I honor religion, you know that, I feel that it is refreshment to many a languishing man. Only—must it be that for everyone?"

[12]*Ibid.*, p. 503.
"And what does that mean that Albert is your husband? Husband! That would be valid for this world. . . . From this moment [the moment of his suicide] on you are mine! mine, O Lotte! I lead the way! go to my father, to your father. He will hear my lament and he will console me until you will come and I'll fly towards you and grasp you, stay with you, before the face of the Infinite One in eternal embraces."

[13]"He who eternally creates—the being which produces everything in himself and through himself."

urgent questions: "... aber, Werther, sollen wir uns wieder finden? wieder erkennen? was ahnen Sie, was sagen Sie?" Werther answers: "... wir werden uns wieder sehen! Hier und dort wieder sehen."[14] Such a conversation actually took place between Goethe, Kestner and the original Lotte; as Goethe reports, they did indeed talk about life after death. If Lotte asked or thought about such questions as we find them in the novel, life, not eternity, gave an answer which was final.

Kestner died in 1800, and in 1816 Lotte came to Weimar to visit relatives. She had not seen her former ardent admirer for forty years. An old man and an old woman met who had little to say to each other. Goethe saw that such a demonstration of dead emotions was unnecessary. He invited her, together with many other guests, to one of his formal dinners and sent her a note offering her his box in the theatre, excusing himself by saying he could not attend. *Lotte in Weimar* is an enchanting novel to those who know Goethe well. But life did not write it, Thomas Mann did.

While Goethe spoke about reunion above the clouds for the ears of pious friends, in the same novel he talks in a different tone, in a modern tone, when he discusses the tragedy of man's existence without mentioning the painkillers of the naïve. Not quite two months before his death, *Werther* writes about the transitoriness of feeling with a tragic resignation reminding one of R. M. Rilke's terse line: *Denn Bleiben ist nirgends.* It is as if Goethe had anticipated in his mind the sober and sad end of his relation to Lotte forty years later:

> Ja es wird mir gewiss, Lieber! gewiss und immer gewisser, dass an dem Dasein eines Geschöpfes wenig gelegen ist, ganz wenig. . . . Und wenn ich mich umsehe, und sehe das Zimmer an und rings um mich Lottens Kleider und Alberts Skripturen und diese Möbeln, denen ich nun so befreundet bin, sogar diesem Tintenfasse, und denke: Siehe, was du nun diesem Hause bist! Alles in allem. Deine Freunde ehren dich! Du machst oft ihre Freude, und deinem Herzen scheint es, als wenn es ohne sie nicht sein könnte und doch—wenn du nun gingst, wenn du aus diesem Kreise schiedest? Würden sie, wie lange würden sie die Lücke fühlen, die dein Verlust in ihr Schicksal reisst? Wie lange?—Oh, so vergänglich ist der Mensch, dass er auch da, wo er seines Daseins eigentliche Gewissheit hat, da, wo er den einzigen wahren Eindruck seiner Gegenwart macht, in dem Andenken, in der Seele seiner Lieben, dass er auch da verlöschen, verschwinden muss, und das so bald![15]

[14]Vol. 4, p. 347. "... but Werther, are we to find each other again? recognize each other again? what do you sense, what do you say?"
    "... we shall see each other again! see each other again here and there."
[15]*Ibid.*, p. 465.
"Yes, I am becoming more and more certain that the existence of a human being matters little, very little. . . . And if I look around and look at the room and all around me Lotte's dresses and Albert's written work and these pieces of furniture with which I am now such good friends, even with this ink pot and think: See what you mean to this house! In every respect. Your friends respect you; you are often their delight and you feel as if life could not go on without them; and yet—if you were to leave now, leave this circle? Would they, how long would they feel the breach which your loss has broken in their destiny? How long?—O man is so transitory that he must flicker out even when he makes the only real impression of his presence, in the memory, in the soul of those who love him, that he must disappear even there and so soon."

That must have been a slap in the face for Jacobi, Lavater, Klopstock and all the others the young author had pacified earlier with his pious talk.

Much more offensive might have been the ethical convictions of this author as they appear particularly in his attacks on the "villains" of his story, had they been able to understand what Goethe was implying. But probably only modern readers, of our own day, fully grasp what this young genius towering over his European contemporaries had to say to them. Twice, human actions put Werther in such a rage that he curses and feels the desire to kill the malefactors on the spot. Even this storm of indignation is caused by something neither church nor state has ever condemned. If the modern reader thinks of the solemn anathemas pronounced in the majestic cathedrals up and down Europe or the Jeremiads in city and village churches, he may at first be startled by the passionate fury a parson's wife provokes in this gentle soul Werther by improving the parsonage in her way and making it possible for her husband to earn a little money on the side:

> Man möchte rasend werden, Wilhelm, dass es Menschen geben soll ohne Sinn und Gefühl an dem wenigen, was auf Erden noch einen Wert hat. Du kennst die Nussbäume, unter denen ich bei dem ehrlichen Pfarrer zu St. . . . mit Lotten gesessen die herrlichen Nussbäume! die mich, Gott weiss, immer mit dem grössten Seelenvergnügen füllten! Wie vertraulich sie den Pfarrhof machten, wie kühl! und wie herrlich die Äste waren! Und die Erinnerung bis zu den ehrlichen Geistlichen, die sie vor so vielen Jahren pflanzten. Der Schulmeister hat uns den einen Namen oft genannt, den er von seinem Grossvater gehört hatte; und so ein braven Mann soll er gewesen sein, und sein Andenken war mir immer heilig unter den Bäumen. Ich sage Dir, dem Schulmeister standen die Tränen in den Augen, da wir gestern davon redeten, dass sie abgehauen worden—Abgehauen! Ich möchte toll werden, ich könnte den Hund ermorden, der den ersten Hieb dran tat. Ich, der ich mich vertrauern könnte, wenn so ein paar Bäume in meinem Hofe stünden, und einer davon stürbe vor Alter ab, ich muss zusehen. . . .[16]

The parson's wife, an unpleasant woman "who has good cause not to take any interest in the world since nobody takes any interest in her," had her reasons for the felling of the trees. She likes sterile order, and the leaves soiled her yard. Besides, the little boys threw stones at the nuts and made her nervous when she was pondering the latest theological publications. There

---

[16]*Ibid.*, p. 462.
"William, I could lose my mind with rage. Why should there be people without sense and without feeling for the few things on earth which still have value. You remember the walnut trees under which I was sitting with Lotte visiting the good old parson of St. . . ., those glorious walnut trees which God knows always delight my soul so much. What a cozy place they made of the courtyard of the parsonage. How cool it was under their glorious branches. And then the memories back to the good parsons who planted them many years ago. The schoolmaster often told us the name of one of them his grandfather had often mentioned; and they say he was such a fine man, and his memory was always sacred to me. I tell you the schoolmaster had tears in his eyes when we talked about it yesterday, that they were cut down—Cut down! I could lose my mind; I could murder the dog who struck the first blow against them. I, who could lose myself in mourning that if two trees like that stood in my courtyard and one of them were dying of old age, I must idly watch."

is also a little financial incentive. The parson and the mayor of the village sold the trees, but the board snatched the money away from them. At an earlier stage of the story Werther had seen and admired these trees and had learned how dear their history was to the old parson and his wife. The younger tree had been planted the day she was born. The memory of the good man who had planted the older tree was sacred to Werther, when he enjoyed their shade. Beside their natural beauty these trees possessed laric values.

The gradual disappearance of the feeling for nature is a process already noticeable to Goethe and other romantics. That is the meaning of the word "still" when Werther speaks of the "feeling for the few things on earth which *still* have a value."

In the two centuries since the walnut-trees fell as victims to the unfeeling pedantry of the parson's wife, the dullness of the woodcutter, and the desire for a little profit, millions of later assailants have almost succeeded in killing this once so beautiful planet. Today, we would hardly call Werther's fury overreaction, but even a few decades ago it seemed like preciousness, excessive romanticism.

Another furious outburst of the hero is caused by the aristocrats who resent Werther's, the commoner's, presence at their party. Worse even than this humiliation is the gossip following it:

> Und da man nun heute gar, wo ich hintrete, mich bedauert, da ich höre, dass meine Neider nun triumphieren und sagen: da sähe man's, wo es mit den übermütigen hinausginge, die sich ihres bisschen Kopfs überhöben und glaubten, sich darum über alle Verhältnisse hinaussetzen zu dürfen, und was des Hundegeschwätzes mehr ist—da möchte man sich ein Messer ins Herz bohren.[17]

A young aristocratic lady, who likes Werther very much, tells him, with tears streaming down her cheeks, how she could only half defend him as her old aunt made disparaging remarks about him and chastised her for tolerating such a low company. Werther rages in his letters: "Ich wollte, dass sich einer unterstünde, mir es vorzuwerfen, dass ich ihm den Degen durch den Leib stossen könnte; wenn ich Blut sähe, würde mir es besser werden."[18]

Particularly significant is the remark made by his calumniators about insolent commoners who think they can disregard class distinctions because they have some intelligence. (Translated into antiquated American that means, does it not: a smart nigger is the worst nigger.) Generally, commentators have seen in all of Werther's outbursts of fury only overreactions of a sick— the more modern ones say neurotic—young man. Emil Staiger, who wrote what I consider to be one of the finest Goethe monographs, calls the scene at

---

[17]*Ibid.*, p. 450.
"And today they all pity me wherever I show myself. I hear that those who envy me are triumphant and say: that's how it goes with the insolent ones, who get ideas because of their little bit of intelligence and believe it gives them permission to disregard all social conditions and more S.O.B. drivel like that. You hear that and you want to bore a knife into your heart.

[18]*Ibid.*, p. 451.
"I wish someone would be impertinent enough to say this to my face that I could run him through with my sword; if I could see blood, I would feel better."

the count's party "eine leicht peinliche Szene."[19] He does not even mention the even more humiliating aftermath of that scene. Nonetheless, the modern reader, it seems, would side with Werther.

There are a few minor characters who reveal additional aspects of evil as that young heretic, Goethe, saw it. For instance, there is the doctor who observes Werther having a tussle with the small brothers and sisters of Lotte. He considers such behavior undignified and spreads the rumor in town that Werther is a bad influence on the children. He earns himself a place on Werther's list of rogues with the title: *eine sehr dogmatische Drahtpuppe.*[20] How insignificant and harmless such utterances must have seemed to older critics! In the meantime our outlook has shifted focus, and we have learned how dangerous such characters can be. What better description than dogmatic, dangling puppets could be found for the millions who believed in the teachings of Hitler and Stalin?

At a party under the beautiful walnut-trees Werther meets the fiancé of the old parson's daughter. He notices that the young man is in a bad humor, and he makes a few remarks about this "vice" which, as he says in another passage, he considers the worst of all vices. A vice according to his own definition is anything with which one harms oneself and others. He even wants the clergy to preach against this vice: bad humor attacked from the pulpits, and then preaches himself:

> Ist es nicht genug, dass wir einander nicht glücklich machen können, müssen wir auch noch einander das Vergnügen rauben, das jedes Herz sich noch manchmal selbst gewähren kann?[21]

The word "noch" (still) occurs here for the first time, indicating a process of inner impoverishment among the people of Werther's time and world. This lament about people losing the capacity of being joyful without an outer cause must have sounded quite superfluous and "romantic" to the men of the hard working industrial age. Perhaps bad humor, ready at any moment to grow into hatred, is today the modern sickness, a pollution of the soul as dangerous as physical pollution. To a greater extent than has been recognized then, *Werther* may be an early work of literature whose author knew what the real sorrows of men are, sorrows quite different from those which church and state recommend for the wellbeing of the soul.

The modern reader has more to learn from this novel than could be discussed here. The errors of the time, time understood as the last two centuries —might even raise such questions as why Lotte is an embodiment of good? Surely, there is more to be found in this great novel about a young man who cried too much. But then, if one thinks about that today, he may have been right, for his sorrows were greater than has been assumed.

Northwestern University

---

[19]Emil Staiger: *Goethe* (Zürich, 1952) I, p. 170.
"a slightly embarrassing scene."
[20]Beutler: *Goethe*, Vol. 4, p. 291.
"a very dogmatic wire-puppet."
[21]*Ibid.*, p. 411.
"Is it not enough that we cannot make each other happy; must we also rob each other of the pleasure which every heart can still at times provide for itself?"

The Infernal Fairy Tale: Inversion of Archetypal Motifs in Modern European Literature

By HORST S. DAEMMRICH

The efflorescence of the fairy tale as genre and the interest in folk and fairy tale motifs during the time of German Romanticism has been documented exhaustively.[1] With the advent of Romanticism in Europe, basic fairy tale motifs have also recurred in literature. Frequently they are not

[1]For excellent bibliographical references see Max Lüthi, *Märchen*, 2nd rev. ed. (Stuttgart, 1964). Relevant to the topic are the well-known studies by Northrop Frye, Carl Gustav Jung, and the following: Antti A. Aarne, *The Types of the Folktale. A Classification and Bibliography*, 2nd rev. ed., trans. by Stith Thompson (Helsinki, 1964); Hedwig von Beit, *Symbolik des Märchens*, 3 vols. (Bern, 1952-1957); Richard E. Benz, *Märchendichtung der Romantiker* (Jena, 1926); Rudolf Buchmann, *Helden und Mächte des romantischen Kunstmärchens. Beiträge zu einer Motiv- und Stilparallele* (Leipzig, 1910); Max Dietz, "Metapher und Märchengestalt," *PMLA*, 48 (1933), 74-99, 488-503, 877-894, 1203-1222; Mimi Ida Jehle, *Das deutsche Kunstmärchen von der Romantik*

recognized, because the fairy tale's familiar setting, timeless characters, temporal unity, and the concurrence of reality and supra-reality are absent. The fairy tale exhibits a distinct pattern: it proceeds from a situation of challenge, disorder, or conflict, to one of resolution or restoration of order. And though the hero is threatened by the possibility of failure he invariably succeeds in his quest and journey. He is rewarded with happiness in life by either remaining innocent, gaining worldly riches, or attaining truth. After being tested he actually experiences the spiritual rebirth promised to the tragic hero in literature in the form of increased self-knowledge. Consequently, the reader who perceives the archetypal form hidden in a fairy tale motif may fail to identify it in a literary work which portrays man's existential situation, his passion and action in a specific historic and cultural setting. Furthermore, fairy tale motifs in fiction or plays are often transformed or completely inverted.

Such inversions can be the result of a deliberate and playful manipulation which sets up a sharp contrast between the universal, ageless archetype and a singular human fate. Inversions can also spring from the conscious or unconscious rejection of the archetype. This pattern, consistent with a tragic or absurd view of the world, is characterized by a demonic modulation which questions the validity of the archetype and transforms the joyous acclamation of life into a somber appraisal of man's destiny. Inverted motifs constitute basic structural units in narratives and plays. Their identification should lead to the recognition of an important structural pattern in literature and consequently enhance critical appraisals. In the light of traditional motifs such inversions should be called infernal fairy tales.

In some tales the demonic imagery seems to express the author's "ironic mode."[2] Frequently, however, it forms the basis for a profoundly pessimistic design of caged man. In the perspective of intellectual history, infernal fairy tales balance the optimistic view of the world expressed in traditional fairy tales; one might even argue that infernal tales express man's existential situation more faithfully than fairy tales, which appear almost as inversions of life.

I shall focus on the inversion of three basic motifs: The Rite of Spring, the Quest for Life, and Spiritual Rebirth. The Rite of Spring has found its most enduring expression in "Sleeping Beauty."[3] The pattern of fertility and ster-

zum Naturalismus (Urbana, Ill., 1933); André Jolles, *Einfache Formen*, 2nd ed. (Halle, 1956); Max Lüthi, *Das europäische Volksmärchen. Form und Wesen* (Bern, 1947); Karl Justus Obenauer, *Das Märchen* (Frankfurt, 1959); Robert Petsch, *Wesen und Formen der Erzählkunst* (Halle, 1934); Vladimir J. Propp, *Morphology of the Folktale* (s'Gravenhage, 1958); Lutz Röhrich, *Märchen und Wirklichkeit*, 2nd enl. ed. (Wiesbaden, 1964); Harry Slochower, *Mythopoesis* (Detroit, 1970); Hans Steffen, "Märchendichtung in Aufklärung und Romantik," in *Formkräfte der deutschen Dichtung vom Barock bis zur Gegenwart* (Göttingen, 1963); Marianne Thalmann, *Das Märchen und die Moderne* (Stuttgart, 1961); Jessie L. Weston, *From Ritual to Romance* (Garden City, 1957); Paul Wolfgang Wührl, "Nachwort," in *Märchen deutscher Dichter* (Frankfurt, 1964), pp. 767-799.

[2]Cf. Northrop Frye, *Anatomy of Criticism* (Princeton, 1957), p. 151.

[3]"Dornröschen," in *Die Kinder- und Hausmärchen der Brüder Grimm. Vollständige Ausgabe in der Urfassung*, ed. Friedrich Panzer (Wiesbaden, 1956), No. 50; this edition is hereafter cited as KHM. See also Johannes Bolte, *Anmerkungen zu den Kinder- und Hausmärchen der Brüder Grimm*. Neu bearbeitet von Johannes Bolte und Georg Polivka. 5 vols. 2nd. ed. (Hildesheim, 1963).

ility points to a seasonal ritual as the basis of the fairy tale which relates how a virgin earth goddess is born, matures, is threatened by death from an opposing season but jubilantly comes forth after she is awakened by light. In the beginning, the queen mother sits in the bath when a crab crawls out of the water and announces that the queen will soon give birth to a daughter. The child is bestowed with gifts of life but also endangered by death. At the age of maturity, Sleeping Beauty grasps a spindle, not only a sexual but also a harvest symbol, begins to bleed, and falls asleep. A hedge of thorns grows protectively around her. Those who attempt to penetrate the hidden grove, reminiscent of the grove of the Eumenides, die wretchedly in the thorns. At the right moment, however, when spring, the prince of light, approaches, the thorns suddenly burst into flowers and invite him to enter. He kisses the earth goddess and awakens the slumbering world to new life.

The fairy tale celebrates the rhythm of life, the awakening of earth through light, and the joys of a fertile soil. The succession of life and death, rainy season and drought, spring and winter represents a crisis. It raises the possibility of the sterility of the land. But the transformation of earth into sleep, into a dormant season, holds the promise of exuberant life bursting forth again. The similarities between Sleeping Beauty and Brunhild (Brynhid), between the hedge of thorns and the wall of flames, between the prince and Siegfried (Sigurd) indicate that the motif was used in Germanic mythopoetic works. It recurs in Richard Wagner's *Ring der Nibelungen* and in a variation in *Tristan und Isolde*. The inverted motif appears in Thomas Mann's *Tristan* (1902), while its demonic modulation dominates Maurice Maeterlinck's *Pelléas et Mélisande* (1892).

Thomas Mann establishes associations between Sleeping Beauty and Gabriele Klöterjahn through a series of detailed characteristics which the fairy tale, because of its concentration on the general type, leaves to the reader's imagination: Gabriele's drowsiness, the tendency of her eyes to close, her sharply marked lips, her queenly attire, and the enchanted grove in which she spent the years of her youth waiting for Prince Charming.[4] In one of her afternoon discussions with Detlev Spinell, Gabriele describes the garden behind her house where she was discovered by her future husband. The place was completely overgrown, surrounded by a mossy wall, and had a fountain at the center around which Gabriele and her friends used to sit. At this point Spinell interjects: A small golden crown blinked in your hair. Gabriele laughs at his idea. Yet two weeks later she asks him: "Then it is true . . . Mr. Spinell, that you would have seen the crown."[5] And later when Spinell urges her to play the fateful music at the piano, that is, precisely before the experience of beauty will truly liberate her and bring about her death, he suggests that the crown can be seen again.

Almost against her father's will Gabriele marries the first and obviously wrong suitor who enters the enchanted garden. It seems as if life itself has come to her in the form of Mr. Klöterjahn, the healthy, robust, loud, and common merchant. But despite the fact that she fulfills her role and bears an excessively healthy child, life fails to awaken her fully. Her already

---

[4]Thomas Mann, "Tristan," in *Gesammelte Werke*, 12 vols. (Berlin, 1956), IX, 131-132.

[5]*Ibid.*, p. 149.

fragile constitution is weakened by the birth of her son, and her intellectual predisposition toward beauty and death finally finds a physical outlet in tuberculosis. When she is brought in the midst of winter to the sanatorium, she meets the real Prince Charming, death, in the form of Detlev Spinell. His outward appearance betrays his nature and mission. He has a round, white, and bloated face, a short fleshy nose, a curved, porous upper lip, large, decayed teeth, no beard, enormous feet, and is usually dressed in a long, black coat. Spinell bares his teeth in a strange, exalted smile, similar to the distorted grimace of death when he first begins to arouse her.

The subsequent action centers on Gabriele's search for her true identity in which she is ever so carefully guided by Spinell. When he finally persuades her to play Chopin and Wagner, he has succeeded. She transcends herself, rejects the world of her husband and Anton, and dies from the kiss of beauty, as Spinell states in his letter to her husband: ". . . if she expires proudly and blissfully from the kiss of beauty it has been *my* responsibility."[6] Gabriele's death at the very moment when spring arrives, the death imagery surrounding Spinell and the sanatorium, and the union of beauty, preciousness, and disease in Gabriele are consistent with the inversion of the motif. The tension which results from the contrast between increasing self-knowledge and impending doom, between aesthetic freedom and physical destruction is resolved by paradoxically contradicting the inverted motif with the Rite of Spring. Though death destroys Gabriele, he cannot eradicate life as such. When Spinell sees Anton, when the messenger of death meets the young Dionysos, life triumphs once again. Thus the dynamic tension between the Rite of Death and the Rite of Spring forms the basic structural pattern of Mann's narrative.

Maeterlinck's *Pelléas et Mélisande* shows a pattern of demonic modulation of the Rite of Spring. The action extends from early spring when Golaud discovers the mysterious Mélisande to late fall, when by wounding her he causes her death. Golaud first encounters the girl at a fountain in a dense, forbidding forest. Mélisande, attired like a princess, with her beautiful long hair, and her large, hypnotic eyes, stands trembling at the water in which she has lost her golden crown. With only vague memories of her past, anguished by the present, and doubtful of the future, she seems suspended in time, the victim of a deep existential fear.

Prince Golaud, a robust, active huntsman, untroubled by the threat of life, rescues Mélisande and marries her but instead of light brings her oppression and destruction. He leads her to his grandfather's gloomy castle, built on a stagnant pool, where she finds herself caged in the deadly atmosphere of dark rooms and halls. Only the "Fountain of the Blind" in the garden of Allemonde's castle seems to hold the promise of physical and spiritual refreshment. She loses her wedding ring in its water and near its edge declares her love for Pelléas, her true prince of light. But the fountain's water of life is also poisoned when the murdered body of Pelléas defiles it, and Mélisande slowly dies after Golaud has jealously stabbed her.

Within this deadly atmosphere, intensified by the imagery of the cage, the forest of darkness, the stagnant water, and repeated predictions of doom, the

---

[6] *Ibid.*, p. 167.

three main characters succeed in finding their true identity by transcending themselves. Pelléas and Mélisande experience hope in the contemplation of light[7] and realize themselves in their love for each other. The fatal consequences of Golaud's passion awaken in him an awareness of responsibility for his action and a hitherto unknown respect and understanding for the feelings of others. Since the action of Maeterlinck's play revolves around a pattern of conflict between self-realization and self-transcendence, existential fear and hope, it also calls forth associations of the archetypal Quest for Life.

The motif of the Quest for Life and its variations are found in many fairy tales, among them, "The Brave Tailor," "Cinderella," "The Three Ravens," and "The Devil with Three Golden Hairs." Its characteristic elements can be perceived most clearly in the tales of "The Princess on the Glass Mountain," "The Raven," and "Prince Swan."[8] The tale of the "Princess on the Glass Mountain" relates how a young man retains his pure heart, successfully overcomes all obstacles, and finally rides up the mountain of glass to win the fair princess. In "The Raven" a man encounters in a dark forest the enchanted princess who implores him to free her. All he has to do is to resist the lure of an old woman and refuse her food and drink in order to stay awake for the princess. Despite her admonition he is enticed to drink on three successive days by the old woman and fails his test. After leaving bread, meat, and wine which will always replenish themselves, that is, symbols of eternal life and rejuvenation, the princess disappears to the mountain of glass. Hopelessly, the man searches for her in a dark forest which symbolizes the existential uncertainty of life. Finally he overcomes three giants, wins a magic horse, rides to the top of the mountain and liberates the princess.

The pattern of the tales reveals a struggle between man's idealistic vision and his earthly, confining instincts which is hidden in the conflict between the fair princess and the evil woman, the virgin and the temptress, or the lion and the dragon. The hero yearns for pure light but falls prey to temptations in his quest for self-realization. The ultimate success of the quest does not depend on heroic qualities nor does it spring from a rebellious assertion against nature. Indeed, the hero frequently needs the help of nature which he receives from friendly animals and insects; just as often he relies on shrewdness or even resorts to trickery. But while he initially fails to surmount the obstacles which he encounters during his trials, he is eventually redeemed because he remains faithful to his ideal during the long, arduous journey in the forests of darkness. By retaining a pure heart and remaining true to his quest he can ultimately scale the shimmering mountain of glass that reaches far into the sky and thus realize his vision.

E. T. A. Hoffmann's narrative "Die Bergwerke zu Falun" (1819) provides an excellent example for the inversion of the motif.[9] Like many of Hoffmann's tales, this story can be interpreted as portraying a central conflict between

[7]Maurice Maeterlinck, "Pelléas et Mélisande," in *Théâtre* (Paris, 1925), II, 79-95 (III, v).

[8]Cf. Aarne, no. 530; KHM, "Aschenputtel" (No. 21), "Von einem tapferen Schneider" (No. 20), "Die drei Raben" (No. 25), "Von einem Teufel mit drei goldnen Haaren" (No. 29), "Prinz Schwan" (No. 59); "Die Rabe" (II, No. 7).

[9]E. T. A. Hoffmann, "Die Bergwerke zu Falun," in *Die Serapions-Brüder*, ed. Walter Müller-Seidel (Darmstadt, 1966), pp. 171-197.

man's demonic vision and reality. The hero Elis Fröbom is driven into a mine by the romantic yearning to discover the mystery of earth and there finds death on his wedding day. The story probes into the dark forces confronting man from within, explores the powerful drives apparently beyond his control, and reverses the theme of freedom to that of compulsion. In Hoffmann's version of the motif, the hero descends to the core of the mountain in search of the secret of life, a mysterious red almandine, but discovers the ultimate truth—death. Indeed, the themes of love and compulsion, self-realization and captivity are woven into a symbolic narration of man's confrontation with death on his journey into his inner being. In "Die Bergwerke zu Falun" the quest for life becomes the quest for death.

Elis Fröbom begins his voyage while his comrades joyously celebrate their return after long months on a ship. He withdraws quietly from the boisterous scene, mourns the loss of his mother, the only person he had loved, and overwhelmed by anguish, expresses the wish to die. Suddenly he sees the figure of an old miner, a figure strangely familiar and comforting. In the ensuing dialogue the miner orders Elis to overcome his indecision and gives direction to his vague premonitions by commanding him to look for truth in the mines of Falun. There the marvelous stones will reflect the secrets hidden above the clouds. The miner proceeds to picture an enchanting, intensely fascinating world to Elis, who feels simultaneously exhilarated and oppressed by the experience because he fears the strange world and yet suspects that he has been there before. That night the vision recurs in a dream but is transformed into an image of seduction inviting him to descend into the earth. Again Elis feels joy and fear. He yearns for the hidden secrets of this world and sees in a flash the universal earth-mother guarding the mysteries of life and death. But he also beholds the old miner, now a figure of molten mineral and gigantic proportions who suddenly warns him, and his rejoicing turns into terror. After a brief vision of life calling from above, an inward force compels him to glance downward again. He awakens, deeply and lastingly affected by his dream. After reliving the same conflict during a daydream, Elis is ready to follow his inner voice. Both the old miner and the temptress in the earth are of a demonic ambiguity. They remind Elis of the necessity for action, lure him with the secrets of self-knowledge but also seem to warn him of the consequence of his search.

Beckoned and guided by the old miner, he arrives at his destination only to be overwhelmed by the sudden fear of death. He decides to leave immediately but forgets his plan when he meets Ulla Dahlsjö, a girl whose eyes promise light, health, and life. Thus Elis has arrived at the crossroads of his quest. He becomes a miner but looks toward life, eager to be greeted by Ulla when he leaves the shaft. One day the vision of the old miner returns to warn him not to forget the true nature of his search. Elis threatens him and rejects the idea. Yet when his love is tested that very day, he makes no attempt to save it. Feeling that he has lost Ulla, he runs in wild desperation back to the mine. For the first time since meeting Ulla, he concentrates with all his power on the inner world and begins to perceive its mysteries. Told later that he can marry Ulla, he struggles desperately with himself and finally resolves his torment on the wedding day when he leaves his bride and life. Looking for the secret of existence, the secret hidden in his own heart, he finds death in the mine.

When the miner had beckoned previously, Elis had always experienced a sensation strangely compounded of terror and joy. In his final hours, however, he embraces death without fear. Yet the true significance of his quest remains veiled to him. In searching for the mystery of life within himself, he fails to see that it was revealed to him in Ulla's love. The warm red light he hoped to find in the almandine glowed in her heart. After fifty lonely years of faithful waiting, Ulla too is rewarded with her ultimate truth: death while embracing the rediscovered body of the man she had loved so much. The old woman's subdued weeping echoes the despair of all victims of life. Elis Fröbom's journey had ended long before the mountain released his body only to fall to dust. He remained true to his quest but failed to realize himself in the world, because his vision led him to death, not life.

Allusions to, demonic modulations and inversions of, the motif of the Quest for Life seem to increase toward the end of the nineteenth and the beginning of the twentieth century. They are apparent in the fiction of Jean Marie de Villiers de l'Isle-Adam, Hugo von Hofmannsthal, and Isak Dinesen (Karen Blixen), to name three authors from different countries. A prevalent pattern in these narratives is the transformation of vistas of life and potential self-realization in the world to visions of alienation, death, destruction, and existential failure. The pattern is frequently enforced by imagery of distortion, oppressive squalor, and the cage. Two tales from Villiers de l'Isle-Adam's collection *Contes cruels* (1883) provide good examples. In "Duke of Portland," the young, wealthy, and popular Duke journeys to the Middle East. Suddenly, without understanding the reasons for his urge, he decides to visit the last victim of the ancient incurable form of leprosy, an outcast banned in horror from society. It seems as if a mysterious demonic fate guides his action: "no one escapes his destiny."[10] Descending into the cave of the leper, the Duke, "bold to the point of madness," insists upon shaking the man's hand and immediately contracts the disease. Thereupon he buries himself in his manor and dies imprisoned in his own cage.

In the narrative "A s'y méprendre!" the basic theme of active self-realization in the world is inverted to a confrontation with death. On a cold, drizzly November day the narrator calls a carriage in order to attend a previously arranged business meeting. While waiting on the threshold of a building resembling all and any buildings in his life, he follows a sudden impulse to step in and greet the hostess. Upon entering, he finds himself confronted by dead businessmen, who are entertained by Death. They had already ended their journey, for they failed to perceive the true significance of life, by confusing activity with existential commitment: "Certainly, in order to escape their harassed existence, most of the people in the room had assassinated their bodies, thus hoping for some more well-being."[11]

Horrified, the narrator tries to escape by leaping into a coach, which has disgorged more dead businessmen. During the ensuing trip through the streets of Paris, he observes that the passing scenery has assumed the appearance of

[10]Jean Marie de Villiers de l'Isle-Adam, *Contes cruels* (Paris, 1923), p. 87.
[11]*Ibid.*, p. 129.

death. Still determined to follow his destiny, he alights at the café designated as the site of the planned meeting, only to find once again a room filled with dead associates. At this point he begins to understand that "in order to escape the burden of their intolerable, nagging conscience, most of the people in the room had long ago assassinated their 'souls,' thus hoping for some more well-being."[12] And yet the narrator-protagonist fails to understand the real significance of his visionary experience. He leaves silently, returns to his home, and renounces his profession and life.

Demonic imagery remains restricted in Dinesen's traditional stories. Her tale "Peter and Rosa" (1942), for instance, contrasts the coming-of-age theme with the crushing power of an inexorable, inexplicable fate that leads a young man and his beloved to death in the icy waters of the ocean.[13] Unlike Dinesen's story, Hofmannsthal's modern fairy tale "Das Märchen der 672. Nacht" (1895) reflects in every detail, image, and picture, the horror of a person crushed by "inescapable life."[14] Apparently prompted by the fear of becoming guilty through action in life, the hero of the narrative has dedicated himself to the contemplation of beauty. Yet he cannot escape reality, because the eyes of his four ever-present servants haunt him as a constant reminder of his failure in the quest for life. Capable of neither self-transcendence nor self-realization he feels his terror increase when he finally ventures into the unknown world. Simultaneously lured and alarmed by visions which combine fragments of archaic inner projections, memories, and fleeting perceptions of reality, the young man gropes his way through a maze of different worlds until he encounters death. His journey ends in a hellish scene, in which he finds himself face to face with brute animal instincts. Kicked in the groin by a horse, cursing his life, hopes, fears, and the accusing eyes of his servants, he dies wretchedly.

The motif of Spiritual Rebirth holds the promise that the tragedies which befall man are only temporary, that his suffering is not in vain, and that guilty or innocent he will be redeemed. The motif seems to affirm the possibility of eternal life. It appears in tales which center on the successful metamorphosis from a lower to a higher form of life. The best-known are probably "The Frog King or Iron Henry" and "Prince Swan."[15] Since the transformation is only possible through love, the motif has erotic overtones, and the tales appear to be variations of the myth of Eros and Psyche. The restoration to life which is expressed in the fairy tales as a return to a prior physical form requires, aside from love, complete faith and devotion from others. These elements are reflected in the loyalty of the servant Henry to his king and the faithfulness of the girl to the prince in "Prince Swan." Even the young princess in "The Frog King" is forced by her father to keep her promise. Thus, while the rebirth takes place visibly in one person, be it a frog, swan or raven, the true heroes or heroines of the tales are those who

---

[12]*Ibid.*, p. 130.

[13]Isak Dinesen, "Peter and Rosa," in *Winter Tales* (New York, 1942), pp. 251-285, simultaneously in Danish as "Peter og Rosa."

[14]Hugo von Hofmannsthal, "Das Märchen der 672. Nacht," in *Erzählungen und Aufsätze* (Frankfurt, 1957), 7-24. Cf. also "Reitergeschichte" (1898) and "Das Bergwerk zu Falun," (1899).

[15]KHM, "Der Froschkönig oder der eiserne Heinrich" (No. 1), "Prinz Schwan" (No. 59), see also "Der Froschprinz" (II, 13). Aarne, No. 440.

experience a spiritual rebirth when confronted with the restoration to life.

Franz Kafka's "Die Verwandlung" (1912)[16] captures the total hopelessness of a situation in which the hero is condemned to an existence in which the promise of physical or spiritual rebirth remains unfulfilled. Even before his metamorphosis, Gregor Samsa lived in a world without love, ruled by fear and suspicion. Actually, his transformation brings his relationship with others into sharper focus, shatters Gregor's false security, and forces him to question the basis of his existence. He has never rebelled against the existing order but passively acquiesced to the lot meted out to him. He dislikes the ever-present, ever-suspicious power of the company-machine for which he slaves, but does not know how to escape from it. Even life at home lacks real understanding and love, though Gregor is the sole supporter of the family. Of intimate relationships he has only a fleeting memory of an affair with a maid in a hotel and his failure in courting a cashier in a hatshop. Gregor's isolation and fear of the world are reflected in his habit of locking all the doors of his room at home, a cell of relative security in a threatening world.

Not surprisingly, in this atmosphere everyone is highly suspicious and assumes Gregor's guilt when he fails to leave his room after his fateful metamorphosis. The comptroller of the company arrives to check on his absence from work. Father, mother, and sister urge him to come out and allay their fear. Even the mother's faint defense that everything will be clarified in a minute, since Gregor is honest and devotes his life completely to his duties as a travelling salesman, of reading railroad time tables and rushing from place to place, has a hollow ring. When he appears in his new shape, which only mirrors his existential plight, their reactions and subsequent adjustment range from the smug Samaritan role of the sister to the father's violent rejection. Gregor's two attempts to break out of his cage end in disaster. The first time his father breaks one of his legs; the second time he attacks him with apples. This symbolic gesture indicates that the father, who in Gregor's eyes represents all fathers in the world, that is, all authority, refuses to acknowledge Gregor's plight.[17] Since one apple remains in Gregor's back and slowly rots away, Kafka seems to hint that Gregor has become aware of his existential situation, but his search for truth proves illusory as long as he does not receive assistance, compassion, and the love of another human being.

This failure on the part of the family, the family of man, becomes most apparent in the inability to provide Gregor with the right food. Immediately after his transformation Gregor is hungry. Repulsed by a favorite dish of former days, he at first gorges himself on leftovers which seem to satisfy his bodily needs. Soon he feels starved, but not for the food that is carelessly thrown into his room. When his sister plays the violin once, he muses that perhaps music is the right food he is looking for: "Was he an animal if music had such an effect upon him? He felt as if the path was opening

---

[16]Frank Kafka, "Die Verwandlung," in *Die Erzählungen* (Frankfurt, 1961), pp. 39-93. Allusions to and inversions of the archetypal motif are also present in Hans Christian Andersen's tales "The Little Match Girl" and "The Little Mermaid." In both stories a true self-realization in the world seems no longer possible.

[17]Kafka, pp. 56, 73-75.

before him to the unknown nourishment he craved."[18] But the aesthetic experience of music as the road to truth, as medium of communication between him and the world is forever withheld from him. Gregor's isolation, reflected in the substitution of haze and fog for sunlight in his vision as he stares blindly out of the window, is complete, and he finally withers away. This picture of a hopeless loss of identity and man's inability and failure to love stands in stark contrast to the hope of self-realization and rebirth expressed in the fairy tale motif.

In the play *Rhinocéros* (1959) Eugène Ionesco creates a dynamic pattern by juxtaposing the archetypal motif with its infernal inversion. The audience, while watching society's spiritual decline and hopeless loss of identity, witnesses the rebirth of a slovenly drunk, unable to cope with life, who becomes a staunch, defiant defender of humanity. The first act opens with a picture of society in which everyone follows his narrow interests. And though people (an alcoholic, a grocer, a café owner, a logician, a housewife) live side by side, they fail to establish a truly human relationship—in the sense of Schiller, Buber, Camus, or Heidegger—because they lack the courage for existential encounter with each other. When their mode of life is threatened by the sudden appearance of a rhinoceros they are momentarily united by a common feeling of loathing and terror.

But as soon as they relate the strange phenomenon to their experience, each individual's perception, reflecting his isolation, becomes a divisive factor. Whereas initially they respond directly to the appearance of the rhinoceros, they soon question its number of horns, its origin, and whether they had seen one or two animals. But as the beasts increase in number and form a herd, united by savage instinct, the people begin to respond to the essence of "rhinoceritis." And while some still argue the necessity of a policy toward the phenomenon, others have begun to embrace the menace. The atavistic relapse into a primitive, instinctive, and pre-human condition holds the promise of salvation for all who are unwilling to develop their spiritual potential and commit themselves to a life which requires respect and love for others. As the action progresses and the metamorphoses spread, the audience becomes painfully aware of the complete renunciation of human values: "Let's demolish all that, we'll feel much better."[19]

While Bérenger, the lone alcoholic, sees person after person, including his friend Jean and his girlfriend Daisy, transformed and absorbed in the indistinguishable herd, he experiences a true spiritual rebirth. Initially unable to face life, he scarcely notices the appearance of the first rhinoceros. But as society changes around him, he becomes deeply concerned for others, offers help and compassion, and finally defends humanity: "Come on, think, you'll realize that we have a philosophy that these animals don't have, an irreplaceable system of values. Centuries of human civilization have built it."[20] When Daisy tells him that the savage beasts are gods he begins to contemplate the riddle of human existence and with her departure he becomes fully conscious of the challenge confronting man: "I am the last man. I will remain so to

---

[18]*Ibid.*, p. 84.
[19]Eugène Ionesco, *Rhinocéros*, in *Théâtre* (Paris, 1963), III, 76.
[20]*Ibid.*, p. 76.

the end! I will not capitulate!"[21] To interpret these last lines of the play as optimistic would express a humanistic view but do injustice to the nature of the archetypal motif. Bérenger, though he understands the essence of the existential commitment, cannot turn toward others and live in the world, because he is left alone. He transcends himself, represents the view of an ennobled man, but stands in total, tragic isolation.

The inversion of archetypal fairy tale motifs shows several common features. Instead of anticipating a happy ending, the motifs arouse a feeling of impending disaster. Joy in life is marred by the finality of isolation or death. The possibility of a successful self-realization in the world is questioned or negated and the theme of enslavement replaces that of freedom. Finally the motifs focus attention on man's existential anguish and the suffering of all those who face a wretched, absurd world. In the process of demonically inverting the motifs from light to darkness and from life to death, these authors have created infernal fairy tales.

Based on the preceding analysis, we can reach two theoretical conclusions. First, a dynamic relationship exists both in the fairy tales and in literature between motifs and contrasting motifs. The affirmation of life in the Rite of Spring is unthinkable without the threat to existence; the successful Quest of Life is endangered by possible failure; the promise of freedom and rebirth is counterbalanced by the possibility of eternal enslavement and darkness. A similar formal relationship between inverted motif and motif is discernible in literary works. Second, we can distinguish between a prosaic and poetic use of the motifs. The fairy tales present simple, unadorned stories in which one motif becomes transparent and assimilates its opposite. The inverted archetypal motif forms the basis of an important dynamic aesthetic pattern in literature, which encompasses tradition and innovation, mythical aspects and individual characteristics, as well as harmony and energy. The motifs are employed to develop contrasts, contradictions, and an ever-increasing tension which stir conflicting emotions in the reader and force him to perceive the mystery of life in the basic incongruity of the motifs and their opposites.

Wayne State University
Detroit

---

[21]*Ibid.*, p. 117.

J. KOSTKA

Par Vagerkvist:
The Dwarf and Dogma

By ROGER RAMSEY

Par Lagerkvist remained a free literary spirit throughout his career. Although he flirted with several modern movements, such as expressionism in the drama and socialism in politics, he cannot be identified with any. By his fiction he is known to the world as a parablist, foregoing realistic detail for the larger effect and setting the scene in remote pasts; yet even these parables are consonant with much of modern fiction, for Lagerkvist's major characters suffer a spiritual anxiety familiar to the readers of Kafka, Joyce and Camus. Especially after the publication of *Barabbas*, in 1950, and the Nobel Prize which followed in the year after, Lagerkvist was in danger of being associated with the swelling existential movement. The rapid growth in popularity of Sartre's ideas made strange bedfellows of a number of writers: Dostoevsky, Proust, Unamuno, Mann, Kafka, Genet; yea, even unto

Celine, Cela and Silone—all have been mined for their existential "elements." The slighting alliteration is intentional, for to ally these writers is to deny the integrity of each and to infringe upon the closed system of ideas that is existentialism. It is to define "existential" as loosely as "personal," "inner," or "separated." These terms do describe the typical Lagerkvist protagonist, but only one of his characters is an "existentialist," in the proper sense of the word.[1]

Lagerkvist has apparently called himself a "religious sceptic." His novels have a curious unfinality about them, for their characters never come to their proper reward, never gain the solace suffering is supposed to bring. In manifestly Christian fiction, the main characters seem completed by their faith, whether that faith has temporal reward or not. In explicit existential fiction, generally the protagonist achieves some sort of pride, even happiness, in his incompleteness. But for the religious sceptic, like Lagerkvist, there is neither fulfillment nor pride. Humility, very human love, tenuous community, striving—these are the "rewards" of such a world. They are universal conditions, but they are not rigidly defined. In other words, they do not congeal into dogma. In the Lagerkvist scheme of things there are no conclusions, no party lines, no givens. As near to Christian as the basic tenets are, they are not locked into doctrine. In *Barabbas*, the Christian enclave ignores and then purges Barabbas, the truer seeker. Christ himself is said to have cursed Ahasuerus in *The Death of Ahasuerus*. And the Christians in *The Dwarf*[2] are generally materialistic and vicious beings, even sadistic in their faith. Lagerkvist consistently attacks those who are so meager of spirit that they accept the narrow word and in consequence reject the spirit of religious law.

The meanest of them all is the dwarf, whose memoirs make up the longest and most complex of Lagerkvist's novels. Everything observed is seen through the jaundiced eye of this creature who could rightly be called cretin, a dialectical form of the French for Christian. The repugnance of his person, his twisted values, his narcissism and contradictoriness and bitterness have

---

[1] It is not Barabbas. Barabbas was the bandit amnestied by the people when they chose Jesus to die instead; literally he has been saved by "Christ." As he learns about the man who died in his place and as he moves in the circle of the new sect, he discovers his own desire to believe that his savior is the Savior. But he is denied even full faith. The Christians ostracize him, the authorities persecute him, his questions remain unanswered and finally, on his own cross, he looks up to a darkening, unpromising sky. The novel ends there. Outcast among men and spiritually exiled, Barabbas seems another image of the prototypical existential character, "the stranger."
The need to believe, the communion with the Christian prisoner Sahak, the thoroughly questioning spirit, even at the moment of death, preserve the religious spirit from the dictates of dogma. Although Barabbas doubts, his doubt never withers into despair. Like Christ, Barabbas withholds judgment and condemnation; unlike Christ, he hesitates because he is unsure. Barabbas condemns neither the Christians nor the authority which punishes him because of Christian markings on his slave's medallion. Instead, he carries the body of the stoned hare-lipped girl to her proper grave. After the death of Jesus, condemnation, judgment, even concrete purpose are no part of Barabbas' nature. For him, the Crucifixion saves him from dogma, not from the immorality which characterized his past life in murder and marauding, but from the dictates of an easy moral system. He then becomes neither Christian nor existentialist, both built on absolute premises, but a sceptic.
[2] A readily available paperback edition in English of *The Dwarf* has been published by Hill and Wang (New York, 1945), trans. Alexandra Dick.

already made him a prime example of evil in the modern world. Even so, exemplars of bona fide evil, in the Miltonic sense, are hard to come by. We shall find that the generalized appellation of "evil" is not very appropriate for the dwarf, for he is specifically, not generally, disgusting and his perversion of truth, as Lagerkvist sees it, is his only—albeit pervasive—sin. In radical opposition to Camus, for whom "Sin is not so much knowing . . . as wanting to know," Lagerkvist defines sin as pretending to know. The world for Camus and many other modern writers is absurd; for Lagerkvist it is mysterious. In the existentialists Lagerkvist found common ground but not common understanding. As Camus expresses it, there is simply no meaning to discover. Whether or not there is ultimate meaning, man in the Lagerkvist world is in no position to find it out. To a sceptic, the existential premise betrays itself to be just as dogmatic and pretentious as the Christian doctrine. Epistemology is the common sphere for sceptics and existentialists, for the problem of knowing the nature of existence is foremost for both. But the schism occurs when existentialism announces the primary truth that existence precedes essence. A sceptic considers this only a possibility, and the religious sceptic doubts it.

As a brief against the acceptance of dogma, *The Dwarf* holds no truth as self-evident. The misapprehension of events by the dwarf serves the important literary purpose of portraying insubstantial knowledge directly; no other technique could as well have evoked the reader's dissatisfaction with answers and judgments. We cannot trust the dwarf, just as we cannot trust the evidence of this world or the "evidence" of an otherworld. Wayne C. Booth has made "unreliable narrator" a watchword of modern literary criticism in his excellent book, *The Rhetoric of Fiction*; Professor Booth writes, "One of the worst results of all this is that it becomes more and more difficult to rely, in our criticism, on the old standards of proof; evidence from the book can never be decisive." It is true that the narrator of *The Dwarf* is an imp of the perverse who obscures facts and intentions; but surely this is not "one of the worst results." Professor Booth has not acknowledged the valuable possibilities of such a narrator nor has he allowed for the full bodying forth of doubt in the very undependability of the speaker. Like Henry James and Vladimir Nabokov in some of their fictions, Lagerkvist has created a narrator whose conclusions leave the reader ill at ease. The brilliant use of the memoir format in *The Dwarf* accomplishes the sceptical attitude in the most immediate, almost visceral way by encouraging doubt in the reader himself. In effect, the unreliable narrator *is* the meaning of the novel.

Even though the dwarf's narration veils some of the actuality in the novel, there will be agreement on a number of his characteristics: his ugliness, his misanthropy, cynicism, pride, shallowness, his love of war and of killing. The common denominator of these is not, however, undifferentiated evil, as Alrik Gustafson avers in *A History of Swedish Literature*. He states that "in many ways" the dwarf is "the very incarnation of evil," and thus far the commentators have agreed. But the dwarf is too closely drawn, too *specifically* malicious to represent all evil. Furthermore, to designate the dwarf as evil incarnate is to imply metaphysical manicheism, a rather simplistic duality which certainly would not appeal to a modern sceptical mind. *The Dwarf* is full of realistic detail unusual for Lagerkvist's novels, and the first-person narrator is also unique; the consequence of these techniques is that we may be confident of determining the dwarf's precise nature. The "evil" is really an overwhelming egoism, a selfishness raised to the highest power, an I-ness such as that touted by the existential philosopher. The dwarf denies any values outside himself; he retreats within, where fickleness, vacillation, and ephemerality have reign. His judgments begin and end in himself, referring at every instance to his own self-serving. So extreme is his egoism that he convinces himself of his authority in the court, though he obviously has none, and of the continuing reliance of the Prince on him, though he is chained in a dungeon. Since his character emanates from the vicissitudes of the "I" he is arbitrary and changeable in his opinions. He adores his Prince but turns against him bitterly; he taunts the Princess and brings about her death although he confesses his love for her; he has unlimited admiration for the leader of the mercenaries and then denounces him. The dwarf's only consistency lies in the inconstant and incontinent ego. His resources located only within himself, and those proving to be insubstantial, the dwarf's career exposes the insipid egoism of the self-ish, in effect a parody of the existential. The "evil" of the dwarf is his inversion of values.

One scene, early in the novel, catches and parodies this self-sufficient "myth" and leads the reader into further versions of its *in*sufficiency. Called to deliver a message to Bernardo, the master engineer and artist, the dwarf encounters in the artist's studio his "deepest degradation." Bernardo, modelled with exactness on Leonardo da Vinci, is a perfect Renaissance man, various in his capacities, fascinated by all things known, hesitant and detached about things unknown. At Bernardo's first appearance, the dwarf is puzzled: "His knowledge seems to embrace everything and everything seems to interest him. He tries to explain it all but, in contrast to the others, he is not always convinced that his explanations are correct." The first words of this Great Master are humble and sceptical ones: "But perhaps it is not thus." Contrary to the harsh judgments of the dwarf, Bernardo's attitudes are "unpretentious"; in sharp antithesis to the dwarf, Bernardo "does not always vacillate" and "is not treacherous." Clearly, even through the warp of the dwarf's memoirs, the artist is fully sympathetic, a foil to the dwarf himself. We are prepared, then, to accept the dwarf's humiliation as justified. And so it is. He deserves the terrible shame of having his likeness drawn in silverpoint by this most critical of all men.

Nothing else happens. Lagerkvist could have played on Leonardo's penchant for grotesquery or on his homosexuality in order to humiliate the dwarf. Even a simple good deed might have irritated him, a word of kindness from the artist, a smile. Instead, Lagerkvist reveals the source of the dwarf's ugliness as he is examined, for the only time in the novel, nude. Shrieking "I can't bear any offense against my body!" the dwarf is stripped and placed on a scaffold for inspection. "I stood there defenseless, naked, incapable of action." He is robbed of all possible pretense and the wellsprings of his false being immediately dry up. He had stated to Bernardo that he would not be portrayed: "I wish to possess my own face." Bernardo explained that one's face, i.e., identity, is possessed by many others; "Nobody really possesses himself." The idea of self-possession is fully understood by the artist who rejects it, for man cannot completely exist by his own sufficiency, nor can he entirely control himself. "But I do," cries the dwarf. "You don't possess yourselves, but I do!" Not without the baggage of baseless egoism, not nude.

Bernardo carefully sketches him and contemplates his work as the dwarf scurries out of the studio in "agony." The philosophical implications of the creature's self-esteem become clear in his response to the painting just begun by the artist, "The Last Supper." Though it is incomplete, the dwarf immediately identifies not with Judas, whose villainy against divine order is not the dwarf's, but with Christ. The dwarf feels that this drawing of him will leave him "exposed to the stares of all, mocked and defiled," like Christ soon after His betrayal. Like Christ, he will be sold for a pittance to "the noble, high-minded people." The dwarf is indeed a christ of a different dogma, a self-ish rather than a self-less christ, a christ of alienation and disgust rather than a christ of communion and mercy, a christ of hate rather than love. In his fantasy identification with the unfinished picture, the dwarf concludes existentially that "Mankind does not like to be violated by God."

This conclusion is a parody of the atheistic existentialism which was gaining popularity in the days when *The Dwarf* was written, the early 1940's. The flimsiness of the view is suggested in the conditional, preferential nature of the assertions: "I *wish* to possess my own face," "Mankind *does not like* to be violated by God," reminiscent of the "I prefer not to" of Melville's Bartleby (a character often considered existential). There are other important levels of the novel, but this is central to the conception of the dwarf. He thinks he is totally free, though he is a servant; he believes he had made himself inviolate, for he has ridded the palace of all other dwarfs, killing the last, whereas he is used by everyone, even the young Angelica, who toys with him. He ends his days putting his memoirs together in a prison cell, welded to the wall, while the entire community celebrates peace and the lifting of the plague. Nothing more clearly indicates Lagerkvist's sympathies than this contrast of communal celebration and wretched loneliness. The dwarf's "freedom" throughout the novel is a parody of existential freedom. For Sartre, as he describes it in the famous essay, "Existentialism and Humanism," the final stage of recognition is the knowledge that each man is condemned to freedom, condemned to utter freedom of choice. This is literally true of the dwarf. But Lagerkvist asks further, who condemns man to this lonely freedom? And the answer is, man does, when and if he choses to do so. As criticism, by means of parody, of the existential position, *The Dwarf* presents the alienated hero limited in vision (the dwarf cannot see the stars which others guide by), shrunken in stature and self-serving. He is, of course, also sterile.

A ghastly scene early in the novel portrays the desperation and sickness of the dwarf's views. He recalls the time he gave "holy" communion to the dwarfs of Mantua court, a Black Mass in which Christ is hailed as savior of all dwarfs—a dwarf Himself—and the wine is transformed into dwarf's blood. Again the dwarf identifies with this Christ: "It is as though I drink my own blood." He concludes the brief episode by thinking, "I am glad to be *alone*," for his perverted communion brought him only the dungeon. Here is communion celebrated in hatred; Christ's body "tastes as bitter as gall, for it is full of hatred." Ultimately, hatred must turn on itself.

> It is my fate that I hate my own people. My race is detestable to me.
> But I hate myself too. I eat my own splenetic flesh. I drink my own
> poisoned blood. Every day I perform my solitary communion as the
> grim high priest of my people. (p. 28)

The dwarf has raised hatred—more specifically alienation—to the level of religion, and he consequently rejoices in any evidence of enmity and hostility. He loves war and is especially proud of killing another dwarf; as he writes, "And during the fight, especially when dealing the death blow, I felt strangely exalted, as though I were performing a rite in an unfamiliar religion." When he kills the enemy leaders with poisoned wine, he calls it his "somber communion feast where they have drunk my poisoned blood, that which my heart drinks daily." Hatred becomes absolute, the religion of hate dogmatic. Accordingly, he is distraught at signs of peace and abhors human love and sexual consummation. Any bridging of the existential abyss which separates people evokes his malice, for the dwarf's view of life disallows communion, sharing, being together, communication. Ironic in the portrait of the dwarf himself, *The Dwarf* here partakes of olympian irony: as a deliberate writer of his own memoirs, the dwarf is in the very process of communication. In thus sharing his experience, in the very intent of offering his life and views to others, he ridicules his own attitude and parodies every "existential" view he holds.

This is the purpose of the form of *The Dwarf*, unique in the Lagerkvist canon. It turns on itself, just as the dwarf's egoistical pretense to freedom of action in the palace and to authority is ironically subverted by his actual status. He is living a lie which he has made dogma. The existential conception of life is just as dogmatic and blind, Lagerkvist suggests, as the most canonical law of any religion, for it invents absolute premises and erects a superstructure of demands onto them. The idea of "existence before essence," first premise of existentialism, is only a possibility; "But perhaps it is not thus." But a dogmatist rushes to aver or argue. The dwarf is quick to accept the idea that "life itself can have no meaning. Otherwise it would not be." He exposes both his basic existentialism and his egoism: "Such is *my* belief" (italics his). Of course, *The Dwarf* is fiction, not a disquisitory refutation of a system of ideas. As Richard Vowles, the first appreciator of Lagerkvist in English, has said, "Lagerkvist is always the artist, seldom the philosopher." In the character of the dwarf is embodied the perversion of truth which dogmatic adherence to existential premises can cause; the novel is a warning from the north of Europe that humanistic scepticism and breadth of vision are endangered by this new dogma.

Neither is *The Dwarf* Christian apologetics. It is frustrating to hear critics and students speak of existential elements in Lagerkvist, although his early pessimism and constant subject, the isolated man, might account for this. No less erroneous is it to ascribe to Lagerkvist doctrinaire Christian principles, although the settings and spiritual questings in his novel might again lead easily to such a conclusion. It is likely that the popularity of the fiction among the general public in America has something to do with this misapprehension.

(The film version of *Barabbas*, for instance, was awfully Christian in tone and in the weight of its sympathies, obviously because of the assumed necessity of appealing to a very large audience.) But a more acute perception of the settings shows that they suggest an atmosphere of turbulence, of conflicting loyalties and insecure commitments. The medieval explicitly compared to the modern rise of totalitarianism in *The Hangman*, the development of a new and promising faith in *Barabbas* and *The Death of Ahasuerus*, the growth of Apollonian thought in the Greece of *The Sibyl*, the components of the title itself in *The Pilgrim of the Sea*—all of the characters are pilgrims, seekers, in the chaos of the sea.

Except the dwarf. Renaissance Italy is a superb selection of setting to invoke the spirits of feudal authority structures and of the rise of liberating humanism. The dwarf calls himself a Christian, and in a sense he is. We have seen that his misanthropic alienation is anti-Christian, in the larger sense, but his dogmatism corresponds to that of a Church at the zenith of its power. Here, about fifteen years before Luther's apostasy, the political and spiritual suzerainty of the Pope is uncontested and every activity requires "religious" sanction. Even in her flaunted infidelity, Princess Teodora cannot conceive of a Christ who would deny her sexual pleasure, for the Church exists only by pandering to the whims of those dangerous to its authority. Like the existential dogma, religious dogma is here parodied as untrue even to itself, toadying and arbitrary. In the Lagerkvist world, rigorous execution of Church law is no less binding to the human spirit than militant egoism, and no less false at its very source. The pointless war, the treachery of the Prince, the murder of Angelica's lover, the scourge-death of the Princess and her deification afterwards, the very vindictiveness of the dwarf—all are sanctified in the ancient manner by the blessing of the Church. In every instance, the Roman Catholic Church is presented as materialistic and opportunistic. The true religious spirit is recommended at the end of the novel, when the campanile is finished and the silver bells, made from the free offerings of the people, ring out the peace of communal solidarity. "It echoed over the town and all felt happier for having heard it."

Except the dwarf. For this is the undogmatic, spontaneous and humble attitude of religion which is antithetical to the proud absolutism and selfishness displayed by the dwarf and the Church. For a religious sceptic like Lagerkvist, even the misguided and dogmatic Church will not deter the proper religious spirit from expressing itself in the people. As always, in literature at least, this truth is discovered only after intense suffering, after war and siege and plague. Man's proud and pretentious character must bow before the ultimate mystery, wherein is located the true spirit of religion.

There is another dogma, curiously relevant to the twentieth century and earlier envisioned by Lagerkvist in *The Hangman*; this dogma is also parodied. It is the pursuit of power at all costs, the gaining of political goals by any means, the Machiavellian dogma. Again, the setting allows Leonardo, Machiavelli, and Machiavelli's model, Caesar Borgia, to exist together near the end of the fifteenth century. They each represent part of the genius of the Renaissance. But whereas Bernardo-Leonardo manifests the genius of human greatness, the Prince-Borgia lives a life of power-hungry ruthlessness and the dwarf-Machiavelli idealizes it. The love of pomp and pleasure, the intrigue of the Prince's court—most of all the machinations—are the conditions of Machiavelli's world. Even the Church is summoned to bless these mean-spirited adventures; all in subsumed into the immediate aim of conquest. More specifically than in *The Hangman*, Hitler (the Prince) and Mussolini (Il Toro, alias Il Duce) provide the modern paradigm of the worship of power. Like Malraux' projected outcome of the Spanish Civil War in *Man's Hope*, Lagerkvist's resolution is wishful thinking. The betrayal of one leader by the other, the retributive plague, the defeat of the Prince were instances of Lagerkvist's faith in man, for neither political, religious nor philosophical dogmatism lead back to man.

Bernardo emerges as the moral center of the novel, for it is only he who maintains the human in its limitations and its glories. The dwarf does not understand him and that in itself is a clue to his significance, as is the fact that he is an artist. We have already noted that he is sceptical; this characteristic is true of his artwork as well. He is insatiably curious about all the things of this world. At one point, he is allowed to examine the entrails of a hanged man, not for prophecy but for information about his anatomy. The lack of doctrine allows him to listen to the astrologers with interest, like Leonardo himself, without committing himself to superstition, and also to prepare original designs for war machinery without himself catching the war fever, again like Leonardo in the court of Ludovico of Milan. He is never satisfied, either with actualities or with imagined creations. Like the real Leonardo, Bernardo cannot complete his paintings; as the dwarf says, he "finds no peace of mind in his work." Only once in the novel does this man have center stage—in the only conversation directly recorded by the dwarf—and his words are those of cosmic scepticism; in Lagerkvist's world they are words of the most noble and generous qualities of mankind because they welcome his only reward: restlessness. The passage is succinct enough to quote almost in full:

> "Are we the happier because we seek the truth? I know not. I merely seek it. All my life has been a restless search for it, and sometimes I have felt that I have apprehended it, I have caught a glimpse of its pure sky—but the sky has never opened itself for me, my eyes have never filled themselves with its endless spaces, without which nothing here can be fully understood. It is not vouchsafed to us. Therefore all my efforts really have been in vain. Therefore all that I have touched has been but partly true and partly completed. I think of my works with pain and so they will be regarded by all—as though it were a torso. All that I have created is imperfect and unfinished. All that I leave behind me is unfinished.
>
> "But is there anything strange in that? It is the fate of mankind, the inescapable destiny of all human effort and all human achievement. Is it ever more than an attempt, an attempt at something which can never be achieved, which is not meant to be achieved by any of us? All human culture is but an attempt at something unattainable, something which far transcends our powers of realization. There it stands, mutilated, tragic as a torso. Is not the human spirit itself a torso?"
>
> (pp. 54-55)

Bernardo's statement defines man. Words like "search," "unfinished," and "attempt" pattern themselves into the shape of Lagerkvist's thinking. Man is limited, even if limited only by the limitlessness of existence. As infinite being impinges upon transient and truncated man, he becomes a "tragic torso," as beautiful in his incomplete state as the ruin of a Greek sculpture, perfectly imperfect, gloriously tragic. Lagerkvist's theme, that life is worthy of man, that man must be worthy of life, sounds a discordant note in contemporary literature, but, like the silver bells of the campanile, it rings untrue only to the warped and belittled senses of a dwarf. Naturally—or rather unnaturally —the dwarf's reaction to the words of Bernardo is, "I do not understand him."

"The Last Supper" is a thoroughly symbolic painting in the novel, for it is left unfinished. So was the original; the famous copy is the work of one of Leonardo's students. The head of Christ was never painted by Leonardo. Lagerkvist has made Leonardo's great defect, his inability to finish his projects, into the greatest of human truths: nothing is final. Leonardo painted the apostles at the moment when Christ has announced that one of them will betray Him. Their faces are alive with questions. Am I to be the one? Who is it? Do I believe in this god? The source of the faith, Christ himself, is not clear; his head was too difficult to paint, for, in the context of the novel, one can never be sure. The selection of this painting as the critical symbol is a master stroke because it reveals the central fact of faith itself, and that fact is doubt. Bernardo, in the fullest way, expresses the questioning and questing spirit that is religious scepticism. One can be no more sure of a human being than of Christ, for Bernardo paints Princess Teodora both as "a middle-aged whore"—the dwarf says, "It is really like her, diabolically so" —and as "a gentle consolatory Madonna," reminiscent of the Mona Lisa. The fact that she is presented as whore and virgin symbolically manifests Bernardo's positive inability to delimit human nature. The description of the latter painting suggests again the tenuousness of truth:

> Most entrancing of all was the enigmatic smile which hovered around her lips, which affected everyone as being something quite heavenly, inexplicable and full of divine mysticism. I understood that the artist had taken that smile from his earlier portrait, the one in which she resembled a whore. (p. 223)

Both pictures exist, one in the cathedral and one in the palace. "And yet," as the dwarf says, "both pictures, despite their great dissimilarity, may speak the truth each in its own way; both show the same vague smile, which the worshipers in the cathedral think so heavenly." As in "The Last Supper," Bernardo portrays possibilities, not sureties. His vast questioning spirit allows no final judgments, no easy iconography, no absolutes. In choosing Leonardo as model for Bernardo, Lagerkvist has portrayed the soul in its most creative unfulfillment; life does not accord even the earnest seeker conclusive answers. Who more than Leonardo da Vinci has sought? And who has been more rewarded in his dissatisfaction?

Even in *The Dwarf*, perverse and unreliable as the point of view is, we may find the positive values that inform all of Lagerkvist's fiction. Dogmatism is antithetical to the human spirit, evidenced in the cruel and severe oppressiveness of the Renaissance Church, machiavellian deviousness, and existential egoism. If we have dwelled on the latter, it is because it has not been noted before. In *The Dwarf*, Lagerkvist isolated a particular kind of evil, one that paralleled the groundswell of totalitarianism in politics; existentialism was as dogmatic as legalistic Christianity and power politics. All of them blind and blinker man's capacity for thought and investigation, a capacity which has as its only reward the pleasures of incompleteness, tentativeness, pursuit. This is man's lot; like Keats' lovers on the Grecian urn, Lagerkvist's heroes are forever searching, never to find, "forever panting" after truth. And this is the beauty man can achieve. Only a dwarf can convince himself that he is happy and whole. His negative example reminds us of the consequences of immediate commitment, the kind that the Pope, the Macchiavel, and the Sartre demand. No commitment is vital or vitalizing in a world ungraced by truth, and so in recognizing the evil of dogmatism, incarnated in the dwarf, we may recoil from it and take refuge in scepticism, affirmative scepticism. We may, with Bernardo, question the meaning of existence and be humble before its silence.

Rockford College
Illinois

Vittorini's Multiple Resources of Style:
Conversazione in Sicilia

J. Kostra.

By BRUCE MERRY

Few writers have exerted such a continuous domination on the literary life of their country as the Italian novelist Elio Vittorini (1908-1966).[1] He wrote

---

[1]His childhood always remained in his memory as a fairy-tale period, incongruously incorporating scenes of poverty and the railway stations in which he spent his early years because of his father's profession. Strongly influenced by books read in his boyhood years, such as *Robinson Crusoe* and the *Thousand and One Nights*, he left Sicily in 1927, settling in Florence in 1930. "He learned his Italy," Ernest Hemingway remarked, "in the same way American boys who ran away from home learned their own country." Vittorini joined the Communist Party, and after drifting through a variety of casual jobs eventually made his way into literary circles at Florence, without having achieved any formal higher education. After the war he became editorial consultant to the newly founded publishing house Einaudi, and eventually found himself in the position of dispensing advice and criticism to a whole post-war generation of Italian prose-writers, notably Pavese, Calvino and the group involved with his journal *Politecnico*.

his masterpiece, *Conversazione in Sicilia*, in 1937-39, constantly harassed by the fascist censors, who managed to detect a coherent political statement in this novel and earlier works which led up to it.

The surface impression of *Conversazione*, however, is a transparently simple plot, with a pervasive air of fable and persistently paradoxical use of language. It was immediately acclaimed a classic and is still considered the purest literary distillation of the anti-fascist experience in Italy. It holds an oblique fascination for Italian writers and intellectuals as a cardinal point which must be accounted for in any attempt to grasp the intellectual directions of modern Italian writing. But is it sufficient to take the book as a political denunciation? And if so, why was it written at such a level of poetic abstraction? The purpose of the present essay is to try to answer these questions by defining the novel as a "polyvalent" text (a technical term borrowed from serial music) and hence to set out four possible "values" which the variables in the text may correspond to, and argue that since no single interpretation can account for the complexities of Vittorini's style, they all merge ultimately in the fourth, which is the level where language is pure literary play. In fact, the "polyvalence" of the plot finds a precise analogue in the multiple (or "polysemous") resources of the style, because the latter refuses to be harnessed to a single meaning, continuously constraining grammar and word-order into unorthodox patterns.

The basic material of the story is organised into five chronologically sequential sections, which hint at pastiche and self-parody. In Part I the hero, Silvestro, a thirty-year-old Sicilian, is agitated by "abstract furies," alarmed by news headlines that "shriek of war and slaughter" and generally depressed by the water in his shoes and the silence of his friends. So when he receives a letter from his father suggesting that he travel back home to wish his mother happy birthday, he buys a cheap train ticket on the impulse. As he travels by train, he converses with a series of eccentrically picturesque figures, most notably a "Great Lombard" who has blue eyes, three fine daughters and mentions the existence of certain "new duties" and the need for a "new cognition" of the world. In part 2 Silvestro walks in on his mother, and they sit down to eat a herring together and reminisce about the family past. Her own father emerges as another "Great Lombard," while her husband (who recently left her) is denounced as an adulterer who wrote poems to other railwaymen's wives, calling them "queen-bees." But when she is cross-examined by Silvestro, she admits that she too acted "like a cow" with various other men. In part 3, they leave the house, as his mother goes to give the round of injections which is her means of livelihood. First he sees injections administered to the starving poor in dark hovels. Gradually the patients' status improves, until she is treating the bared buttocks of richer women—and querying her son as to whether he finds them "appetising." In part 4, he separates from his mother and joins a group of working-class men who decide that the world is "deeply offended" and needs "live water" to wash away its woes. He gets drunk with them in the tavern of Colombo, a "shameless gnome of wine." In part 5, his brother, recently killed in battle, now a phantom in a cemetery, incapable of accepting a cigarette, seems to talk with Silvestro, increasing his nostalgia for their common childhood. But his mother informs Silvestro that he had been imagining things while drunk. He tells her that she is as glorious as Cornelia, mother of the Gracchi, and stumbles out of the house to a war memorial, around which he meets all of the secondary characters of the novel. In an epilogue, he sees his mother washing her returned husband's feet, and bids her goodbye without addressing a word to his father. The author then remarks that the hero is in no way autobiographical, and that the text is set in Sicily only because that name sounds better than Persia or Venezuela. In any case, he imagines that all manuscripts are washed up in a bottle.

The author's appended remark is illuminating at two levels. Firstly, it typifies the whole tone of *Conversazione* as a closed non-referential literary act in which the language amounts to a verbal *jeu* rather than the vehicle for a formal message. Secondly, it conforms to the axiom of serial composition which holds that the aesthetic fabric of a work is principally a tacit analysis of its own creative resources. The Italian critic Umberto Eco has summed up this attitude in a lecture on the Italian avant-garde, which was recently delivered at Yale:

> Tout message met en question le code, tout acte de parole constitue une discussion sur la langue qu'il engendre; à la limite tout message pose son propre code à lui, tout oeuvre d'art est la fondation linguistique de soi-même, la discussion sur sa propre poétique, la libération des liens qui avant elle prétendaient la déterminer, toute oeuvre d'art est la clé de sa lecture.[2]

It is true of no modern Italian novel so much as *Conversazione* that the written page presents a continuous "discussion of its own poetics," for the individual effect achieved by a particular episode always tends to be a self-conscious exaggeration of its literary possibilities. Where a page is by intention narrative, it has a marked inclination towards narrative in the grand manner. Descriptive pages present the symptoms of the set piece or the purple passage, and where there is symbolism, Vittorini deploys many of the devices of classical rhetoric to accentuate and pinpoint the lower surfaces of meaning.[3] Thus, the writing in *Conversazione* always follows the logic of its intent and may strike the reader as unrelieved across individual episodes, in spite of its manifest over-all economy. As the sum of a wide range of disparate parts, it recalls a doctrine propounded by the Russian theorist V. Sklovskij on style: "The quality of a style consists in its ability to express the greatest possible number of ideas with the least possible number of words."[4] If a written text achieves its effects by self-conscious striving, that is to say by following the logic of its intent in individual passages rigorously, then it is most likely to expose this intent at every turn of the narrative. This is especially true of *Conversazione*, the self-sufficient story in a washed-up bottle, which consistent-

---

[2]The lecture is adapted and translated as an article in *Twentieth Century Studies*, no. 5, (1971), pp. 60-71.

[3]Vittorini's use of rhetorical devices is analysed in my article "Vittorini's *Conversazione in Sicilia* as an Exemplary Stylistic Process," in *Association of Teachers of Italian Journal*, no. 6, Summer, 1971, pp. 22-31.

[4]The expression is reported by V. Sklovskij in the opening chapter of his *O teorii prozy*, (Moscow, 1929). I translate from the Italian translation *Una teoria della prosa*, (Bari, 1966).

ly offers what Eco calls *la clé de sa lecture* within itself. At times the 'key' is made explicit, rather than left to be deduced from the tonal emphasis of a particular passage. For example, after Silvestro has recognised his brother Liborio in the cemetery, he is still unaware that the figure talking to him is the ghost of a dead soldier, and so he asks Liborio if he is pleased to be resting among the graves:

> He sighed once more. "How can I be happy? For thirty days I've been lying on a field covered with snow and blood."
> "But what is this nonsense you're telling me?" I shouted.
> "You're right," said the soldier. "Please forgive me. It was my metaphorical way of talking."[5]

The last sentence of the soldier's response is an internal miniature of the potential response which the author could make, if charged with having consciously sought mystification in the book: "the reader will forgive my pure, metaphorical way of writing." However, if the common reader can suspend his curiosity about these hermetic prevarications, he will still derive a cumulative satisfaction from accepting *Conversazione* as a traditional descriptive story, since the surface level of the text clearly presents a sensitive evocation of Sicily. At every point in the narrative, Vittorini offers vignettes and sketches of the island, although he was at pains, in the epilogue of the book cited above, to profess a complete lack of authorial concern for the geographical coordinates of his ostensible subject. The style is, in fact, admirably fitted to a straight sequential narrative spaced out with descriptive glimpses of the character's environment: Vittorini employs a matter-of-fact Italian prose built out of nouns and verbs, actions and their agents, with a limpid and transparent syntax that can be mastered so easily that the reader transfers his concentration to the choice of words. The main line train "sped clattering between orange groves and the sea;" the country train "entered a rocky gorge and then a wood of prickly-pear trees." A boy yells out at "the scampering train, and the sun blazed down on his cries, the red flags, and the station-masters' red caps." When he arrives in his mother's village, "not a soul was about except children with bare feet ulcered by chilblains." Silvestro glances round his mother's kitchen "and saw the stove with the cracked earthenware pot in it, and next to it the bread-bin, the water-jug, the sink, the chairs, the table, and the old clock said to belong to grandfather on the wall."

In parts 3 and 4 of the book, where Silvestro is visiting houses and wandering in the streets of the village, the description creates a sense of ritual permanence by repeating the same glimpses many times: children's makeshift kites fly in the cold air, crows caw overhead, a herd of goats sound their bells, sheep bleat, or a shepherd's pipes are heard from a nearby hill. Vittorini is at pains to describe the interior of each house which Silvestro enters with his mother. Some are pitch-black, built into the rock, with damp smells and a single pane of glass above the door. He feels the warm skin of a goat

---

[5]*Conversazione in Sicilia*, (Torino, 1966), p. 163. A number of the following translations are taken from Wilfrid David's English edition of the novel (London: Lindsay Drummond, 1949).

as he gropes across the icy dark of the single room. In others, he dimly perceives a group of women dressed in black, sitting round a bucket full of black snails, sucking them up and throwing the empty shell back into the pail as an invalid lies silent on his bed. He also detects "that old smell of must typical of wealthy Sicilian households," the way the prosperous widow offered marsala and cakes, and spoke with "a rich chest-voice that rose from her ample bosom, and had black eyes and black hair."

Above all, it can be said that Vittorini's descriptions serve to convey a special sense of the privileged childhood landscape, which is an aesthetic temptation for all novelists and consists in recalling a particular scene so acutely that all other scenes seem momentarily irrelevant:

> I could remember myself and the train in a kind of special relationship like a dialogue, as if I had been speaking with *him*. The sound of goods trains with wagons bumping into each other while they were being shunted. . . . I remembered the winter time, the immense solitude of a surrounding bowl of countryside, without trees, lacking foliage, with the ground exhaling its tang of melon, and the noise of the shunting trains.

> "We were happy," I said, and I thought it too, imagining the tomatoes left out to dry in the sun during the summer afternoons, without a living soul about in the vast encircling countryside. It was dry, sulphur-coloured country, and I recalled the endless humming of summer and the engulfing silence, and again I reflected how happy we were.[6]

However, the primary task of the novelist is to make what he describes seem exceptional at deeper levels than that of the privileged landscape, so that Vittorini is immediately faced by the task of transforming a mass of purely descriptive material into a narrative of universal significance.

The solution is by way of symbols, by turning the actions and images of his characters into symbols of recurring actions and recurring characters, and the identification of this process of universal symbolism in *Conversazione* offers the second main line of approach to the text. Once again it is made clear in the text itself that there is a simultaneous co-existence of different layers of significance in the narrative body of *Conversazione*:

> She kept on examining the herring, holding it up in the air, first on one side, then on the other, no part of it burnt yet burnt all over, and the herring too provided a memory and an additional actuality. Everything had this two-fold reality, the memory and the present actuality, . . . real twice over and transposed into a fourth dimension during the journey.[7]

This aspect of the fourth dimension, an extended dimension over and above the physical realism of the surface narrative, is what makes the general symbolic reading of the novel most persuasive to some critics. Thus F. Bernardi went so far as to propose (in an article the draft of which was read aloud to Vittorini just before his death[8]) that Silvestro's journey represents a voyage

---

[6]*Conversazione*, p. 61; p. 48.
[7]*Conversazione*, p. 46.
[8]In *Lingua e stile*, 1-2, 1966, pp. 161-190.

of ritual initiation, progressing through the series of functional stages analysed by Vladimir Propp in his *Morphology of the Folktale*.[9] Bernardi's analysis breaks up *Conversazione* into three parts. At the outset, there is the preparation and summons to adventure, which consists of the letter from Silvestro's father and his meeting with a wizard who knows the terms of the quest, the "Great Lombard." Secondly, there is the journey through ritual tests. Here Silvestro accomplishes a descent into the underworld with his mother as guide, and achieves the mystical revelation that humanity is offended. He undergoes a ritual initiation to femininity (by his mother's injections to denuded clients) and is diverted with fresh guides into an unoffended sector of humanity, until he is admitted to a meeting with Death, constituted by the ghost of his brother in the cemetery. The third section of the Russian folktale was summarised by Propp as the re-integration of the hero. In Silvestro's case this involves absorption into a procession of humanity around the symbolic statue of war, his confrontation with his father, and his successful return from the quest to the world of the living.

This Proppian analysis of the hero's quest is accepted by the writer Calvino in a more recent assessment,[10] which attempts to show that each of Vittorini's novels is a search for powers that allow the hero to "emerge from his initial incompleteness and acquire those attributes which define a fully-fledged man." Calvino then proposes that Vittorini envisaged the novel as a kind of literary triad: "Its mythical form is the journey, its stylistic form is the dialogue, its conceptual form is the Utopia."

Nevertheless, even without being seen as an allegorical fable in which the hero is the subject of a succession of mythically significant functions, *Conversazione* still retains its level of universal symbolism. The clothier, Porfirio, for example, falls down drunk "in the womb of wine, and he was naked in blissful slumber, though still standing on his feet; he was the laughing, slumbering ancient who sleeps through the centuries of man's history, old father Noah of wine." This makes one inebriate the symbol of intoxication down the ages of men. An analogous lyrical expansion is performed on Silvestro's mother, who is transformed into the symbol of toiling motherhood: "I watched her as she busied herself about the coffee-pot and the stove, isolating herself in her tasks as every woman does." Here Vittorini fulfills exemplarily what the Russian formalist critic V. Sklovskij saw as the primary function of art in his *A Theory of Prose*: "Art exists to give us sensation of a thing which is *vision*, not just *recognition* or acknowledgement that it is there. To do this it uses two devices: the estrangement of subjects and the complication of their form. By these devices it makes our perception of them occur at a higher level and last longer."[11] His theory requires that people, objects and landscapes in literature must be transferred to a different level of values by the constant operation of "semantic shift." Sklovskij's term "semantic shift" covers all the linguistic devices by which the reader is forced to abandon his normal associative reactions and perceive a thing "as if it is being seen for the first time." In Vittorini the process is one of eccentric universalisation: a knife-grinder, clothier and tavern-keeper are perceived in such eccentric attitudes

[9]Translated by L. Scott (University of Texas Press, 1968).
[10]Translated in *Twentieth Century Studies, op. cit.* pp. 25-30.
[11]In the opening chapter already cited.

that they become emblems of the working class. Their individual uniquenesses are developed so far, semantically, that they are forced on the reader's perception as universally related elements:

> The lady appeared, tall, with her light head, and I recognized my mother perfectly, a tall woman with chestnut hair which was almost blonde, and a tough chin, a hard nose, and those black eyes.

> It was only when we got inside Colombo's that Porfirio acquired shape and colour. He stood over six feet tall and three feet broad, clad in brown fur-cloth, with a fine head of hair, some of it white, some of it black, blue eyes, chestnut beard and red hands: truly a huge St. Bernard dog with a welcoming face.[12]

A different way of looking at *Conversazione* altogether is to isolate the voices and dialogue which make up so large a part of the book. In this way, they suggest a series of formal choral settings in which the various antifascist messages seem to fall into a fugue pattern throughout the narrative, for it is true that the weight of spoken material offers the strongest ground for a straight political reading of the text. The "abstract furies" that haunt Silvestro at the opening of the novel represent his impotent rage at the whole spectacle of fascism and the Spanish Civil War, and make up the Fugue Subject. Silvestro is thus, in technical terms, the first voice, stating the introductory melody decisively in chapter 1. The second voice, giving the responsive entry in another key, is the "Great Lombard," who introduces the theme of "new and different duties" in chapter 7.

A third voice now enters in the original key, that of Silvestro's mother, who declares in chapter 20 that her seducer took part in an anti-government strike and hence, in other words, he was like a "Great Lombard." The cumulative effect of Vittorini's fugue now becomes apparent. In the musical fugue, when a new voice takes over the subject, the preceding voice can take up a countersubject, rather than a mere string of accompanying notes. Thus, the main subject of rage at fascism is constantly accompanied by the successive countersubjects of superseded voices, singing on themes such as poverty, hunger, illness and unemployment. The main subject occurs as a countersubject at chapter 31, where Silvestro declares that at the age of seven one does not "know the evils of the world, nor grief and hopelessness; one is *not* possessed by abstract furies but one knows a woman."

The fourth voice to take up the subject is Calogero, the knife-grinder, who declares in chapter 34 that it is wicked to offend the world. The other voices accompany this idea in successive countersubjects and develop it for several chapters (35-39), singing contrapuntally of the suffering of the offended world, how it must be washed with live water, how the individual must suffer not for himself but for everyone, how the world is beautiful and must be enjoyed only by those who have blades (for a knife-grinder to sharpen) or live water. The fifth voice comes in at chapter 43, where Silvestro's dead brother, the emblematic victim of fascism, declares that he has to suffer much, "millions of times, for every printed word, for every spoken word, for every quarter-inch of erected bronze."

---

[12]*Conversazione*, p. 44; p. 145.

Towards the end of a fugue, the entries often overlap one another and are drawn together in a device called *stretto*, by which the voices tend to sing on top of each other as a means of intensifying excitement. Thus, the last three chapters of *Conversazione* (47-49) see the five voices of the novel singing their cumulative anti-fascist subject in *stretto* around the fascist war memorial, until the returning first voice of the hero breaks down and weeps with mingled grief and drunkenness. In this way the "abstract furies" of the Fugue Subject receive their concluding contrapuntal expression and the enduring impression of the novel is a chorally constructed political protest.[13]

And yet the salient feature of experimental literary work is often a built-in resistance to the commonsense view that the text must develop its ideas in a coherent way. Ambiguity of intention may well be the factor which produces plurality of effect, so that the pure element of mystification in *Conversazione* can be both serious and gratuitous at once. The plot of the novel may be interpreted as combinative play, and its language as polysemous and unresolved; so that there is, in fact, no particular *signifié*, other than the incantatory power of words, in such a declamation as

> Ah, the night in those days! Everywhere, from the earth's parallels, placed at horizons, dogs barked. The seven invisible heavens and the mountains of the Milky Way burst out with jasmin. There were ten stars, then fifteen, yet we could sense the fragrance of a million in the air.

And when the workers make their impassioned pleas for the world, their characteristic listing of the elements in creation refers to everything at the same time as it means nothing in particular:

> "Trees and fresh figs, pine needles," the knife-grinder went on, "stars in respected hearts, myrrh and incense, sirens of the deep sea. Free legs, arms and chests, and the hair of body and head streaming freely in the wind, with races and all-in wrestling uh! oh! ah!"[14]

Some of the characters' names are classical, like Calogero and Porfirio, others biblical (Ezechiele, Concezione), or historical (Costantino, Silvestro) apparently for no other purpose than to achieve the effect of their association of mystification. In the same way Colombo has nothing to do with discovery, but possibly there is a kind of "donation of Constantine to Pope Sylvester" in the letter from Costantino to his son Silvestro which causes a transfer of location. Neither of these associations is certain; they are simply inherent potentialities of the language. Again, Concezione is seen to behave in a way opposed to the connotations of her name; or, alternatively, the connotations themselves are being insulted by the fact of her behaviour. The author refuses to clarify which innuendo is justified, because his concern is not that of clarifying the innate equivocations of his language. We may not even be sure

---

[13]M. Forti has suggested in a persuasive article in *L'approdo letterario*, Vol. 35, 1966, pp. 37-42 that the fascist vs. socialist interpretation of *Conversazione* is substantially correct but must be broadened to a political commentary on all human conflict. Silvestro's journey is a "displacement in the horizontal direction of space but also in a vertical interiorised direction of time."

[14]*Conversazione*, p. 158.

that the innuendo is present in the first place. When the knife-grinder swears a massive curse at the fine on his vending trolley, "the third time in a month! Scissors, awls, knives, pikes and archibuses; mortars, sickles and hammers, cannons, more cannons, and a hundred thousand volts" (chapter 36), the reader easily detects the communist insignia of the hammer and sickle given in the plural. But he may well wonder if those symbols are there consciously at all. If so, do they carry a political or anti-fascist message, and, more important, are they placed among a set of like tools and instruments in order to distract the reader, or to make him wonder whether he is being deliberately distracted?

The actual events of the plot can be examined in the same kind of way, and invite us to form a similar conclusion. The work becomes a "polyvalent" text, in that it acquires a spread of possible meanings, possibly contradictory but no one of them to the exclusion of any other. The juxtaposition of one incident with another may be designed to produce a joke, or a frustrated expectation in the reader, rather than a link in the narrative chain. Costantino, for example, has left his wife, and by the combinative logic of folk narrative at least, one is entitled to anticipate that he will return to her. There has been separation because the plot is leading to reconciliation; for there to be reconciliation at the end, there must have been a preceding separation. In the case of *Conversazione* it becomes unclear which of the two narrative elements has logical priority. Again, Silvestro is forced to catch the inland train from Syracuse, because, if he posted his mother's birthday card at this point in his journey, it would not arrive in time (chapter 8). It is half implied that he visits her simply because his greetings would otherwise arrive too late for her birthday, so that the card itself becomes a combined motive for the visit. In this kind of narrative, where a combined motive seems to carry more weight than a psychological reason, the justification for an event is the event itself. The reason need not be plausible or true, but it may be anything from gratuitous and trivial to intentionally misleading. Thus Silvestro goes to talk with a knife-grinder because the knife-grinder just happens to be standing there when he stops talking with his mother. It is only later that he pulls out a knife for the man to grind. Or again, because he is drunk, Silvestro is conducting a conversation with his dead brother. This at least is the reader's point of view, but the reader may be seeing things from a sophisticated standpoint which fails to take into account the logic of combinative narrative; in point of fact, the author makes Silvestro drunk so that the crazy dialogue with his brother can be staged. Combinatively he is intent on presenting the dialogue: the drunken dream setting merely serves to render a surrealist sequence plausible in the realistic terms of the rest.

In sum, language and plot move on two parallel lines in *Conversazione*, polysemous and polyvalent in partnership. Neither line can be coerced inside any one of the various interpretations which have been outlined above. However, to adopt the fourth and view Vittorini's masterpiece as an extended combinatory *jeu*, a novel in which form completely dominates content, is the interpretation which the text has been seen to insinuate as the key to itself. Beyond its realistic and political dimensions, Vittorini's novel is also a gratuitous literary act inside literature, and with the characteristic paradox of experimental writing presents itself as an anti-novel disguised within the tradition of novel. In this double posture it confirms another of Sklovskij's remarkable insights in *A Theory of Prose*:

> In fact there is no such thing as a great novel which is not also an anti-novel: the process began with Cervantes, continuing with Sterne and Flaubert, until we reach Tolstoi. There emerges from the inside of their novels a clear polemic about the status and entity of the novel, sometimes by the introduction of emblematic figures who dissociate themselves by a series of significant repudiations from the very novel they are part of.[15]

University of Kent
England

---

[15]Sklovskij, *op. cit.* p. 84.

The Primitive World of
Giovanni Verga

By S. B. CHANDLER

Giovanni Verga's elevation to second place behind Alessandro Manzoni in the hierarchy of Italian novelists began with Luigi Russo's essay of 1919, three years before the author's death. In redeeming his fellow Sicilian from the narrow classifications of *verismo*, regionalism and imitation of Zola, Russo revealed the deep complexity of Verga's world of primitives in the novels and short stories and the compassion that underlay the impersonality of the technique. In particular, he identified the "religious" character of the archaic community of Aci Trezza in *I Malavoglia* (1881), with its hallowed "laws" founded on ancestral experience and its sanctuary in the family and house governed by the oldest member as patriarch. Infringement of these laws entailed inevitable catastrophe for the offender and his family, a feature that led Francesco Flora to recall Greek tragedy. Russo preferred *I Malavoglia* to

Mastro don Gesualdo (1889), Verga's other major novel, because he judged it a unity, a quality required by the Crocean canon since it represented a unitary lyrical intuition. Subsequent idealist criticism tended to stress the lyric element in *I Malavoglia*—characters embodying Verga's own feelings and problems, natural descriptions, comments on the transience of life—without troubling overmuch with other aspects and characters or with the society in which they lived. Unity was preserved through partial neglect. After the demise of Fascism in 1945, new social and political experiences provoked a search for social meaning in Verga's work within the general context of economic conditions in post-Risorgimento Sicily. More recently, a realization of the originality in style and structure of *I Malavoglia* and, to a less extent, of other works has produced contributions from stylistic critics, including Leo Spitzer himself and Giacomo Devoto; and also, partly through the intervention of Marxist critics, a new interest in Verga's relationship to the political, social and cultural conditions of his day has produced a need for their precise definition and his attitude to them, with a further need for an inquiry into his own cultural formation. An important consequence of these investigations has been the revaluation of the fundamental conflict in Verga between acceptance of reality and pursuit of illusion. I believe that its interpretation in purely social and political terms—inevitable within the Marxist position—disregards sections of the evidence and, by categorizing Verga with some of his disillusioned contemporaries, overlooks his true individuality.

This conflict had already motivated Verga's earlier novels. The typical scheme had consisted of the chief character's rejection of his normal life through the irresistible attraction of an elegant woman moving in refined society, the failure of the attempt to escape owing to the non-correspondence of this experience with his preconception of it and finally the return to the drabness of life, defeated and incapable of new efforts. The woman is not viewed as a source of sexual pleasure: indeed, such an association would destroy the dream of attaining the intangible. It is significant that, at the beginning of *Eva* (1873), Eva is described as the dream of a young man made into a woman. In *Tigre reale* (1874) and *Eros* (1875), however, occurs a shift in position: reality is no longer disillusioned emptiness but is expressed in "normal" women devoted to home life and capable of genuine affection. In contrast, their antitheses have become *femmes fatales* derived from literary excess rather than from any conceivable source in real life. The manifest impossibility of realizing the dream does not prevent its pursuit, but the alternative now offers the modest satisfaction of family life. Giorgio La Ferlita of *Tigre reale* is spared by the opportune death of the Russian Countess Nata from consumption—the occupational disease of late Romanticism—and resumes domestic life; but Alberto of *Eros* abandons his proposed marriage with the quiet Adele through infatuation with Velleda and, after the latter's marriage for self-seeking motives into the aristocracy, travels for a lengthy period until, on his return, he might still choose the stability of domestic life with Adele, yet is prevented from doing so by the reappearance of Velleda. With all practicable options blocked, he commits suicide.

It seems to me that, despite the different context and immense disparity in artistic value between *Eros* and *I Malavoglia*, Alberto's final position prefigures that of 'Ntoni. He rejects what he realizes in the end is the only possible choice and this initial error brings its own inevitable punishment, in that the second opportunity presents only an apparent choice: Alberto has reached an understanding of things, yet is so changed in the process that his return to the fold is precluded. In the primitive atmosphere of Aci Trezza suicide was out of the question, but wandering through the world, which is 'Ntoni's penalty, is equated elsewhere in the novel in its terminology with death itself. In Verga's secular religion, repentance does not open the way to a new life.

Much emphasis has been laid in recent years on a few passages condemning the new materialist civilization created by the commercial interests of banks and industrial companies, with its goals of wealth, well-being and success. The growing industrialization of Northern Italy was creating a marked imbalance between city and agricultural countryside and, to an ever greater degree, between the North and the impoverished, agrarian South. Citing one such passage in the preface of *Eva*, the Marxist critic Vitilio Masiello[1] contrasts this new society, dedicated to material things and stripped of all sacred elements, with the Romantic world of Verga and his characters, a world that had now lost its faith and certainty. It may be objected that, by definition, a "Romantic world" lacked faith and certainty and that the Romanticism lay in the duality between acceptance of the "real" world and a yearning for something beyond. This yearning in Pietro Brusio of *Una peccatrice* and Enrico Lanti of *Eva* seeks satisfaction in the very society condemned by Verga and its failure, therefore, is predictable. Furthermore, this *Sehnsucht* had existed in the Romantic period earlier in the century when industrial capitalism was scarcely known in Italy. In *I Malavoglia* we shall note the same quest for the unknown even though the society is pre-industrial. It is not clear that Lanti, apart from his initial devotion to art, Brusio, La Ferlita and Alberto ever had many ideals to lose, let alone a sensation of inner emptiness, as Masiello suggests. Apart perhaps from La Ferlita, they reflect personal psychological problems of Verga himself in his constant search for something undefined and, not least, in his relationship with women and in his conception of them. As for La Ferlita, he settles down in a solid middle-class home and Alberto wishes he could do likewise.

That Verga, the Sicilian in Florence and, especially, Milan, was unhappy with city life emerges from his own statements, but again, the features he criticizes are not confined to capitalist cities; in fact, his observations indicate the typical aversion to urban bustle of one from his background though, in his case, felt more strongly since he recognized that his aim of success meant inevitably his immersion in this "movimento incessante." Here he is describing Florence, "il centro della vita politica e intellettuale d'Italia," during its period as capital of Italy, so that this movement hardly stems from an industrial society. Movement connotes a series of emotions, "e per noi altri infermi di mente e di nérvi, la grand'aria è la vita di una grande città, le continue emozioni, il movimento."* Verga's absorption in this movement—and thus in present time—prevented him from standing back and seeing it in perspective, in a pattern. His experience foreshadows the similar disorientation

---

[1]Vitilio Masiello, *Verga tra ideologia e realtà* (Bari; De Donato, 1970).

*"and for us, sick in mind and nerves, the finest air is the life of a great city, the continual emotions, the movement."

of 'Ntoni Malavoglia when he is exposed to a mass of simultaneous new experiences in Naples, except that, unlike 'Ntoni, Verga preserves an ambivalent attitude which causes him to create heroes whose actions flow from a confidence that the apparently chaotic conditions of such a society will permit escape from normality through the realization of their desires and longings, while, at the same time, he expresses his doubt of any such satisfaction by having them fail. As Sandro Briosi has commented, cynicism and heroism coexist in Verga's work and tend to cancel each other out in turn.[2]

The antithesis of constant movement and spiritual oscillation is a uniform calm: thus Verga tells Luigi Capuana on 13 January 1875, "felice te che puoi fare qualche cosa, pensare a qualche cosa, felici coloro per cui la vita scorre uniforme e tranquilla."[3]* Three years later, however, he expresses to Capuana the impossibility of happiness and rest: "Tu hai la nostalgia di Milano ed io quella di Sicilia, così siam fatti noi che non avremo mai posa e vera felicità."[4]** On 14 March 1879, he explains to Capuana his intentions in composing *I Malavoglia*:

> Anch'io faccio assegnamento su Padron 'Ntoni, e avrei voluto, se la disgrazia non mi avesse perseguitato sì accanitamente e spietatamente darvi quell'impronta di fresco e sereno raccoglimento che avrebbe dovuto fare un immenso contrasto con le passioni turbinose e incessanti delle grandi città, con quei bisogni fittizii, e quell'altra prospettiva delle idee e direi anche dei sentimenti. Ma forse non sarà male dall'altro canto che io li consideri da una certa distanza in mezzo all'attività di una città come Milano o Firenze.[5]***

Verga yearns for the tranquillity of Sicily, but now introduces a new motive to explain his absence and as self-justification—"la fatalità"—and, as in *I Malavoglia*, it is loosely identified with God. To his aunt Giovanna he writes on 20 December 1879:

> Ma che farci ora che la maledizione di Dio ci ha colpito? Mi duole per te, povera e cara vecchiarella; mi duole per tanti altri; ma tu sai che la

---

[2]Sandro Briosi, "Sullo stile del Verga," *Lettere Italiane*, 21 (1969), 201. The references to Florence occur in a letter of Verga to his mother of early 1869, quoted by Dorothee Böhm, *Zeitlosigkeit und entgleitende Zeit als konstitutive Dialektik im Werke von Giovanni Verga*, (Münster Westfalen: Aschendorffsche Verlagsbuchhandlung, 1967), 17. Dr. Böhm comments perceptively on the question of movement.

[3]*Opere di Giovanni Verga*, a cura di Luigi Russo (Milano-Napoli: Ricciardi, 1955), p. 115.

*"happy are you who can do something, think of something, happy are those for whom life flows uniformly and calmly."

[4]Böhm, 170, note 11.

**"You have a nostalgia for Milan and I for Sicily, we are so made that we shall never have rest and true happiness."

[5]*Opere*, ed. Russo, 119-20.

***"I, too, am counting on Padron 'Ntoni, and I would have wished, if misfortune had not persecuted me so doggedly and ruthlessly, to give it that stamp of fresh and serene concentration which ought to have made an immense contrast with the stormy and unceasing passions of great cities, with those artificial needs, and that other perspective of ideas and I would say of feelings also. But perhaps it will be no bad thing on the other hand for me to consider them from a certain distance in the midst of the activity of a city like Milan or Florence."

fatalità mi ha scacciato da Catania, e dalla nostra casa, e mi condanna alla lontananza.[6]*

His sister and mother had died in the recent past. A letter of 20 October 1879 to his uncle emphasizes the polarity of remembered "tranquille delizie" with his family and the stormy existence to which he has condemned himself;[7] and on 24 February 1880, again to his uncle, he contrasts the battle which he fights against the future with repose in the calm peace of past days that were almost happy.[8] Life's disturbances and struggles are associated with time itself; consequently, tranquillity and happiness belong to the absence of time. The stage is set for *I Malavoglia*.

The short story *Fantasticheria*, published on 24 August 1879, is recognized as a key work in Verga's development since it marks the rejection of urban, bourgeois society, its empty conventions and its self-centred neglect of the poor and humble. In his address to the fashionable young woman who had expressed from the train a wish to stay a month in Aci Trezza but who had succumbed to boredom in only two days, a boredom indicative of a total lack of human feeling towards the inhabitants, Verga displays compassion for their hardships, but no moral indignation and no thought of ameliorative political action. He differs from socially minded contemporaries in that he assimilates this world of the humble to his own spiritual problems and re-created it in *I Malavoglia*—"ricostruzione intellettuale," as he defined it—as a function of his renewed search for a solution, just as earlier with the urban society of Florence and Milan. Verga's repudiation of this society, then, is due, not to its defects, but to its incapacity to provide a medium for the solution of his problems. The primitive world of Sicily will eventually disappoint him also but, for the moment, he can delude himself to the contrary. In *Fantasticheria* he writes: "Sembrami che le irrequietudini del pensiero vagabondo s'addormenterebbero dolcemente nella pace serena di quei sentimenti miti, semplici, che si succedono calmi e inalterati di generazione in generazione.**

Here the rootlessness has been transferred to thought itself. Thought will not be refuted but lulled to sleep by unquestioning acceptance of traditional propositions. Symbolically, this new situation is externalized in the subsequent sentence: "Sembrami che potrei vedervi passare, al gran trotto dei vostri cavalli, col tintinnío allegro dei loro finimenti e salutarvi tranquillamente."[9]***

---

[6]Lina e Vito Perroni, "Storia de *I Malavoglia* da lettere inedite," *Nuova Antologia*, 75 (1940), 107.

*"But what can be done now that the curse of God has struck us? I feel sorrow for you, poor and beloved old lady; I feel sorrow for so many others; but you know that fate has driven me from Catania, and from our home, and condemns me to be far off."

[7]*Ibidem.*

[8]*Ibid.*, 108. Emerico Giachery, *Verga e d'Annunzio* (Milano: Silva, 1968), p. 156, suggests that the land of his ancestors is really the solid and firm land within Verga himself, the centre, the authentic element, that which persists in time and has remote and sure roots, and he compares Jung's realization of the self, the centre towards which the process of individuation is oriented; cf. also p. 160.

**"It seems to me that the anxieties of roaming thought would gently fall asleep in the serene peace of those mild, simple feelings, which succeed each other calm and unchanged from generation to generation."

[9]In *Tutte le novelle*, I (Milano: Mondadori, 1962), p. 123.

***"It seems to me that I could see you pass, with the fine trot of your horses, with the gay jingle of their trappings and could greet you in perfect calm."

In *I Malavoglia*, then, we should expect a humble, struggling society, unchanging from one generation to the next as it conforms to ancestral schemes of life, and such a society is indeed portrayed, though Verga's ambivalence does not permit a simple portrayal thereof, nor would a novel have otherwise resulted. We may recall Russo's "genesi polemica." The society is somewhat of a hybrid.

It is of interest to define this primitive society of Aci Trezza, outside time and previously untouched by history, and to compare it with the findings of Mircea Eliade.[10] Society is absolute and total reality, with nothing outside it. Its members have the roots of their individuality within it alone[11] and in their acceptance of its past proven acts and decisions which stand absolute, commanded by their ancestors. There is no abstract moral sense, apart from the Malavoglia group's inexplicable and anachronistically premature ethic, so that religion is identified with the conventions and ritual events of society. Consequently, religious terminology is associated with the traditional scheme.[12] When Alfio Mosca asks Mena if it is true that her grandfather is arranging her marriage, she replies "Sarà come vuole Dio!"[13]* which equates the will of God not only with that of the family patriarch, but also with her unhappiness. In a similar situation, when Alfio is on the point of leaving Aci Trezza, Mena repeats "Ma così vuol Dio"** (p. 125); her mother, la Longa, had said a few moments before "Le ragazze vanno come Dio le ha destinate,"*** which identifies the divine will with marriages arranged for economic reasons. Mena's final rejection of Alfio is preceded by "Mena si strinse nelle spalle, perchè era avvezza fare la volontà di Dio, come la cugina Anna"**** (p. 289). When 'Ntoni questions the necessity of their life of hardship, his grandfather bids him "Ringrazia Dio piuttosto, che t'ha fatto nascer qui; e guardarti dall'andare a morire lontano dai sassi che ti conoscono"***** (p. 192): as the proverb says, "Bisogna vivere come siamo nati"****** (p. 14). Later, after 'Ntoni has given up working, padron 'Ntoni tells him they have never had money, "Non ne abbiamo avuti mai, e ci siamo guadagnato il pane come vuole Dio"******* (p. 233): unremitting labour has been ordained by God, but he also eases matters by arranging different

---

[10]Giachery, *Verga e d'Annunzio*, p. 162, introduced Eliade into the subject in a passing reference, but he mistakenly attributed Eliade's "terror of history" to Aci Trezza: in fact, this is completely absent since the inhabitants know nothing of history's existence.

[11]Cf. Mircea Eliade, *Myth and Reality*, translated from the French by Willard R. Trask (New York: Harper Torchbooks, 1968), pp. 6 and 24-5.

[12]Cf. Eliade, *Cosmos and History. The Myth of the Eternal Return*, translated from the French by Willard R. Trask (New York: Harper Torchbooks, 1959), p. 34.

[13]*I Malavoglia* (Milano: Biblioteca Moderna Mondadori, 1952), p. 111. All quotations from the novel are drawn from this edition.

*"It will be as God wills!"

**"But such is the will of God"

***"Girls go as God has destined them!"

****"Mena shrugged her shoulders, because she was accustomed to do the will of God, like cousin Anna."

*****"Thank God rather, who caused you to be born here; and take care you don't go away to die far from the stones that know you."

******"We must live according as we were born."

*******"We've never had any, and we've earned our bread as God wills."

colours for the sea so that sailors may know when to sail without preoccupations as to impending weather (pp. 152-3).

It is the ancestors, however, rather than archetypal gods, who established
permanent norms, "Perchè il motto degli antichi mai mentì"* (p. 14), where
we note an approximation to the classical Greek use of the gnomic aorist in
moral maxims. The doctrine of these *antichi* has been preserved in oral
proverbs rather than in sacred writings and there are no original actions
elevated into myths and ceremonially renewed, when men live again "in illo
tempore," as Eliade calls it: such a procedure would conflict with the in-
significance of individual man in that society. The projection of the "antichi
nell'oggi e dell'oggi nell'antico"** of Alberto M. Cirese tends to suggest an
"illud tempus."[14] Original—and subsequent—acts are distilled into incontro-
vertible proverbs. Ritual occasions as such are rare: the *visita pel marito*
after Bastianazzo's drowning, in which behaviour is to some extent ritualized,
as in the necessity of a joke which Don Silvestro supplies, to the disgust of the
pharmacist's wife whose city origin does not allow her to understand, or *la
spartizione dei capelli* of Mena. Conformity to ancestral wisdom is a moral
duty whether gain accrues or not—another similarity with Christian teaching.
The Malavoglia family of the house by the medlar tree had prospered through
adherence to padron 'Ntoni's proverbs and thus he was considered a "testa
quadra." Luca, when called to the navy after 'Ntoni's return therefrom, did
his duty there as he had done it at home and was content (p. 109); padron
'Ntoni informs 'Ntoni that he himself had always done his duty, as had la
Longa in her sphere, the house (p. 192). The old man, confronted with the
unprecedented problem of his grandson's reluctance to do his "duty" can
allege, inadequately, only fear as his motivation. Even certain perils form an
integral part of this society and are unhesitatingly accepted as such, with no
possibility of individual withdrawal: "Il mare è amaro ed il marinaro muore
in mare"*** (pp. 64 and 75). Recovery from disasters can lead only to the
re-establishment of the original position. After the loss of Bastianazzo and the
Provvidenza, people affirm with the certainty of there being no conceivable
relief or assistance that new troubles are beginning for la Longa's house:
the future is fixed.

In family affairs the authority of the ancients devolves in pontifical succession upon padron 'Ntoni as head of the household. Thus he can make
absolute decisions, expressed in almost lapidary form, as binding as those of
the ancients: Mena tells Alfio Mosca that the family will go to the city for
All Souls Day if the affair of the lupins prospers, "l'ha detto il nonno"****
(p. 28) and padron 'Ntoni repeats a dictum to 'Ntoni, "Prima deve maritarsi
tua sorella Mena"[15]***** before 'Ntoni himself can marry.

For the inhabitants, Aci Trezza is the only reality and so the only fixed

---

*"Because the word of the ancients never lied."
**"ancients into today and today into ancient time"
[14]Alberto M. Cirese, "Il mondo popolare nei *Malavoglia*," *Letteratura*, Anno 3,
Numero 17-18 (Settembre-dicembre, 1955), 86.
***"The sea is bitter and the sailor dies at sea."
****"grandfather said so"
[15]Cf. Cirese, 84.
*****"First your sister Mena must marry."

point and the centre of the world.[16] Outside are movement and instability. Critics have emphasized the symbolic importance of the carts that are heard passing on several occasions, but I believe the point has escaped notice that Aci Trezza also represents life and that the outside world is death. The circumlocution for death is a journey to Alexandria in Egypt but, when Nunziata's father abandoned his family to seek his fortune outside, he too is described as having gone to Alexandria (p. 28) and everyone knows he will never return. Padron 'Ntoni regards his grandson's desire to leave as a temptation to go through the world like a gypsy, for the old man can admit no fixed point outside (p. 193). The correlative in family terms to Aci Trezza is the house, the fixed point, with which is associated the term "nest." It is interesting that Mircea Eliade quotes the *Pañcavimsha Brāhmana* to the effect that "nest" implies flocks, children and home and symbolizes the world of the family, of society, of gaining a living.[17] In addition to the proverbs "A ogni uccello il nido è bello"* and "Beato quell'uccello, che fa il nido al suo paesello,"** padron 'Ntoni compares being born, living and dying in his own house with the custom of sparrows which have always nested nearby, will always do so and have no wish to go away—that is, with an ordinance of nature. Eliade's reference to the house as a symbol of gaining a living finds a correspondence in the association of the Malavoglia house by the medlar tree with their boat, the *Provvidenza*, their means of livelihood. At the outset, the Malavoglia are identified as "quelli della casa del nespolo, e della *Provvidenza*" (p. 13) and, immediately afterwards, we learn that the storms which had scattered other branches of the family had passed over the house by the medlar tree and the boat without much damage. Finally, the two are unified: all expedients are needed to send forward "quella barca della casa del nespolo" (p. 20). The loss of the *Provvidenza* inevitably entails the loss of the house. At the end, Alessi and Mena, the two survivors of the "storm"— perhaps a reminiscence of the myth of the flood—with Nunziata, redeem the house and restore the initial position.

The frequent religious references in *I Malavoglia* are usually superficial, conventional phrases with no moral significance or are obviously hypocritical as in the case of zio Crocifisso. The only genuine morality in the Christian sense is practised by the Malavoglia and their circle. Given the rigid structure of the primitive society of Aci Trezza, for which Christianity seems a late and ineffective intervention powerless to disturb established patterns governed by the economic motive, the origin of the Malavoglia ethic is unexplained. Critics unite in calling them "heroes" but Aci Trezza thinks otherwise when it sees them struggling to settle the debt of the lupins with zio Crocifisso despite the absence of any legal obligation. An examination of three crucial passages yields mixed results: two depend on past family custom, the third is founded on a proverb whose observance would scarcely be common in Aci Trezza and in none does any specific moral vocabulary occur.

---

[16]Cf. Mircea Eliade, *The Sacred and the Profane. The Nature of Religion.* Translated from the French by Willard R. Trask (New York; Harper Torchbooks, 1959), p. 22.
[17]*The Sacred and the Profane,* 183.
*"For every bird its nest is best."
**"Happy that bird, that makes its nest in its own little village."

No! rispose padron 'Ntoni,—no! chè bisogna pagare il debito allo zio Crocifisso, e non si deve dire di noi che "il galantuomo come impoverisce diventa birbante"* (pp. 56-7).

È vero, i lupini ce li ha dati, e bisogna pagarli .... Questo poi no! questo non l'hanno mai fatto i Malavoglia. Lo zio Crocifisso si piglierà la casa, e la barca, e tutto, ma questo poi no!** (p. 84).

In this second passage, padron 'Ntoni sets the very basis of his existence, the centre of family life, as the price of his honesty. The third passage shows padron 'Ntoni endeavouring to get the habitually drunken 'Ntoni to bed unnoticed by the others because "questo non c'è mai stato nei Malavoglia!"*** (p. 223). One rotten apple spoils the others, a sentiment expressed at about the same time by Emile Zola.[18] Nunziata, cugina Anna and Grazia Piedipapera also share feelings of neighbourly charity, sometimes buttressed by proverbs, and thus distinguish themselves from the general population. It appears that Verga baulks at the relentless logic of his own creation and, in mitigation thereof, inserts concepts of the individual derived from his own society.

An unchanging society stands, by definition, outside time and history, though its component members are transient within time. In this pre-industrial world, the present is not divided into small units according to the clock and the exigencies of labour, nor are the past and future. The fishermen operate in daily, repetitive periods according to dawn and sunset, the Sabbath, the seasons and religious festivals. In the minds of the people, past and present are interwoven.[19] The past is a prefiguration of the future and, in view of the immutability, knowledge is experience of the past and older persons are wiser. The view advanced by some critics that the society of Aci Trezza moves in spirals rather than in cycles does not distinguish between individuals and society and suggests an evolution which is precluded by the basic condition of immutability. Individuals flourish or fall, grow old and die, but the overall structure remains invariable. Alfio Mosca's reiterated statements of change relate to individuals only (pp. 123, 274, 275, 285). They are expendable units whose roots and sole existence lie in that society and thus personal survival after death is irrelevant and impossible. Eternity is Aci Trezza itself. The dead are forgotten: when 'Ntoni returned from the navy, the courtyard

---

*" 'No!' replied padron 'Ntoni, 'no! because we must pay the debt to zio Crocifosso, and it must never be said of us that 'when he grows poor the honest man becomes a rogue.' "

**" 'It's true, he gave us the lupins, and we must pay for them .... Not this! the Malavoglia have never done this. Zio Crocifisso will take the house, and the boat, and everything, but this we won't do!' "

***"the Malavoglia have never had this sort of thing!"

[18]Emile Zola, *Le roman expérimental* (Paris, 1893), p. 26, in the preface written in September 1880.

[19]Cf. Böhm, 51; see also, for the question of time in *I Malavoglia*, Wido Hempel, *Giovanni Vergas Roman I Malavoglia und die Wiederholung als erzählerisches Kunstmittel* (Köln-Graz; Böhlau, 1959) and Peter de Meijer, "La Sicilia fra mito e storia nei romanzi del Verga," *Rassegna della letteratura italiana*, Anno 67 (1963), 116-28; though he does not mention Verga's work, Hans Meyerhoff, *Time in Literature* (Berkeley and Los Angeles; University of California Press, 1960), has many observations that bear upon it.

of the house was thronged with people as after the death of Bastianazzo, "tempo addietro, che nessuno ci pensava più,"* except la Longa (p. 69); and, towards the end, when Alessi is planning to marry Nunziata. "Così anche i parenti dimenticano quelli che non ci sono più"** (p. 275). Existential "angst" is completely lacking. As Mircea Eliade points out, personal memories of the dead are of no importance in archaic societies, since only modern man with his "historical consciousness" considers impersonal survival a real death and feels himself diminished by it.[20]

A timeless society outside history presupposes isolation through poor communications and a consequent delay in learning of external events, if these ever become known at all. This non-contemporaneity contrasts with the modern diffusion of widely scattered and disconnected events, even as they are occurring, and the almost inevitable disorientation through inability to absorb and adjust oneself to them. Reports of historical happenings reach Aci Trezza by chance. Two sailors in transit describe the Italian naval defeat at Lissa in 1867 during the Austro-Prussian War. The unreality and temporal and spatial remoteness of the battle is conveyed by comparing the sailors to "quelli che raccontavano la storia d'Orlando e dei paladini di Francia alla Marina di Catania"*** (p. 132). The clerk at the Catania naval base evinces surprise that the Malavoglia had not heard of an event more than forty days old.

We have seen that virtue in this primitive society is equated with conformity to the indisputable schemes established by the *antichi* which define reality itself. Accordingly, non-conformity is a sin and brings its own penalty of suffering. In the Preface (p. 11) Verga alludes to the stigmata of sin borne by the Malavoglia, Mastro don Gesualdo and the protagonists of his other projected novels in the cycle of *I Vinti*. The first deviation is committed by padron 'Ntoni himself, unwittingly, in response not simply to a bad fishing season but to the unprecedented impinging of history through 'Ntoni's being drafted into the navy of the new United Italy. He transgresses one of his own proverbs by overstepping the limits of his fisherman's trade to become a transporter of lupins. The wreck of the *Provvidenza* and the resultant crushing debt push this previously compact family on to the path of suffering and disintegration. The "theological" condemnation of padron 'Ntoni's decision is pronounced by la Longa: "I lupini li abbiamo presi tutti!—mormorava la Longa,—e il Signore ci ha castigati tutti insieme col prendersi mio marito"**** (p. 84) and a more mundane contribution from padron Cipolla: "Al giorno d'oggi . . . nessuno è contento del suo stato e vuol pigliare il cielo a pugni"***** (p. 44). As padron 'Ntoni had earlier observed, he who commands has to render an account, though he did not specify to whom (p. 15).

---

*"time passed and no one thought of it any more."

**"Thus even relatives forget those who are no more."

[20]*Cosmos and History*, p. 47.

***"those who tell the story of Orlando and the paladins of France on the seashore at Catania."

****" 'We all took the lupins!' murmured la Longa, 'and the Lord has punished us all together by taking my husband.' "

*****"Nowadays . . . . nobody is contented with his condition and wants to punch his way into heaven."

The fundamental "sin," however, is committed by young 'Ntoni, the significance of whom is complex indeed. His experience at Naples suggests questions to him and then doubts. If conditions are different elsewhere, if other "centres" exist, then Aci Trezza is not absolute reality and change is possible. In Eliade's words, 'Ntoni falls into time and duration;[21] his eventual imprisonment for five years compels him to savour every moment of the time and duration he has chosen. It is worth noting that the only specific date in the novel, December 1863, refers to 'Ntoni. He loses his link with the society of Aci Trezza and with his family which mirrors it, so becoming an autonomous individual who has cut away the only possible root which could give him identity. Severed from the past, he is poised towards a different future of anticipated material improvement. Why should some people inherit wealth and enjoy themselves in idleness while others "tirano la carretta coi denti per tutta la vita?"* We are all sons of God and should have equal shares (pp. 226-7). Why was he unlucky enough to be born into a family of fishermen? (p. 216). All the blame was due to his being born in that condition (p. 226). Their misfortune is the work of the devil (p. 233). 'Ntoni knows the world better—"veniva da lontano, e il mondo lo conosceva meglio degli altri"** (p. 77)—and can see injustice in everything. He calls it "ingiustizia sacrosanta," which implies an awareness of the true situation but from an inverted point of view. The irony is that in the real nineteenth century world 'Ntoni's criticisms hit the mark precisely. He envied two young men who one day appeared at the inn, well supplied with funds, and thinks of their happy fortune of wandering through the world.

'Ntoni does not understand that it is precisely the eternal repetition of paradigmatic actions which confers meaning on life; the eternal return to the *antichi* preserves life from nothingness.[22] Repetition devoid of its "sacred" basis implies a frightening lack of purpose. 'Ntoni's departure to make his fortune is presented as a solemn public event with forebodings of impending disaster: Nunziata twice recalls a well remembered previous occasion—the departure of her father. The renunciation of reality is attended with due ritual and awe. Unknown to himself, 'Ntoni is proclaiming his desire to leave the world, his refusal of every worldly situation, through his abandoning the centre, the "casa."[23] It is significant that his mother's death opens the way for 'Ntoni's departure: in his letter to his aunt Giovanna of 20 December 1879, Verga had said, "il pio desiderio della nostra povera mamma era sempre di saperci uniti."[24]*** La Longa is the real centre, "e gli erano attaccati al cuore, che glielo strappavano a pezzetti, ora l'uno ora l'altro"**** (p. 196). 'Ntoni's return in rags banishes all hope for the future: he has deprived himself of a past and is now reduced to the sole present, thoughtless

---

[21]*Cosmos and History*, pp. 85-6.
*"pull the cart with their teeth for their whole lives."
**"he came from afar, and knew the world better than the others."
[22]Eliade, *The Sacred and the Profane*, p. 107.
[23]Eliade, *The Sacred and the Profane*, pp. 183-4.
[24]*Nuova Antologia*, 75 (1940), 107.
***"the pious desire of our poor mother was always to know that we were all united."
****"and they were attached to her heart, and were tearing it from her in little pieces, first one then the other."

of causes and consequences. His degradation by way of the tavern, smuggling, and wounding don Michele of the customs guards ends with five years in prison. On his return to Alessi, Nunziata and Mena in the house by the medlar tree, he is inhibited from rejoining the reality he has rejected despite his longing to do so: it is the Dantesque desire without hope. He must leave and wander through the world, the punishment being the sin itself: again for Verga, repentance earns no redemption, for his secular deity is not a personal and merciful God. His three relatives realize the inevitability of his renewed departure. In the final tremendous scene, 'Ntoni stands alone at dawn, alone over against the universe, each element of which, from the stars to the people of Aci Trezza, is performing its repetitive function. The usual pilgrim's role is reversed: 'Ntoni does not go forth in quest of the truth, because he has already found it and his former boast of knowing everything has come tragically to fruition. His pilgrimage thus conducts him away from the truth, a pilgrimage as devoid of meaning as he had once thought the society he must now forsake.

It would be ingenuous to regard 'Ntoni as merely the young man from a primitive society who is thrown into history and destroyed. He certainly embodies one side of Verga's dichotomy, his yearning for something beyond, the unknown, that could not be stilled, even when he was creating a world of certainties in order to escape from this yearning, by making the individual a part of a larger whole wherein everything was determined. But another character represents an apparent solution of the dichotomy. Mena, too, had glimpsed a vision of happiness in her love for Alfio Mosca, a genuine love unknown to Aci Trezza's ritually economic viewpoint: Mena, who can contemplate the stars and the moving clouds and be carried far away in her thoughts. In the end, she adapts herself to circumstances and renounces the marriage offered by Alfio Mosca: "e così ella era salita nella soffitta della casa del nespolo, come le casseruole vecchie, e s'era messo il cuore in pace"* (p. 290). She has set her heart at peace. It is too simple. She solves the problem at the expense of her life, for she acknowledges that she belongs to the past and that is a form of death. 'Ntoni suffers alienation in space, Mena in time, and she is the most tragic of them all.

University of Toronto

---

*"and so she had gone up into the garret of the house at the medlar tree, like the old pans, and had set her heart at peace."

Les Paliers de Décompression (1922–1972)

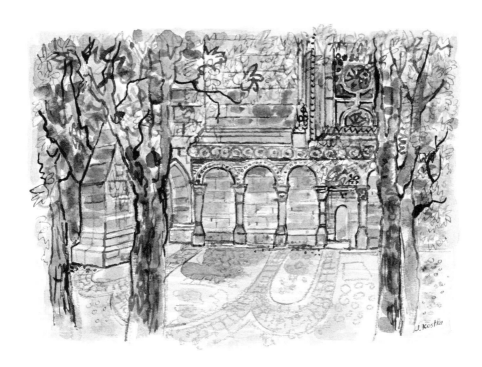

Par Claude Mauriac

Paris, 24 quai de Béthune,
dimanche 23 janvier 1972

Il n'existe d'autre roman concevable pour moi, en ce moment, que "le roman de ma vie," d'une vie, je l'ai déjà noté ici, "où il ne se passe rien mais où passe le temps": c'est à dire *Le Temps immobile.*

Ma vie, grâce aux éléments que je trouve dans mon journal—ou que j'y ajoute à la date du jour où j'écris—est composée comme un roman,—moins un vrai roman qu'un roman vrai, mais roman aussi, dans la mesure où il y a construction, à l'exemple d'un livre de fiction. La différence avec mes romans, qui étaient déjà des montages au sens cinématographique du mot, est que je monte ce film du temps immobile avec des fragments de journal où jamais, tout au moins consciemment, je n'ai menti, triché ou inventé. Roman vérité comme il y a un cinéma vérité. Même si, dans le montage que j'ai effectué aujourd'hui et que voici, il n'était pas question des romans que j'ai écrits ou que je me propose d'écrire, ces pages trouveraient sans abus leur place dans la revue *Mosaic*. *Le Temps immobile*, s'il est une sorte de roman, est aussi et surtout une mosaïque.

Paris, 38 avenue Théophile-Gautier
samedi, 23 janvier 1932

Composition de français. Je choisis un sujet sur Rousseau. Je donne à Jean Davray un autographe de papa, il en est enchanté. Après un interminable voyage en métro, puis en train, Bruno et moi arrivons à Survilliers où l'auto nous attend. Nous mangeons dans la voiture en regrettant l'absence de notre grand-mère, retenue à Vémars par ses rhumatismes au bras qui la font souffrir depuis le jour de l'an. Chasse à courre assommante. La fin, pourtant, est ravissante: à travers de hauts roseaux nous apercevions un splendide cerf qui se débattait dans l'eau sombre, alors qu'un des membres de l'équipage, dont la vive couleur rouge mettait un point clair sur la grisaille des arbres, l'épaulait . . .

Très agréable soirée avec grand-mère et Bruno à qui je lis ma conférence sur Pascal. Nous entendons à la T.S.F. la retransmission du spectacle du Châtelet, *Nina-Rosa*. Je commence *Le Fleuve de Feu*.

Paris, 24 quai de Béthune
dimanche, 23 janvier 1972 (écrit à la suite de la note précédente)

Trente ans déjà, pensais-je hier, en lisant cette page, anodine, de mon *Agenda* 1932. Et soudain, vertigineusement: mais non, quarante, quarante ans. Mis devant cette évidence, moi que hante la fuite du temps, je prends conscience, à nouveau, de mon refus, viscéral, de l'accepter réellement. Pour la première fois peut-être, confronté à ces pages si anciennes, je me reconnais . . . J'hésite à écrire: vieux. Et pourtant, qu'aurait pensé Claude Mauriac, le samedi 23 janvier 1932, de l'inimaginable Claude Mauriac du 23 janvier 1972 qui, dans un inimaginable futur, laisserait un jour sa trace sur cette page restée blanche quarante années durant?

Paris, café Royal Saint-Germain
jeudi 22 janvier 1942

Mauvaise tenue de ce carnet et, peut-être, probablement, sûrement, de ma vie. Ne puis m'intéresser ni à l'un ni à l'autre dans ces conditions de désordre et d'inintelligence. Je sais qu'il faudrait peu de chose pour remettre en place et mon existence et les notes que je prends à son sujet. Je ne me sens à l'aise dans ma vie quotidienne que s'il y a, entre elle et mon journal, synchronisme (. . .) Je voudrais retrouver le rythme double et unique qui, de mes journées, se prolonge dans mon journal. Tout ce que j'ai écrit ici (sur ce carnet-ci) me paraît désaccordé. Et je ne sais ce qui sonne le plus faux, de ma vie ou de ce journal. Le loisir évidemment me manque de repenser mon existence, de lui imposer cette unité, ce sens à défaut desquels elle est incohérente. La vie de bureau impose à mes heures de liberté une sorte d'hébétude. Il m'arrive, par éclair, de mesurer mon inintelligence présente: le hasard d'une lecture, d'une méditation volée à mon engourdissement, me fait connaître, un moment, la richesse intellectuelle d'autrefois, ce foisonnement d'idées et d'émotions, cette lucidité joyeuse. Hier soir, quelques pages de Balzac m'initièrent de nouveau au secret oublié: il s'agissait des premières lignes de *La femme abandonnée*. En retrouvant Mme de Beauséant, dont je ne savais plus rien depuis *Le père Goriot*, une émotion me saisit qui délivra mon esprit emprisonné. De Mme de Beauséant, à qui je pensais comme à une femme que j'aurais connue, je sautai à d'autres héros balzaciens, puis à mon essai ébauché sur Balzac (automne 1940). Dans la rue du Dragon où je regagnai mon hôtel, je me sentis, en un instant, infiniment riche et fort. Ne plus perdre cette confiance. Ne pas laisser mourir ce foyer ranimé. (. . .)

A la suite des lignes qui précèdent, dans le même café, (Royal Saint-Germain, où je ne vais jamais, mais j'ai voulu fuir les Magots, Flore, Lipp: être tranquille) repris mon Balzac dans la joie et *merveilleusement travaillé*.

Paris, 24 quai de Béthune,
dimanche 23 janvier 1972

Saut de dix ans, après mon commentaire de l'*Agenda* 1932. Trente ans cette fois, oui, trente ans . . . "Remettre en place et mon existence et les notes que je prends à son sujet."—"repenser mon existence, lui imposer cette unité à défaut desquelles elle est incohérente," accorder, synchroniser ma vie et mon journal: nostalgie de toujours, plus ou moins consciente et qui trouve dans *Le Temps immobile*, (si peu ébauché soit-il, et dont la nature est de demeurer, quoi qu'il en soit, inachevée) un commencement de réalisation. Le loisir, je l'ai, malgré mes travaux (qui ne sont plus de bureau depuis longtemps). Hier soir, quelques pages de Balzac (*Splendeurs et misères des courtisanes*), oui, hier soir, 22 janvier 1972, Balzac, comme "hier soir," 21 janvier 1942 . . . J'ai le loisir, mais il n'en rend que plus aiguë l'inhibition en présence de l'amoncellement de ces pages mortes.

Paris, Hôtel Palissy, 24 rue du Dragon,
vendredi 23 janvier 1942

Mon père craignait hier que la mort de quelque académicien ne vienne empêcher la séance du jour, où il se proposait de faire une significative intervention, racontant l'incident de l'autre soir, prévenant ses confrères d'où lui viendrait le coup, en cas de malheur, et faisant une allusion précise à M. le Secrétaire perpétuel, André Bellessort, qui chaque semaine écrit dans *Je suis partout* où ses amis couvrent de boue et menacent plusieurs de ses confrères . . . Or j'apprends, en ouvrant le journal, ce matin, qu'André Bellessort est mort hier à 13 h., 30 . . . Tête de mon père? Mais il l'a, en somme, échappé belle: si Bellessort était mort non pas une heure avant mais une heure après la séance de l'Académie, on eût ajouté aux divers surnoms de François Mauriac (les salauds!) "déterreur de nonnes," "belliciste," "tartuffe" etc, celui "d'assassin d'innocent vieillard!"

Paris, 24 quai de Béthune,
lundi 21 janvier 1952

Depuis quinze jours, ma belle-mère m'a confié en dépôt, tandis qu'on achève sa bibliothèque, les manuscrits de Proust. Ainsi dormons-nous dans la pièce où reposent les nombreux cahiers d'*A LA RECHERCHE DU TEMPS*

PERDU, les lettres du jeune Marcel à sa mère, maints inédits. Parfois, j'ouvre un cahier, au hasard, trouvant, par exemple, une curieuse lettre de l'original d'Albert(ine)—avec, au dos, des notes de Proust pour son roman.

Rien de particulier à noter, ces jours-ci. Déjeuner et dîner, hier, avec le R. P. Couturier. Ma bibliothèque enfin achevée, je vais pouvoir travailler sans menace perpétuelle de dérangement. Mais je ne suis fait ni pour le luxe, ni pour la possession. Un jour peut-être, je me sentirai *chez moi* quai de Béthune, mais ce jour n'est pas venu.

Paris, 24 quai de Béthune,
dimanche 23 janvier 1972

... n'est pas venu, est venu, a disparu, n'est jamais venu, est toujours là pourtant. Si je me suis jamais senti chez moi, quai de Béthune, c'est dans la mesure très relative, où je puis, où que ce soit, croire à quelque permanence, à quelque sécurité que ce soit. Et la possession, si relative soit-elle, m'est plus que jamais une gêne et, peut-être, une honte.

Nouveau palier de décompression dans ma remontée à l'air libre du présent.

J'en arrive à 1962,—si près, si loin! Déception: aucun journal daté des 21, 22 ou 23 janvier 1962. Mais, surprise, don admirable du hasard, ces pages du 29 janvier 1962, les premières que je trouve, se rapportent explicitement aux 22 et 23 janvier 1962 et à un projet de roman, "cellule originelle" de ce qui devint, cette même année, *L'Agrandissement.*

Ce qu'il entre d'imprévisible dans les collages du *Temps immobile* m'enchante: il me plaît de contrôler ce qui est par nature incontrôlable; de bâtir, avec des matériaux de hasard, aussi solidement et aussi nécessairement que si je les avais choisis.

Paris, 24 quai de Béthune,
lundi 29 janvier 1962

A Megève je disais à Marie-Claude (ce devait être lundi dernier, 22 janvier):

—Dans quelles conditions naît et se prend la décision de commencer tel roman précis? Par exemple, quand ai-je vraiment décidé de commencer *La Marquise sortit à cinq heures*? Je n'en ai aucun souvenir ...

Le lendemain, 23 janvier, nous prîmes dans la matinée, n'en pouvant plus d'être séparés de nos enfants, la décision de partir le soir-même—c'est à dire sept jours plus tôt que la date prévue. Et dans le train, me vint une idée de roman qui s'imposa, se précisa, exigeant à maintes reprises dans la nuit que, sur ma couchette supérieure, je rallume pour prendre des notes. Huit jours après, je suis moins sûr de mon projet, mais comme il s'agit peut-être de la cellule originelle d'où naîtra mon quatrième roman, je ne crois pas inutile de lui consacrer ce "journal." (...)

Il s'agirait, d'abord, sous sa première apparence, d'un ouvrage critique où serait étudiée l'oeuvre de Bertrand Carnéjoux—c'est à dire la mienne, mais sous les titres parallèles donnés dès *TOUTES LES FEMMES SONT FATALES* qui s'appelait, pour Carnéjoux, *METAPHYSIQUE DE L'AMOUR PHYSIQUE*, le roman suivant s'intitulant non plus *LE DINER EN VILLE* mais *LE DEJEUNER AU BISTROT*. Quant à *LA MARQUISE SORTIT A CINQ HEURES*, son titre pourrait être *LE CARREFOUR DE BUCI*, ou

LE CARREFOUR DES SIECLES, ou, mieux *LES BARRICADES DE PARIS*. Resterait enfin un quatrième volume, *VALROME*, qui serait (en partie) celui-là même que le lecteur lirait—le quatrième—et qui dans le "livre de critique" porterait un autre titre si ce roman devait réellement s'intituler ainsi. Ainsi me référerais-je à trois livres existants, dont je donnerais des citations non pas textuelles mais parallèles, les situations et surtout les intentions étant respectées (ce qui me permettrait de signaler tout ce qui dans cette trilogie échappa aux critiques et qui était, qui demeure pour moi capital)— et à un quatrième qui serait celui alors publié et lu (...)

Je dois reconnaître dans cette idée un de mes plus anciens projets (il date des premières années de l'occupation, peut-être même de plus tôt encore) celui de *l'ESSAI DE CRITIQUE PURE*. Mais ce n'est que la première apparence d'un livre beaucoup plus subtil dont je n'ai pas encore trouvé, je le sens bien, l'exacte définition, mais qui, dès la nuit du train, pouvait s'exprimer ainsi: peu à peu, à certaines incertitudes dans le ton, à certaines failles dans le récit, à certains répétitions, le lecteur devrait s'apercevoir qu'il ne lit pas un livre de critique comme les autres, étant même entendu qu'il s'agit de la critique par le romancier et grâce à un subterfuge, de sa propre oeuvre romanesque. Dans mon idée (encore insuffisante, imprécise) il s'agirait en réalité d'une rêverie, d'une rêve ou d'un délire de Bertrand Carnéjoux, dormant ou malade, au sujet de ses livres—par exemple d'une sorte de demi-rêve obsessionnel où il tâcherait d'expliquer et de s'expliquer ce qu'il avait voulu faire dans son oeuvre et qu'aucun lecteur, aucun critique n'avait compris. L'idée essentielle, à rendre plausible, à matérialiser, étant celle-ci: le véritable sujet de ce livre serait un livre lui-même, *le LIVRE* que lirait le lecteur. Mais c'est ici que je demeure, je le sais, dans les ténèbres.

Ce recul me permettrait en tous cas d'éviter le reproche de prétention, car Bertrand Carnéjoux serait le premier à se dire et à dire, à la fin, qu'en réalité rien de ce qu'il a écrit n'a la moindre importance, qu'il s'est grisé de mots pour essayer désespérément de croire à son oeuvre—plus qu'aucune autre insuffisante et manquée. Jugement qui n'était pas tellement le mien, il faut oser l'avouer, dans la nuit du train—où me grisait mon projet grâce auquel serait, selon mon plus grand désir, récupérées, liées, épanouies mes oeuvres romanesques précédentes dont je ferais ainsi de façon indubitable, même aux yeux des tiers mal intentionnés—ou simplement objectifs, *une oeuvre*. Mais depuis lors j'ai été ramené à plus d'humilité et voici pourquoi.

Avant-hier, en fin de journée, Nathalie Sarraute réunit chez elle, à la demande d'Ilya Ehrenbourg de passage à Paris (elle venait de le voir à Moscou) quelques représentants du "nouveau roman." En l'absence d'Alain Robbe-Grillet et de Michel Butor, se trouvaient là Claude Simon, Claude Ollier et Jérôme Lindon, devant un Ehrenbourg phraseur, sarcastique, buté, bien décidé, sans nous entendre et alors qu'il ne nous avait pas lus, ne connaissant que notre légende, à considérer comme vérifiées ses idées à notre sujet.

Tant que dura la réunion je fus, comme mes camarades, agacé par l'incompréhension et le parti-pris systématiques d'Ehrenbourg, que je voyais pour la troisième fois de ma vie. A Moscou, cet été, dans les jardins de l'Ambassade de France—, il m'avait rappelé (quelle mémoire!) notre première rencontre, au bar du Pont-Royal, peu après la Libération.

Après l'avoir trouvé longtemps très bête, avec ses questions du genre: "Quelle est la valeur sociale de ce que vous écrivez?", je m'avisai qu'il faisait bien plutôt la bête et que, compte-tenu de ses positions idéologiques et de son manque d'objectivité, il en savait tout autant, sinon bien plus que nous, vieux lion malin ayant survécu à tout, même à Staline, et ayant bien connu une époque dont nous ne savions que les fastes prestigieux: celle de l'après-grande-guerre. Nous avions beau être pleins d'humilité et lui opposer précisément notre humilité, disant: "Nous ne prétendons à rien d'autre qu'à faire le mieux possible nos livres, comme nous les concevons. Ce n'est qu'après coup, dans longtemps et nous ne serons plus là, que certains d'entre nous seront peut-être récompensés par "la reconnaissance d'utilité publique" que vous posez, vous, au départ comme un postulat." Et je disais: "Ce n'est point parce que vous avez décidé d'écrire des romans qui peuvent être utiles à vos contemporains qu'ils le sont. On ne saura cela que bien plus tard." Donc tandis qu'il parlait, parlait (ah! l'ennui soviétique), je me disais qu'il avait assurément raison (nous l'avons admis bien volontiers) en affirmant que les romanciers des années 20 (je disais même: tous les meilleurs écrivains, toujours) avaient eu exactement les mêmes ambitions que nous, mais qu'il avait hélas sans doute, en ce qui me concernait tout au moins, bien plus raison encore que je ne l'aurais souhaité: bref, peu à peu, ma pauvre petite "oeuvre," tout à fait ignorée de lui (qui n'avait rien lu d'aucun de nous) était par lui niée au point que j'étais le premier à en admettre, à en reconnaître en moi-même la totale nullité.

J'en fus—et j'en demeure attristé. Mais ce manque de complaisance à l'égard de mes tentatives personnelles est excellent: si je dois commencer mon roman, il est bon que ce soit avec l'idée très nette de mes insuffisances—ce qui de la suffisance me gardera.

Dès la nuit du train, j'avais du reste considéré comme un des avantages de mon projet la possibilité qu'il me donnerait non seulement de corriger dans la mesure du possible (par additions) les romans précédents, (par exemple en introduisant de nouveaux textes, le moins possible, sur le carrefour de Buci), mais encore et surtout de marquer mon désaccord sur certains points fondamentaux: notamment sur la lettre (bien souvent) et l'esprit (toujours) de *TOUTES LES FEMMES SONT FATALES* dont la partie "amour physique" me paraît aujourd'hui d'un inintérêt presque total et d'un certain ridicule (...) Ainsi donc, sans rien changer à ce qui fut et demeure écrit, imprimé, aurais-je la possibilité de rectifier le tir et de juger moi-même avec recul, donc avec objectivité, ce qui, dans ce moi-même et dans ces moi-mêmes d'autrefois et de naguère, me déplaît.

Dans le désert qu'est devenue ma vie personnelle, dans ce vide désespéré de l'âge et de sa lucidité terrible (où il ne me reste que mon amour *éperdu*—voir le dernier "journal" de Du Bos—pour ma femme et mes enfants, amour qui ajoute plus de douleur peut-être que de bonheur à mon désenchantement), cette mise au point d'un long journal m'apporte une chaleur, une lumière qui me réconfortent. Je ne croyais plus en rien—et surtout en rien de ce qui me touchait moi-même. C'est à peine si j'existais. Pour le passé, je n'avais pas existé. Et voici que ces pages me font retrouver un moi qui, s'il est tué peu à peu par le temps, lui échappe quant à l'essentiel: du moins aussi longtemps qu'il est vivant. Voici que je puis faire un peu plus que semblant de m'intéresser à moi-même—notamment à cette "oeuvre" dont l'inanité, je m'en aperçois, est la plus constante de mes certitudes—et c'est pourquoi, justement, j'essayais en me proposant d'ajouter un livre aux livres précédents, de sauver ce qui pouvait être sauvé, de récupérer au dernier moment (et pour peu de moments) ce qui allait à jamais m'échapper, s'échapper—se dissoudre et se perdre.

Paris, 24 quai de Béthune,
dimanche 23 janvier 1972

Hier encore, comme il y a dix ans, je parlais à Marie-Claude du roman qu'il me faudrait écrire et dont je n'avais, dont je n'ai toujours aucune idée ...

Rien ne distingue ces pages, tapées il y a dix ans, de celle que, sur la même machine, je compose aujourd'hui—et surtout pas mon opinion, inchangée, sur *Toutes les femmes sont fatales*, paru à la fin de 1971 en Livre de Poche. Seul progrès: j'ai, depuis, conçu et commencé de réaliser, la grande et belle idée du *Temps immobile*, oeuvre que je laisserai sans doute à peine ébauchée et à laquelle, qui sait, tel ou tel exégète proposera, dans l'avenir, de possibles solutions de détail en utilisant quelques-unes des milliers de pages de ce journal léguées à une bibliothèque ...

C'est le même papier, la même disposition, les mêmes écrits et les mêmes cris—avec cette seule et considérable différence: dix ans ont passé, j'ai maintenant près de cinquante-huit ans ... Avec plus de quarante ans de journal à ma disposition.

Plus de quarante ans, donc ... Mais que dis-je! Je me souviens que je puis plonger plus profond, non pas seulement en 1932 mais en 1922 ...

Si loin dans mon passé (j'avais huit ans) les ténèbres sont presque totales. Je ne puis m'attendre à trouver des dates précises, des textes intéressants— leur seule existence suffisant à les rendre, pour *Le Temps immobile*, importants.

Car il existe—et je vais le chercher—un petit carnet saumon où, sur la couverture, je lis mon nom, la date 1922 et la mention "Pour tout." Carnet où je me revois écrire, dans le bureau de travail, à Vémars, émerveillé, enchanté, grisé de cette découverte (je revis, aujourd'hui encore, cette griserie, cet enchantement, cet émerveillement): la possibilité de m'exprimer et même (je ne le formulais pas, mais c'était cela): de créer.

Je revois la précise, l'exacte lumière de ce jour d'hiver. Cette pièce n'était habitée que l'hiver. Mais une preuve m'est inutile: c'est un soleil hivernal qui à jamais éclaire les pages de ce carnet.

Les pages 4 et 5 sont consacrées à ce qui était—déjà—un roman et qui porte cette seule indication: "histoire par Claude Mauriac." Cela commence par "Nous étions à Breste que nous v. yames un bateau qui semblé saproché" et se termine par *à suivre*, après: "Le capitaine lui reponda que ce mot: bon. il averti un marin d'aler Nous donner une cabine. On Nous conduisies dans une chambrette. Nous y déposâmes notre petit paquet." J'ai respecté l'ortho-graphe. Il y a un accent circonflexe sur l'a de déposâmes ...

Paris, 24 quai de Béthune,
lundi 24 janvier 1972

Je voudrais éviter la tentation d'enchaîner sur la suite des 24 janvier abolis.

Mais comment ne pas noter qu'une idée de roman m'est enfin venue ce matin, aussi différente sans doute de ce que sera réellement ce roman, s'il doit être jamais, que l'embryon de *L'Agrandissement* recueilli dans mon journal du 29 janvier 1962, "Cellule originelle" si fragile encore que je n'ose encore n'en rien dire ici. (Extrait inédit de *Le Temps immobile*).

Paris, 1972

"Quelqu'un" in Robert Pinget's Fiction

By STEVEN G. KELLMAN

From *Entre Fantoine et Agapa* (1951) to *Passacaille* (1969), Robert Pinget has published fifteen volumes of fiction and drama. Yet only now is he beginning to attract a sizeable audience on this side of the Atlantic. Vivian Mercier, tracing some important developments in the contemporary French novel, situates Pinget in the company of Raymond Queneau, Nathalie Sarraute, Alain Robbe-Grillet, Michel Butor, Claude Simon, and Claude Mauriac. And Robert Pinget himself expresses his own preoccupations in terms of:

> ... la passion de l'auteur pour l'invention, son obsession des destins individuels, sa hantise de l'imagination et des efforts à accomplir pour sonder la seule réalité qui soit, son âme, et enfin son amour illimité de la langue française.[1]

[1]Mercier, Vivian, *The New Novel* (New York, 1971), p. 145. Pinget's statement is quoted by Mercier from a private letter sent by the author on July 14, 1965, making it roughly contemporaneous with *Quelqu'un*.

Like his more celebrated compatriot Alain Robbe-Grillet, who abandoned a career as an engineer to become a novelist, Robert Pinget began as a lawyer and then defected to painting before finally retiring to his "pension" of literature in the early fifties. *Quelqu'un* (Les Editions de Minuit) appeared in 1965. It occupies a central position among Pinget's novels to date, and, specifically, it offers distinct parallels with two earlier works, *Graal Flibuste* (Les Editions de Minuit, 1956) and *Baga* (Les Editions de Minuit, 1958).

Quelqu'un follows the proprietor of a boarding house through all the paltry details of one day in his life. As opposed to the novelistic tradition of intricately patterned plot, nothing happens in *Quelqu'un*. The narrator descends from his bedroom, goes into the garden, engages in meaningless and repetitive conversations with the boarders, and eats meals about which his most vivid observations have to do with the number of teaspoons of sugar each person takes in his coffee. The narrative is continually being halted in order to backtrack over trifles that have already been described over and over again. It is in fact the record of a futile search for a lost scrap of paper containing information which would enable the narrator to write a botanical treatise. The effect which emerges is that of a severely limited existence which never leads anywhere and of a network of language which circles around itself without ever achieving a resolution.

However, after uttering an involuntary pun, the narrator of *Quelqu'un* observes that words can create "rapports, choses qui sont très proches et on ne le sait pas, personne ne le sait, et on les sort comme ça et un monde, un univers entier nous est révélé, des gouffres, des enfers" (p. 177). *Quelqu'un* portrays and is itself a desperate attempt to create links between the narrator and the other characters and between the narrator and the reader, even if the universe which arises as a result is an infernal one. The title of the novel itself appears to demonstrate this awesome power of words. The word "quelqu'un" effectively emblematizes the major concerns of this work, as well as of Pinget's fiction in general. Perhaps through a study of "quelqu'un" in *Quelqu'un*, a whole world will pop out at us.

Ten years before the novel begins, the narrator of *Quelqu'un* left his office job in the city to establish a boarding house in the suburbs with his school chum Gaston. There is a vague reference to the narrator's failure in love. Aside from these facts, very little specific information is advanced about the narrator, and we never even learn his name. Instead, the title of the novel suggests that he is simply "Quelqu'un," someone but no one in particular.

It is easy to see this Someone as a type of the alienated contemporary anti-hero plagued with the usual problems. As such, his anonymity is both descriptive and functional. It indicates his mediocrity; and, while denying him status as a rounded, independent personality, the narrator's anonymity also emphasizes his role as surrogate for the reader, making Quelqu'un, if not a contemporary Everyman, at least a type of contemporary man imprisoned within the suburban limbo between city and country and doomed never to meet Rivoire, his neighbor.

The narrator self-consolingly repeats the fact that "Je suis un garçon honnête, un peu niais, sans envergure" (pp. 38, 58). In Aristotelian terms, he is thereby neither above us nor below us and can thus function as a communal someone. "J'ai une vie pénible et rasante comme tout le monde"

(p. 193). This someone who could be anyone is anxious throughout the novel to demonstrate the universality of his own petty experience. Observations on events in his own life are frequently followed by "Il paraît que c'est partout la même chose" (p. 7), "Mais ça doit arriver partout" (p. 122), and "Ça doit être partout comme ça" (p. 250). But the use of such words as "paraît" and "doit" suggests a note of uneasiness, as if the narrator is uncertain about the existence of an external world and can only hope that he is not alone.

If the alienated Quelqu'un does succeed in functioning as a species of Everyman, then a paradox has been realized. As a representative for all of us, he must communicate the fact that we are all separate and incapable of converging and communicating. To do this, his presentation must fulfill Roquentin's requirement that a novel "fasse honte aux gens de leur existence," which is similar to the purpose for writing given by the narrator-king in Pinget's *Baga*: "Pour dessiller les yeux des gens, pour les dégoûter de leurs nids. Ils sont infects" (p. 74). A communal act has been performed without a community, and the universal reality of solipsism has been shared. This is an accomplishment somewhat akin to that of Rivoire's manuscript, which explains how to be happy and solitary but which is bequeathed to other people.

In any case, Quelqu'un—like Pinget himself—was born in July (p. 148), perhaps indicative of his locus in the post-Revolutionary world. No act or title of nobility is available to him any more. In this respect, he is reminiscent of the narrator-king of *Baga*, king "de ma crasse" (p. 7), who makes the very unregal confession that "Je ne suis pas fait pour les grands desseins" and follows it with a tragicomic soliloquy detailing just how much of a rogue and peasant slave this scion of Père Ubu really is:

> J'ai la tête grosse et bourgeonneuse. Des enflures, des boutons. Mes cils tombent dans mes yeux. J'ai le nez en pomme de terre et les oreilles en feuilles de chou. . . .
> Mon ventre est gonflé à partir de l'estomac. Autrefois je le rentrais comme tout le monde, maintenant plus. Je ne vois mon sexe qu'en me penchant. La surprise n'a rien de fou. Du poil un peu moins jaune que sous les bras, une verge trapue et les bourses qui se détendent. Ça tombe. En leur tirant la peau en remontant on peut m'en recouvrir tout le bas-ventre. C'est le jeu de mes femmes. Les cuisses sont grêles et le derrière énorme. Quand je me regarde dans la glace j'ai l'air d'un gros ver blanc (pp. 66-7).

One chapter in *Baga* portrays the intimidated little king being forced to account to a man whom he refers to throughout as "mon président." At the end of the chapter, the narrator is led away, condemned. This theme of interrogation is also conspicuously present in *L'Inquisitoire* (1962), a novel by Pinget which consists entirely of the responses by the old caretaker of a house—once again a house—to the imperious questions of an unidentified voice. Quelqu'un, like the other narrators, is a trivial figure born under the wrong star. Never more than "quelqu'un," he anonymously functions as a representative of the anonymous world which has replaced a universe of personal glory. "Quelqu'un" thus suggests "a nobody" at least as much as does Jules Romains' *Mort de Quelqu'un*.

But the word "quelqu'un" also has honorific connotations, as in the expres-

sion "Il se croit quelqu'un." There is a very trenchant irony to this suggestion
of the word applied to the insignificant lives in *Quelqu'un*. At one point, the
narrator explicitly calls attention to this irony in mocking Gaston's foolish
dedication to the epic task of buying a washing machine. "Pour lui c'est une
espèce d'aventure, peut-être qu'il se dit qu'il est quelqu'un de bien de se
tourmenter pour ça, uniquement pour être moderne, et actif?" (p. 142).
Rather than the no one that each one is condemned to be, each character
yearns to be a someone, to assert himself meaningfully. Yet the narrator
remains conscious of the limitations of such efforts and even recognizes
that refusal to assert oneself can also proceed from an inflated conception of
oneself as "quelqu'un." "Je ne pouvais même plus leur parler, j'avais tout le
temps peur de croire qu'ils croient que je me prenais pour quelqu'un"
(p. 183). The title of the novel thus acts as a commentary on the pretensions
of a cast of petty characters. However, through his awareness, the narrator
is able to transcend his shortcomings. Although the irony of "quelqu'un"
is directed at least as much against him as against anyone, the narrator also
merits the sense of admiration in the word "quelqu'un," if for nothing else
than his endurance in a supremely dismal cosmos.

"Quelqu'un," someone, also suggests some *one*, emphasizing the feeling of
solitude pervading the novel. The narrator can never escape the fact that he
is one person alone, and we as readers are perpetually aware of the fact that
we are confined to the first person narrative of one mind which can do
nothing but circle around itself. The title *Quelqu'un* thus supports the intolerable sense of separation and of imprisonment within the trivial existence
of some one. The narrator frequently expresses his wish to "m'en débarrasser"
but concedes "je sais que je n'en sortirai jamais" (p. 193). He is condemned
forever to be some one.

At one point in the novel, the narrator makes a casual allusion to having
been rejected in love, "plaqué" (p. 32). And the neighbor, who more and more
emerges as a projection of the narrator himself despite the gulf between the
two, has likewise been jilted. "Oui, il venait de me dire qu'il était fiancé en
quatorze et que sa fiancée l'avait plaqué pour un Anglais, il ne s'en était
jamais remis, il était resté célibataire" (p. 80). Each of them thus remains
alone without even any satisfactory communication between the "quelques-
uns."

The characteristic reaction to rejection is a movement toward withdrawal,
ironically toward further isolation. This is seen in the narrator's removal
from the affairs of society to a secluded and shabby *pension*, from which he
ventures out less and less, allowing himself to be dominated more and more
by Marie and Gaston, just as the king allows himself to be governed by his
prime minister Baga. This tendency is in fact not very far removed from the
paranoia and xenophobia of the narrator of *Baga*, who declares fatalistically
"Mais l'impression qu'on fait aux gens n'a aucune importance. Même si je
me tenais royalement qu'est-ce qui empêcherait les voisins de me déclarer la
guerre?" (p. 35). This attitude receives its extreme expression in the king's
maxim "Mais sache que tout ce qui vient de l'étranger est funeste, tu entends,
funeste" (p. 40). Quelqu'un, furthermore, directs himself to "penser mai-
greur" and has high praise for the most dramatic of illnesses, cancer: "Il y a
de nos jours cette merveilleuse maladie du cancer qui fait maigrir rapidement

les vieux pour la simple décence devant la mort mais voilà qu'on se met à lutter contre, que les croulants veulent grossir jusqu'à la dernière minute" (p. 224).

However, such a death wish ("J'ai envie de mourir" [p. 221] is only part of the total ambivalence exhibited by the narrator. This ambivalence is perhaps most succinctly expressed in Pinget's echo of the final lines of Samuel Beckett's *L'Innommable*, "Je ne peux pas continuer. Je continue" (p. 168). And in describing his attitude toward his boarders, the narrator declares, "Quand je me sens vibrer de la glotte ou suinter de la paupière je crois que je les aime. Et une minute après j'ai envie de mourir ou de battre" (p. 31).

Likewise, after relinquishing his kingdom to become a poor hermit in a forest, the narrator of *Baga* discovers "C'est depuis mon installation solitaire que je découvre combien j'aime les autres" (p. 69). His inclinations are so contradictory that "Si je n'étais pas ermite je serais voyageur" (pp. 73-4). And the ambivalence in Quelqu'un also parallels that in *Graal Flibuste*, in which the Induction represents a realistic balance and undercutting to the flights of fancy in the body of the novel. In the Induction to *Graal Flibuste*, a drunkard is shown abusing his cat in an apparent effort to get rid of it. Yet paradoxically when he thinks that he has succeeded, "J'ai donc avalé ce chat, se dit-il, me voilà bien seul. A l'évocation de sa solitude, l'ivrogne se met à pleurer" (p. 8). He is like the lonely monarch of *Baga* who confesses to his hypothetical nephew-readers "Votre oncle a tout le temps envie de pleurer" (p. 31). In *Quelqu'un*, although Rivoire's manuscript explains how to live happily alone, it is left as a legacy to someone else, and, although the narrator withdraws within himself, it is ironically in reaction to others and in the hope that by doing so he might possibly reach others.

Clearly, the narrator as "quelqu'un," some one, is not enough. He needs someone else. Within the fictional world, this explains his obsession with meeting and communicating with his neighbor, even if he has to talk about scarecrows, weather vanes, or garbage pails to do so. And it explains the poignancy of the Captain Corcoran idyl with Fonfon, as well as of the attempts throughout the novel at genuine conversation with Gaston, Reber, and Apostolos. "Quelqu'un" as emphasizing someone other than the narrator is suggested in his dream of himself as aged and living in the public square while other people come to consult him about recovering their lost articles (p. 89).

In addition, the narrative itself represents a desperate reaching out for "quelqu'un." The reference of the title thus shifts from the first person to the second person, from narrator to reader; we become the someone capable of breaking the circle of the writer's isolation. This meaning of "quelqu'un" recurs throughout the novel, notably in the plaintive requests "Si seulement j'avais quelqu'un! Quelqu'un qui lise par-dessus mon épaule, mais ça serait trop beau" (p. 195), "Je voudrais que quelqu'un, au moins quelqu'un se rende compte de mon état mais je sais bien que c'est impossible" (p. 151), and "Qu'on me comprenne, qu'on se mette à ma place. Je me demande si quelqu'un voudrait. Quelqu'un" (p. 52).

Quelqu'un as direct address to "quelqu'un" is thus related to the epistolary nature of both *Baga* and *Graal Flibuste*. The king-narrator conceives of his narrative as, in effect, a series of letters to his nephews, thus placing it within the tradition of aids to the education of royal heirs. The sterile king, of course, has no children of his own and no prospects for any, but even the existence of any nephews soon becomes very questionable, and the narrator is made to conclude: "Tout mon temps je le perds à rédiger ces mémoires imbéciles, commencés pour laisser à mes neveux un témoignage de ma grandeur mais continués sans but" (p. 172). At one point within the narrative itself, the king becomes a hermit writing letters, which are intercepted by a king named Gnar. And the narrator as hermit in the forest endeavors to communicate with a "chat-tigre," suggesting the ferocity with which Pinget's characters paranoically endow others in their own minds. Every day he writes some letters and leaves them outside his hut, where the tiger-cat takes them, although that animal is unable to read. The tiger-cat eventually utters one word—"correspondance," significantly—and the narrator kills him. The universe of *Baga* is not a "temple" of "de vivants piliers."

And *Graal Flibuste* apparently proceeds as the dream of the drunkard shown in the Induction. He conceives of himself as a noble warrior awaiting an important letter in vain: ". . . rien au monde à part le chat qui me traque n'a plus d'importance, que cette lettre au fil de l'eau" (p. 9). The Induction ends thus:

> L'ivrogne s'endort sur la table et le vin l'emporte au pays des cadavres de lettres. Beaucoup de lettres n'atteignent pas leur destinataire, elles attendent dans les postes, puis l'ange des lettres les assassine. C'est l'ange ennemi de l'amour, l'ange sec aux ailes de papier (p. 9).

Like *Baga* and like *Quelqu'un*, *Graal Flibuste* is an attempt to recover a lost communion, an attempt which illuminates its own futility. It is the dry angel of letters with wings of paper who destroys the form of communication counted on by the drunkard.

"Quelqu'un" as both apostrophe to the reader and approach to other characters in the novel is embodied in the figure of "la chouette." The screech-owl is very comforting to the narrator.

> Elle m'apaise parce j'ai comme l'impression qu'elle sait que je suis là à ma table, elle voit la lumière, elle me jette un cri, t'en fais pas je suis là aussi, il n'y a pas que toi qui t'escrimes, on est deux qui s'escriment à débarrasser le jardin de ses rats . . . (pp. 168-9).

The screech-owl represents *someone else* and, despite the bleakness of the situation and the folk conception of screech-owls as harbingers of evil, the cry which it emits is a form of communication and a recognition that the two of them are united in a common effort, however fruitless. In regard to the narrator-reader relationship,

> Elle m'apaise parce que j'ai comme l'impression que les choses se transforment quand elle crie, tout devient un peu chouette, un peu vagabond, un peu ratier, le jardin frissonne pour faire sauter ses rats, la pagode Rivoire cherche quelque chose de toutes ses mansardes comme des yeux dans l'anthracite du marronnier, la girouette du voisin esquisse une manœuvre, elle a envie de repartir sur la côte ou ailleurs, bref un

mouvement partout tant que crie la chouette, sitôt qu'elle s'arrêtera tout redeviendra immobile, elle nous tient en éveil, elle me trouble, je sens une excitation, une fièvre (p. 169).

Like Wallace Stevens' Key West girl or his Man with the Blue Guitar, the screech-owl is able through its music to transform the world and to give it unity despite the omnipresence of vermin. It is an analogue of the narrator striving to have a similar effect, to reach out directly to someone else.

Then, too, bothersome rats seem to provide a constant background for the universe inhabited by Pinget's narrators. It is the territory of Chanchèze in the narrator's kingdom which occasions the fateful war with Novocordie in *Baga*. Chanchèze, like Camus' Oran, is overrun by rats. They cross the border with Novocordie, and the Novocordians use this as a pretext to annex the area and begin a war with the narrator-king. Apparently, the same Chancheze is in question at the very beginning of the narrative proper of *Graal Flibuste*: "Le Chanchèze est une vallée morne et peuplée de rats" (p. 11). And, like Quelqu'un's garden, Chancheze also has its birds in *Graal Flibuste*. "On dit que ces oiseaux se nourrissent de rats. Mais Porphyreus affirme qu'ils ne sont pas carnivores, ils se contentent de tuer les rongeurs" (p. 12). Whatever their actual motivations for battling the rats, the birds, like the screech-owl and like Quelqu'un, engage in a continual effort to transmute a chaos of vermin.

Ultimately, the perfect reader, the final "quelqu'un," becomes God. There are some twenty occurrences of the word "Dieu" and many others of such words as "Seigneur" and "le ciel" in the ostensibly incongruous context of this novel. Yet, among other things, *Quelqu'un* is a novel of frustrated mysticism. The narrator sees himself as Joan of Arc (p. 18), Saint Anthony (p. 61), and the Virgin Mary (p. 178). He spends a large portion of the narrative either holding or looking for a book on Thérèse Neumann, the twentieth century German peasant mystic. There is therefore some significance to Reber's apparently naïve remark to the narrator, "Dieu vous entende" (p. 106). The narrator in fact has a strong impression that he is responding to questions, that he is answering someone who is "informulé mais présent" (p. 17). God becomes the primal "quelqu'un," and the narrator's failure to communicate with the divine presence becomes even more tragic.

Of course, the context of mysticism is the basis for a good deal of irony in *Quelqu'un*. There is certainly a disparity between the apostolic tradition of transcendent vision and the sordid reality of the diarrhetic Mme. Apostolos awaiting tidings of Paradise from her canary, perhaps influenced by Flaubert's Félicité. Similarly heretical is the episode in *Baga* in which the narrator-king goes into retreat and becomes a nun, miraculously changing sexes and becoming "Sœur Angèle." He-she joins his-her blood sister Louise and a girl Marie, whom they have seduced into entering the monastic life, forming a rather unorthodox *ménage à trois*. And the king's withdrawal into the woods as a hermit which culminates in his murder of the tiger-cat would not have been likely to please St. Francis of Assisi.

As the title *Baga* might emphasize, Pinget's narrators are and are concerned with "bagatelles." Through the power of their language, their "bagou," they must attempt to overcome this; those brief moments which present some glimmer of success have the mystical quality of genuine divine possession. Like

Quelqu'un, the king at one point becomes aware of the power of his words to create a vital experience which is more than a mere record of past actions: "Des fois j'imagine que je suis en train de faire ce que j'écris. Il y a là un pouvoir inexploité. Il vient du droit divin, probablement" (pp. 42-3). Of course, he is also sharply undercut here; not even Bossuet would attribute divine right to this wretched man. Pinget's narrators are in some sense vatic, transmitting through their words all of the power necessary to hold and convert us as someone else. But what their words do is essentially depict their pettiness. The narrators thereby assume the position of the sorcerer encountered in the country of trees without roots in *Graal Flibuste*: "Mon pays est aride, dit l'enchanteur, et je suis impuissant à lui donner de l'eau. Mon pays a soif, le désert l'envahit, les vergers se dessèchent la pierre affleure le sol. A quoi me sert de changer le ciel en armée de grenouilles, les hommes en potirons, les bêtes sauvages en gravier? Ma puissance est dérisoire" (pp. 26-7).

In a way, Quelqu'un is a solitary pilgrim, a devoted contemplative retreating to the suburbs from the sinfulness of the world, but the narrative also makes it clear that he is a terrified and isolated little man. He is some one cut off from someone; he inhabits a world irrevocably divorced from the divine and must cultivate a garden made barren by factory soot. Solitary, he can only begin, with no hope of consummation, in the direction in which Dante started and where Yeats found that all ladders start. The narrator can only ferret through the trash can of his existence and become conscious of its contents:

> Toutes les épluchures de courgettes et d'aubergines, le pourri des tomates, les nerfs recrachés du bifteck, les dégueulasseries des casseroles, les trognons de salades, les coquilles d'œufs, les restes moisis de ratatouille, c'est vrai qu'elle ne se conserve pas, les effilochures du foutoir mélangées à des grosses boules de poussière déjà toutes grasses du jus des assiettes, des papiers restés collés au fond depuis Dieu sait combien de temps, tout, j'ai tout regardé (p. 214).

Surely someone can admire that.

University of California at Berkeley

Bernanos— Un "Dostoïevsky Français?"

J. Kostka

Par WILLIAM BUSH

On a souvent comparé Bernanos à Dostoïevsky.[1] Certes, les affinités sont nombreuses entre ces deux romanciers également préoccupés par le conflit que se livrent en l'homme les forces antagonistes du bien et du mal. Ils partagent en outre la même prédilection pour les thèmes de la misère, de la souffrance et de l'innocence trahie. On sait enfin que Bernanos s'est passionné pour

---

[1]A. Bellessort, "Un Nouveau romancier," *Journal des Débats*, 21 avril 1926; Albert Béguin, *Critique*, septembre 1948; Luc Estang, *Présence de Bernanos* (Plon: 1947), pp. 37-45; Claude-Edmonde Magny, "La Part du Diable dans la littérature contemporaine," dans *Satan* (Desclée de Brouwer: 1948), pp. 573-606; Rima Drell Reck, "Bernanos et Dostoïevsky: le dépassement du roman policier dans UN CRIME et CRIME ET CHATIMENT," *Etudes Bernanosiennes* 6, pp. 73-83; Ernest Beaumont, "The Supernatural in Dostoïevsky and Bernanos: A reply to Professor Sonnenfeld," *French Studies*, XXIII, no. 3, July 1969, pp. 264-271.

l'oeuvre du romancier russe.[2] Néanmoins, on peut se demander si ces points de ressemblance suffisent à faire de Bernanos un "Dostoïevsky français."

i

Bernanos, comme Dostoïevsky, s'intéresse d'abord et avant tout au fond psychique de l'homme. Comme lui, il a compris que les contradictions de l'âme humaine ne s'expliquent pas par de vagues forces psychologiques mal définies mais, dans une autre perspective, par la lutte qui oppose, au coeur même de l'homme, Dieu et Satan. Condamné par la Chute à subir la mort— cette manifestation souveraine du mal—, l'homme de Bernanos, comme celui de Dostoïevsky, demeure néanmoins capable d'exprimer la lumière incréée du divin aussi bien que la puissance ténébreuse du démoniaque. Pour ces deux romanciers, en effet, l'homme est un théâtre où se heurtent la lumière et les ténèbres: sa vie intérieure est modelée par le choc de ce que Baudelaire a si justement appelé les "*deux postulations simultanées.*"[3] Chez l'un et l'autre auteur, la lutte se solde tantôt par la transfiguration de l'homme dans la puissance et la gloire de Dieu, tantôt par le chaos de la comédie trompeuse du démoniaque.

Peu de romanciers sont capables de mettre en jeu un tel conflit et moins encore d'en soutenir la tension tout au long d'un roman. Face à un Bernanos ou à un Dostoïevsky, les auteurs les plus vantés de ce que l'on a appelé "le roman catholique français" semblent bien médiocres. Le romancier catholique français, imprégné d'une tradition littéraire qui favorise l'analyse lucide du conflit entre la raison et les passions, se trouve certainement plus gêné qu'un auteur russe lorsqu'il lui faut affronter le problème du démoniaque. L'auteur français craint—et il s'agit d'une crainte atavique—que la portée du démoniaque ne soit plus vaste et plus universelle que la portée de la raison.

Les auteurs catholiques français éludent généralement le problème en se contentant de présenter un Satan de théâtre, celui d'un Huysmans par exemple, c'est-à-dire celui qui nourrit le satanisme traditionnel. En ce qui concerne la présentation de Satan, Bernanos fait donc exception à la règle. Dès son premier roman, *Sous le Soleil de Satan*, il nous présente le mal dans une optique tout à fait conforme à l'expérience humaine: c'est toujours derrière le masque de nos propres traits que Satan se cache.

En soulignant le rôle authentique à accorder au démoniaque dans la vie de l'homme, Bernanos et Dostoïevsky rejoignent tous deux la tradition des pères du désert, qui enseignaient que tout homme a besoin de Dieu pour être délivré de la puissance du démon. Cette optique commune aux deux auteurs,— source même de leurs oeuvres respectives—s'exprime pourtant de deux manières tout à fait différentes dans leurs écrits romanesques.

ii

La plupart des romans de Bernanos présentent un nombre limité de personnages. On peut même dire que plus il est fidèle à lui-même, plus

---

[2]En juillet 1957 Madame Georges Bernanos m'a confirmé que son mari ne connaissait le monde russe que par ses lectures. Cette lecture des auteurs russe a sensibilisé Bernanos à la complexité de l'âme russe, comme en témoigne le personnage énigmatique de Fiodor dans *La Joie*.

[3]*Mon Coeur mis à nu*, XI.

Bernanos restreint le champ de sa vision, jusqu'à centrer tout l'éclairage sur un seul personnage. N'est-il pas significatif que le dernier roman qu'il ait conçu, *La Nouvelle Histoire de Mouchette*, soit aussi le plus réussi du point de vue du style? Le drame de l'adolescente humiliée s'y déploie dans toute sa force, les autres personnages ne servant qu'à faire valoir la figure centrale de la jeune Mouchette. Même dans un roman aussi riche que *M. Ouine*, Bernanos ne parvient pas toujours à relier entre eux les fils des divers drames qu'il réunit. Le drame de Steeny à la recherche d'un père, celui de M. Ouine au château de Wambercourt, le drame familial des Devandomme, la névrose d'Arsène, et la solitude du curé paraissent mal intégrés les uns aux autres, même si l'on accorde au meurtre du petit vacher une fonction unificatrice.

D'autre part, plus Dostoïevsky est fidèle à lui-même, plus ses romans fourmillent de personnages. Par exemple, lorsque le héros de *Mémoires écrits dans un souterrain* deviendra Raskolnikov, le romancier russe aura fini par l'entourer de tout un monde de personnages, monde avec lequel Raskolnikov essayera de se réconcilier en expiant son crime. Le héros de *Mémoires écrits dans un souterrain* ressemble beaucoup d'ailleurs à un héros de Bernanos. Néanmoins, ce personnage est aussi, pour Dostoïevsky, le point de cristallisation de tout un univers romanesque, le point de départ d'un grand roman: *Crime et Châtiment*.

Bernanos n'a jamais su étendre ainsi son imagination créatrice. La deuxième Mouchette n'est que la première Mouchette épurée; Simone Alfieri d'*Un Mauvais Rêve* reprend Evangéline d'*Un Crime*. Le drame demeure toujours centré sur le conflit personnel plutôt que sur le conflit cosmique.

En effet, Bernanos en est resté plus ou moins là où il avait commencé, n'arrivant pas à élargir sa vision. Dominé par un petit nombre de rêves qui se répètent de roman en roman, il a puisé la plupart de ses personnages dans deux sources principales: le rêve du prêtre—bon ou mauvais—et le rêve de l'adolescent. Donissan, Mouchette, Chantal de Clergerie, Chevance, Cénabre, le curé d'Ambricourt, Olivier Mainville, Steeny, André Gaspard, la nouvelle Mouchette sont tous ou des adolescents ou des prêtres. L'univers de Dostoïevsky par contre offre beaucoup plus de diversité. Si l'on s'en tient aux principaux personnages des quatre grands romans du maître russe, on voit qu'ils ne se ressemblent pas: qu'est-ce que Raskolnikov, les quatre Karamazov, le prince Mychkine ou Stavroguine ont en commun?

Il n'est pas question de nier le génie de Bernanos—son incarnation de Satan dans *Sous le Soleil de Satan* dépasse de loin celle de Dostoïevsky dans *Les Frères Karamazov*—mais seulement d'en constater les limites, ou plutôt la spécificité. Bernanos n'a pas su—ou voulu—multiplier et diversifier ses personnages. Pourquoi? Pour répondre à cette question il faut situer Bernanos dans sa propre tradition littéraire et spirituelle.

iii

Enfant de souche française, Bernanos était nourri d'auteurs classiques tels que Racine et Corneille, même si c'est de Balzac qu'il se réclame au début de sa carrière.[4] L'idéal classique, c'est-à-dire la présentation du drame intérieur sans trop de références au monde extérieur, se retrouve d'ailleurs dans l'oeuvre

---

[4]*Le Crépuscule des Vieux* (Paris: Gallimard, 1956), pp. 63-64.

de Bernanos. Le conflit intérieur présenté, tout est joué. Par exemple le drame de Simone Alfieri dans *Un Mauvais Rêve* est certainement aussi vraisemblable que celui de Raskolnikov. Mais Simone n'est pas rachetée[5] par l'amour et l'expiation comme c'est le cas pour Raskolnikov. Il semble que Bernanos ait été incapable d'envisager son héroïne dans un monde autre que celui dont elle sort une fois pour toutes en assassinant la tante d'Olivier. Remarquons que la réincarnation de Simone dans le personnage d'Evangéline d'*Un Crime* est toujours centrée sur la culpabilité et non pas sur le rachat.

La vision cosmique de Bernanos serait-elle plus noire que celle de Dostoïevsky? Les grands romans de Dostoïevsky se referment sur une sorte d'acceptation du monde, de la vie de l'homme, de son existence tragique et de sa propension à la souffrance. Une telle vision n'est évidente que dans un seul roman de Bernanos: le *Journal d'un curé de campagne*. Mais l'obscurité dans laquelle se terminent *Sous le Soleil de Satan*, *L'Imposture*, *La Joie*, *Un Crime*, *Un Mauvais Rêve* et *Nouvelle Histoire de Mouchette* n'est guère rassurante. D'ailleurs même le *Journal d'un curé de campagne* a paru suffoquant à de nombreux lecteurs, surtout aux non-croyants. A ces mêmes lecteurs, la mort de la Prieure dans *Dialogues des Carmélites*, l'oeuvre la plus lumineuse de Bernanos, paraît également scandaleuse et peu en accord avec une vision chrétienne du monde.

Il est remarquable, par ailleurs, que le même lecteur non-croyant ne soit pas choqué par la vision chrétienne de Dostoïevsky, telle qu'elle s'exprime dans le personnage du Starets Zosime ou celui d'une Sonia dans *Crime et Châtiment*. Sans doute est-ce parce que l'intrigue romanesque n'est pas centrée sur ces personnages. Même Aliocha dans *Les Frères Karamazov* n'est qu'un des frères de ce nom.[6]

Dostoïevsky nous présente toute une gamme de personnages, et les chrétiens dans l'ensemble de cette présentation, comme dans le monde réel, ne semblent pas tout dominer. Bref, on n'a jamais accusé Dostoïevsky d'avoir écrit des "romans orthodoxes." Car l'orthodoxie n'est qu'un aspect de la vision cosmique du romancier russe, bien que la foi orthodoxe demeure l'élément unificateur de cette vision. On peut se demander, dès lors, si l'orientation même de la spiritualité orthodoxe ne pourrait expliquer le caractère cosmique de l'univers dostoïevskien.

La spiritualité orthodoxe, comme le culte ou la piété populaire, ne s'est jamais fixée sur une image exclusive; elle est caractérisée, au contraire, par la diversité de ses images religieuses. Alors que l'Eglise romaine s'est orientée vers une piété officielle et cléricale centrée sur le Saint Sacrement comme Image suprême, les Orthodoxes n'ont rien changé à leur culte de l'icône. En outre, pour l'Orthodoxe, l'Eglise du Christ n'est pas centrée non plus sur le "Vicaire du Christ sur la terre" qui, lui aussi, a fini par devenir l'Image suprême de la vérité chrétienne pour les Catholiques. Cette concentration de la spiritualité sur une image exclusive n'est peut-être pas tout à fait étrangère à la création et à la conception du personnage chez Bernanos.

---

[5]Voir notre article: "Un Problème de Structure: *Un Mauvais Rêve*, conclusion d'*Un Crime*," *Etudes Bernanosiennes* 11, pp. 7-13.

[6]D'après Paul Evdokimov même Aliocha ne représente qu'une époque de la vie de Dostoïevsky lui-même. Voir *Gogol et Dostoïevsky ou la descente aux enfers* (Paris: Desclée de Brouwer, 1961), p. 269.

Dans les deux oeuvres les plus lumineuses de Bernanos, *Journal d'un curé de campagne* et *Dialogues des Carmélites*, les deux personnages principaux sont officiellement liés à l'Eglise. On a l'impression que Bernanos nourrissait encore le rêve de réconcilier l'Eglise avec le monde.[7] Ces mêmes personnages principaux, le curé d'Ambricourt et Blanche de la Force, sont d'ailleurs tous les deux bien cornéliens: ils s'efforcent de se réconcilier avec leur honneur. Ces deux êtres s'étant donnés à Dieu par vocation, les attaques sur l'honneur de cette vocation ne sauraient en rien empêcher leur rachat à la fin. Car Bernanos, lui, est sûr de cet honneur.

Une telle certitude reste étrangère à l'esprit de l'auteur russe. L'honneur personnel n'est jamais certain chez ses personnages. Certes, chez Bernanos l'honneur d'un Donissan est mis en doute lorsqu'il est condamné à se retirer dans un monastère après son "imprudence," mais nous savons que son honneur personnel prévaut finalement, malgré le miracle raté à la fin du roman. Ainsi en sera-t-il aussi de l'honneur du curé d'Ambricourt, pourtant mis à l'épreuve par la situation ambiguë dans laquelle il mourra (sans sacrements, chez un défroqué) après avoir bravé ses supérieurs ecclésiastiques, pour protéger le secret de la dernière confession de la comtesse. Ainsi encore de l'honneur de Chantal de Clergerie ainsi que de celui de son confesseur, l'abbé Chevance, que menace Cénabre.

Bernanos se montre donc assez fidèle non seulement aux données de Corneille, mais aussi aux données du christianisme occidental où tout un code d'honneur a fleuri et où la chevalerie chrétienne est devenue une sorte d'idéal, celui de la fusion sur cette terre et d'après les lois humaines, des valeurs temporelles et des valeurs éternelles. On sait que Bernanos tenait beaucoup à cette fusion terrestre. Il a même exprimé son espoir dans *Les grands cimetières sous la lune* de voir renaître la chevalerie chrétienne du sol français ainsi que du sol allemand.[8]

Un tel idéal chez un tel auteur sera naturellement réfléchi dans ses écrits, et l'on peut s'attendre à constater une fusion terrestre du temporel avec l'éternel. Cette fusion s'opère d'ailleurs de préférence chez les personnages ecclésiastiques. On ne trouve pas la marque d'une telle préoccupation chez Dostoïevsky. Sans doute est-ce parce que le christianisme de Dostoïevsky, c'est-à-dire celui de l'Eglise orientale, n'a jamais connu de "chevalerie chrétienne." Un saint Alexandre Nevsky pouvait bien défendre l'Orthodoxie contre le Catholicisme allemand et polonais, mais l'idée d'allier l'honneur temporel à l'Eglise est loin de la spiritualité russe qui reste plutôt personnelle. Ce n'est donc pas une question d'honneur, mais de péché et de rémission du péché qui alimente le drame des personnages de Dostoïevsky. Au fond de la vaste vision cosmique de l'Orthodoxie universelle, le pécheur et le saint s'assoient *ensemble* au banquet des noces mystiques du Christ ressuscité.

Bernanos, malgré l'authenticité de sa vision chrétienne, n'est jamais allé aussi loin. Aucun personnage chez lui n'embrasse la terre comme le font

---

[7]Dans l'interview de 1926 publié dans *Le Crépuscule des Vieux*, Bernanos exprime l'idée que Balzac "ne s'est pas élevé à la notion la plus générale, universelle, de l'humain, au réalisme catholique" (p. 64). De même il parle de "reprendre de ce point de vue toute l'oeuvre de Dostoïevsky, par exemple, ou celle de Balzac même" (p. 83). Notons bien que Bernanos y défend l'idée du *réalisme catholique*.

[8]*Les Grands Cimetières sous la lune* (Paris: Plon, 1938), p. 359.

Aliocha et Raskolnikov. Les personnages de Bernanos, comme les personnages de Corneille, restent au centre de leur propre drame et il n'est pas toujours évident que ce drame finisse en Dieu. Ce qui est certain chez Bernanos, c'est que le drame demeure centré sur le personnage principal; il ne s'étend pas aux dimensions de l'univers, où le personnage principal ne jouerait qu'un rôle bien personnel. Quel contraste avec les romans de Dostoïevsky, où on trouve une sorte de panorama du cosmos entier plutôt que la seule analyse d'un personnage particulier, comme microcosme de la race humaine.

iv

Le monde romanesque de Bernanos baigne donc dans une atmosphère ecclésiastique. Chez Dostoïevsky, par contre, l'Eglise en tant qu'institution ne joue pas un rôle prépondérant. Ce sont le plus souvent des êtres en marge de l'Eglise visible qui parlent pour le Christ. La certitude de trouver la vérité dans le monde autour de lui plutôt qu'au sein d'une institution, semble donc émaner, chez Dostoïevsky, de la conviction que le rôle de l'Eglise du Christ dépasse tout système—surtout celui de Rome.

Bernanos était certainement tenté par un tel point de vue, comme le manifestent les incarnations de Mouchette: la première est rachetée par un prêtre, la deuxième ne l'est pas. Mais sa formation catholique l'a emporté. C'est ce qui explique, à mon sens, le fait que le prêtre demeure l'incarnation privilégiée de ses obsessions créatrices. Bernanos semble même avoir été incapable d'envisager un monde où l'Eglise romaine serait dépourvue de toute puissance temporelle. Sa tentation de surmonter cet obstacle, de sortir de cette donnée étroite d'un monde *encadré* par l'Eglise visible, demeure néanmoins évidente. Dans *La Nouvelle Histoire de Mouchette* c'est l'auteur lui-même, en tant que chrétien, qui représente l'Eglise en confiant, dès la page dédicatoire, son personnage à la miséricorde de Dieu.

On peut donc affirmer que si les deux auteurs se rejoignent par l'importance qu'ils accordent à l'Evangile dans leur vision chrétienne, ils se distinguent l'un de l'autre par leur expérience de l'Eglise. On ne saurait s'étonner du fait que Bernanos, formé dans sa jeunesse par des prêtres—voire des jésuites— essaie de rester fidèle à la présentation d'une image suprême de la vérité chrétienne. Rien d'ailleurs dans la tradition classique française, ne s'opposait à ce que cette présentation soit faite à partir d'un conflit personnel de type cornélien.

Bernanos est donc demeuré fidèle à sa formation française, tant littéraire que chrétienne. Ce qui est curieux chez lui, c'est qu'il semble parfois, en partant de ces deux données, s'égarer dans la direction des frontières de la littérature russe et de la spiritualité orthodoxe. C'est sans doute ce qui lui a valu d'être appelé, de temps en temps, un "Dostoïevsky français."

University of Western Ontario
London, Ontario

La Nausee and the Avators of Being

By Eugenia N. Zimmerman

Students of twentieth century literature are familiar with the classical position of Academia: namely, the only good author is a dead author. Such an attitude is understandable. A living author is dangerous, since he may, at any moment, send crashing down about their ears the cherished, yet problematic, constructions of his interpreters. And few are more dangerous than Jean-Paul Sartre, who, as he has frequently told his readers, delights in contradiction, in bastardy and betrayal, refuses to be bound by his past work, and looks to the future for meaning and value.[1] Yet Sartre criticism proliferates, and the scholars, although

---

[1]For Sartre's attitude to the future, see *L'Etre et le Néant* (Paris: Gallimard, 1943) and *Les Mots* (Paris: Gallimard, 1964). For Sartre's notion of the traitor and the bastard, see *Saint Genet: comédien et martyr* (Paris: Gallimard, 1953) and Francis Jeanson, *Sartre par lui même* (Paris: Seuil, 1961).

handicapped by Sartre's stubborn refusal to give up the ghost as well as by the absence of published correspondence, diaries and critical editions, can nevertheless make statements, at least about some of the texts, which have a chance of remaining valid in the years to come.

Such a text is *La Nausée*. With publication in the early 1960's of Simone de Beauvoir's *La Force de l'âge* and *La Force des choses* and of Sartre's own autobiographical essay *Les Mots*, certain limits have been imposed upon interpretive criticism. It is no longer possible to say, as did Iris Murdoch in 1953, that in *La Nausée*, "[Sartre] is patently uninterested in the esthetic solution."[2] We now know from Simone de Beauvoir's description of Sartre's attitude to literature and from Sartre's own analysis of his childhood[3] that the esthetic solution, far from being a mechanical device to finish off the story, is the very substance of *La Nausée*.

The argument of the novel is familiar. Antoine Roquentin, after what appears to be an adventurous past, settles in Bouville with the intention of doing an historical study of the Marquis de Rollebon. He leads a solitary life, with few human contacts, on the fringe of all social and institutionalized activities. When he is not doing research in the municipal library, he wanders through the town and observes the behavior of its inhabitants and, specifically, the *bourgeoisie* whom he calls *salauds*. Sporadic nausea, provoked in him by the world of things as well as by his own body, reveals to him what he terms "Existence" while, contrapuntally, a recording of an American popular song, "Some of These Days," gives him intimations of what he learns to define as "Being." In the course of these experiences, he gives up as vain his attempt at historical reconstruction and projects instead the creation of a work of art—a novel—as his only hope for salvation: deliverance from the horrors of Existence and access to the blessed realm of Being.

Unwillingly, and at the price of progressively increasing discomfort, Roquentin is thrown into a symbolic voyage, in the course of which revelations are offered him concerning the nature of Existence and the nature of Being. When the voyage ends, illusory appearances are destroyed and Roquentin perceives fundamental, previously hidden realities.

The revelation of Existence is gradual and fairly straight-forward. It imposes itself on Roquentin with greater and greater insistence. Deepening in intensity, signaled by recurrent bouts of nausea, it culminates in the ecstatic cry of the visionary fulfilled: "Et tout d'un coup, . . . le voile s'est déchiré, j'ai compris, j'ai *vu*."[4]

Roquentin has seen and understood that the world of things and the world of his own body are in a state of gratuity, bereft of significance, characterized by aimless proliferation: "Nous étions un tas d'existants . . . embarrassés de nous-mêmes, nous n'avions pas la moindre raison d'être là . . . chaque existant . . . se sentait de trop par rapport aux autres." (p. 181) Roquentin is as much implicated in Existence as any phenomenon of the world of things. His status as *Homo Sapiens*, that privileged being created in God's image and given dominion over the earth has been gradually eroded:

---

[2]*Sartre: Romantic Rationalist* (New Haven: Yale University Press, 1967), p. 13.

[3]See *La Force de l'âge* (Paris: Gallimard, 1960).

[4]Jean-Paul Sartre, *La Nausée* (Paris: Gallimard–Livre de poche). All quotations are from this edition. Unless otherwise noted, all italics are Sartre's own.

> En vain cherchais-je à *compter* les marronniers, et les *situer* ...
> à comparer leur hauteur avec celle des platanes: chacun d'eux s'échappait
> des relations où je cherchais à l'enfermer ... Ces relations (que je
> m'obstinais à maintenir pour retarder l'écroulement du monde humain,
> des mesures, des quantités, des directions) j'en sentais l'arbitraire; elles
> ne mordaient plus sur les choses. (p. 181)

Inherent in the destruction of the human world of definitions and relationships is the destruction of language. Just as man was privileged, so was language the sign of his privilege: Adam dominated the universe by his capacity to name. Language gave the world form and kept it under control: "Je murmure: c'est une banquette, un peu comme un exorcisme. Mais le mot reste sur mes lèvres: il refuse d'aller se poser sur la chose. ... Les choses se sont délivrées de leurs noms. ... Ça paraît imbécile de ... dire quoi que ce soit sur elles: je suis au milieu des Choses, les Innomables." (p. 174) When language loses its power, the world of things returns to primeval chaos and drags man along with it into the obscenity of being *de trop*: "Et *moi* [sic]— veule, alangui, obscène, digérant, ballotant de mornes pensées—*moi aussi j'étais de trop.* (p. 181) Such, then, is the world of Existence, a world with which Roquentin must come to terms, since he, as an incarnated consciousness, is not exempt. His attempt at coming to terms with Existence takes the form of an anguished search for Being.

Being is all that Existence is not: "... dans un autre monde, les cercles, les airs de musique gardent leurs lignes pures et rigides. Mais l'existence est un fléchissement." (p. 181) Being is not the natural world, nor is it the world of things nor the world of human bodies. It does not lie within the province of biology nor of physics; it cannot be scientifically proven. It is quite probably not phenomenal at all, but rather numinous in origin.[5]

The search for Being, free of nausea, is physically less painful than the experience of Existence. It is, however, spiritually more difficult. The revelations granted are ambiguous, the dissipation of appearances, tortuous and subtle. The problem of appearances is complicated by the fact that Roquentin must learn to distinguish between false idols and the true reality. Until the idols are broken, reality will not be correctly understood.

Consequently, Being, which holds forth the promise of salvation, can be attained only when pseudo-Being—inauthentic Being—is unmasked and its falsehoods repudiated. Since Roquentin is obliged to explore not only the uncleanliness of Existence, but also the shifting forms of Being, it is proper to consider *La Nausée* as, among other things, a study in the avatars of Being.

Inauthentic Being takes two forms: deliberate inauthentic Being, and accidental inauthentic Being. In relation to the former, Roquentin is a lucid and caustic observer; to the latter, an honest, if bewildered and erring seeker.

Roquentin identifies deliberate inauthentic Being with the *Salauds*, the *bourgeoisie*, a class Sartre has all his life hated with fierce consistency. The *Salauds* are the chief and unforgivable offenders since they have manufactured inauthentic Being through their bad faith. As Sartre showed in "L'Enfance d'un

---

[5]On one occasion, however, the phenomenal world seems to offer Roquentin a quality similar to Being: the Boulevard Noir, "inhumain. Comme un minéral." (p. 43).

chef,"[6] the *bourgeois* is he who refuses to accept responsibility for the creation of his identity through acts freely chosen, but prefers rather to believe that what he does corresponds to a preestablished framework in which he need only insert himself and to a preestablished code of values he can unthinkingly follow:

> [Les dames en noir] jettent de côté des regards . . . sur la statue de Gustave Impétraz. . . . Elles . . . voient bien que ce fut quelqu'un du beau monde. . . . c'est un peu comme si leur grand-père était là . . . coulé en bronze. . . . Au service de leurs petites idées étroites et solides il a mis son autorité . . . Les dames en noir se sentent soulagées . . . les saintes idées, les bonnes idées qu'elles tiennent de leurs pères, elles n'ont plus la responsabilité de les défendre; un homme de bronze s'en est fait le gardien. (pp. 45-46)

Another aspect of inauthentic Being promulgated by the *Salauds* is the concept of Rights. It is brought out clearly in the section devoted to Roquentin's visit to the Bouville museum: "[Jean Parrotin] avait la simplicité d'une idée. Il ne restait plus en lui que des os, des chairs mortes et le Droit Pur. . . . Quand le Droit s'est emparé d'un homme, il n'est pas exorcisme qui puisse la chasser; Jean Parrotin avait consacré toute sa vie à penser son Droit. . . ." (p. 128) To believe we have fixed, immutable Rights that establish our essence once and for all and that need never be called into question is to deny that terrifying reality whose name is Existence: "Tout est gratuit, ce jardin, cette ville et moi-même. . . . voilà la Nausée; voilà ce que les Salauds . . . essaient de se cacher avec leur idée de droit. Mais quel pauvre mensonge: personne n'a le droit; ils sont entièrement gratuits, comme les autres hommes, ils n'arrivent pas à ne pas se sentir de trop." (p. 185) Inauthentic Being, as brought into the world by the *Salauds*, is therefore intellectual dishonesty and moral cowardice, willful choosing of false perceptions and conscious distortion, through fear and laziness, of the revealed truth.

There is, however, a more comprehensive form of inauthentic Being. It is the philosophy of Humanism. Humanism, as Sartre defined it in the 1930's,[7] is a set of generalities and abstractions which permit us to ignore the concrete reality of men, all of them gratuitous existants, in favor of the false intellectual construction, Man: "Ce que ces toiles sombres offraient à mes regards, c'était l'homme repensé par l'homme, avec . . . la plus belle conquête de l'homme: le bouquet des Droits de l'homme et du Citoyen. J'admirai sans arrière-pensée le règne humain." (p. 129)

Humanism is not only the property of the *Salauds*; it is also the point of view advocated by that pathetic figure, the Autodidact. Roquentin's attitude toward the Autodidact is ambivalent. He is disgusted by his philosophical position, but he cannot help pitying him as an eventual victim of the *Salauds*. Unlike the *bourgeoisie* who uses Humanism both to avoid facing reality and to justify its position as a ruling class, the Autodidact uses Humanism to escape from his loneliness:

---

[6]*Le Mur* (Paris: Gallimard–Livre de poche, 1939), pp. 131-249.

[7]Sartre's attitude to humanism later changes. In his pamphlet, *L'Existentialisme est un humanisme* (Paris: Nagel, 1946), he gives this term a much more favorable sense.

> Je contemple l'Autodidacte avec un peu de remords: il s'est complu toute la semaine à imaginer ce déjeuner, où il pourrait faire part à un autre homme de son amour des hommes.... Au fond il est aussi seul que moi ... Seulement il ne se rend pas compte de sa solitude.... ce n'était pas à moi de lui ouvrir les yeux.... Je rage ... mais pas contre lui, contre ... les autres, tous ceux qui ont empoisonné cette cervelle.... L'Autodidacte est ... quelqu'un de mon bord, qui a trahi par ignorance, par bonne volonté!" (pp. 171-72)

Thus, the presence of the Autodidact allows a more subtle delineation of inauthentic Being. Inauthentic Being is not always the result of vicious error; it can also be caused by good-natured weakness and basic emotional needs.

Roquentin himself is not completely guiltless in this respect. In his flight from Existence, he inadvertently makes other forms of inauthentic Being appear. These forms of inauthentic Being are accidental. They are caused neither by the deliberate bad faith characteristic of the *Salauds* nor by the intellectual confusion emanating from the Autodidact. They come rather through misinterpretation, deceptive appearances or disappointed hopes.

One of these forms is the *aventure*. For Roquentin, an adventure is less a question of content than of manner. That he has traveled in Asia and led what others might consider an adventurous life is not enough for him: "Je n'ai pas eu d'aventures. Il m'est arrivé des histoires, des événements, des incidents, tout ce qu'on voudra. Mais pas des aventures." (p. 58)

Thus, an adventure is inauthentic Being not because it is undesirable, but because it promises falsely a quality of experience impossible on the level of lived reality.

Similar in nature to the adventure are the *situation privilégiée* and the *moment parfait*. They are explicated by Roquentin's former mistress, Anny: "[Les situations privilégiées] étaient des situations qui avaient une qualité tout à fait rare et précieuse, du style ... (p. 207) [;] la situation privilégiée ... entre dans la vie des gens. Alors la question se pose de savoir si on veut en faire un moment parfait." (p. 208)

Just as Roquentin was forced to admit that he had not really had any adventures, so did Anny come to realize that there are no privileged situations:

> "Je croyais que la haine, l'amour ou la mort descendait sur nous, comme des langues de feu du Vendredi saint.... Quelle erreur! ... je pensais que ça existait "la Haine," que ça venait se poser sur les gens et les élever au-dessus d'eux-mêmes. Naturellement, il n'y a que moi, moi qui hais, moi qui aime. Et alors ça, moi, c'est toujours la même chose, une pâte qui s'allonge ..." (p. 211)

Anny and Roquentin use the same terminology—*qualité rare et précieuse* —to describe what once had given meaning to their lives; they have undergone parallel experiences: "C'est ça, c'est bien ça. Il n'y a pas d'aventures— il n'y a pas de moments parfaits ... [*sic*] nous avons perdu les mêmes illusions, nous avons suivi les mêmes chemins." (p. 210)

What Anny and Roquentin had seen as transfiguring and redemptive experiences, they now perceive as self-deceptions. Under the façade of inauthentic Being lies the terrible insipidity of Existence.

Yet another form of inauthentic Being remains to be examined. Roquentin not only learns to do without the comforts of the past—the notion of adventure—, he also reluctantly gives up his hope in the present: his historical study of the Marquis de Rollebon.

The Monday after his visit to the museum, he noted: "Je n'écris plus mon livre sur Rollebon: c'est fini, je ne *peux* plus l'écrire. Qu'est-ce que je vais faire de ma vie?" (p. 136) To write such a book was for him not merely an act of amateur scholarship, but an attempt to avoid the gratuity of Existence: "M. de Rollebon . . . s'était emparé de ma vie pour me *représenter* la sienne. Je ne m'apercevais plus que j'existais, je n'existais plus en moi, mais en lui . . . chacun de mes mouvements avait son sens au-dehors, là, juste en face de moi, en lui . . ." (p. 141-142)

With M. de Rollebon no longer furnishing justifications, Roquentin loses hope of escaping Existence: "La chose, qui attendait . . . a fondu sur moi . . . la Chose, c'est moi. L'existence, libérée, dégagée, reflue sur moi. j'existe." (p. 141) The triumph of Existence seems complete. Roquentin, incapable of accepting the inauthentic Being of the *Salauds* or the Autodidact, is equally incapable of living by the inauthentic Being of adventure or of historical reconstruction.

There is, however, in *La Nausée*, one realm in which Existence has no power. It is the esthetic, the realm of the work of art, the only authentic incarnation of Being. Intimations of the esthetic appear throughout the novel, in the very formulation of pseudo-Being itself. Indeed, the inauthenticity of certain forms of Being lies precisely in the fact that esthetic criteria are wrongly applied to lived reality, and lived reality, judged by such criteria, is found wanting.

Thus, Anny discovered privileged situations through engravings: "[Les situations privilégiées] étaient celles qu'on représentait sur les gravures. C'est moi qui les appelais privilégiées, je me disais qu'elles devaient avoir une importance bien considérable pour qu'on eût consenti à en faire le sujet ces images si rares." (p. 206) Roquentin, for his part, saw the concept of adventure as linked to that of narration: "pour que l'événement le plus banal devienne une aventure, il faut et il suffit qu'on se mette à le *raconter*." (p. 60)

It is only when Roquentin renounces the world of lived reality and turns to the world of the esthetic that he glimpses the possibility of salvation. For him, the basic revelatory experience is music. In the recording of "Some of These Days," he finds the perfect image of Being: "Il y a un autre bonheur: au-dehors, il y a cette bande d'acier, l'étroite durée de la musique, qui traverse notre temps de part en part, et le refuse et le déchire de ses sèches petites pointes; il y a un autre temps." (p. 37) The time of the phenomenal world, irrevocably in bondage to Existence, is overcome by the time of the numinous world of true Being, of rigor and of grace.

Toward the end of the novel, Roquentin sees the full implications of the numinous world: "Cette petite douceur de diamant n'existe pas, puisqu'elle n'a rien de trop: c'est tout le reste qui est trop par rapport à elle. Elle *est*." (p. 244) The song "Some of These Days" belongs to the realm of Being, and through its intercession, the composer and the singer responsible for it are saved: "En voilà deux qui sont sauvés . . . Ils sont un peu pour moi comme des morts, un peu comme des héros de roman: ils se sont lavés du péché d'exister. Pas complètement, bien sûr—mais tout autant qu'un homme peut faire." (pp. 247-48)

The composer and the singer, once drawn into the world of the esthetic, become esthetic figures themselves, characters in a novel, and it is to something very much like the novel that Roquentin directs himself when he contemplates his own possibilities for esthetic creation: ". . . il faudrait qu'on devine, derrière les mots imprimés . . . quelque chose . . . qui serait au-dessus de l'existence. Une histore, par exemple, comme il ne peut en arriver, une aventure. Il faudrait qu'elle soit belle et dure comme de l'acier et qu'elle fasse honte aux gens de leur existence." (pp. 248-249)

La Nausée, as do all of Sartre's significant literary and philosophical texts, bears witness to the presence of two antithetically different modes of reality: the reality of Existence and the reality of Being.[8] Yet *La Nausée* occupies a particular position in what will one day be the Sartrean canon. Although Sartre deals with the work of art in other contexts,[9] nowhere but in *La Nausée* does he allow it such a privileged role. Nowhere else is it permitted to monopolize the world of Being in quite the same way.

It is *La Nausée*'s deification of the work of art that makes Sartre, at least in the early part of his literary career, the reluctant disciple of a writer for whom he has expressed considerable dislike—Marcel Proust.[10] The esthetic solution is the *raison d'être* of *La Nausée* just as it was the *raison d'être* of *A la recherche du temps perdu*. In both cases, salvation comes from the work of art. Marcel was offered the possibility of escape from Time through the recapturing of lost Time, and Roquentin, the possibility of substituting for the Time of Existence the Time of Being.

Yet neither in *A la recherche du temps perdu* nor in *La Nausée* did the protagonist come to his knowledge of salvation lightly. Marcel had to painfully learn to renounce the illusion of the social world before the definitive esthetic revelation was given him. Roquentin was prepared, by a series of overwhelming experiences, for a new and dearly-bought awareness of the double nature of reality: Existence, concommitant with nausea, and Being, limited to and concommitant with the work of art.

Carleton University
Ottawa, Canada

---

[8]Sartre's conception of Being is modified in his later writing. In *L'Etre et le Néant*, Being cannot be attained at all; in *Saint Genet*, it is placed in an unfavorable light, linked to the Good, the *status quo* and the *bourgeoisie*.

[9]See for example, the conclusion of *L'Imaginaire* (Paris: Gallimard, 1940); the fourth part of *L'Etre et le Néant*: "Avoir, Faire et Etre; *Situations II* (Paris: Gallimard, 1948).

[10]See *Situations II*, pp. 20-21.

J. Kostka

Cocteau's
Les Enfants terribles
As a Blind Text[1]

J. Kostke

By Leon S. Roudiez

At the outset of *Les Enfants terribles* "La cité Monthiers" provides both
the first words of the text and the setting for the first (unnumbered) chapter

[1] I have borrowed the idea of a "blind text" from Julia Kristeva's notion of *texte
clos*. Such a text is essentially expression or *mimesis* (as opposed to a text conceived
of as "productive"), circumscribed by an ideological system within which the narrator
himself is located; as the system posits that meaning must precede statement, there is no
way the latter can break out. Trapped in the system, the text is blind to any possibility
that might lie outside of it. See Kristeva's *Le Texte du roman* (Paris: Mouton, 1970) and
the chapter "Le Texte clos" in her *Recherches pour une sémanalyse* (Paris: Seuil, 1969).
I use the word "blind," for which I find conceptual justification in Louis Althusser's
Lire le Capital (Paris: Maspero, 1970), in order to distinguish this concept from that
involving the open/closed nature of a text as developed by Umberto Eco in his *Opera
Aperta*, which I read in the French translation, *L'Œuvre ouverte* (Paris: Seuil, 1965).

of the narrative. The *cité* is a microcosm of the contemporary world, although it is an ambivalent one. When filled with school children, it emphasizes the primitive violence of that world (note the words or phrases like *instincts animaux, rites obscurs, victimes, jugements sommaires, supplices,* and *sacrifices humains* on pp. 5-6);[2] at other times it is a quiet enclave of bourgeois culture that is protected against anxiety. But while that area is protected it is also caught within the confines of the city it seeks to negate: "La cité Monthiers se trouve prise..." Those initial half-dozen words stand as a microcosm of the entire narrative, which both portrays an attempted escape from reality and inscribes it in a circular pattern caught in the prevailing ideology from which it cannot escape.

Prise indirectly suggests the snuffing of tobacco and also of heroin. On the fourth page of the book a heavy snowfall is described; in both English and French, snow (*neige*) is slang for cocaine. Drugs are thus present at the start of the narrative, appearing in the text in the fashion of a watermark and seen only in its transparency. They characterize the kind of escape from the world that is involved here; they also point to the futility of such an escape. As the snow keeps falling, the *cité* becomes a ghostly salon (*salon fantôme*, p. 7). Death is introduced into the text through the connotations of *fantôme* and by a textual echo as well. Late in the narrative, the hall in the town house that belonged to Michael, who is dead at that time, conjures up memories of the first snowfall and of "the whole of the *cité* Monthiers, which the snow had reduced to the size of a hall" (p. 146). The *cité* is where Paul is hurt, the hall is where he dies. The very words *drogue* and *opium* make their appearance in the text, but as they do those signs deny their referents: "Taking drugs, for them, would have been like adding white to white or black to black ... But drugs existed. From the time of their birth Elizabeth and Paul carried those fabulous substances in their blood" (p. 123). That is typical of the entire text of a novel in which meaning is constantly at odds with statement.

As all readers of Cocteau's novel will remember, the story is caught between two very similar events. They are so similar, in fact, as to make the final one seem like a repetition of the first. Early in *Les Enfants terribles* Paul falls victim to what the narrator calls a "dark blow" (*un coup sombre,* p. 12). He has been struck by a snowball aimed at him by Dargelos, whose cheeks are flushed with fire (*les joues en feu*). Gérard saves Paul, so to speak, by taking him home to Elizabeth and the famous "room"; in other words, Gérard has led him to a metaphorical death where he will remain, sheltered from reality. Toward the end of the book Dargelos sends Paul a dark ball (*boule sombre*, p. 192), presumably a poison or a drug (corresponding to the *neige* of the earlier ball); its inside is reddish in color (echoing that of Dargelos' cheeks), and it is delivered by Gérard. The latter thus "saves" Paul a second time, in a degraded fashion, as he unwittingly pushes him in the direction of actual death. Inserted into the middle of the narrative, like a *mise en abyme*, the event is symbolically restated as Agathe "strikes" Paul with a snapshot of Dargelos. In effect, both Dargelos and Agathe are symbols of a reality that fascinates Paul, in the full meaning of the

---

[2]References throughout are to *Les Enfants terribles* (Paris: Grasset, 1929). The translations are my own.

verb, but with which he is powerless to cope. The ending of the narrative confirms the beginning as metaphor becomes fact: since one cannot change reality, he tries to escape through the poetry of death—but poetry does not afford sufficient protection, and the only true escape is death itself.

The white snowball contrasts with the ball of poison just as the room of Paul and Elizabeth does with reality; it is only fitting that the snowball leads the reader into the room. The narrative appears to gravitate about those two poles of black and white (or darkness and light), eventually sinking toward the former; as it does, red emerges as a possible solution to the implied conflict, and it constitutes a correlative to the room itself. There can be no solution in Cocteau's narrative, however, for if red is at the beginning associated with passion (*le feu de Dargelos*, p. 20) it is later sublimated in the theatrical rituals of the room (when a red cloth is used to cover the lamp) and finally enrobed in black and bound with death (the inside of the ball of poison). Never, of course, does it come anywhere close to suggesting revolutionary change. A couple of pages before the end, brightness, red, and darkness appear in characteristic interplay within one sentence: "The harsh light of the lamp took the place of dusk, except in the direction of Elizabeth upon whom shone the crimson of the red cloth strip; she remained there, protected, spinning a void, hauling Paul towards the darkness from which she watched him, as he lay in full light" (p. 213). Life or reality is too harsh to bear and Elizabeth attempts to draw Paul into the safety of poetry; but red and darkness have in that sentence become practically synonymous, with the latter about to engulf the room and its two protagonists.

In order to enter the room a person needs to sever his connections with the world, a circumstance that stresses the analogy between the room and death. Paul's and Elizabeth's father is dead, their mother is dying; by the time the reader reaches page 62, she is dead. Gérard is an orphan, and so is Agathe. From Cocteau's standpoint, such details could well have been introduced as a means of respecting verisimilitude, but the effect is quite opposite. It becomes even more striking where Michael is concerned. "At first glance one knew he belonged on earth; that is where he owned everything he had, and only his racing cars occasionally made him dizzy" (p. 135). He could not cut his ties with the world without ceasing to be what he was; therefore he must undergo real death in order to enter the room. "The living scarf, in strangling him, had opened the doors of the room to him. He never would have entered otherwise" (p. 142). Something similar happens to Dargelos. After he throws pepper into the principal's face, he is expelled from school and almost literally disappears. As Gérard explains, "People like him don't leave addresses" (p. 53). The exclusion from school amounts to banishment from the world—school, after all, is the children's world. In what at first may seem no more than irony, the narrator says that Dargelos was expelled because there is no death penalty in a *lycée*.[3] On the operative level of the text, however, it seems clear that the statement sets up the analogy: expulsion = death. As a result of such a "death," "all that is left" (p. 53) of Dargelos, a photograph, is placed in the room's treasure chest.

---

[3]There is a narrator in this novel, whose links with the author I shall not presume to unravel, who reveals his existence when he writes, *nos jeunes héros* (p. 68); *Est-il presque besoin de l'écrire?* (p. 140); *Nous avons parlé d'une aptitude* (p. 141).

In most cultures, death is a highly ritualized event. Thus, and although such rituals were most probably conceived as poetic shelter against life, it comes as no surprise to find strong ritualistic features attached to the room. Again, statement, which suggests poetry, is at odds with meaning, which points toward death. The word *rite* actually makes its initial appearance when activities of the school children in the *cité* are described; at the same time, there are references to the "dark instincts of childhood" and to "animal instincts" (p. 5). The rites are *obscures* and are likened to those of a primitive religion. The pattern of the narrative, which was set in the first line of the text, is thus confirmed. Caught within a bourgeois, romantic ideology, it can only go back, not forward. Blinded by the wrongs of the present it can only move in a circle and oppose to them a Golden Age of the past. In this instance it is a myth of primitive society that is embodied in childhood, the childhood of individual man corresponding to an early stage of society. With the word *obscure*, however, the seed of destruction is inserted into the rituals that attempt to revive a lost paradise—and the rituals in the narrative must end in death. In the room itself, they begin by losing touch with reality. Cocteau's exalted childhood is "a serious, heroic, mysterious reality" (p. 22) that is assimilated to an "enchantment" (*féerie*) practically within the same breath as its reality is stated. In that enchanted realm it is impossible either to conceive of death or to comprehend life to the fullest (p. 20).

As Gérard takes Paul back to Elizabeth after the snowball incident, another word is used to refer to childhood rites, the "game"—"that is what Paul called the semi-conscious state into which children immerse themselves" (p. 23). During the brief taxi ride the brightness of street lights, the whiteness of the snow, memories of Dargelos' "fire" and of Paul's blood, and the red glow of a fire truck combine to negate the evening darkness and act as an introduction to the room; words such as *noir*, *nuit*, or *sombre*, all of which one might have expected under the circumstances, are absent from the text. The firemen suggest at the same time the rescue mission they are engaged in and the conflagration or possible tragedy they are driving to; they constitute a correlative to the narrative, which attempts a rescue and ends up in death. Red fails to reconcile white and black, possibly because within the ideology of *Les Enfants terribles* the dialectic process cannot function; only black is real—which is to say that reality is unacceptable. White, through the slang meaning of "snow," is degraded into a drug, that is, a form of escape in which reality can be ignored. Red becomes theatrical—something of a game, a shift made possible by the ambiguity of the French word *jeu*—as the fire horn accompanies it with a "human, inhuman" sound and the firemen are transfigured into allegorical representations—"men with golden helmets, set up like allegories" (p. 23). Gérard, thinking back to that preliminary leg of a journey that will take Paul and Elizabeth out of this world, characterizes it with the word *fabuleuse* (p. 33). In other words, it is a journey leading into a fairy world of the past.

The event that triggers the narration (the snowball thrown by Dargelos) has an unsettling effect and patterns do not fall into place at once. Paul and Elizabeth's room does of course reveal some of its basic characteristics. It is windowless, hence a correlative to Elizabeth's virginity, her protected status. The lack of windows also symbolizes its isolation, a feature that is emphasized when it is likened to a shell (*carapace*, p. 46); it is set apart from everyday reality—"one might have mistaken it for a lumber room" (p. 28), where people store things for which they no longer have any use. Its values are different, too, as demonstrated by the pictures that are displayed on its walls: movie stars, boxers, and murderers, all apparently on an equal footing. The treasure chest is mentioned; the objects it contains have acquired a meaning no longer related to their everyday use (p. 39). One's first impression of the room is one of a true haven, in spite of its peculiarities. But its rites cannot yet be enacted (see pp. 41 and 49); when they are, their falsity will lead to its destruction. Words like *blancheur, neige, éclat, pâle, lumière*, and *blanche* coexist with *ombre, pénombre*, and *rayon noir* and restate the black and white poles of the narrative. At this point, however, there is no red. The two alternatives, acceptance and withdrawal, are present, but there is no attempt either to choose or to reconcile.

With Dargelos' sublimation (his expulsion from school and the promotion of his image into the treasure chest) the situation changes. Ritual now enters the room by means of theatrical references (*grande tragédienne*, p. 54; *geste théâtral, lourde traîne*, p. 56). At the same time, the other-worldliness of the room, as opposed to its mere separateness, is openly stated. Paul and Elizabeth have a rhythm of life that "did not belong to this world" (p. 57). Their room is a place where "the air was pure and brisk" and "nothing heavy, base, or vile could penetrate" (p. 66)—which is to say that it negates reality. The vacation they spend with Gérard and his uncle reveals their ability to take the atmosphere of the room with them wherever they go and calls attention to their "otherness." "Elizabeth hated to associate with people, she despised *the others*" (p. 78). The families that have come to the resort hotel are described as "black, ugly" (p. 79); again the reader is told that "black" is closely linked with reality, that reality is ugly and unacceptable. Withdrawal is hence necessary.

As a consequence, after the children's return from vacation, "the room put out to sea" (p. 87). Everyday reality having been introduced and shown to be incompatible with the spirit of the room, it can be discarded from the narrative. The word "opium" is now directly associated with the activities carried out in the room (p. 87). Theater is no longer alluded to, it is a daily performance with Gérard playing the role of a spectator—"the beds dominated him, like the stage of a theater" (p. 88). Because of the piece of crimson cloth thrown over the lamp, the room acquires a reddish hue. Rituals begin, primitive and unconscious at first: "Perhaps these unsophisticated souls, obeying some order, carried out an operation as disturbing as the one that, at night, closes the petals of a flower" (p. 95). In such a statement, the idea of withdrawal in the presence of darkness is again obvious. It is Elizabeth, conscious or no, who is in charge of the performances, and she is gradually transformed from a common virgin into a virgin priestess, uttering oracles "on those nights when she felt in top condition, under the spell of a god, on a tripod" (p. 97). Later in the text she is the "virgin of the temple" (p. 137) and the "sacred virgin" (p. 144).

Paul, at the same time as he regains his physical strength, comes closer to death. Early in the book, references to him were accompanied by such words as *pâle, triste, infirme, victime, malade*, and *lassitude*, and obvious, physical weakness led to what in this essay has been called metaphorical death. Now, metaphors of death specifically applied to Paul adumbrate the ending. His going to bed resembles an embalmment (p. 94), and as he is about to go to sleep he is pictured as being "delivered, hands and feet bound, to the river of the dead" (p. 99). He no longer breathes the same air as others do (p. 99); he is like a man with his head cut off (p. 99), or like a dead child (p. 100); he sleeps in a sarcophagus (p. 116).

The metaphor of the room sailing the high seas functions in two different ways. Since, within the ideology of the narrative, there is no hope for the future (the golden age always lies in the past), it suggests that eventually the ship must be wrecked. Allusions to sinking or falling are accordingly introduced, in romantic antithesis to images of rising or floating. On the one hand, "the air in the room was lighter than air" (p. 66), and on the other, "the room was sinking" (p. 103). Of special interest is the presence of the word "dark" (*sombre*) within the word "to sink" (*sombrer*), even though there is no etymological connection. Midway through the narrative the reader understands that Elizabeth's fate will be the same as Paul's: she, too, will go down into the darkness "like a captain on board his ship" (p. 103). The sailing metaphor plays, in addition, an intertextual role, introducing the sea and ships of Baudelaire's poetry along with the myth of the *poètes maudits*. It also sends Paul out into the streets—not into reality, however, but in quest of a girl "who might resemble Baudelaire's sonnet" (p. 103).

He does not find her, but eventually Elizabeth does. The orphaned Agathe thus makes her appearance, and the two girls, at first, become united in a "fatal friendship" (p. 114). Paul then recognizes Agathe's name as being the one that "rhymes with frigate in one of the finest poems in existence" (p. 114); the poem, as one might have guessed, is by Baudelaire. Agathe also resembles Dargelos, and when she holds up the latter's picture, which seems like a white blot in the reddish darkness of the room, Paul feels as though he has been hit again. That symbolic blow, coming at the end of part one of the narrative, mirroring the initial event, heralds the intrusion of reality into the room, just as reality had intruded upon the quiet atmosphere of the *cité*. This time it is sexual desire that manifests its presence; on the contrary, the real blow struck by Dargelos at the beginning was linked to "a desire that was chaste, without sex or purpose" (p. 11). The symbolic repetition also foreshadows the final event and sets the stage for a playing out of the conflict between myth and reality that will end with the death of Paul and Elizabeth.

Incidents leading to the double suicide now follow in rapid succession. In keeping with the same antithetical pattern that is imposed upon most of the narrative, as death moves away from the domain of metaphor and comes closer to reality, the imagery that characterizes the setting shifts from primitive religious ritual to contemporary secret societies and to a theater that, whatever its origins might have been, has degenerated to a superficial form of theatricality. The "stage" is set for a repetition of the initial event as the hall in Michael's town house is likened to "la cité Monthiers." Footlights are even provided, as well as "theatrical moonlight" (p. 146). Paul, entering the hall, has an impression of "*déjà vu* derived from a previous life" (p. 152).

The reality of sex separates Paul and Agathe even more than he realizes. "Paul dreamed his love, and at first he did not associate Agathe with it under any terrestrial shape" (p. 158). When he writes to her, he actually addresses the envelope to himself. He is fully identified with the white pole of the narrative; typically, "His white gown brightened the darkness" (p. 180) during one of his sleepwalking spells. As in the beginning, words like *malade* and *langueur* are again tied to Paul. When Gérard brings Dargelos' black ball, Paul imagines himself back in school, a slave to Dargelos (p. 195). On a Sunday, as the snow falls and Elizabeth dreams that Paul is dead, the reader knows that the end is at hand. In the dream, Paul's answer to his sister could be said to describe their idealized life in the room: "Yes, I am dead, but you have just died; that is why you can see me, and we shall always live together" (p. 198). In the hall where Paul is dying, there is "a funeral stench, a black, reddish stench" (p. 200) that metaphorically rejects reality and any possible compromise with it (black and red), calling both evil (stench), but equally unable to avoid a greater evil (death). White reflections from the snow give Paul a "livid mask" with contrasting dark shadows. About him, "the room was sliding down to its doom on a vertiginous incline" (p. 210).

In the meantime, Elizabeth has been following her own downward path. She is both virgin priestess and dramatic actress, and there is tension if not antagonism between those two functions. As soon as theatrical references accompany descriptions of her actions, the connotation of sham also enters the text. At one point the narrator notes, "She was obstinate, she became the part she was acting" (p. 68). While the word *mensonge* is first connected with Paul, Elizabeth's doings become increasingly deceitful until the moment when the reader is told that "she fed on nothing but lies" (p. 186). When she dies, bringing the furniture down with a loud crash, she "transforms the secret room into a theater open to an audience" (p. 214). She has gone from falsehood to sacrilege.

Cocteau no doubt realized that he had told the story of two mythomaniacs whose "life" was a lie. In *Opéra* he also made his famous statement, "I am a lie that always tells the truth." That, however, is not very convincing, for the "truth" of *Les Enfants terribles* is an affirmation of despair. On the one hand, the text extols the impossible values of a lost paradise of childhood; on the other hand, it condemns the contemporary world on account of its ugliness and evil. But Elizabeth and Paul demonstrate that the lost paradise is a myth. Those who survive, in the text, Dargelos, Gérard, and Agathe have, especially the first two, made their peace with the world and joined the "system." Dargelos is in the automobile export business and Gérard has inherited his uncle's industrial plant. Agathe seems less tainted, but in the final sections of the book she stands apart from what the room exemplifies. When the black ball of poison is introduced, she experiences a "bourgeois revulsion" (p. 191); she "remained at the other end of the room" (p. 192); she lives in a "petty atmosphere" (p. 196); during the last moments of Paul and Elizabeth, she "screamed in another place, at another time" (p. 213); and in the last sentence of the narrative, she appears as part of Paul's vision as "a little lady standing on a safety island" (p. 215). She and the stench of the black ball are all that remain as the room disappears—and the stench condemns her, along with Gérard and Dargelos. The choice between total rejection, which can only be achieved in death, and total compromise, which means corruption of the individual, represents the truth that the text proclaims. Love, too, can be attained only in death, which here is clearly a sexual act: "For Elizabeth, as a lover postpones his pleasure to await the partner's, her finger on the trigger, waited for her brother's mortal spasm . . . watched for the splendid moment when they would belong to each other in death" (p. 214). On another level, poetry effects the same kind of rejection of reality—that is, the escapist poetry of a number of romantic writers, of the *poètes maudits*. Nearly everyone, including Cocteau himself, speaks of poetry when discussing this novel; it belongs, like the others, to his *poésie de roman*. One is encouraged to read it as a poem of fate, of which Dargelos would be the personification and Agathe its agent, as suggested by the "fatal" friendship already referred to. One would accept that only if "fate" were to be used as a synonym for ideology. For such an assimilation, however, the word "karma" would be far more apposite. The narrative of *Les Enfants terribles* is caught blindly spinning in the closed circle of its bourgeois ideology. Cocteau claimed to have been surprised by its success, but he need not have been. In this book, he depicted the only truth most of his readers knew, that of their own doom, and they wallowed in it.

Columbia University

Delinquent Parents:
Jules Vallès and *L'Enfant*

By W. D. REDFERN

If there are any teeth in that old saw that French novelists are moralists, who favour universal types, and that English novelists excel rather at the creation of comic eccentrics, then Vallès is closer to the Anglo-Saxon than to his own tradition. What he admired in Dickens, the genius for locating "le côté douloureux des farces et le côté plaisant des tragédies,"[1] reveals his own preferences; and the two writers are further linked by the obsessive theme of martyrised childhood conveyed often by hallucinatory inflation of details. In

---

Page numbers in brackets refer to the edition of *L'Enfant* by Editeurs français réunis (Paris, 1964; Vol. 1 of the *Oeuvres complètes*). Other volumes are designated by the initials *O.C.* in the footnotes.

[1]*O.C.*, Vol. 11, p. 177.

contrast, other French writers on comparable subjects, like Daudet or Jules Renard (sometimes considered to have plagiarised *L'Enfant*; Léon Daudet called him "Poil de Vallès"), seem anaemic, the first by reason of a fey facetiousness, the second because of an authorial neutrality stemming perhaps from emotional aridity. One who at times matches the power of Vallès' writing, a man, as the French has it, "rotten with talent," Hervé Bazin, does so (in *Vipère au poing*) at the expense of piling on the agony for his hero with such precise relish that the sadistic indictment of the mother comes to seem curiously masochistic. What Vallès offers is an often comic recital of suffering, which yet communicates real distress, all the more compelling for being shared out amongst the unhappy trio of father, mother and son.

The negative pole of Vallès' deepest conviction is his hostility to authority in all its forms: parental, pedagogic, governmental, ideological, literary. And the positive pole: an unkillable urge for justice, on behalf both of the self and others. In *L'Enfant*, the boy Jacques Vingtras expands from self-pity, first to commiseration and then to an effort to whip up resistance amongst his fellow-sufferers (to whom the book as a whole is dedicated). He knows another lad, who still wets the bed, who is ashamed, and whose shame is doubled by the ritual display of the damp sheet every day before the eyes of the entire village. Jacques has not only a heart that bleeds for such victims, but fists that clench for them, and his later explosions of physical militancy spring to a large extent from this early acquaintance with the ill-use of children. Simply, Jacques learns to think of, as well as the many who are better off, those worse off than himself. His primitive but unswerving hunger for justice demands that, even in his charges against his own parents, he still explains and motivates their delinquency. (In Jules Renard's *Poil de Carotte*, the mother's *méchanceté* is given, unexplained: an essence). It is not they who are wholly, or even mainly, at fault. It is social pressures which condition, stunt and all but wreck them as human beings. One of the major reasons why *L'Enfant* is so vivacious a book is that its child narrator is a fully-fledged, though at times almost skinned-alive, member of a family unit, as he is of various small-scale community units. Hence the gossipy tone, the sense of shared experience, of reciprocal aid or malevolence. The family trio itself is, severally and collectively, accident-prone. No project ever properly works out for them. From this grows, despite the continuous arguing and beatings, a rough fellow-feeling, fluctuating mutual support, the vestiges of loyalty. Not, then, a facile matter of Me versus Them, but, more profoundly, of the lot of us in a communal soup.

That is the final balance of the book's account-sheet. But, in details, the scales bang up and down stridently. The boy's earliest and dominant memories are of savage beatings, so much so that he exclaims at one point that his miserly parents have never let him have anything for himself, not even his own skin. The mother, in particular, yields to an almost physiological need to hit Jacques, a need natural as "the tail-wagging of the wagtail, or the ducking under water of the mallard" (p. 94). The playfulness of the wording here is not, as in Renard or Daudet, due to an incorrigible tendency to joke reality away, but rather to a mixture of bitter sarcasm and a half-conscious wish to find a reason for irrational behaviour, as a first step perhaps towards forgiving it. On the one hand, he asks the loaded rhetorical question "What can take a mother's place?"—to which he replies *"Mon Dieu! une trique remplacerait assez bien la mienne!"* On the other, when he describes his bruises as "the marks of her solicitude," he is admitting, alongside the sardonic gag, the possibility that she really, however tortuously, worries for him. More truly harmful, anyway, than her blows is her depriving him, as a punishment, of his friends' company. Some ambiguity enters into the whole business. When at one stage Jacques dreams of running away to sea and says that he welcomes his father's thrashings, for they harden his skin and make it ready for the tough life of a sailor, it is not at all clear how much this is heavy irony, how much a defence tactic of making virtue out of necessity, or how much un-controlled hyperbole. Jacques learns two key lessons from his experience of violence in his own family and in others': that it merely sets up a chain-reaction of vengeance (Bergougnard savages his son who terrorises smaller kids); and that, in this as in other ways, it has its perverse logic. His mother, for instance, has a system which she believes in and applies. She beats her son "for his own good," as a deterrent. And, deviously, he even enjoys her tyranny, for it proves he is a rebel and that flatters his ego. But she brain-washes him so unrelentingly that it takes all the instinctive strength of his own desires not to believe with her that *"il ne faut pas gâter les enfants."* Is his view of himself as an ugly and filthy wretch a genuine self-appraisal, or what he has been instructed to think of himself? A conditioning programme, Pav-lovian in its rigour, forces him over five years to eat what he most loathes: onion hash. The day he can stomach it without looking queasy, his mother stops cooking it, for it is training of the will, self-denial, that she has been trying to drum into him. After so much mind-stuffing (not only from parents but also from books, to which Jacques lends over-much credence), he has to work on himself to *unlearn*; for example, to see the chasm between the Catho-lic myths about Protestants as ogres, and an actual Protestant he glimpses for himself. Brainwashing can set up a divided nature, training versus instincts, with falsity as the end-product. Thus the mother's pseudo-genteel strictures on table-manners cause Jacques, when visiting, to respond hypocritically to offers of tasty food.

In fact, she spoils every sport, foreseeing danger or damage before it has a chance to occur: *tristis ante coitum.* Like many another mother, she makes a great show of self-sacrifice, twisting facts to suit the myth of herself as the self-abnegatory pelican, or as the virtuous Roman of boys' story-books. Her very solicitude is stifling, killing. She piles it on thick, whether nagging and striking Jacques, or devising for him impossible clothes. In her desire to escape her peasant origins, she hooks on to petit-bourgeois, vulgar gentility, (saying not *"cul de bouteille"* but *"chose de bouteille"*); she foists lessons of deportment and etiquette on to her providentially maladroit son, for she wants him to become a "gentleman." It is partly through cussed reaction against this ambi-tion that Jacques clings to his love of the country and the peasantry.

In truth, he has inherited something of the country way of life from both his parents, who are afraid that he will regress to the level above which they have lifted themselves. Their social climbing is unsure-footed, anyway. At a ball in his school, the mother suddenly erupts into loud-mouthed Auvergnat folk-ditties and heavy-soled stomping. For once in her dowdy life, she lets her hair down in coquettish if clumsy exhibitionism. It is a sad spectacle, for sartorially the poor woman, like her son, who is almost charmed and is certainly less embarrassed by her performance than the onlookers, is always a sight. She is especially pathetic as she knows she is in the process of losing her husband to an attractive and well-dressed other woman. Though most often monstrous in her cruelty, meanness and posings, on occasion she collapses into simplicity, drops her guard, and treats Jacques almost tenderly. Her private tragedy is that she is blind to the fact that this sporadic humanity, if expanded, would have disciplined her son far more effectively than her harshness ever has. But "ma mère tordait le cou au premier mouvement pour se livrer au second" (p. 101). Only towards the end, in her misery at being abandoned by her husband, does her sadness soften Jacques' justifiable resentment. Only when he is old enough to speak up, to articulate his real feelings, is a kind of bond created which could not exist as long as he was mutely withstanding her drubbings. Before, she had often referred to him in the third person, a way of distancing him and reducing him to the status of an object. At the end, there is the direct and quieter, though still painful, contact of two linked persons.

On the whole, she is shown as worse than the father, who is more often pitied than condemned. Like his son, Monsieur Vingtras has had choices made for him as a child, and all his adult life he has had to submit to the humiliating imposition upon him of lowly work and status. Jacques, himself subject to the unnatural strain of being a pupil in his father's class, always strives to explain his father's bitterness: "Il voyait tout à travers le dégoût et la fureur" (p. 186). He feels both a sense of guilt and of duty, lest his father lose his miserable but indispensable job, despite the fact that, when he has been criticised by the principal for neglecting his wife, the father takes over the mother's rôle as child-beater. As with the mother, an element of posturing enters into his attitude towards the boy: "Il s'épuise à la fin, à force de vouloir paraître amer" (p. 320). Meeting him again after a separation, Jacques experiences the same old awkwardness, the grating and the noncoincidence of two sensibilities. The one time that the pair of them share anything occurs when the mother is asleep, and they escape to enjoy food, wine and gaiety. Here Jacques sees the evidence of the other side of his usually grim father. Similarly, when Bergougnard, an old schoolmate, on reunion tells the father (and it is a parody of the meeting of Frédéric and Deslauriers in Flaubert's *Education sentimentale*) that he embodies "*l'Imagination folle*," whereas Bergougnard is "*la Raison froide*"—though pompously stated, this notion contains some truth, for the father's other side visibly struggles to get out, in his affair with Mme. Brignolin.

Until this disruptive event, the family atmosphere had been marked, except in the explosions of violence, by the parents' corseting of their emotions. Not even tears, never mind laughter; just griping. When the infidelity comes to light, a fishy, a hurtful situation develops: "Il parle à ma mère d'une voix blanche, qui soupire ou qui siffle; on sent qu'il cherche à paraître bon et qu'il en souffre; il lui montre une politesse qui fait mal et une tendresse fausse qui fait pitié" (p. 184). Vallès is ever alert to the real meaning underlying fake emotions, the inner divisions which they unwittingly unmask. The trio is atomised by the event: Jacques is stretched between two enemies. Throughout, the parents had taken it in turn, to become human or inhuman. At the end, it is the father's turn to be savage, since his wife has by this stage sunk her pride. The father's guilt at his own extra-marital conduct, his son's failure to pass his examinations, and his subsequently expressed wish to become an artisan—an ambition which negates all that the father had counted on and the little he had achieved—these combine in an explosive mixture. It seems a damned and doomed household. Jacques feels that the father has never given him a shred of trust or credit and, worse, that he has lied to his son, to salvage his self-esteem which was threatened by his own irresponsible actions. In a fight, where he rains nearly murderous blows on Jacques, the lad at last resists, having formed the clear question in his head: why should parents have such unjust rights over their children? (In the 1880s, Vallès was to propose a League for the protection of children's rights).

Even so, and even after battling with him, Jacques physically defends his father against the irate parents of a pupil he slapped in class, by fighting a duel against the enemy's oldest son. After this undeniable evidence of his son's loyalty, Monsieur Vingtras at long last turns, partly at least, honest: "Ce professorat a fait de moi une vieille bête qui a besoin d'avoir l'air méchant, et qui le devient, à force de faire le croquemitaine et les yeux creux . . . Ça vous tanne le coeur. On est cruel . . . J'ai été cruel" (p. 343). He does not say this to the face of Jacques, but the boy overhears his parents' shamefaced mutual admissions. The father fears telling his son himself, for it might "*blesser la discipline.*" He is as pedantic domestically as he is at school: "*Je lui parlerai toujours comme à un écolier*"; and he asks the mother to act as go-between and to tell the boy that the father is, against all the evidence, fond of him. He is a pathetic case of *déformation professionnelle*, a distortion aided and abetted by a flawed, diminished but still recognisable nature. Jacques also discovers that he was at the time of the duel on the verge of having his son locked up. The law of the land grants him this prerogative. And it is against this and other noxious laws that Vallès, beyond the father himself, is striking. In a letter written to a friend while writing *L'Enfant*, Vallès declares: "Je hais l'Etat avant tout. C'est même l'Etat qui fait les pères féroces en sanctifiant l'autorité, en mettant au-dessus de la tête d'enfants comme des têtes d'insurgés un droit providentiel, une religion indiscutée, le respect de père en fils du respect de la loi."[2] Here again, like Dickens, he attacks the wider evil behind the local crime. The parents are depicted throughout as more ignorant and incompetent than definitively wicked. Though they attempt to invalidate him as a distinct person, their efforts arise less from a refusal than from a failure to understand him. The boy himself survives, partly because he always hangs on to an idea of how his childhood *should* have been treated. Is this an instinctive criterion, or one learned from his readings, or from his observation of other, happier families (the shoemaker's clan, for instance, bonded by an underlying love despite periodic quarrels)? Perhaps, simply, he gets the idea from the *truces* in his misery. Perversely perhaps, the despotism of the parents at least instructs the boy in the art of survival, and his resilience owes something to them as well as to his own endowments.

What of the child himself, who in talk, as distinct from in action, cannot

---

[2]*O.C.*, Vol. 4, p. 143.

be separated from his progenitors? For good and bad, Vallès was never cured of his childhood. Whereas Daudet in *Le Petit Chose* sees the child with the adult's eyes as another person, an object, in *L'Enfant* Vallès relives his past so intensely that he rebecomes the child he was and still remains in actuality. There is in Jacques a peculiar admixture (but perfectly recognisable to readers who acknowledge the aberrant in themselves) of raging injured innocence and acceptance of guilt, when his father lacerates his hand while carving a toy for his five-year-old son and the mother instantly blames the mishap on the child. Perhaps a child can see the effect better than its cause. And accidents are hardly a childish concept, except as an alibi for breakages, for children believe in a deterministic universe. Vallès is as interested in the bitty but persistent logic of the child's mind as in the no less unreliable adult version. Jacques betrays touches of that sadism which springs, as much as from an inherent capacity for evil, from the young child's inability to make connexions, except when the suffering of others affects him directly. (It is totally different in kind from Renard's *Poil de Carotte*, where the whole family is alien to the reader and where the young hero himself stonily tortures and massacres little animals at great length.)

Jacques, at another turn (and unlike the biologically snobbish Petit Chose of Daudet), is kind to the deprived. He revels in the company of a deaf-and-dumb aunt, whose entire body speaks for her and who thus creates a much more dynamic relationship with her observers than speakers usually establish with listeners. Very child-like, too, is the repeated emphasis on faces as counters of the inner self. But Vallès deals with fantasies as much as with everyday realities. At Mass, after passing pork-butchers' shops full of Christmas fare, the bored and hungry child sees images of pigs' tails in the candle flames and incense fumes. The hyperbole of a child's disappointment is beautifully caught in Jacques' comparison of the leaves in a new and disliked landscape with the sickly hue of a consumptive's ears; even the cabbages look apoplectic.

At school, Jacques shares his father's humiliation, which helps him to understand the man's bitterness. Against his mother's over-estimation of the teaching profession, Jacques is entirely disabused: a teacher's lot is squalid. Jacques himself oscillates between being "*une bête à pensums*" and "*une bête à concours*"; whether it is impositions or examinations, school is a tread-mill and a rat-race. Like today's youth, he asks all the time: what is the relevance of this study to me, or to the present day? (He has a solid case: French colleges in the mid-nineteenth century taught the classics in a proportion of 16:1 to French.) *L'Enfant* carries a running joke about the enforced reproduction of classical writers' styles in essays: "Ce n'est pas dans les latrines de Vitellius que je vais quand je sors de la classe" (p. 255). How can he "put himself in the place of Scaevola," when he does not have a charred wrist? One day he meets a real, present-day Roman, a political refugee, who gives him direct-method *leçons de choses* (visual and tactile aids to study). Throughout, Jacques' true education (acquired *against* his official indoctrination in school) takes the form of a contest between common-sense and fakery in which pretensions are cut down to size. Similarly, his psychological growing-up entails the yielding by superstitious fears of the unknown to authentic fears of the known: the world of oppression. It is a loss of innocence, but

more importantly a loss of naïveté. Appropriately, his adolescence is registered
as an irritation, an irking of the senses. He welcomes the sensuous friction of
noisy, smoky, strong-smelling bars and other places of voluntary public congress; he detests the cold, musty, ink-stinking atmosphere of compulsory
institutional life.

It might seem strange that *L'Enfant*, rather than the bohemian *Le
Bachelier*, should be the most sensual volume of the Trilogy. The hinted but
eloquent sexuality of the lad's feelings for a pretty aunt or for Cousine
Apollonie (clinging on horseback to her, he feels her flesh firm up as he grips
hard), the pastoral idyll with other girl-cousins; episodes like these give the
lie to Claude Roy's remark: "Vallès (sauf dans sa correspondance) ne sait pas
ce que c'est que parler à mi-voix."[3] In the main, it is older women who are
most attracted to the growing boy; and in the final relationship with the flirting,
pouting, scheming Mme. Devinol, Jacques is perhaps saved from an un-
pleasantly adhesive fate by the involuntary disclosure of their affair and the
subsequent family scandal. Other truces, oases of joy or escape in his otherwise largely bleak young life, come when Jacques occasionally achieves still-
ness, pure existence, usually out of doors. He needs these moments of peace,
as well as brusque outbursts of violent exertion; he needs solitude as well as
crowds. Even as a child, he is addicted to nostalgia as often as to great
expectations. Recurrent holidays on the land clear his lungs and open his
eyes. Tramping through ploughed fields, rolling in the hay, he immerses
himself "dans la vie familière, grasse, plantureuse et saine" (p. 85). His love
of country life extends to hard work in the fields, for even in his utopia he
includes industriousness: "les pays où l'on souffre, où l'on travaille, mais
où l'on est libre" (p. 115). And, always, the comparison with home: his
father, who scorns peasants, has to bow and scrape to superiors far more than
they; he is worse off, in terms of self-respect, than a hired hand. In this whole
area of truces, Vallès reveals his faith in alternation, his sense of seasonal
changes, his overall view of life as an affair of swings and roundabouts. It
injects hope into despair, but it reminds joy that it is menaced.

Dressed all in black, in frock-coat and top hat, "J'ai l'air d'un poêle"
(p. 52). As well as the prosecution, often broadly satirical, directed against
the parents, the balance of this novel insists that Jacques himself be subjected
throughout to frequent mockery, at his own or onlookers' hands. Sartorial
fiascos are one means of self-deflation. Jacques feels exiled from his fellows
by the clothes devised for him by his mother, ludicrous to look at and abrasive
to wear. At a children's ball, he is greeted with something akin to horror by
the other guests. This self-monstrification stems no doubt in part from Vallès'
freely admitted passion for circus freaks. At the same time, Jacques' lack of
social graces is a kind of saving grace. After his mother's efforts to civilise
him with paid lessons, the best he can manage is a kind of stage-etiquette,
bowing like a theatrical bumpkin. He presents himself, not unflatteringly in
the long run, as a yokel-hero, disembowelling the principal's carpet with the
nail protruding from his shoes: a perfect vaudeville number. Here as elsewhere, he lets himself and his mother down, but it is largely because she has
hoisted him up to a false height. On his father's birthday, he spills his present,

---

[3]C. Roy, *Le Commerce des classiques* (Paris: Gallimard, 1953), p. 253.

a potted plant, all over his father and is booted out of the room for his pains. He is the fall-guy, the drudge on whom are loaded his parents' woes and, when they travel, their always excess baggage. In his own life, reports present Vallès as an expert at clanging gaffes; so often, after a successful run in a job, he was fired for putting his foot in it. Yet this tactlessness is the most endearing part of Vallès, this speaking out of turn, this thinking aloud.

What form does this thinking aloud habitually take? As Vallès works principally by moods and by associations, his novel can hardly be linear in structure. Often, when it appears that a situation is about to evolve in a certain direction, the narration sidesteps or backtracks to something else. This shifting pattern may well reflect Vallès' conviction of the messy randomness of life. He is a moody, often broody writer (cf. the refrain of some idea or person "*qui me botte*" or "*qui ne me va pas.*" This stress on being *suited* comes from the preference for instincts and the dislike of intermediaries). Apart from the temperamental reasons, his journalistic experience likewise often encourages him to write in a feverish manner. He starts an incident with a phrase as arresting as a headline, which is then explicated jerkily by the following narrative. The use of the present tense, too, promotes the illusion that everything is just now happening. The book is strongly polarised: the mature author identifies with himself as a child, and the mother is both magnet and Moloch. Vallès inserts a nice chiasmus-figure in the already mentioned episode of the father and son desporting themselves in the mother's absence: "Ma jeunesse s'éveille, ma mère dort . . . Ma jeunesse s'éteint, ma mère est éveillée" (p. 206). This polarisation and his own flaunted love of word-play could easily lead Vallès astray into purely gratuitous exaggeration. In fact, this rarely happens. Repetition is used often as a branch of compassion, for the effort to dwell on someone else presupposes an interest, the beginnings of tolerance; for example, the junior teacher's minor sin of brandy-tippling: "C'est son péché mignon, sa marotte humide, son dada jaune" (p. 113). Vallès' fondness for puns is intimately linked with his outlook on life; for him, excruciation is a common experience. When Jacques approaches another maltreated boy he hopes to recruit for a rebellion, he says: "Je tâte Ricard; quand je dis je tâte je parle au figuré: il me défend de le tâter (il a trop mal aux côtes)" (p. 163). Tightening screws is a hazardous operation, and here it may well be that Vallès turns them too tight for the pointed joke to be fully effective. He knows only too well how hit-and-miss an affair is the art of expression. What Jacques says of his school-essay style is true also of Vallès': "Pour la *narration française*, je réussis aussi par le retapage et le ressemelage, par le mensonge et le vol" (p. 256). How many of us have a style to call our own? In an essay called *Victimes du Livre*, where Vallès' attack on fiction as the misleader of the public is mingled with a confession of his own voracious readings, he argues that, just as we check our watches against public clocks, so "*on règle son coeur sur le volume.*"[4] For a long period of his childhood, Jacques lives in his imagination the life of Robinson Crusoe; Defoe's novel is a true lifebuoy of a book to the suffocating child. To combat the prison-grey of his family-life, Jacques turns thirstily to bright colours;

---

[4]*O.C.*, Vol. 7, p. 145.

even an impish sunbeam dancing on a row of dormitory chamber-pots can delight him.

With so open-hearted a writer, the charge of sentimentality has to be confronted. Now, this is one of those terms which resemble a peasant's bedsock: into it may be accommodated gold currency, or just smelly feet. If proved in Vallès' case, sentimentality would be mainly a matter of over-persuasiveness (bludgeoning, nudging the reader hard in the ribs) than of under-conviction (far-fetched situations or events). In *L'Enfant*, coincidences are generally exploited as a joke: for instance, when Jacques unwittingly eats the rabbit which he has earlier won at a fair, carried painfully inside his shirt like the legendary Spartan, and eventually allowed to escape. One scene, however, veers close to the kind of sentimentality for which Dickens is notorious; the death and disposal of a cherished dog: "un être qui m'avait aimé, qui me léchait les mains quand elles étaient bleues et gonflées, et regardait, d'un oeil où je croyais voir des larmes, son jeune maître qui essuyait les siennes" (p. 195). This I take to be sentimental, not because it is not true to certain experiences, but simply because it is the kind of wishful thinking we do not wish to hear. A sentimental episode, however, need not scupper a whole book. But what of another scene, Dickensian in its power to revolt the reader against the cruelty it relates as well as in its unabashed emotionalism, the scene where the mindless, gratuitous and reiterated brutality of a father (Bergougnard, "*la Raison froide!*") eventually kills his young daughter before Jacques' agonised gaze? Her fruitless begging for mercy makes the scene all the more distressing to read. Jacques can usually find some justification for, or consolation in, his own punishments, but witnessing this example of human savagery, he can only respond by an urge to eye-for-an-eye revenge: the father should be buried alive alongside his victim. This vicious demand for vengeance perhaps introduces some balance, hysterical but understandable, in what might otherwise have proved an overloaded scene.

Finally, one clear instance of blatant sentimentality. Having read about the French Revolution and the poor classes who had helped to engender it, Jacques says: "Et je n'aimais que ces gens-là, parce que, seuls, les pauvres avaient été bons pour moi, quand j'étais petit" (p. 311). Like the slack tolerance of Camus' *La Peste* towards the end, this is sentimental because patently untrue to the previous facts of the book, in which several well-off people treated him kindly and several poor people refused him help. Despite a few such aberrations, however, his most persevering energy goes towards the pursuit of truth. Vallès greatly admired Daumier and Dickens, other cartoonists, for cutting everyone down to size and for capturing people at their most salient and crucial points (cf. the view sometimes expressed that Dickens renders people in the way that children see grown-ups, with disproportionate features). What sentimentality remains is the dross, the excess of a generous nature.

In *Le Bachelier*, a friend says of Jacques' father that he had "*une nature d'irrégulier,*" but that he had been trapped in "*un métier de forçat.*" It is precisely the desire to safeguard and to extend his own irregularity of temperament and political outlook that drives Jacques to want to avoid like the plague ending up in that profession. In fact, for a period and out of the necessity to support a widowed mother, he later succumbs. The experience reteaches him what he already knew as a child: that, at that time, the insecurity of tenure and the ignominy of the junior teacher's position had helped to madden a man already sickened and impoverished materially and spiritually by defeating work. As Jacques says in *L'Enfant*: "Etre libre? Je ne sais pas ce que c'est, mais je sais ce que c'est d'être victime, je le sais, tout jeune que je suis" (p. 313). His only qualifications for a career are his suffering, and in this he resembles his father, and less directly but by contagion, his mother. In his case, to understand is not to forgive all, but it is to mitigate resentment and to feel compassion. At the open-ended conclusion to *L'Enfant*, Jacques, on his sick-bed after being wounded in the thigh in the duel, talks as one who has earned the right to independent speech, as one who has finished at least this particular apprenticeship of bondage. As always, however, the mother has the last word; next time he fights a duel, she warns, he must remember to put an old pair of trousers on.

There might seem to be a certain perverseness, as well as charity, in Jacques' seeing some good (or less evil) in his parents, despite their obvious ill-treatment of him. It is true that Vallès always goes against the grain, *à rebours*, even more than Des Esseintes in his private realm (Vallès and Huysmans were mutual admirers). But Vallès believed that if you fight for justice, it must be justice for all. And in literary terms, the reminder that there is generally more in other people than meets the cursory eyes is surely one of the prime functions of a good novel. It is not so much a matter of "ambiguity" (a term over-used, since Freud at least, as an automatic pat on the back), for ambiguity can result from the author's mental or moral laziness. In Vallès' case, the complexity arises from a genuine insight into the wayward variousness of human motivation and behaviour. It was in an article on Dickens that Vallès once exclaimed: "*Comme si la grandeur n'était pas dans le mélange et la lutte des éléments divers.*"[5] In some ways, the greatest French novelist is Montaigne. In his writings as in his life, Vallès was equally as capable of great warmth as of biting and kicking; he saw and lived life as a scrum. He knew his own deficiencies. Of *L'Enfant* he said: "J'ai voulu faire un livre de sensations, presque de pensées, primesautier, coupé—avec une leçon terrible au bout malgré les ironies voulues, les grossièretés de parti-pris. Il y a sans doute des répétitions."[6] He knew that, as a polemist, he lacked allusiveness (that joy to sophisticated readers), and worked directly, more like a pirate than a smuggler.[7] His explosive loquacity springs from years of having to hold his tongue, at home, at school, in hack jobs, as a journalist under the Second Empire. As much as anything else, *L'Enfant* is a release from verbal straitjacketing. Though something of a fairground barker by temperament, he believed he ought to restrain himself from bullying the reader into acquiescence: "*Je crois que je ne devrais pas dicter la colère . . . C'est le lecteur qui, je l'espère, criera ce que je n'ai pas crié.*"[8]

Vallès would have rejoiced to have the close connexion with his reading public enjoyed by Dickens. At least, he clung to the belief that "*la vie des*

---

[5]*O.C.*, Vol. 11, p. 168.
[6]*O.C.*, Vol. 9, p. 110.
[7]*O.C.*, Vol. 10, p. 225.
[8]*O.C.*, Vol. 4, p. 202.

autres est un morceau de la vie de chacun."[9] He held out for naïve realism; he loved books, paintings which the reader or spectator felt he could walk into. His own art has this concreteness (*"la vie nous serre de près!"*[10]), this feeling for the physical texture of life, less common in the French than in the Anglo-Saxon novel tradition. Vallès succeeds in executing Robert Graves's (diabolical) advice to storytellers: "Make the whole read human and exact."

University of Reading
England

---

[9]*O.C.*, Vol. 4, p. 131.
[10]*O.C.*, Vol. 11, p. 278.

L'Evangile Social de *Travail:* un anti-*Germinal*

Par Henri Mitterand

S'il existe chez Balzac des personnages reparaissants, on pourrait parler, à propos de l'oeuvre de Zola, de thèmes reparaissants et de situations reparaissantes, avec bien entendu des personnages récurrents, qui, s'ils ne portent pas un seul et même nom, s'ils ne forment pas un seul et même personnage du point de vue de l'état-civil, se ressemblent en tout cas fortement. L'inventaire de ces récurrences est relativement aisé. Il pourrait déboucher sur une étude approfondie des rapports d'intertextualité qui relient les uns aux autres les vingt romans du cycle des *Rougon-Macquart*, et, au-delà, l'ensemble des romans de Zola. Dans son livre sur *Zola et les mythes*, Jean Borie a montré que des modèles se dessinent, qui transgressent la clôture de chaque oeuvre prise à part, comme si, des romans de jeunesse aux *Quatre Evangiles*, on n'entendait qu'un unique et intarissable discours, où s'accumulent les variantes de quelques situations fondamentales.

La fin de *La Fortune des Rougon* renvoie à celle de *La Débâcle*. *L'Argent* est une suite de *La Curée*. *Au Bonheur des Dames* est en correspondance thématique avec *Le Ventre de Paris*. *Le Rêve* est pour une part analogique de *La Faute de l'Abbé Mouret*. *Paris* fait pour la vie parlementaire de la République ce que *Son Excellence Eugène Rougon* avait fait pour celle de l'Empire. *Fécondité* est une réponse à *Pot-Bouille*, et aussi à *La Joie de Vivre*, et j'en passe.

Le cas le plus frappant est celui de la résurgence des thèmes de *Germinal* à travers *Travail*. *Germinal*, on le sait, n'était lui-même que le troisième maillon d'une chaîne, le long de laquelle on trouve également *La Bête humaine* et *La Débâcle*, pour certains de leurs thèmes. Après 1871, Zola a ajouté à la liste des sujets de romans qu'il avait proposés à son éditeur, et parmi lesquels figurait un roman sur le monde ouvrier qui deviendra *L'Assommoir*, un deuxième roman ouvrier, plus particulièrement politique. Celui-ci devait mettre en scène "l'ouvrier de l'insurrection, de la Commune." L'ébauche de *Germinal* déviera, en réalité, vers un autre sujet. Etienne Lantier deviendra, non pas l'ouvrier parisien des barricades de mai 1871, mais le militant des luttes syndicales et politiques sur le lieu de travail. Mais Etienne devait être aussi le héros du roman judiciaire, la violence meurtrière se confondant pour un temps, dans l'esprit de Zola, avec la violence révolutionnaire. En réalité, quelques pages après le début de l'ébauche de *La Bête humaine*, qui est le roman de la folie homicide, on voit Etienne s'effacer et céder la place à un substitut hâtivement imaginé pour les besoins de la cause, un troisième fils de Gervaise Macquart, qui se prénommera Jacques. Le personnage d'insurgé n'est pas oublié pour autant: on le trouvera, sous un autre nom encore, dans la dernière partie de *La Débâcle*.

Si *La Bête humaine* et *La Débâcle* sont des rameaux poussés sur la même branche où s'est greffé *Germinal*, cette dérivation n'est repérable que pour des aspects isolés, et à l'aide d'une étude génétique et diachronique. Avec *Travail*, c'est tout autre chose, et l'on pourrait presque parler d'homologie de structures, ou en tout cas de larges analogies, qui sautent aux yeux par la seule comparaison des textes.

Les deux oeuvres représentent, à un certain degré, la société industrielle et ses décors: les mines de charbon, dans *Germinal*, l'industrie métallurgique, dans *Travail*. On sait que l'action de ce roman, le deuxième des *Quatre Evangiles*, publié en 1901, oppose symboliquement deux entreprises: celle des Boisgelin, l'*Abîme*, dirigée par l'ingénieur Delaveau, qui fabrique des canons et des obus, des engins de mort, par les moyens de la métallurgie traditionnelle, et celle des Jordan, la *Crêcherie*, dirigée par l'ingénieur Luc Froment, qui substitue les fours électriques, découverte de la technique moderne, aux anciens hauts fourneaux, et qui fabriquera des rails, des ponts, des charpentes métalliques, des machines, des "oeuvres de vie." Le nom de *L'Abîme* a plus d'un trait sémantique avec celui qui désigne le puits de mine de *Germinal*, le Voreux.

Dans les deux romans, trois classes sont en présence: celle des propriétaires de la terre et des instruments de travail, et de leurs collaborateurs directs, les directeurs de puits de mine ou d'usine et les ingénieurs; celle des travailleurs manuels; et une classe intermédiaire, qui regroupe les commerçants, les fonctionnaires, les militaires, les prêtres, etc. Chacune de ces classes s'incarne dans des personnages qui symbolisent ses conduites et ses langages typiques, et qui sont saisis dans des scènes ou des situations caractéristiques: le dîner, par exemple, pour les bourgeois. Le dîner chez les Boisgelin, au début de *Travail*, fait pendant au dîner chez les Hennebeau, dans *Germinal*.

Les analogies de personnages sont multiples et frappantes. A la fragile et chlorotique Catherine Maheu, de *Germinal*, correspond, dans le premier livre de *Travail*, Josine. Celle-ci, qui vit en concubinage avec l'ouvrier Ragu, est battue et maltraitée par son amant, comme Catherine l'était par Chaval. Ragu lui-même, type de l'ouvrier buveur, querelleur, brutal, facilement traître à ses camarades, est pour une part une réincarnation de Chaval. Le triangle se complète, comme dans *Germinal*, avec Luc Froment, qui, de même que Lantier face à Josine, jouera le rôle ambigu du protecteur, du séducteur, et du rédempteur. Josine deviendra sa compagne et son inspiratrice, comme Catherine aurait pu le devenir si elle n'était morte au fond de la mine inondée après s'être donnée à Lantier. Les correspondances jouent ainsi non seulement d'un personnage à un autre, mais d'un groupement à un autre. Notons que le couple adultère et complaisant que constituent, dans *Germinal*, Hennebeau, le directeur de la mine, et sa femme, réapparaît dans *Travail* sous les traits du couple Delaveau, également directorial et également adultère. Je ne puis poursuivre l'inventaire, car la population est fort nombreuse dans l'un et l'autre roman, mais il resterait beaucoup de réapparitions semblables à signaler. L'anarchiste Lange rappelle évidemment Souvarine, et le père Lunot le Vieux Bonnemort, de *Germinal*. Comme lui, il est perclus de rhumatismes, comme lui, il survit sans ressources, recueilli par ses enfants, comme lui enfin il aime ressasser ses souvenirs de vieil ouvrier et l'histoire de l'usine où il a travaillé.

Les procédés narratifs et descriptifs se répètent également. Par exemple, les deux romans commencent par l'arrivée du principal personnage sur les lieux de l'action: Un homme qui vient d'ailleurs—Etienne Lantier venait de Lille, Luc Froment arrive de Paris—et qui marche. Il pénètre lentement au sein d'un décor qui lui est inconnu et qui l'effraie, et qui d'emblée apparaît lourd de misère et d'inhumanité: les brasiers qui brûlent dans la nuit du terri de Montsou, d'un côté, et de l'autre "l'amas sombre des bâtiments et des hangars" de l'Abîme, avec "les poussières, les vapeurs, qui s'exhalaient sans cesse de lui, qui lui faisaient une continuelle nuée de la sueur de sa besogne." Un peu plus loin, le défilé des grévistes vaincus porte les mêmes marques que celui des mineurs de Montsou: le silence, la résignation, l'amertume, l'espoir informulé de la revanche:

"Le patronat, l'autorité bourgeoise avait pu avoir raison des salariés; mais les esclaves domptés restaient si menaçants dans leur silence passif, qu'une affreuse amertume empoisonnait l'air et qu'on y sentait souffler tout l'effroi des vengeances, des grands massacres possibles."[1]

Je terminerai ce bref et très incomplet inventaire en indiquant l'existence des correspondances de symboles. Je n'en cite que deux: la lapidation du héros, et le viol sacrificiel. Lorsque Lantier, après l'échec de la grève qu'il a conduite, réapparaît dans Montsou, il reçoit des pierres. Luc Froment, pour avoir gagné le procès qui lui avait été intenté par un commerçant de Beauclair,

---

[1]*Oeuvres complètes* (Paris, Cercle du livre précieux 1960-67), t. VIII, p. 550.

est poursuivi lui aussi par une populace qui ne comprend pas le sens de son action, et lapidé. Les deux personnages ne sont à ce moment-là que deux variantes d'une même figure, celle du sauveur incompris de ceux-là mêmes pour lesquels il se sacrifie: "Qu'avait-il donc fait, depuis quatre ans, pour que tant de haines se fussent amassées contre lui, au point d'être ainsi traqué, hurlant à la mort? Il s'était fait l'apôtre de demain, d'une société de solidarité et de fraternité, réorganisée par le travail ennobli, régulateur de la richesse . . . Et cela suffisait, la ville entière le considérait comme un malfaiteur, il la sentait derrière cette bande qui aboyait à ses trousses. Mais quelle amertume, quelle souffrance, dans cette aventure commune du calvaire que tout juste doit gravir, sous les coups de ceux mêmes dont il veut le rachat!"[2] Quant au viol de la belle Mme Delaveau par l'ouvrier Ragu, il me paraît du même ordre que dans *Germinal* la castration de Maigrat, le meurtre du petit soldat ou l'étranglement de Cécile Grégoire par Bonnemort: ce sont des sacrifices symboliques, des gestes de fous, d'isolés ou de marginaux, qui singent et dévoient la violence proprement révolutionnaire, qui substituent la revanche ou la compensation individuelle à la lutte collective, l'acte-simulacre à l'action pratique.

Comment expliquer ces réduplications, qui, on le voit, foisonnent à tous les niveaux du roman? On peut avancer plusieurs hypothèses. La plus simple serait de les attribuer à une baisse de pouvoir inventif et au réemploi de modèles et de noyaux narratifs dont l'efficacité avait été une première fois démontrée. Une autre hypothèse est celle qu'avance Jean Borie, en s'appuyant sur la psychanalyse: *Les Quatre Evangiles* répondent aux *Rougon-Macquart* comme les romans du salut à ceux de la nausée. Un mythe de rédemption et de résurrection succède aux mythes de saccage, de sang et de mort. Josine sauvée remplace Catherine dégradée et perdue. "Dans *Travail*, écrit Jean Borie, Luc sauve la mère humiliée, remplace le père et s'érige en messie. Sauveurs de la mère et sauvés par elle, il n'est pas étonnant que les Evangélistes célèbrent l'harmonie, la justice et l'équilibre du monde nouveau qui s'organise autour du héros."[3]

Mais enfin, il n'est pas étonnant que quinze ans après *Germinal*—et entre temps il y a eu à Fourmies, la célébration du 1er mai, la constitution du mouvement syndical, l'entrée des socialistes au Parlement, les succès de Jaurès, les attentats anarchistes et le vote des lois scélérates, l'Affaire Dreyfus et le renversement de la majorité, la poussée du mouvement ouvrier à travers toute l'Europe—il paraît assez naturel que Zola tente une nouvelle fois de faire le point sur le sens et l'évolution des conflits sociaux, et de scruter l'avenir de la société française. *Travail* est à cet égard le deuxième dossier d'une même énquête, le deuxième reflet d'une même curiosité et d'une même anxiété.

Les différences entre les deux oeuvres n'en sont que plus frappantes, et plus pertinentes quant à l'évolution du romancier. C'est ce que je voudrais maintenant rapidement montrer.

---

[2]*Ibid.*, p. 727.
[3]Jean Borie, *Zola et les mythes* (Paris: Ed. du Seuil, 1971), p. 190.

Travail, je l'ai dit à l'instant, reprend l'étude de la condition ouvrière la où *Germinal* l'avait laissée: à la fin d'une grève manquée, "l'ouvrier forcé par la faim, grondant, forcé de reprendre le licou." Cependant, après quelques dizaines de pages, la rupture d'optique et de ton devient éclatante.

Certes, j'ai essayé de le montrer ailleurs, la leçon de *Germinal* est ambiguë."[4] Le contenu historique et social y est débordé par l'imagerie biologique et cosmique. Les crises de la société contemporaines y sont assimilées aux cataclysmes naturels qui affectent périodiquement l'ordre du monde, sans en modifier les structures profondes. Il reste que dans ce roman l'accent est mis sur l'antagonisme des classes; l'économie capitaliste est clairement désignée comme la source de la misère ouvrière; les mineurs prennent conscience de leur situation économique et politique, et de leurs possibilités de lutte, dans la pratique même de leur travail; la lutte pour le pain devient la lutte pour le socialisme, même si les idées de Lantier, et, partant, celles de Zola, sont encore singulièrement confuses sur ce sujet; les forces de l'Etat apparaissent essentiellement sous leur aspect répressif, à travers le rôle de la gendarmerie, de l'armée, du préfet; c'est dans son nombre et son organisation que le prolétariat trouve sa force; et même, si l'on admet qu'en Etienne Lantier se confondent, au moins pour un temps, l'ouvrier et le dirigeant, le travailleur manuel et le militant qui a réfléchi, on voit que Zola a compris la nécessité d'une interdépendance entre l'organisation pratique de la classe ouvrière et la recherche théorique sur les structures et l'histoire de la société. La grève échoue. Mais l'évangile qu'annonce la dernière page de l'oeuvre est celui qu'annonçaient les titres primitifs du roman, tels que *La Lézarde, La Maison qui craque, Château branlant, Le Feu qui couve*. Il affirme le caractère fondamental et inéluctable de la contradiction entre le capital et le travail, et la permanence d'une "lézarde," d'une déchirure qui traverse la société contemporaine et y oppose deux classes, avec, de période en période, des affrontements violents, dont nul ne peut prévoir la cessation.

Au contraire, quinze années plus tard, *Travail* est construit sur l'hypothèse inverse: la grève qui s'achève dans les premières pages du roman, loin d'en préfigurer d'autres, sera la dernière de l'histoire, par le miracle de l'association du capital, du travail et du talent. "Luc, écrit Zola, ébaucha à grands traits son rêve, tout ce qui avait germé en lui de la récente lecture de Fournier, une association entre le capital, le travail et le talent. Jordan apporterait l'argent nécessaire, Bonnaire et ses camarades donneraient les bras, lui serait le cerveau qui conçoit et dirige."[5] L'entreprise réussit, après quelques péripéties. L'ouvrier Bonnaire a conservé son attachement au collectivisme, Mais c'est Luc l'ingénieur, qui parviendra à créer une société harmonieuse, après la destruction accidentelle des usines de l'Abîme, symbole de la disparition de l'ancien capitalisme et de l'ancien salariat.

L'harmonie règnera également entre le peuple paysan et le peuple industriel. Les petits propriétaires, cédant à la persuasion de Luc, mettent leurs champs en commun. "Ils se procuraient les outils et les machines à la Crècherie, en échange du pain, du vin, des légumes, qu'ils lui fournissaient. Ce qui faisait

---

[4]Voir "L'idéologie du mythe dans *Germinal*," dans *Problèmes d'analyse textuelle* (Paris: Didier, 1971), pp. 83-90 et "*Germinal* et les idéologies," *Les Cahiers Naturalistes*, no 42, 1971, pp. 141-152.

[5]*Oeuvres complètes*, t. VIII, p. 670.

leur force, c'était justement de n'être plus isolés, d'avoir noué le lien solidaire, désormais indestructible, entre le village et l'usine et c'était la réconciliation rêvée, longtemps impossible, du paysan et de l'ouvrier, le paysan qui donne le blé nourrisseur de l'homme, l'ouvrier qui donne le fer pour que la terre soit ensemencée et que le blé pousse."⁶ Les petites gens de la ville se fournissent aux magasins de l'usine. Seuls, les commerçants en pâtissent, mais c'est justice. "C'était la mort du commerce, tel qu'on l'avait entendu jusque-là, l'intermédiaire entre le producteur et le consommateur, renchérissant la vie, vivant en parasite sur les besoins des autres."⁷

Si *Germinal* est un évangile d'affrontement, *Travail* est donc un évangile de réconciliation. A la fin de l'oeuvre, de multiples fêtes, à la Crêcherie, à la mairie de la ville, dans les villages voisins, marquent les différentes étapes de la pacification universelle. La lutte des classes n'est plus qu'un mauvais souvenir, elle a cédé la place à "cette fête géante de tout un peuple attablé là, en une seule et fraternelle famille."

Ce renversement de perspective a des conséquences directes sur la structure et la dynamique narratives du roman. Aux oppositions idéologiques correspondent des oppositions formelles et fonctionnelles. En l'occurrence, la forme, la structure, n'est pas neutre. Le point de vue de romancier sur la société est en incidence directe non seulement sur la substance de son roman, mais aussi sur sa structure formelle. A l'inverse de *Germinal*, les personnages principaux de *Travail* appartiennent à la bourgeoisie, tandis que les prolétaires n'ont aucune initiative romanesque. D'un roman à l'autre, les rapports entre les personnages et l'action dramatique ont basculé. Fait remarquable: à un roman dont la première personne, le sujet actif, à travers le personnage de Lantier, était la classe ouvrière menant combat contre le patronat, a succédé un roman qui confère la fonction principale, l'initiative, la conduite des événements, à un représentant du patronat, menant combat pour la classe ouvrière, mais sans elle et même malgré elle. Du même coup, le langage du héros et celui du romancier se confondent, ce qui n'était pas le cas dans *Germinal*, le sujet de l'énonciation rejoint le sujet de l'énoncé.

Conséquences, également, sur le plan de la temporalité et de la logique romanesques. La durée romanesque, dans *Germinal*, est à la fois resserrée sur une brève période et rythmée par l'alternance des saisons et celle des péripéties. Sa courbe présente une montée de la tension dramatique, progressive, mais marquée de temps forts, jusqu'à une forte akmê, dont le point culminant est la répression sanglante de la grève. Dans *Travail*, malgré l'apparente dialectique des trois livres successifs: "la peinture noire de ce qui est," "l'effondrement de la société qui meurt," et "la nouvelle organisation du travail," la progression s'opère par un lent pourrissement des structures anciennes et l'implantation concomitante des formes nouvelles de la société, le long d'une durée qui s'étale, dans un temps irréel, achronique, anhistorique, et au fond, par le seul jeu de la succession des générations les unes aux autres, tandis que Luc et Jordan s'acheminent sans à-coups vers leur centième année, toujours plus satisfaits et plus dignes de l'être.

---

⁶*Ibid.*, p. 794.
⁷*Ibid.*, p. 797.

Tout ceci ne va pas, du reste, sans un choc en retour sur le contenu. Les relations de personne et de temps, dans un roman, sont à la fois effet et cause, et elles participent directement à la production de la mythologie sociale. La longévité de Luc Froment, bâtisseur et bénisseur de la cité nouvelle, fait songer à celle de ces vieux dictateurs qui n'en finissent pas de mourir de nos jours, ici et là. Zola est peu explicite sur les institutions politiques de la *Cité* fondée par Luc. Mais on ne force pas le sens du texte en observant que tous les pouvoirs demeurent concentrés entre ses mains. Jusqu'au terme de sa vie, il veillera aux destinées de son peuple, en véritable monarque, ou, si l'on préfère, en père, voire en Dieu. Dès l'heure où il a jeté les bases de son apostolat, il est apparu comme le nouveau Christ de l'humanité. Lors de son procès, il a reçu au visage les crachats de la foule. Son sang a coulé, comme celui de Jésus, pour le salut de l'humanité. Il vivra désormais entouré de saintes femmes, comme celles qui ont accompagné le Christ dans sa Passion. Après avoir souffert par les hommes et pour eux, il deviendra leur sauveur. Son pouvoir est charismatique, tout procède de son intelligence, de sa bonté, de sa parole, de son pouvoir de persuasion, de son génie organisateur et fédérateur. "Il était le Fondateur, le Créateur, le Père, et tout ce peuple en joie, tous ces convives à toutes les tables, où l'on fêtait, avec le Travail, les fécondités de l'été, étaient son peuple, ses amis, ses parents, sa famille sans cesse élargie, de plus en plus fraternelle et prospère. Et une acclamation accueillit le voeu d'ardente tendresse qu'il portait à sa ville, monta dans l'air du soir, roula de table en table. Tous s'étaient mis debout, levaient à leur tour leur verre, buvaient à la santé de Luc et de Josine, le couple de héros, les patriarches du travail, elle, la rachetée, glorifiée comme épouse et comme mère, lui le rédempteur, qui, pour la sauver, avait sauvé de l'iniquité et de la souffrance le misérable monde du salariat."[8]

La société ici rêvée est une utopie, certes, mais l'utopie d'une dictature paternaliste, dont l'idéologie paraît en fin de compte assez proche de cette Révolution nationale qui inspirait les institutions de l'Etat français entre 1940 et 1944 et s'ornait du sigle "Travail, Famille, Patrie." L'utopie de *Travail* n'est pas très éloignée non plus, me semble-t-il, de celle de *Tête d'Or*, ou plutôt de *La Ville*, ce drame claudélien qui, après l'effondrement de l'ancienne société, reconstruit une cité idéale sur des bases théocratiques.

Un mythe de fraternité et de prospérité s'est substitué dans *Travail* aux images d'apocalypse par lesquelles *Germinal* avait traduit la misère et la révolte du prolétariat. Ce mythe s'aventure jusqu'aux frontières d'un courant de pensée sociale et politique qu'on n'a pas l'habitude d'associer au nom de Zola. La recherche, sur ce point, serait fructueuse pour la connaissance des structures idéologiques de la France à la fin du XIXe siècle, et aussi bien que pour la compréhension de certains langages politiques, entre 1930 et 1945.

Il est d'autres mirages auxquels l'auteur de *Travail* s'est exposé. Le personnage de Jordan croit en l'électricité comme en une magie nouvelle, sans se poser à aucun moment les problèmes économiques et politiques que soulève le progrès technique. Si dans *Germinal*, la grève et l'insurrection sont com-

---

[8]*Ibid.*, p. 938.

parées à des catastrophes passagères, mais dont le retour régulier est aussi inévitable que celui des inondations ou des tremblements de terre, *Travail* nous propose un mythe inverse et complémentaire: les progrès continus de la science et de la technique donneront aux réformateurs la double maîtrise des forces naturelles et des forces sociales. La conversion du collectiviste Bonnaire en témoigne: "C'est vrai, on a fini par me convertir. Je croyais à la nécessité d'une brusque révolution, d'un coup de main qui nous aurait livré le pouvoir, avec la possession du sol et de tous les outils du travail. Mais comment résister à la force de l'expérience? Depuis tant d'années, je vois ici la conquête certaine de la justice sociale, de ce bonheur fraternel, dont le rêve me hantait!"[9]

Les sources de ces mirages sont livrées par le dossier préparatoire du roman: les théoriciens de l'anarchie, Kropotkine et Grave, d'un côté, et de l'autre, Fourier. Zola a tempéré les uns par l'autre. Il a escamoté le thème de la révolution violente et celui du partage des biens, chers aux anarchistes, et leur a substitué l'idée fouriériste de l'association volontaire du travail, du capital et du talent, et le rêve d'une construction progressive de la commune sociétaire, dont le seul exemple ferait peu à peu dépérir l'ancien monde. Il se garde de donner des détails précis sur ce qu'il entend par cette association: il fait le silence sur l'organisation économique de la Crècherie, sur le régime de propriété qui y est en vigueur, et sur la manière dont y sont répartis les capitaux, les salaires et les profits. Seul demeure le louable désir de concilier l'inconciliable: la conservation de la propriété privée des moyens de production et la suppression de l'exploitation de l'homme par l'homme.

On voit mal également comment la mise des terres en commun, qui implique une modification du statut de la propriété décidée par les propriétaires eux-mêmes et ne concernant qu'eux, peut résulter d'un acte analogue à celui qui régit, à la Crècherie, les rapports du capital et du travail, autrement dit des propriétaires des instruments de production et des salariés.

En fait, le "socialisme" de Zola se définit d'un côté par "l'intéressement" des ouvriers aux bénéfices de l'entreprise, en second lieu par la constitution de coopératives de production agricole, et enfin par la substitution, au petit commerce, de grands magasins de distribution eux-mêmes dépendant de l'entreprise industrielle. Zola ne semble pas voir que la création des grandes chaînes commerciales, préfigurée par son roman, repose sur une organisation capitaliste et a pour fin, non point le "bien-être de tous," mais l'accroissement des profits de quelques-uns.

De plus, il a retenu la méfiance des anarchistes à l'égard des organisations politiques, de l'Etat et du collectivisme: l'action de Luc s'exerce entièrement à l'écart des syndicats, des partis, des hommes politiques. En revanche, Zola emprunte à Fourier la vision d'une société rigoureusement organisée, sous la houlette d'un Père.

Dans *Travail*, on voit donc la vaticination anarchiste se marier sans difficulté à l'imagerie évangélique et à un bricolage socio-politique hérité des rêveries fouriéristes. C'est un extraordinaire dérapage idéologique, par

[9]*Ibid.*, p. 918.

rapport à *Germinal*, et par rapport aux tendances les plus vivaces du socialisme de 1900, auxquelles Zola croyait pourtant, de bonne foi, se rattacher. A Jean Jaurès, venu lui rendre visite pendant son exil à Londres, il avait dit: "Pour moi, je lis, je cherche, non pas pour imaginer un système nouveau après tant de systèmes, mais pour dégager des oeuvres socialistes ce qui s'accorde le mieux avec mon sens de la vie, avec mon amour de l'activité, de la santé, de l'abondance et de la joie." De *Germinal* à *Travail*, les figures mythiques du social et du politique, souvent analogiques dans leur forme, comme nous l'avons vu, ont changé de signe. *Travail*, qui emprunte tant de leitmotivs à *Germinal*, est par le fait un anti-*Germinal*. Il resterait à expliquer ce renversement. Je dirai seulement qu'il ne faudrait pas s'étonner d'une contradiction entre les intentions exprimées par le romancier, voire entre ses actes publics, et telle ou telle des significations profondes de son oeuvre. Il n'est pas le premier ni le seul écrivain chez qui l'on ait à constater cette discordance. Car il existe dans toute oeuvre un inconscient idéologique. Le langage de la générosité utopique peut être aussi celui de la régression. C'est d'ailleurs de cette "fêlure" que sont souvent faites les grandes oeuvres. Et c'est ce qui donne à l'histoire littéraire un certain intérêt de pathétique.

Université de Paris VIII

Zola's *Thérèse Raquin:*
A Re-Evaluation

By Lilian R. Furst

Few writers have suffered such vicissitudes of critical evaluation in the course of the last hundred years as Emile Zola. Fortunately, the days are long since past when die-hard moralistic traditionalists castigated Zola as a depraved purveyor of pornographic filth. *Le Manifeste des Cine,* for instance, published in *Le Figaro* of 18 August 1887 by five renegades to Naturalism in protest against the excesses of *La Terre,* accused Zola of seeing nature not "à travers un tempérament," as he had phrased it in his well-known formula, but rather "à travers un *sensorium morbide.*" The pervertedness of Zola's view of man is also the prime object of Brunetière's attack in *Le Roman naturaliste* (Paris, 1902, p. 13), where he rejects Zola as a mutilator of nature through "les grossièretés révoltantes et malsaines" of his portrayal of the human condition.

While this moralizing approach is now well and properly outdated, it is not so long since critics presented Zola simply as a Naturalist, in the light of his own programmatic theories. He was repeatedly characterized as a detached observer and objective painter of reality who drew the material of his novels from a conscientious and deliberate collection of so-called 'documentation.' This image of Zola was buttressed and spiced by the many anecdotes that grew out of his ride on a railway-engine (in preparation for *La Bête humaine*), his descent into a coal-mine (as background to *Germinal*) or his rapid trip into the country to look at farming methods (for *La Terre*). His compulsive note-taking in every situation and his passion for factual detail prompted George Moore's delightful, possibly even true, story of Zola, while amassing information for *Nana*, being taken to the house of a famous *demi-mondaine* and promptly rushing into her bedroom—to measure its precise dimensions! Moore, however, was an Irishman with a satiric sense of humor and his tongue always in his cheek. Most of Zola's other contemporaries, as well as subsequent critics, took his zeal for 'documentation' at its face value and emphasized the mimetic fidelity of his depiction of reality. So he came to acquire the reputation of being a kind of super-realist who explored areas of existence beyond the ordinary or the exotic customary in the nineteenth century, and who reproduced what he had observed—often, incidentally, 'shocking,' 'lower-class' environments—with photographic accuracy.

The portrayal of milieu was, of course, only one segment of Zola's Naturalism, for according to Naturalistic doctrine man was determined by the combination of heredity, milieu, and what Taine called "le moment," i.e. the pressure of immediate circumstance. These are the forces at work in Zola's *Les Rougon-Macquart*, that sequence of twenty novels designed to trace the "histoire naturelle et sociale d'une famille sous le Second Empire," to quote its sub-title. Zola made great play, particularly in this series, of his scientific pretensions. Just as he based his method on Claude Bernard's *Introduction à l'étude de la médecine expérimentale*, which he read soon after its publication in 1865, so he discovered much of his actual material in Dr. Prosper Lucas' *Traité philosophique et physiologique de l'hérédité naturelle dans les états de santé et de maladie du système nerveux, avec l'application méthodique des lois de la procréation au traitement général des affections dont elle est le principe*. Zola was evidently much impressed by this curious work which he studied in 1868-9, annotating it copiously. In his formulation of his literary theory, notably in *Le Roman expérimental*, one of the cardinal points, of course, was the parallel between the novelist and the scientist both as objective observers and as 'experimenters' with human life. It was in this light that the majority of critics examined Zola's works for many years. Guided by Zola's own (misleading) pronouncements, they assiduously analyzed his documentation and commented on his scientific conception of character. Zola was reputed to have proceeded 'geometrically,' in part no doubt as a result of his own heritage from his engineer father. Admittedly, critics who adhered to this line did encounter certain difficulties when they were unable to squeeze Zola's monumental novels into the corset of his narrow theory. But with a blindness and a mental rigidity that should be an awful warning to academic critics, they tended to conclude that the flaw lay in an insufficiency of science: Zola had not grasped his medical sources well enough, had not been "consistent" enough in putting his scheme into operation. For example, Martineau in *Le Roman scientifique d'Emile Zola* (Paris, 1907) criticized Zola for his incomplete understanding of Lucas' treatise, while Desprez pondered, in *L'Evolution naturaliste* (Paris, 1884), whether Zola had achieved the best balance between observation, logic and deduction. At its worst, this type of criticism virtually turned Zola's novels into mechanical artifacts devoid of aesthetic interest.

But other voices too were raised, and not only in the last twenty years, as some recent critics seem to think. As early as 1882, in a polemical article "Für und gegen Zola" (published in *Kritische Waffengänge*, number 2; reprinted in *Literarische Manifeste des deutschen Naturalismus*, edited by E. Ruprecht, [Stuttgart, 1962]), the brothers Hart questioned the validity of Zola's literary theories, which they dismissed as "nebulae," whereas, in contrast, they praised Zola's novels as truly shining stars. This line was much further developed by Brandes in his brilliantly perceptive article on Zola, which is hardly known even today because it appeared in the *Deutsche Rundschau* (number *liv*, January 1888, pp. 27-44) in German. Brandes, who envisaged Zola as the "Dichter der Kehrseite" (the poet of the reverse side of life), gave a sensitive appreciation of his artistry, especially his use of symbols.

Parallel to Brandes' appraisal, and almost contemporaneous with it, is the excellent essay by J. A. Symonds on *La Bête humaine* in *The Fortnightly Review* of October 1891. Sub-titled "A Study in Zola's Idealism," the essay opens with these words: "It is one of the *mauvaises plaisanteries* of the epoch to call M. Zola a realist. Actually, he is an idealist of the purest water;" and the first paragraph ends with the comment: "The fact is that Zola, like Whitman, approaches his art-work in the spirit of a poet." Beside Symonds' radical arguments in favor of Zola's so-called "idealism," much supposedly avant-garde modern criticism seems relatively timid. Its direction, however, is clearly that of Brandes and Symonds in its repeated insistence on Zola's greatness as an essentially mythopoeic poet, who transformed reality into poetry by his subtle elaboration of a complex web of symbols.[1] It is not on the scientific and mimetic, but on the lyrical, visionary, symbolist aspects of Zola's writing that the spotlight now falls.

This revaluation of Zola has centered on the *Les Rougon-Macquart*, and rightly so, since the series includes such masterpieces as *Germinal* and *L'Assommoir*. To conceive them merely as documents of the lives of miners and laundresses determined by their physical appetites and their environment strikes us as patently grotesque. They have been rescued from this reading, as well as from moralistic censure, by the recognition of the grandiose

---

[1]This is not the place to indulge in a detailed review of Zola criticism. Suffice it to say that foremost among the exponents of this aesthetic approach are Robert Baldick ("Zola the Poet" in *The Listener*, number *liv*, 8 December 1955), Jean Cocteau ("Zola, le poète" in *Les Cahiers Naturalistes*, number *xi*, 1958), Harry Levin (in *The Gates of Horn*, N.Y., 1963), S. Max (in *Les Métamorphoses de la grande ville dans les Rougon-Macquart*, Paris, 1966), H. Petriconi (in *Das Reich des Untergangs*, Hamburg, 1958), Guy Robert (in *Emile Zola*, Paris, 1952), P. Walker (in "Prophetic Myths in Zola" in *PMLA*, *lxxiv*, number 4, September 1959) and the contributors to both *Présence de Zola* (edited by Marc Bernard, Paris, 1953) and the special Zola issue of *Yale French Studies* (number xliv, June 1969).

mythic structure that turns them into epics of forceful originality. A rescue operation of sorts has also been attempted for Zola's early work by John Lapp in his book *Zola Before the Rougon-Macquart* (Toronto, 1964), which discusses themes, images and attitudes of the mature work already incipient in the early stories, and suggests—not always very convincingly—that they were a preparatory foreshadowing of *Les Rougon-Macquart*.

In all these efforts at rehabilitation, *Thérèse Raquin* has largely been by-passed. Even so astute and thorough a Zola specialist as Guy Robert skates over it in a page or so, pretty well accepting the traditional assessment of it as a pioneering, but not very good, example of Naturalism. Yet *Thérèse Raquin* marks a crucial stage in Zola's development, and for this reason, quite apart from possible artistic considerations, it deserves closer attention than it has hitherto been given. For with *Thérèse Raquin* Zola made the decisive break away from the saccharine sentimentalities of the *Contes à Ninon* (1864) and *La Confession de Claude* (1865) which seem in places horribly like an unintentional parody of Musset's *La Confession d'un enfant du siècle*. Suddenly, possibly as a result of the encounter with Claude Bernard's *Introduction à l'étude de la médecine expérimentale*, a completely new astringency comes into Zola's writing. *Thérèse Raquin* in fact represents the first steps in a new direction and, as with a child's first steps, there are signs of both faltering and impetuosity. But here is a work squarely set on the road that was to lead, before long, to *Les Rougon-Macquart*. It lacks the stature and the finesse of Zola's mature work, and it would be rash to advance excessive claims in its favor; yet its very shortcomings in themselves are highly significant, for they reveal that *Thérèse Raquin* is by no means the straightforward prototype of Naturalism that it is generally assumed to be.

If *Thérèse Raquin* has been constantly misinterpreted as the Naturalistic novel *par excellence*, the fault must in part be ascribed to Zola himself, for this is the image that he fostered in his preface. Like Wordsworth's programmatic 1800 preface to the *Lyrical Ballads*, the preface to *Thérèse Raquin* was added to the novel's second edition. Again, as in Wordsworth's case, it was specifically designed to counter criticism of the work by a systematic statement of artistic intent. Not surprisingly, Zola's unabashed portrayal of adultery and murder had provoked an outcry in the staid France of the mid-1860s; in *Le Figaro* of 23 January 1868 Louis Ulbach had condemned it as "putrid." Hence, Zola sought primarily in his preface to defend himself against this charge which exasperated him because he was genuinely convinced of his innocence. Indeed, Zola seems as shocked at his readers' failure to understand his purpose as they were at his supposed immorality; the word "comprendre" recurs no fewer than eight times in the six little pages of the preface, and it is "pour éviter à l'avenir tout malentendu"[2] (p. 8) that Zola decides to outline his aims and his method.

The crux of the preface—and of his self-defence—lies in the proclamation of his scientific approach: "mon but a été un but scientifique avant tout" (p. 8); his ultimate goal, like that of the scientist, has been, simply and grandiosely, "la recherche du vrai" (p. 9), and with this in mind, he has used "la méthode moderne," i.e. "l'analyse scientifique" (p. 11). Here Zola

---

[2]All quotations refer to Livre de Poche edition, (Paris: Fasquelle, 1968).

already foreshadows the explicit parallel he will later draw in *Le Roman expérimental* between the novelist and the medical man. He portrays himself as "un simple analyste" (p. 9), working "comme un médecin" (p. 9) and "avec la seule curiosité du savant" (p. 10). His novel is defined as "une étude physiologique" (p. 11), carried out on "pièces d'anatomie nues et vivantes" (p. 12). The whole scientific scaffolding to *Thérèse Raquin* is epitomized in one strange sentence: "J'ai simplement fait sur deux corps vivants le travail analytique que les chirurgiens font sur les cadavres" (p. 9). The fundamental questionability of Zola's program is hinted, to my mind, in the confusion of the living with the dead, the healing surgeon with the dissecting pathologist. Be that as it may, the scientific costume admirably served Zola's immediate need in that, as he was quick to point out, "le reproche d'immoralité, en matière de science, ne prouve absolument rien" (p. 10).

Although the scientific approach was originally championed by Zola to counter the allegation of putridity, in the long run it had quite other, very far-reaching implications for his technique as a novelist. This development is already evident in the preface to *Thérèse Raquin* in which the emphasis shifts from the defence against immorality to the fundamental question of characterization, and specifically the writer's relationship to the figures he is depicting. The quintessence of the scientific method lies in its innate objectivity, its total and cold neutrality vis-à-vis the matter of its enquiry. This kind of detachment from his characters is advocated by Zola as the ideal stance of the 'experimental' novelist who should engage in a dispassionate "analyse du mécanisme humain" (p. 9). That word "mécanisme" gives an important clue to Zola's view of man. For the icy gaze of the scientist, by definition, strips man of his humanity, and sees, instead of quirky individuals, classifiable products of physiological, chemical, and social pressures. This may be an over-simplification, even a slander of the scientist. But what is important is not so much the questionable validity of this conception, as the fact that Zola clung to it in all sincerity. He categorically believed, and repeatedly maintained, that his attitude was that of the scientist, and for him that meant an objectivity so radical that it amounted almost to an emotional deadness. It is significant, in this context, that he compared his analysis of character to that of the medical man on *corpses* ("cadavres"). Thus he claimed that "l'humanité des modèles disparaissait" (p. 9), that he was sketching "des tempéraments et non des caractères" (p. 8), "des brutes humaines" (p. 8) in whom "l'âme est parfaitement absente" (p. 8), who are "souverainement dominés par leurs nerfs et leur sang, dépourvus de libre arbitre, entraînés à chaque acte de leur vie par les fatalités de leur chair" (p. 8), and who, since they have no soul or feelings, suffer from "détraquements cérébraux" (p. 8), "un simple désordre organique" (p. 8) as a consequence of the murder they have perpetrated (I am deliberately avoiding here the word "committed" because this implies a far more active role than Zola would have admitted).

This is, at least in theory, an infinitely more intense degree of objectivity than that customary in mid-nineteenth century Realism. Not only is the novelist turned into an insensitive manipulator, but also character is reduced to a mere scheme in which man is conceived as the passive product of heredity, milieu, and the pressure of momentary circumstances. Yet this is what Zola was suggesting when he described his novel as "l'étude du tempérament et des modifications profondes de l'organisme sous la pression des milieux et des circonstances" (p. 12). And this is, strange to say, the light in which *Thérèse Raquin* has generally been interpreted: as the prototype of systematic Naturalism in accordance with Zola's avowed program. Quite recently, for instance, Guy Robert wrote (*Emile Zola*, Paris, 1952, p. 19): "Zola s'arme bien d'un scalpel en face de Thérèse et de Laurent, de leur amour, de leur crime, de leurs remords et, n'étant pas l'homme des ménagements, d'emblée il prive d'âme ses personnages pour ne voir en leur comportement que le résultat de phénomènes d'ordre purement biologique." While this judgement is not to be disputed fundamentally, nonetheless it seems dangerously blinkered, for it reduces *Thérèse Raquin* to Zola's own formula. It is for this reason, of course, that Robert dismisses *Thérèse Raquin* as "simpliste, artificiel" (*op. cit.*, p. 19). But if we can only rid ourselves of the brain-washing effect of Zola's preface and read the text with an unprejudiced mind, *Thérèse Raquin* proves a much more complex, paradoxical and interesting novel than is commonly thought. Its potential for controversy lies quite elsewhere than in questions of morality or even of fidelity to the Naturalistic program.

At first sight the opening pages of *Thérèse Raquin* are likely to impress the reader as a realistic description of milieu, particularly if he comes to them fresh from the impact of the preface. The location is cited in the very first sentence with the utmost precision: "Au bout de la rue Guénégaud, lorsqu'on vient des quais, on trouve le passage du Pont-Neuf, une sorte de corridor étroit et sombre qui va de la rue Mazarine à la rue de Seine. Ce passage a trente pas de long et deux de large, au plus; etc." There is no need of a map of Paris to find and recognize the Passage where the Raquin shop is sited; the 'documentation,' as the Naturalists would call it, is a model of its kind. The description of the Passage and of the shop extends over three or four pages, concentrating throughout on visual details. The technique is in fact remarkably like that of the cine-camera, with the lens focused at the outset on the whole Passage, then zooming in on to the Raquin shop and finally coming to rest on the two women seated behind the counter. By the end of the short opening chapter, the reader has seen and experienced the world of Thérèse Raquin; in other words, the milieu, that vital factor in a Naturalistic novel, has been drawn. But the reader's experience of milieu here is by no means exclusively visual, because the cameraman does more than merely select certain telling details chosen to evoke the sinister, eerie atmosphere of his subject, such as its gloom, desolation, decrepitude: "des boutiques obscures, basses, écrasées, laissant échapper des souffles froids de caveau" (p. 15); "une boutique dont les boiseries d'un vert bouteille suaient l'humidité par toutes leurs fentes" (p. 17); "la muraille monte, noire, grossièrement crépie, comme couverte d'une lèpre et toute couturée de cicatrices" (p. 16). In each of these phrases—and there are many more similar ones—the objective notation of detail has been heightened, indeed superseded, by an alien element. The cold, cavernous breaths emanating from the shops, the humid sweating of their walls, and their leprous, pock-marked surface: these amount not just to an anthropomorphizing of the dead object, but also to an emotional response to its inner character as well as to its outer appearance. Gradually it becomes obvious that the Passage and shop are not being photographed by a camera, nor described by a detached scientist. The words themselves betray the presence of feeling: "une clarté blanchâtre tombe des vitres sales et traîne *misérablement* dans le passage. Par les vilains jours d'hiver, par les matinées de brouillard, les vitres ne jettent que de la nuit sur les dalles gluantes, de la nuit *salie* et *ignoble*" (p. 15—italics are mine). On two occasions there are even direct judgements on the part of the author: when the walls are described as "peintes d'une *horrible* couleur brune" (p. 16) and the merchandise in the shop "jauni et fripé, était *lamentablement* pendu à un crochet de fil de fer" (p. 17—italics are mine). Under the guise of an objective painting of milieu Zola is in actuality giving a potent atmospheric evocation of an unsavory spot. "Le passage prend l'aspect sinistre d'un véritable coupe-gorge" (p. 17), and this is due to its illumination by Zola's imagination. Though he attempts the task of the cameraman, he does so under the lighting of his poetic imagination.

The opening chapter also breaks the bounds of realism in its repeated allusions to death and in the associated tension between darkness and light. These are to be cardinal themes of the novel, and as such it is artistically appropriate that they be introduced in the first pages, although here again Zola infringes on the standards of scientific detachment which he advocated in his preface. The whole Passage Pont-Neuf, from its elongated, narrow shape to its darkness and decay, seems to hint at the grave. In the Raquin shop that image is particularly strong, for it is a bare and glacially cold hole "où la nuit habite pendant le jour" (p. 17) and where the goods have faded to a murky grey, rotted by dust and damp. The figures themselves seem curiously static and almost dead in their pallor and lethargy. Even though they move out of the still-life tableau in which they are first glimpsed, their actions are described significantly in the imperfect tense which conveys a sense of repetitiveness, of a sterile ritual continuing to all eternity—as if in fact it were already eternity. No wonder that Thérèse later tells Laurent she had felt buried alive in that shop. In its sombre, mysterious and vaguely threatening quality this is a masterly opening to the 'closet drama' to be enacted in *Thérèse Raquin*. No amount of objective observation and documentation could have produced so haunting an effect: that is the prerogative of the poetic imagination.

Throughout *Thérèse Raquin* a similar substratum of emotion flows powerfully beneath the apparent objectivity, coming to the surface in words, phrases, and images incongruous in a scientific report. It is not possible, within the space of this article, to analyze other sections in the same detail as the opening chapter which serves as a prototype example of Zola's approach. Again and again, often even more persistently than in that first description of milieu, the purportedly sober, scientific prose vibrates to an almost lyrical strain. This is evident in the scenes by the river just before the murder, when the consonance of mood between man and landscape is reminiscent of Romantic writing:

> Les feuilles tombées faisaient à terre une couche rougeâtre qui craquait sous les pieds avec des frémissements secs. Les troncs se dressaient droits, innombrables comme des faisceaux de colonnettes gothiques; les branches descendaient jusque sur le front des promeneurs, qui avaient ainsi pour tout horizon la voûte cuivrée des feuillages mourants et les fûts blancs et noirs des trembles et des chênes. Ils étaient au désert, dans un trou

mélancolique, dans une étroite clairière silencieuse et fraîche. Tout
autour d'eux, ils entendaient la Seine gronder (p. 78).

The threatening sound of the river, the hints of death in the falling leaves,
the allusion to the grave in the "trou mélancolique," the silence, the desolation and isolation: all these add up to a hauntingly evocative setting for a
crime. And when Zola writes, immediately before the murder: "La campagne,
brûlée par les rayons ardents de l'été, sent la mort venir avec les premiers
vents froids. Et il y a, dans les cieux, des souffles plaintifs de désespérance. La
nuit descend de haut, apportant des linceuls dans son ombre" (p. 84), his
words inevitably bring to mind Rousseau's famous autumn *paysage état-
d'âme* in *Les Rêveries du promeneur solitaire*. The parallel is striking both in
the harmony of the prose and in the underlying belief in the pathetic fallacy.
And this proximity to Rousseau's *Rêveries*, the very incarnation of Romantic
prose-lyricism, is surely a telling comment on Zola's attempted disguise as a
scientific writer.

Nor does Zola in practice shun such thoroughly poetic devices as images,
symbols and recurrent leitmotifs. Even when the images are incidental to
the fabric of the novel, they are of a dimension that rises far above mere
decoration: "l'insomnie les couchait sur un lit de charbons ardents" (p. 125);
"le furieux serrement de main qu'ils échangeaient était comme un poids
écrasant jeté sur la tête de Camille pour le maintenir sous l'eau" (p. 93);
"l'étalage, jauni par la poussière, semblait porter le deuil de la maison" (p.
102). Such images make *Thérèse Raquin* quiver with the primordial vigor
of the potent and original imagination inspiring it. What is more, a Wagnerian web of leitmotifs is woven out of certain crucial symbols that are at the
very heart of the narrative: the joined hands, the cat, the river spring to mind
immediately. The most important and obvious, however, is Laurent's wound
on his neck, sustained when Camille bites him as he is being thrown into the
river. References to this wound punctuate the rest of the story. It heals slowly
and badly, leaving a nasty scar that turns an angry red in moments of stress.
Both Laurent and Thérèse become obsessed by it. For Laurent it is the Cain-
like mark of his guilt; which he tries first to conceal, and later, when he has
come to fear that it is eating him up (as indeed his guilt is), persuades himself that only Thérèse's kisses *on* the wound itself can cure it. But Thérèse
refuses point-blank, recoiling in growing horror from Laurent's stigma, which
thus becomes one of the chief sources of their physical alienation from each
other. Only at the very end, as she drops dead on to Laurent's corpse, "la
bouche de la jeune femme alla heurter, sur le cou de son mari, la cicatrice
qu'avaient laissée les dents de Camille" (p. 246). This is more than a parting
shot of horror, or even a symbolic reconciliation in death; it reveals the
beginnings, still in somewhat primitive fashion admittedly, of that mythopoeic
imagination that was to shape *Les Rougon-Macquart*.

The structure and narrative technique oscillate as much as the expression
between a façade of objectivity and an inner involvement on the part of the
author. *Thérèse Raquin* was, of course, based on a real happening. Significantly, the title originally proposed, the heavily ironical *Un Mariage d'amour*,
was changed to the neutral *Thérèse Raquin*. The novel is predominantly

dramatic in structure, consisting as it does of a series of scenes with a strong emphasis on visual details. Often, as at the beginning and at the end, Zola presents a tableau such as would admirably suit the rise or the fall of the curtain in the theatre. The treatment of time too is revealing in its concentration on climaxes and its telescoping of the lengthy intervening periods, so that it is closer to the tautness of drama than to the discursiveness of the leisurely nineteenth century novel. It is worth recalling that *Thérèse Raquin* was turned into a play (and into a film) and in spite of its poor reception at its first run in Paris in 1873, it enjoyed considerable acclaim in Italy, Germany and Scandinavia, and modest success on its return to the Parisian stage in 1892.

It was not only in outline but also in actual technique that Zola aspired to the condition of drama in *Thérèse Raquin*, and this is where difficulties arise. According to Naturalist theory, the novelist should "disparaître complètement derrière l'action qu'il raconte. Il est le metteur en scène caché du drame. Jamais il ne se montre au bout d'une phrase" (*Les Romanciers naturalistes*, Paris, 1923, p. 109). The formula was coined in this explicit manner some fourteen years after the writing of *Thérèse Raquin*, in 1881. But it is already inferred in the preface to this early novel when Zola defines his method as "l'analyse scientifique" (p. 11), which implies objectivity, impersonality, a cold, aloof detachment from the material. This notion marks one of the points where the Naturalistic ideal is simply unfeasible, certainly as far as the novel is concerned. I cannot here go into the whole problem of the vanishing narrator, the so-called 'well-made novel' à la Henry James. Whether any novel can, or indeed should, wholly fulfil such demands is a moot question. What is certain is that *Thérèse Raquin* does not. Zola clearly endeavours to present rather than to tell, and it would be misleading to deny that he succeeds, to some extent, in so doing. Nevertheless he is far from the total objectivity that is supposedly characteristic of the scientist.

In a variety of ways we are aware of the presence of a narrator, an omniscient narrator at that, who knows his figures from the inside and who shifts his viewpoint at his own convenience. Sometimes it is no more than a single word that betrays his refracting presence between the object and the reader, as in those subjective reactions "horrible" and "lamentablement" noted in the opening chapter. Or there is the implied moralistic judgement as when Thérèse's and Laurent's career is termed a "vie de boue" (p. 245) and their marriage "le châtiment fatal du meurtre" (p. 205), and their struggle with Mme. Raquin as "odieuse" (p. 223). In other instances he both presents *and* states: for example at the end of chapter V, when Laurent's disturbing impact on Thérèse has already been admirably shown, Zola adds this superfluous remark that really weakens the foregoing scene: "La nature sanguine de ce garçon, sa voix pleine, ses rires gras, les senteur âcres et puissantes qui s'échappaient de sa personne, troublaient la jeune femme et la jetaient dans une sorte d'angoisse" (p. 44). The trick of ending a chapter on a telling punch-line is indeed one of Zola's favorite forms of intervention. The narrator also becomes manifest in the ironies that punctuate the novel: the irony of Laurent's first, as well as his later, portraits of Camille, all of which make him look like a drowned corpse; the irony of the foolish Thursday guests with their utterly mistaken view of the situation; the irony of Mme. Raquin's incitement to the marriage of Thérèse and Laurent: all these reveal Zola's manipulation of his story in place of the pure observation and recording he purported to practice.

But these 'lapses' are relatively slight compared to the frequent occasions when Zola steps out of his narrative in order to comment on it quite openly, as if to satisfy an irrepressible urge to explain the drama being enacted before our eyes. Thus we stumble on to interpolated sentences such as "C'était l'hypocrisie maladroite de deux fous" (p. 163), "Ce fut une révolte superbe de brutalité" (p. 166), or again, "Il y avait là une contradiction de conduite" (p. 241). These comments stand like boulders in the smooth path of the narrative, and what is more, they increase in number and tend to grow in size as the novel progresses.

> Le plus étrange était qu'ils ne parvenaient pas à être dupes de leurs serments, qu'ils se rappelaient parfaitement tous deux les circonstances de l'assassinat. Ils lisaient des aveux dans leurs yeux, lorsque leurs lèvres se donnaient des démentis. C'étaient des mensonges puérils, des affirmations ridicules, la dispute toute de mots de deux misérables qui mentaient pour mentir, sans pouvoir se cacher qu'ils mentaient. Successivement, ils prenaient le rôle d'accusateur, et, bien que jamais le procès qu'ils se faisaient n'eût amené un résultat, ils le recommençaient chaque soir avec un acharnement cruel. Ils savaient qu'ils ne se prouveraient rien, qu'ils ne parviendraient pas à effacer le passé, et ils tentaient toujours cette besogne, ils revenaient toujours à la charge, aiguillonnés par la douleur et l'effroi, vaincus à l'avance par l'accablante réalité. Le bénéfice le plus net qu'ils tiraient de leurs disputes, était de produire une tempête de mots et de cris dont le tapage les étourdissait un moment (p. 211).

In an explanatory sequence such as this Zola is close to the traditional novelist, interpreting the inner dilemmas of his characters and mediating between them and his readers. There is here more of the old-style, intuitive psychologist than of the new-fangled, dispassionate surgeon.

This passage also raises the crucial problem of the characterization. It is in this field, more than any other, that critics have tended to accept Zola's contentions and to hail *Thérèse Raquin* as the prototype of the scientific analysis of character. This hypothesis proves rather more tenable for the first part of the novel than for its later sections, though even the beginning is not without its contradiction.

It can be argued convincingly that Thérèse herself is the product of heredity and milieu, and that she acts under the pressure of circumstances, at least until the murder of Camille. Since the facts are so clearly presented in the text and have, moreover, been so frequently adduced by critics in support of a Naturalistic interpretation of *Thérèse Raquin*, it seems superfluous to rehearse them here in any detail. Suffice it to say that from her adventurous seafaring father and her mysterious, beautiful North African mother, Thérèse has inherited a passionate temperament that she has had to stifle during her upbringing in the cloying, sick-room atmosphere of Camille's nursery. So from her childhood onwards, "elle tenait soigneusement cachées, au fond d'elle, toutes les fougues de sa nature. Elle possédait un sang-froid suprême, une apparente tranquillité qui cachait des emportements terribles"

(p. 24). To marry this wild animal to the languid, effete Camille was already to court trouble, and the dark, dank, musty shop where Thérèse was doomed to spend her days turns this marriage into a living death for the young woman. Heredity and milieu have thus played their part before the appearance of Laurent who is, in his coarse physical strength, the diametric opposite to Camille. With her repressed, frustrated sexuality Thérèse is inevitably attracted to him. More so than he is to her. At this stage Laurent's heredity and present milieu come into play. For he is "un vrai fils de paysan" (p. 39), a crude, self-seeking nature impelled by a pricking sensuality, yet prevented by his financial straits from buying his pleasures from prostitutes. So, ugly though Thérèse strikes him at first sight, "l'économie lui conseillait déjà de prendre la femme de son ami" (p. 47). Thus far the characterization is predominantly 'scientific' and quite credible; in fact, it satisfies the demands both of the physiological and of the psychological view of man.

In the motivation of the drowning, however, certain discrepancies begin to appear. The major emphasis is still squarely on the Naturalistic approach, which presents the murder of Camille as the inescapable outcome of 'le moment.' The pressure of circumstance is undoubtedly of very great importance, for unless Camille is disposed of, Laurent's meetings with Thérèse must cease. And by this time Laurent is physically so enthralled by Thérèse that he cannot forego her passionate embraces. In the frequent references to burning blood, trembling nerves, and to Thérèse's female smell, Zola brings out the role of sensuality in the motivation of the murder. Here the physiological jargon of vibrating flesh, pallor and sweating, all the *sang, nerfs* and *chair* that punctuate *Thérèse Raquin*, is indeed well-placed. Yet in the last resort, murder merely as a kind of conditioned reflex is unacceptable, however logically demonstrated are the steps leading to it. At some point, at two points as it turns out, Laurent does make a choice: first when he decides, after some thought, to take Thérèse to be his mistress (p. 47), and again when he weighs up the pros and cons of murder during a sleepless night:

> Tous ses intérêts le poussaient au crime. Il se disait que son père, le paysan de Jeufosse, ne se décidait pas à mourir; il lui faudrait peut-être rester encore dix ans employé, mangeant dans les crémeries, vivant sans femme dans un grenier. Cette idée l'exaspérait. Au contraire, Camille mort, il épousait Thérèse, il héritait de madame Raquin, il donnait sa démission et flânait au soleil.(p. 70)

What is this other than a man making a choice? Guided by self-interest and thinking with peasant logic certainly, but deliberately choosing murder, money, and comfort in preference to hard work, misery, and deprivation. I do not wish to labor this matter of choice since I have examined it in some detail elsewhere,[3] but it is vital to note this conscious, volitional element in the murder of Camille as well as the instinctive, physical urge. Nor does Laurent himself try to evade his responsibility; the verbs in the relevant passage are in the active (i.e. he is 'doing,' not 'it happens'), and afterwards he openly admits to himself, "il avait tué Camille" (p. 94). The final suicide too involves

---

[3]"A Question of Choice in the Naturalistic Novel," *Proceedings of the Comparative Literature Symposium* (Lubbock, Texas, 1972).

the exercise of some choice; as my students have pointed out to me, *Thérèse Raquin* should, by Naturalistic logic, have ended in the madhouse.

But then, *Thérèse Raquin* does not proceed with Naturalistic logic. What follows the murder become increasingly difficult to interpret in keeping with the Naturalistic conception of man. "La succession fatale des événements" (p. 243) leading from the drowning of Camille to the suicide of the murderers is perfectly coherent psychologically, but it cannot be explained by sheer physiology as Zola attempts to do when he posits that "la nature sèche et nerveuse de Thérèse avait agi d'un façon bizarre sur la nature épaisse et sanguine de Laurent" (p. 158), infecting him with her own jittery tenseness until the stolid peasant was "jeté en plein éréthisme nerveux." The hallucinations that plague Thérèse and Laurent call not for a neuro-surgeon, but for a psychiatrist. The physiological approach simply breaks down in the latter half of the novel. Laurent's "remords étaient purement physiques. Son corps, ses nerfs irrités et sa chair tremblante avaient seuls peur du noyé. Sa conscience n'entrait pour rien dans ses terreurs" (p. 160), Zola assures us. But this is flatly contradicted by Laurent's, and also by Thérèse's, behavior: her cringing self-accusations before the mute Mme. Raquin, her self-castigation, their hallucinations, their desperate efforts to distract themselves in dissipation, and finally, their suicide; what can these be other than the manifestations of a guilty conscience? They cannot in all seriousness be read purely as physiological reactions divorced from the inner man. And there comes a point—in the description of Laurent's repeated, obsessive portrayal of drowned men— when Zola virtually confesses the failure of his method: "Il est difficile à l'analyse de pénétrer à de telles profondeurs" (p. 184). His subject matter had in a sense outgrown the limitations of his Naturalistic method, as indeed it was to do in *Les Rougon-Macquart*.

To speak of the 'failure' of Zola's method is not to imply an adverse judgment on his artistry. In *Thérèse Raquin*, as I have been trying to show, he did not fulfill the program he outlined—*post facto*, incidentally—in his preface. He did not, in other words, write a Naturalistic novel in the strictest sense of the term as he himself defined it. But this is not by any means to the detriment of *Thérèse Raquin*. The imaginative evocations of atmosphere add a poetic dimension to this novel such as no wholly objective documentation could ever have done. Similarly, instead of a physiological schema, the latter part of the novel offers an acute and often fascinating insight into the workings of guilt-ridden minds. The love-hate relationship of the two accomplices, alternately shunning and clinging to each other, resisting and, at the same time, welcoming their disintegration, is illumined with brilliant intuition. Zola also more than hints at a streak of perversion in Thérèse and particularly in Laurent in the constant association of love and death. They appear to derive a deeper satisfaction from the murder than from their love-making which, significantly, peters out after the killing because, like cannibals who have savored human flesh, they have acquired other tastes. Their attempts to kill each other as well as their eventual suicide could be interpreted as further manifestations of that perversion. All this, of course, draws *Thérèse Raquin* into the realm of psychopathology and distances it from the commonplace that is supposed to be the province of Naturalism. In response perhaps to Taine's criticism that the characters are too 'extraordinary,' Zola concedes in his preface: "*Thérèse Raquin* est l'étude d'un cas trop exceptionnel" (p. 12). The brothers Goncourt, in a letter to Zola on 5 February 1868, call the novel an "étude presque pathologique." Astutely, they refrain from the censure in which many of their contemporaries indulged in the name either of morality or of Naturalism. After an interval of some hundred years we are free to admire Zola's penetrating portrayal of the drift into psychopathology, without the prejudice of moralistic considerations or of literary ideologies.

This relative freedom of ours should indeed enable us to reassess *Thérèse Raquin*. It is evidently not the incarnation of doctrinal Naturalism, as Zola suggested in his preface and as so many critics have since assumed. Although it adheres to some extent to the principles of Naturalism, more so at the beginning than later, there are too many radical departures from Naturalistic theory to warrant the label that has all too often been attached to it. In many ways the second half of *Thérèse Raquin* has a greater affinity to the Gothic than to the Naturalistic novel. The extended description of Laurent's visits to the morgue, the hints of vampirism in the vigils with the spectre of Camille, the ghoulish intervention of his decomposing corpse in the marital bed, the motif of the staring cat, the mute witness of Mme. Raquin, not to mention the novel's closing sentence:

> Les cadavres restèrent toute la nuit sur le carreau de la salle à manger, tordus, vautrés, éclairés de lueurs jaunâtres par les clartés de la lampe que l'abat-jour jetait sur eux. Et, pendant près de douze heures, jusqu'au lendemain vers midi, madame Raquin, roide et muette, les contempla à ses pieds, ne pouvant se rassasier les yeux, les écrasant de regards lourds.

—all these surely are close to the world of Edgar Allan Poe and have little in common with the sobriety of the scientist. Zola's tendency to inflate and to exaggerate, at times into the monstrous, which is discernible in *Les Rougon-Macquart* too, increasingly gains the upper hand in *Thérèse Raquin*.

Thérèse Raquin is certainly no masterpiece. Quite apart from its other defects, it comes in places perilously near to the *kitsch* of *Madeleine Férat* which was written only a year later. In many respects parallel to *Thérèse Raquin*, it reveals fully the dangers latent, and sometimes apparent too, in the slightly earlier, and by and large better novel. Many of the excesses are quite simply the flaws of youth. *Thérèse Raquin* is the product of a violent and lurid imagination not yet under sufficient control; but it is unmistakably the same imagination that was to create *L'Assommoir* and *Germinal*. We may well dismiss Zola's scientific pretensions as mere clap-trap, and we probably concur with Sainte-Beuve's judgement that "Il est certain, que dans *Thérèse Raquin*, les choses sont poussées au cauchemar, et que la vérité stricte est en deçà de tant d'horreurs" (*Documents littéraires*, Paris, 1890, p. 226). But as soon as we cease to envisage *Thérèse Raquin* as the prototype of Naturalism, why, after all, should we demand or expect "la vérité stricte?" As an imaginative tale, it is hauntingly effective.

Such a re-assessment of *Thérèse Raquin* does, however, raise further questions, too thorny and far-reaching to answer here. If *Thérèse Raquin*, which has generally been cited as the very model of the Naturalistic novel, departs so far from the prescribed pattern, is this true of other so-called Naturalistic novels too? Is the discrepancy between theory and practice too great to warrant the use of the term at all? Is not 'Naturalistic' largely meaningless and misleading as a critical concept?

Dartmouth College

A Triad of Images:
Nature in *Madame Bovary*

By MARGARET CHURCH

For a writer with the detachment of Flaubert, the image is a particularly fitting device because, as Benjamin Bart shows, it has a "natural place within the character portrayed."[1] Flaubert was, he himself said, "devoured by comparisons as beggars were by lice."[2] M. D.-L. Demorest offers perhaps the most complete treatment of imagery in the work of Flaubert.[3] Demorest goes beyond the scope of earlier discussions of Flaubert's imagery (such as those by Brunetière, Faguet, Maynial) by studying the grouping of imagery in the works, or the techniques and tendencies apparent in Flaubert's use of imagery.

[1]Benjamin F. Bart, *Flaubert* (Syracuse, 1967), p. 351.
[2]*Ibid.*, p. 350.
[3]D.-L. Demorest, *L'Expression Figurée et Symbolique dans l'Oeuvre de Gustave Flaubert* (Genève, 1967).

One grouping noted by M. Demorest is that of nature imagery, but he goes little further than to indicate that Flaubert consistently employs the banal natural object "que nous environne de toutes parts"[4] as M. Brunetière had already shown in his work on Flaubert.

Claudine Gothot-Mersch, in the chapter "Une Symphonie" in her book on the genesis of *Madame Bovary*, writes of the series of structural schemes which give *Madame Bovary* its unity. She goes on to point out that although a study of the technique of contrast in *Madame Bovary* is beyond the scope of her work, the oppositions in the book respond to a tendency in the temperament of the author.[5] One of the structures mentioned by Mlle. Gothot-Mersch is that of the triad. *Madame Bovary* is, of course, written in three parts; there is also a relatively obvious grouping of episodes into three stages.

What is not noted is that the nature imagery employed by Flaubert generally falls into three main groupings. These groupings are constantly acting as foils for one another and as foils for the characters themselves. Situations and people in the novel are, as Mlle. Gothot-Mersch shows, continually defined by opposition.[6] Water or liquid imagery, one central grouping of the nature imagery, universally symbolizes the vital and flowing quality of experience. Yet Flaubert's water images are often either sentimentalized or muddy, stained or medicated as a result of man's intervention. Significantly, in Table V, given at the end of M. Demorest's work, water imagery far outnumbers all other elemental images listed; Demorest counts a total of 259 water images in *Madame Bovary*.

A second grouping of images, vegetation images (Demorest lists 101 in *Madame Bovary*) symbolizes both fertility and growth. But Flaubert continually contrasts the flowering natural beauty of the Norman countryside with the squalid existences of those who live within its beauty and who convert its grasses to coarse stubble and its flowers to dried bridal bouquets, or who sentimentalize the exotic lemon tree of distant lands.

The third important grouping of natural imagery is that of animals and insects (Demorest lists 205), living counterparts to man himself. The virility and the simple instinctual nature of the animal stand in opposition to man, who harnesses the animal for his own purposes which are frequently tawdry and lacking in real direction. As Flaubert wrote to Louise Colet (*Corr.* III, 269): "Le style est autant *sous* les mots que *dans* les mots."[7]

These three groups of images are skillfully alternated throughout each of the three parts of the book. Part 1 predominates in vegetation imagery, Part 2 in animal imagery, and Part 3 in water symbols. But in each part, the two groupings which do not predominate provide counterpoint for the central image grouping. The myth of *bovarism* is the myth of sterility and civilized deformity. Natural productivity is constantly seen in the light of man's efforts to pervert its force. At the end of the book, the natural cycle continues although individual man dies as a result of his own misdirected efforts. The central thematic concern of the book—the cleavage between real and ideal, which controls it on many levels (as well as controlling its author)—is seen

---

[4]*Ibid.*, p. 426.
[5]Claudine Gothot-Mersch, *La Genèse de Madame Bovary* (Paris, 1966), p. 224.
[6]*Ibid.*, p. 223.
[7]Nouvelle Edition.

as a cleavage created synthetically by the mind of man, a schizophrenic pattern appearing also in *Don Quixote*, which Flaubert read as a child and which dominated his imagination for a long time.[8] Neither real nor ideal has meaning for nature itself which incorporates both in its very being. Emma and Charles Bovary are perhaps grotesque shadows of Don Quixote and Sancho, and they present for the reader two alternative extremes of human behavior, two extremes which Flaubert treats ironically (even scathingly) by means of nature imagery.

It is possible to examine in detail the employment of Flaubert's three groups of symbols. The vegetation images in Part 1 are sometimes arranged so that they form the positive pole of Part 1 with which the negative pole, represented by nature distorted by man, interacts. For example, in Chapter 1, Charles thrives like an oak; later he imagines the coolness of a beech grove in the country. Yet the stream by which he lives is stained yellow and purple by dye factories, and as he pursues his studies he is like a mill-horse walking blindfolded in a circle. On old Rouault's farm in Chapter 2, the houses, occupied by man, are dark stains by comparison, with even the leafless trees and the birds ruffling their feathers in the cold. As Charles' courtship of Emma progresses, the pear trees flower, although old Rouault wishes someone would stew pears for him. In these early chapters, where vegetation images are often used to suggest natural innocence, water and animal symbols are seen in a negative context, contorted by man.

Yet in the wedding scene in Chapter 4, it is as if all nature, even the vegetation, stands in opposition to this marriage. Coarse grasses and thistles attach themselves to Emma's wedding gown, the birds for long distances are frightened away by the sound of the fiddle, and foaming cider mugs and brimming wine glasses take their revenge on humans rather than on flies.

At Tostes, the vegetation imagery, which had at the Rouault farm been a positive force, begins to be replaced by the imagery of Emma's fantasy world in which nature is contorted and idealized. The dried wedding bouquet of the first wife, some scrawny rose bushes, a thorn hedge are all that remain of Rouault's flowering pear, and Emma longs for a fountain and a fish pond to indulge her vanity. As Flaubert points out, her temperament was "plus sentimental qu'artiste cherchant des emotions et non des paysages."[9] Fish and water are both rerouted to this end.

In Chapter 6, the chapter taking the reader back to Emma's youth, Flaubert relates how she had rejected country life with its lowing herds, its animal-like simplicity, and replaced it by the sea, which she loved only for its storms, and by vegetation, which she loved only when it grew among ruins. In this paragraph, the triad of vegetation, animal, and water is clearly apparent. Here it is the passive animal imagery which retains its original innocence, whereas water and vegetation are seen aslant through the eyes of the heroine. Later in the chapter, the three natural elements are all contorted as Emma imagines turtledoves in Gothic bird cages, "une forêt vierge nettoyée" (p. 36), and a sunbeam quivering perpendicular in water.

---

[8]Marianne Bonwit, "*Gustave Flaubert et le Principe d'Impassibilité*," University of California *Publications in Modern Philosophy*, XXXIII, No. 4, 286.
[9]Gustave Flaubert, *Madame Bovary, Moeurs de Province* (Paris: Garnier Frères, 1961), p. 34. All later quotations in the text from *Madame Bovary* refer to this edition.

A contrasting triad is formed as Emma's sentimental daydreams continue; she conjures up a honeymoon in which "les clochettes des chèvres," "le bruit sourde de la cascade," and "le parfum des citronniers" (p. 38) coincide. Here it is the combination of the three images which is contrived, thereby sentimentalizing the scene.

From the idealized world of Emma's daydreams, we return abruptly to another world in Chapter 7, to the dull landscape of Tostes with its sharp-edged rushes, to boredom ("araignée silencieuse"), and to sea winds filling the country with a salt smell. The central animal image at Tostes, however, is Emma's bitch, Djali, representing nature tamed and domesticated by man, yet also yearning for its freedom. Symbolically the dog's Indian name, in addition to its exotic connotations, suggests the distances for which it longs. Flaubert is also obviously aware of the prosaic nature of Emma's name compared with the poetic name of the dog. Like Emma's thoughts, Djali strays, for in captivity she exists in an unnatural mode. Yet unless nature is held captive by man, it can threaten man's very being. The ugliness which Emma sees near at hand in Tostes and in her marriage to Charles is merely the same benevolent captivity in which Djali is held. But like Djali, Emma runs away. The animal imagery which begins to move into the foreground at this point leads smoothly into Part 2 where this second image group predominates.

But before this occurs, we turn to Vaubyessard, which offers a curious parallelism with Rouault's farm, which had introduced the vegetation imagery in Part 1. Vaubyessard points to the close of the circular pattern of this section. The triad at the opening of Chapter 8 consists of cows, shrubbery, and a flowing stream. The grazing cows represent the same sort of simple bucolic setting Emma had rejected at Les Bertaux, but which is exalted in her eyes by its proximity to the château. The variegated shrubbery and the bridge under which the stream flows are, of course, man's improvements on nature. Furthermore, the elaborate dinner prepared at Vaubyessard sharply contrasts with the simple but abundant wedding dinner served at Les Bertaux. Instead of an entire suckling pig, meat is brought on in slices; in place of cider, the marquis serves champagne; and pineapples and pomegranates replace the almonds, raisins, and oranges. What has changed is the quality of the relationship to food, which is less direct at Vaubyessard than at Les Bertaux. The categories of food served are similar, but the means by which they have been obtained differ, adding to their character a romantic appeal. Parallelism, however, is established by Emma herself, who is reminded of the farm at Les Bertaux as she sees the faces of the peasants pressed against the panes. She conjures up the muddy pond, the apple trees, and herself skimming cream with her finger. The ironic contrast with the scene at Vaubyessard is marked. Back at Tostes there are onion soup and veal for dinner, and Emma stares in amazement at fruit trees and flower beds once so familiar.

The use of the triad device enables Flaubert to create a variety of effects. Parallels may exist both within the triad and between triads. Thus the differences noted in the two landscapes are reinforced by the differences in the two meals. Every detail inserted by Flaubert is calculated, so that the reader participates in Emma's mounting frustrations. At the same time Emma's memories of Les Bertaux stress the muddy pond and her menial task, whereas her vision of Vaubyessard ignores the ugliness of the Marquis' father-in-law, Marie Antoinette's lover, who sits dribbling gravy from his mouth.

Next spring at Tostes when the pear trees burst into bloom, Emma finds it difficult to breathe. Man and his institutions are seen to be stunted by comparison with the regular and luxuriant flowering of nature, the pear trees which had been associated with Charles' courtship of her. The liquids in this final chapter of Part 1 consist of camphor baths and valerian drops, concoctions for the ailing, and vinegar, Emma's means of losing weight. The animal, Djali, becomes in Emma's sick imagination a confidante, and to the dog she tells many secrets. The burning of the bridal bouquet at the end of Part 1 is a symbolic rejection of the flowering and growth of the vegetation which dominates Part 1. It is fitting that this imagery accompanies the announcement of a pregnancy Emma hates. From now on we will note the gradual development of the animal imagery in Part 2 which is dominated by this image cluster. At the end of Part 1, portions of the burned bridal bouquet fly up the chimney like black butterflies, suggesting both the metamorphosis in the imagery as well as the metamorphosis in Emma's nature, as she becomes more debased, more animal-like, and as the name, Bovary, becomes more and more fitting.

II.

Although the animal imagery increases with the intensity of Emma's appetites, Part 2 opens with a nature passage stressing vegetation and tying this part with the one that precedes it. The pastures, the grain fields, and the streams extend below the oaks of the Argueil forest. This is the same kind of landscape Flaubert has visualized near the Marquis' chateau and has connected with Emma's childhood on the farm. The cider presses also are a link with Les Bertaux. On the outskirts of Yonville, the image triad consists of aspens and hedges, cider presses and distilling sheds, and window panes with a bull's-eye in the center of each. The pear trees are espaliered and scraggly, supplying a note of foreboding and contrasting with the blooming pears found early in Part 1.

However, the character of the imagery in Part 2 is suggested by the Gallic cock on the top pediment of the town hall. This image, aggressive and assertive, contrasts with the more passive vegetation images of Part 1 and points to the growing sensual nature of Emma's affairs in this part. Furthermore, the name of the hotel in Yonville is Lion d'Or, clearly reinforcing the central motif. Both Léon and the Lion d'Or, however, represent somewhat less virility than the king of beasts. On the main street of Yonville, we encounter a dry goods shop and a pharmacy, the sterile companions of the golden lion. As the Hirondelle (the swallow) pulls up before the inn, we learn that Djali, Emma's greyhound, has escaped. Emma, like Djali, is soon to escape the mould of the dry society which she despises, for with the freeing of Djali comes the freeing of Emma's passions as she stretches out her foot toward the leg of mutton turning on the spit and talks to Léon of idealized natural settings, pastures at the top of bluffs, huge pine trees, roaring streams, and infinite oceans. Although Charles is always on horseback in the course of his work, for Léon "rien n'est plus agréable, il me semble; quand on le peut, ajouta-t-il" (p. 75). It is clear from these examples that animal imagery plays the central role in Part 2 as vegetation and water symbols take second place. Yet the three kinds of symbols are still usually found in conjunction with one another. Thus from Emma's new bedroom, we have a view of the tops of trees and of moonlight on the river, but inside the room we find the disorder left by two moving men, nature's serenity in contrast to animal-man's confusion.

The wet nurse, in Chapter 3, whose role is that of the animal provider for Emma's baby, lives in a house surrounded by a scraggly garden, a walnut tree, and a trickle of dirty water. Returning from her house, however, Emma and Léon walk by a swiftly running river, long grasses bending in the current, and spidery-legged insects poised on lily pads. This particular scene is brightly lighted by sunbeams, a positive force; Emma's sentimental dreams are often lighted by the rays of the moon.

As Emma's passion for Léon grows, both lovers tend hanging gardens in their windows. At the same time, love is compared by Flaubert to an engulfing thunder storm leaving its pools of rain on roofs, pools which may pose a danger to the house. It is water imagery which accompanies Emma's downfall in Part 3.

A bouquet of straw and wheat, tied to the peak of one of the gables at the new flax mill introduces Chapter 5. This image of dried vegetation sharply contrasts with the hanging gardens, the swift streams, the long grasses which have accompanied the initial phase of the love affair; the bouquet also reminds one of the two dried wedding bouquets in Part 1. Emma's carnal desires, her inner storms, continue for the moment, but the dried bouquet of vegetation suggests an outcome ironically different from that signified by the earlier image —the Gallic cock.

Chapter 6 brings us full circle to another April with its flowers, its full streams, and its grazing cattle. It was April when Emma had arrived in Yonville. Nature, imperturbable and indifferent to human activity, continues its fruitful cycle although the cycles of man are full of interruptions and reverses. Although nature flowers, Léon departs for Paris. The Agricultural Show, at which the animal theme receives its culminating emphasis, serves to bridge Emma's two affairs in Part 2, for Homais announces the event at the end of the chapter in which Léon leaves.

The affair with Rodolphe abounds in various animal symbols. In fact, the emphasis on this imagery increases. After Léon's departure Emma has looked back with "une mélancolie morne" at the water and flower scenes which accompanied her romance with Léon, but her hopes are now "comme des branchages morts" (p. 116). By contrast blood imagery accompanies the meeting with Rodolphe, the forceful and animal spurt of blood from the peasant's arm. The name, Rodolphe, of course, connotes red, a different red from that of the blood Emma has been spitting during her depression over Léon's removal. Life and death are curiously knotted in this scene of blood letting. Both Justin and the peasant faint, temporarily die as the animal stream gushes forth, but Emma and Rodolphe remain conscious, for their roles are connected with the "undoing" of life.

The Agricultural Show represents the obvious climax of the animal theme in Part 2. Even the townspeople at the show are described by Flaubert by means of animal symbols. The legs of Binet seem to contain all of his vital energies, like the legs of a horse, or Homais' reverse-calf shoes represent the character of the apothecary, an "inside-out" animal who poses as a man of civilization. Water and vegetation are overwhelmed in this chapter by a proliferation of human animals and domestic beasts, even though the pediment of the town hall has been looped with ivy, a sign of perennial plant vitality. Pigs, calves, cows, rearing stallions, mares are lined up to be judged by a group of gentlemen who advance "d'un pas lourd." Horses and Hippolyte (a name derived from the Greek word for *horse*) go off together towards the stables. And Emma and Rodolphe, sitting on the second floor of the town hall, half listen to the speeches, while Rodolphe argues that casting off the animal skins of savage ages cost man more disadvantages than benefits. The planting scenes cited by Monsieur Derozerays are accompanied by Rodolphe's eulogies of the instinctive animal man and by the imagery of water as he compares his inclinations and Emma's to two rivers at their confluence—another variation of the nature triad basic to the imagery of the novel. The merging of man and animal is made total by the appearance of Catherine Leroux, who through living among animals has taken on "leur mutisme et leur placidité" (p. 141). Yet Catherine Leroux is an authentic figure by contrast with the studied savage reversion suggested by Rodolphe. Her life has been one of service to man and to animal; Rodolphe's and Emma's aim is temporary gratification of both vanity and the senses. Man's fireworks, like those stored in Monsieur Tuvache's cellar (*vache*, of course, meaning cow), are damp and will not go off.

Homais' article, which concludes the chapter, combines once again all three nature images. The topic is, of course, the Agricultural Show, but a show transformed by his pen beyond recognition, a show festooned by garlands of flowers and attended by crowds rushing "comme les flots d'une mer en furie" (p. 143). Flaubert makes it perfectly clear in this chapter that authentic animal existence has no relation to the sick and contorted image made by social man. Catherine Leroux with her fifty-four years of service wins her medal by means far more honorable than Homais' methods in winning "la croix d'honneur." The animal imagery in this chapter counterpoints the activity of man in the same way that the vegetation imagery at Les Bertaux and La Vaubyessard counterpointed the petty idealisms displayed by humans who inhabited these places and who tampered with nature for their own selfish and narrow ends. Yet man is finally defeated in his foolish pursuits, whereas nature, like Catherine Leroux, persists, and the cycle of seasons produces ever new vegetation, new foals and calves, and spring freshets. These for Flaubert stand in stark contrast to the fevered imaginings and cerebrations of Emma Bovary and her lovers in their sterile and short-range affairs. The irony of this chapter is sharp because of the abrupt animal-man contrasts brought out by the well-known counterpoint technique. The very name *Bovary* suggests that these contrasts were to be of major importance in Flaubert's novel.

After this point in Part 2, animal imagery commences gradually to recede in favor of water imagery, which is to dominate Part 3. (In the same way, the dog Djali in Part 1 foreshadowed the animal theme in Part 2.) Although the love making between Emma and Rodolphe is connected with horseback riding, their union takes place in the woods, in the midst of vegetation, by a little pond. Emma's blood flows like a river of milk. Earlier in the scene Emma has felt as if she were swimming "sous des flots d'azur" (p. 149). It is a sense of becoming submerged that overcomes Emma in the final portion of the book and that makes the water symbolism appropriate for Part 3. It should be noted in this connection that, according to M. Demorest's Table V, water is the dominant nature image in the entire book.

The waning pleasures of Emma's love affair with Rodolphe are compared in Chapter 10 to the ebbing of the water of a river. At the same time the yearly gift of a turkey and an accompanying letter from M. Rouault remind Emma of foals whinnying and galloping in the fields, of bees and beehives. M. Rouault has planted a plum tree under Emma's window at Les Bertaux, but in Yonville-L'Abbaye, Lestiboudois rakes up the cut grass. Although at the Agricultural Show and in the love-making scene, horses had played an immediate and vital role, now foals are memories for Emma, as are the bees. Likewise the new plum tree is far removed from Emma's present window under which not planting but cutting and raking (performed by the sexton who will dig Emma's grave) is taking place. Furthermore, the cock to be sent by M. Rouault will be a dead cock. The ebb of water is symbolically removing both plant and animal life, all growth, from Emma and her environment. The cock imagery is particularly appropriate at this point, for it recalls the Gallic cock on the pediment of the town hall at the beginning of Part 2, an image used to prefigure the more virile nature of this section. However, it is clear by Chapter 10 that the cock is doomed to die, and that by next year Emma may need more than M. Rouault's gift of a dead bird.

The horse imagery, which has been part of the entire episode involving Rodolphe, forms the basis, indirectly at least, of the next chapter concerning the operation on Hippolyte's foot. Horses appeared at the Agricultural Show; Emma and Rodolphe rode out to the consummation of their affair. Now an operation is about to be performed on a man whose name bears at least two associations with horses. *Hippos* is, of course, the Greek word for horse. Furthermore, Hippolytus in Greek mythology was dragged to his death by horses after Theseus had petitioned Poseidon for punishment. The use of the name Hippolyte suggests complex but unmistakable mythical overtones. Hippolyte himself is hardly more than a horse, very like the horses he tends. Moreover, like his mythical forebear, he receives an unjust punishment at the hands of the gods. The modern Phaedra is Emma Bovary, who is using Hippolyte for her own selfish and vain ends. Hippolyte is maimed as Hippolytus had been killed. Dark liquid oozes from his leg. This operation symbolically injures the very root of his existence, for to the horse the leg means survival, and he is destroyed when his legs no longer perform. The operation and the ensuing amputation also symbolically indicate the excision of the thematic concern with animals in Part 2.

In the evening after the amputation, Emma meets Rodolphe in the garden on the lowest step of the river stairs. As Brunetière has pointed out, Flaubert's nature imagery is often so banal that it goes unnoticed. Yet after the animal screams of Hippolyte, which have rent the village that day, the simple and idyllic conclusion involving a garden and a river provides welcome relief. Although the horses of pain and passion have been stilled, the passive garden and river persist and remain as backdrop for the imprudent enterprises of man. The animal, the dominant concern of Part 2, is destroyed or maimed when it is used as it has been by Emma for her own vain ends. And yet ironically it is this very animal that serves man most faithfully. Rather than frightened horses, it is the raging sea of Poseidon, the sea of passion, which will cause Emma's death. (Still, the myth element remains. Out of the sea comes the bull [symbol of lust] that terrifies the horses; it is, thus, the sea that is the source of death in the myth, also. The irony is that Emma has offended not Aphrodite, but Athena). Meanwhile the river threatening and writhing like a serpent flows in the background at Emma's last meeting with Rodolphe, although their memories are concerned with the silent rivers, the perfumed syringas, and the prowling night animals they have seen in earlier days. After Emma's desertion by Rodolphe, she feels as if she were on a pitching ship. She develops an aversion to her garden and has it re-land-scaped; her horse is sold.

The tumult of a storm at sea (the kind of storm she had dreamed of in the safety of the convent) descends upon Emma in the final chapter of Part 2. The animal-man is now in the clutches of Poseidon as the double basses at the opera (cf. the operation) remind Emma of the cries of shipwrecked sailors "dans le tumulte d'une tempête" (p. 209). And yet the animal motif is not entirely submerged, for among the crowd at the opera Emma meets Léon (lion). The elements of the nature triad—vegetation, animal, and water —will continue to interact in Part 3. M. Demorest has called Flaubert's writing of *Madame Bovary* a "new and perilous voyage of discovery."[10] Surely Flaubert's complex use of imagery proves Demorest's point. Rarely in novels do we find such a conscious and calculated use of common objects to enrich thematic patterns.

III.

The waters of Part 3 are not, however, always the crashing and tumultuous storms of Emma's youthful dreams. Still, the tempest evoked at the opera is skillfully carried over by Flaubert into Chapter 1 of Part 3 through the comparison of the carriage in which Emma and Léon make love to a ship tossing at sea. (At the same time Flaubert echoes the scene of love-making in Part 2, for horses have carried Emma and Rodolphe to that scene as horses now draw Emma and Léon). Accompanying the image of the sea and completing the triad are the torn bits of paper (thrown from the cab by Emma) which are compared to white butterflies alighting on a field of red clover. The sea image here, however, is the dominant image—the butterflies and the clover evoking merely pastoral quietude. (The white butterflies may also recall the black butterflies which floated up the chimney as Emma burned her bridal bouquet and thus suggest the theme of metamorphosis). Thus Emma's resolution to reject Léon is discarded, as are the vegetation and animal symbols of Parts 1 and 2, in favor of the tossing cab, the stormy sea, to which the heroine abandons herself. This final love affair with Léon is accompanied not by images of growth and life, plant and animal, but by the inanimate elements.

---

[10]Demorest, p. 418.

However, instead of romantic storms at sea, the liquid imagery in Part 3 is often of a medical or chemical nature, as the function of Homais' Capharnaum becomes apparent. The liquids of Chapter 2 are the acids and alkaline solutions of the pharmacy. The chapter opens with a description of jelly-making in the village, not with the boiling ocean but with the sticky, boiling jelly of the kitchens of Yonville. This picture corresponds to the pictures of foaming cider in Part 1, but the temperature of the juice is now at the boiling point. The arsenic, with which Justin absentmindedly threatens the lives of Homais and his family, could have combined with the juice to bring destruction. This boiling cauldron of liquid is the dominating image of the chapter, rather than the maimed Hippolyte who stumps in with Emma's bags or the fragile violets brought by Léon. Vegetable and animal life now play secondary roles by comparison with the role of liquids in Part 3.

Chapter 3 of this section is full of water imagery. The hotel where Emma and Léon stay is on the river front. At dusk they drift downstream (suggesting the direction of their affair) on a river polluted by great oily patches. The river flows toward the ocean, but Emma and Léon land on an island where vegetation imagery once more predominates, the grass, the poplars, and the breeze in the branches, reminiscent of Part 1, as if Emma's progress toward death, toward the ocean, were temporarily halted. Left behind in the city is the barking of dogs, the animal theme of Part 2 which has been associated with Rodolphe.

When the lovers next meet, it is in Yonville during a thunderstorm. Again the suggestion of inundation by water occurs, and the scene takes place, of course, in the garden.

But in the city where Emma goes to take her "music lessons," the trees are leafless, and Rouen has "l'air immobile comme une peinture" (p. 244). The islands in the river look like huge black fish, and smoke pollutes the air as oil has polluted the water. In the city, nature is despoiled as the result of man's presence. But the three galloping horses which draw the Hirondelle bearing Emma into the city take us back to the imagery of Part 2, and the bed in the form of a boat, in which she and Léon sleep, to the tossing cab, now unyoked, at the beginning of Part 3. Liquids flow not only in the rivers and fountains in Chapter 5, but in the running sores of the blind beggar and in the perspiration of Emma as she hurries through the streets of Rouen. Finally the triad of absinthe, cigars, and oysters (liquid, vegetable, animal)—smells in the Rue Nationale—symbolizes in microcosm the larger imagery pattern in the book.

As adultery begins to pall, Emma's thoughts return to the protective elms near the convent of her youth and to her rides in the forest. Vegetation scenes and animals exist now only in memory, and "la rivière livide frissonnait au vent" (p. 271). It is as if even the water shivers before the coming storm which will engulf Emma. At the beginning of her desperate search for money, she is threatened once by crowds, pouring out of the cathedral like a river, and again by prancing black horses, driven by a man who reminds her of the vicomte. Nature itself seems to collaborate in her downfall, for Emma has long courted the destructive forces of life. After her attempt to borrow money from Rodolphe fails, night falls and crows fly overhead, dismal harbingers of her death.

Although arsenic is the immediate means of Emma's suicide, the entire section describing her death is dominated symbolically by the imagery of the storm at sea. The convulsive movements which accompany Emma's final hours, her heaving body and rolling eyes, her gasping breath and her flowing tears, become a horrible parody of the romantic storms at sea she has envisaged and of the scenes of passion with her lovers. The storm reaches its peak in the death scene, and Emma's ship at last shudders and succumbs to the furious waves. Flaubert writes: "tout semblait disparaître dans le sourd murmure des syllabes latines" (p. 302).

In the final chapters of the book, it is clear that nature continues to be employed by man in foolish ways to abet his vanity. Thus Charles' desire for three coffins, one of oak, one of mahogany, and one of lead, exemplifies man's frivolous attempt to forestall decay and separation. For ironically, the arsenic which was chosen by Emma for her destruction is related to the lead chosen by Charles as a means of preserving her body. Likewise the herbs, the camphor, the benzoin, and the chlorine water contributed by Homais are futile gestures, as is the holy water sprinkled by the priest. These pharmaceutical and religious panaceas seem trivial beside the joyous sounds of spring which accompany Emma's burial.

Here, once again, the three elements of the nature triad are united, as colts bolt off under apple trees and dewdrops shimmer on the thorn hedges. Nature persists and recurs, indifferent to, and despite, man's failures. Appropriately Emma's bier moves through the cemetery "comme une chaloupe qui tangue à chaque flot" (p. 313). The sea of passion which has submerged her cannot rest until her body is interred, but meanwhile spring is rejuvenating the earth with new vegetable life, new animal life, and fresh streams of water, beside which the holy sprinkler of Bournisien seems like a gaudy trinket. The destructive imagery of the ocean accompanies Emma's burial to the very end, when Charles drags himself toward the grave "pour s'y engloutir avec elle" (p. 314).

With Emma's death a final sterility seems to settle on human activity in the last chapter. The natural cycle continues as Charles sits grieving in his arbor, but the blind beggar (the animal) is locked up to satisfy Homais' political ambitions; Homais designs even the grass in his garden to reflect his own glory, the Legion of Honor; and Charles' mind is flooded by futile memories. The capping irony is the cotton mill where little Berthe is sent by her aunt to work. It is as if the vegetation symbolism of Part 1 were here purposefully revived in the form of a dead fiber (like the dead wedding bouquets and the bouquet of wheat and straw on the flax mill) to remind the reader of the sterile nature of Emma's legacy. Moreover, the dry goods dealer, M. Lheureux, has had a hand in luring Emma to her destruction.

The details studied in the course of this essay, numerous as they are, simply serve to indicate the tremendous conscious complexity of Flaubert's techniques. More still could be said, but proof here is sufficient to show the skill with which Flaubert manipulated these three image groups. In reading *Madame Bovary* one has a feeling as M. Demorest has well expressed it: "un peu comme celle que l'on a en écoutant une très belle et très solide tentative symphonie, jouée par un orchestra intelligent et sympathique, sous un directeur de génie."[11]

Purdue University

[11]*Ibid.*, p. 480.

The Rhythm of Memory: Mood and Imagination in The *Confessions* of Rousseau

J. Kostka

By STANLEY CORNGOLD

Rousseau conceived his *Confessions* as an original project, and he was quite clear about the way in which it was to be original. In the *Ébauches des Confessions* he wrote: "j'écris moins l'histoire de ces éve[ne]mens en eux-mêmes que celle de l'état de mon ame, à mesure qu'ils sont arrivés" (1150).[1] The autobiography conceived as a history of one's moods at once entails imaginative writing, for what is distinctive about moods is the fact that they defy mimetic representation. Rousseau acknowledges the special demand placed on style by such a project: "Il faudroit pour ce que j'ai à dire inventer un langage aussi nouveau que mon projet [. . .]; mon style [. . .] fera lui-

---

[1]Numbers in parentheses refer to pages of *Oeuvres complètes de Jean-Jacques Rousseau*, Tome I, Bibliothèque de la Pléiade (Paris: Gallimard, 1959).

même partie de mon histoire" (1153-54).[2] The language of the *Confessions* is complex because the act of interpreting moods is complex: "En me livrant à la fois au souvenir de l'impression receue et au sentiment présent je peindrai doublement l'état de mon ame, savoir au moment où l'évenement m'est arrivé et au moment où je l'ai décrit" (1154). Thus the language of this auto-biography has a dimension having nothing to do with memory, for it includes the mood of the act of writing. The self of the *Confessions*, as a history of moods, has an ideal dimension, which suggests the inadequacy of memory for truthful self-reflection. This dimension is one which a history of moods shares with poetry and fiction. Like fiction, the Rousseauvian autobiography *constitutes* a self through acts of interpretation, and points to an absence at the heart of experience.

And yet this conclusion must seem paradoxical, because Rousseau cele-brates at the same time unmediated experiences of great self-sufficiency. In the *Cinquième Promenade* he records a moment in which "on se suffit à soi-même comme Dieu" (1047).[3] An examination of the *Confessions* ought to clarify the relation in Rousseau between the experience of mood and the imagination. For the moments which Rousseau describes in the *Confessions* as especially fulfilling are remarkable for the beauty and the degree of conscious elaboration of their style.

Because the *Confessions* is informed by a general concern for self-interpre-tation, it is not bound to a chronological sequence of empirical events. We enjoy the same freedom from chronology as we pursue its organizing principle.

Book Four of the *Confessions* opens with a movement of experience with which the reader of that work will by then be familiar: it describes Rousseau's infidelity (to M. le Maitre), and then proceeds to justify it; it recounts his forgetting Mme. de Warens but reveals his taste for romance. A life unfolds to the basic rhythm of remembering and the interpretation of memory. The reader is lulled by the alternation of his pleasure in anecdotes and in ideas which serve to justify a self. Then suddenly, within the banal motion of dis-traction and brooding, a dawn breaks, a fresh beginning:

> L'aurore un matin me parut si belle que m'étant habillé précipitam-ment, je me hâtai de gagner la campagne pour voir lever le soleil. [. . .] La terre dans sa plus grande parure étoit couverte d'herbe et de fleurs; les rossignols presque à la fin de leur ramage sembloient se plaire à le renforcer: tous les oiseaux faisant en concert leurs adieux au printems, chantoient la naissance d'un beau jour d'été [. . .] (135).

The dawn is a dawn of intimacy between things. In this intimacy each being introduces into the other a movement through which it is magnified. In the same way that Rousseau's agile awareness penetrates the elements, so these beings enter into intimate responsiveness with each other. The nightingales

---

[2]E. T. A. Hoffman noted à propos of the *Confessions*: "My thoughts too get confused when it becomes a matter of grasping feelings in words." E. T. A. Hoffman, *Dichtungen und Schriften*, ed. W. Harich (Weimar, 1924), XIV, p. 193. Cited in Rudolf Buck, *Rousseau und die deutsche Romantik* (Berlin, 1939), p. 19.

[3]A claim which Hölderlin in his poem *Der Rhein* called "foolish." Friedrich Hölderlin, "Der Rhein," *Sämtliche Werke*, ed. Friedrich Beissner (Frankfurt am Main, 1961), p. 328.

magnify their song; the birds, the beauty of the season and the day. This intimacy is a language—the figurative language which each being speaks in response to the movement of the dawn within it. The dawn is the dawn of a language which, that day, never ceases.

"J'entens derrière moi," writes Rousseau, "des pas de chevaux et des voix de filles [. . . ;] on m'appelle par mon nom [. . .]" (135). Named, Jean-Jacques is brought more deeply into this dawn: he is present fully as himself. The world to which he is present is his own: "[J]'approche, je trouve deux jeunes personnes de ma connoissance [. . .]" (135). He acknowledges the human world, as the birds acknowledged their world of mornings and seasons. This human world is an intimacy, it does not brook separation. "[J]e voulus saluer ces Demoiselles et m'en aller comme un benêt: elles se dirent quelque mots tout bas, et Mlle de Graffenried s'addressant à moi; non pas, non pas, [. . .] on ne nous échappe pas comme cela" (136). A mutual emotion arises in the spirit of figurative language.[4] As the human world fills with the sentiment of intimacy, it expresses itself in the figures of the idyll and of romance: "il faut s'il vous plait venir avec nous, nous vous arrêtons prisonnier. Le coeur me battoit, je regardois Mlle Galley: oui, oui, [. . .] prisonnier de guerre, [. . .] nous voulons rendre compte de vous" (136). The war of Eros ends at its beginning in a gesture of union and restraint; the object of Jean-Jacques' glance takes him prisoner. In a world close to the origin, the players make a fresh beginning: "nous sommes seules;" no danger of division threatens: "nous revenons ce soir, et vous reviendrez avec nous. [. . . J.-J.] trembloi[t] de joie." Their being together in intimacy exacts and finds for its balance a certain formality: "cette décence nous ne nous l'imposions point du tout; elle venoit toute seule, nous prenions le ton que nous donnoient nos coeurs" (138). The balance of "la plus grande liberté" and "la plus grande décence" reflects itself in the continuous transparent utterance of feeling. "La gaité du voyage et le babil de ces filles aiguiserent tellement le mien, que jusqu'au soir et tant que nous fumes ensembles nous ne déparlames pas un moment. Elles m'avoient mis si bien à mon aise que ma langue parloit autant que mes yeux [. . .] (136)." They dine perpetually; their appetite renews itself in the consciousness of being satisfied—donnée of an omnipresent "sensualité." Their intoxication is neither lessened nor heightened by the absence of wine; the "heart" itself feeds the intoxication. The mingling of restraint and freedom creates within "la tendre union" a continuous state of innocent desire. Desire is innocent because it seeks only to preserve itself (as "volupté pure," "chasteté brûlante"), not dissolve itself by its accomplishment.[5] "L'innocence des moeurs a sa volupté qui vaut bien l'autre, parce qu'elle n'a point d'intervalle et qu'elle agit continuellement" (138). The presence of "deux charmantes personnes" (one of whom invites the idea of total freedom, the other, the idea of total restraint) is less the external guarantee of innocence than a figurative expression of the inner nature of a *"volupté* pure." Innocence is the

---

[4]"The spirit of the original figurative language of passion" is, for Wordsworth, the source of poetic language (Preface to the *Lyrical Ballads*). William Wordsworth, *Preface to the Lyrical Ballads, The Poetical Works of Wordsworth*, a new edition revised by Ernest de Selincourt (London, 1956), p. 740.

[5]Phrases in parentheses are by Marcel Raymond. Marcel Raymond in *Oeuvres complètes de Jean-Jacques Rousseau*, Tome I, Bibliothèque de la Pléiade (Paris: Gallimard, 1959), p. 1297.

condition of an absolutely sustained sentiment whose memory is a pure reflection of the future.

Like the perfectly achieved poetic act, the idyll returns, replenished, to its beginnings. "Je les quittai à peu près au même endroit où elles m'avoient pris. [. . .] Avec quel plaisir nous projettames de nous revoir!" But the hope of identical effortless repetition is naïve! The desire for repetition of such an instant must aim not towards the same instant, but towards its source, whose character, as possibility, is to repeat itself. This point emerges through the naïveté of the episode, which confuses sensuality—the experience of fresh sensation—with intersubjectivity—the non-sensory experience of being for another. Neither category of experience is accorded here the philosophical presentation which it receives in Rousseau's novel *la Nouvelle Héloïse*. The novel stresses the dialectical character, and the only apparent stability, of the relation between the sensation and the sentiment.

For the mature Rousseau the experience of pure sensation requires solitude —detachment from others and from the memory of others, as in the *Deuxième Promenade*. Sensuality is typically welcome in the "return" from the plenary ecstasy of imaginative contemplation. But the sensuality of this episode is sustained and diluted by the romance of erotic desire whose principle, whose "lie," is the inexhaustibility of passion. And erotic intersubjectivity, for Rousseau, is never elsewhere a symbol for the freshness of sensation. Apart from the question of their priority, their distinction appears in the article "Unité de mélodie" in the *Dictionnaire de musique*: "Le plaisir de l'Harmonie n'est qu'un plaisir de pure sensation de la Melodie et du chant, est un plaisir . . . , mais le plaisir d'interêt et de sentiment qui parle au coeur" (1629).

The "nuit delicieuse" spent on a road beside the Rhône presents more truly the destiny of the sensation:

> Il avoit fait très chaud ce jour-là; la soirée étoit charmante; la rosée humectoit l'herbe flétrie; point de vent, une nuit tranquille; [. . .] le soleil après son coucher avoit laissé dans le ciel des vapeurs rouges dont la réflexion rendoit l'eau couleur le rose; les arbres des terrasses étoient chargés de rossignois qui se répondoient de l'un à l'autre (168-69).

Not dawn, dusk: but an hour of passage, the advent, again, of an origin, as an intimacy whose purest expression is the intimacy of the self and its vision. "Je me promenois dans une sorte d'extase livrant mes sens et mon coeur à la joüissance de tout cela [. . .]" (169). But without an Other to help sustain it, the sensuality of the scene fades into a mild regret; Rousseau is alone, "soupirant seulement un peu du regret d'en joüir seul" (169). Regret names the absence within a present plenitude. Through this experience of the negative, the original sentiment is succeeded by a purer consciousness of the self, an "amour de soi." "Absorbé dans ma douce rêverie je prolongeai fort avant dans la nuit ma promenade sans m'appercevoir que j'etois las" (169). Sensual scenes arouse the young Rousseau erotically, not reflectively. They make him need an Other; in the absence of the Other, the passion recognizes itself as empty, and becomes philosophical regret. This is a crucial development.

This new consciousness reapproaches the sensual scene with a new intention. Here is the origin of the genuine revery, in which the scene once sensual now yields only transparent emblems of the mind. Things are important now in being present to an experience whose significance is not in them, in being witnesses.

The language with which Rousseau describes the revery is necessarily self-conscious. "Je me couchai voluptueusement sur la tablette d'une espéce de niche [. . .] enfoncée dans un mur de terrasse: le ciel de mon lit étoit formé par les têtes des arbres, un rossignol étoit précisément au dessus de moi; je m'endormis à son chant" (169). It is impossible not to see this scene as an emblem of the genuine idyll in which sensation and reflection peacefully co-exist. "Une nature maternelle," notes Marcel Raymond, protects him; while the solitary song of the mind self-creating, self-delighting—sustains itself overhead.[6] The song of the nightingale is itself an emblem—of a movement of consciousness which transposes, through the absence of the Other, sensation into emblem, into language.

The achieved idyll of reflection prepares the vision of the next morning; "le réveil," writes M. Raymond, "sera comme une naissance au sein d'un monde tout neuf où les choses atteindront leur plus haut degré de présence [. . .]."[7] "Il étoit grand jour; mes yeux en s'ouvrant virent l'eau, la verdure, un paysage admirable." A moment of transparency projects itself as a mood, as Rousseau's "bonne humeur"; from this mood he sings, appropriately, a highly conscious music, a cantata of Batistin. And then something happens which the reader remembers from the idyll at the Château de Toun: "Dans mon meilleur train d'aller et de chanter j'entens quelqu'un derrière moi, je me retourne; je vois un Antonin qui me suivoit, et qui paroissoit m'écouter avec plaisir. Il m'accoste, me salue [. . .]" (169).

The mind's intimacy with the sensuous object—passing through critical stages of the absence of the Other, and the revery—fulfills itself in happy intersubjectivity. Jean-Jacques is summoned from behind and in effect is named himself. Ahead of himself in thought, he is pleasantly detained on the earth by the recognition of another man. The moment of successful inter-subjectivity closes the circle of the revery by stressing the moral significance, the general value, of the movement which sacrifices sensation for language.

This episode contains in embryonic form, yet with a completeness that is striking, the themes of sensuality, revery, and friendship. An intimacy of nature with itself, of human perception with the natural world, finally, of consciousness with its own figurative language, incorporates, through successive *dépassements*, yet without apparent pain, and with the pathos of completion, the intimacy of two subjectivities. A paragraph later Rousseau intervenes with striking effect: "Depuis lors mes finances ont souvent été fort courts, mais jamais assez pour être obligé de jeuner. Je marque cette époque avec un coeur sensible aux soins de la providence. C'est la dernière fois de ma vie que j'ai senti la misère et la faim" (170). A fullness of pastoral experience consummates itself, after a rich reflective development, in the banishment of social need.

But it would be wrong to stop on this sanguine note. Rousseau's truth is more complex, more dialectical than this. This idyll diminishes too easily

---

[6]Raymond, *op. cit.*, p. 1310.
[7]*Ibid.*

the pain and the importance of the absent woman: "Je me répéte, on le sait; il le faut. Le prémier de mes besoins, le plus grand, le plus fort, le plus inextinguible, étroit tout entier dans mon coeur; c'étoit le besoin d'une societe intimé et aussi intime qu'elle pouvoit l'être: c'etoit surtout pour cela qu'il me falloit une femme plustot qu'un homme, une amie plustot qu'un ami" (414). On the other hand it praises too hastily the abrogation of poverty. To be beyond poverty is no unambiguous boon; witness this typical statement of Rousseau some thirty-five years later: refusing the offer of a pension from the king of England he writes: "Tant que j'ai vécu pauvre, j'ai vécu heureux et ce n'est que quand rien ne m'a manqué pour le nécessaire que je me suis senti le plus malheureux des mortels" (xlvi). There is in this idyll a certain opacity, an unwarrantable sufficiency, which arises, in fact, from a suppression of the temporal consciousness which Rousseau in the future will not be able to forget; for here, "[j]e n'avois pas le moindre souci sur l'avenir" (168). The result of this innocence is the absence, in the Rhone nocturne, of any tragic note. There is no consciousness of the painful sacrifice of immediacy which prepares the palingenesis of poetic language.

This consciousness does appear in the tense idyll at Eaubonne, in which Rousseau consummates in poetic language his love for Madame d'Houdetot. This idyll has a history.

> Je faisois ces méditations [sur moi-même] dans la plus belle saison de l'année, au mois de juin, sous des boccages frais, au chant du rossignol, au gazouillement des ruisseaux. Tout concourut à me replonger dans cette molesse trop séduisante pour laquelle j'étoit né mais dont le ton dur et sévére où venoit le me monter une longue effervescence m'auroit dû délivrer pour toujours. J'allai malheureusement me rappeller le diné du Château de Toun et ma rencontre avec ces deux charmantes filles dans la même saison et dans les lieux à peu près semblables à ceux où j'étois en ce moment. Ce souvenir, que l'innocence qui s'y joignoit me rendoit plus doux encore, m'en rappella d'autres de la même espèce. [. . .] Mon sang s'allume [. . .] (426-27).

The absolute reality of these memories ("[l]'ivresse dont je fus saisi [. . .] fut si durable et si forte") requires the completing action of the imagination —the only tenable way to "communiquer enfin ce feu dévorant mais stérile dont depuis mon enfance je sentois en vain consumer mon coeur" (427). The richness of the passages which follow belongs to reimagined memories of moments which in themselves imagine memories.

So central, now, to Rousseau's life is the poetic activity, that the intrusion of other men is only an occasion for spleen. "Quand, prêt à partir pour le monde enchanté je voyois arriver de malheureux mortels qui venoient me retenir sur la terre, je ne pouvois ni modérer ni cacher mon depit [. . .]" (428). We have witnessed a full development of the content of the naïve idyll: all the "nature" which Rousseau can tolerate now is the image which sentiment engenders, and the language which keeps the image. "L'imagination créatrice" has absolute primacy; from this source, most immediately present in the world of *la Nouvelle Héloïse*, Sophie d'Houdetot will take her aura. When she arrives, "je la vis, j'étois ivre d'amour sans objet, cette ivresse fascina mes yeux, cet objet se fixa sur elle, je vis ma Julie en Mad^e d'Houdetot, et bientot je ne vis plus que Mad^e d'Houdetot, mais revétue de toutes les perfections dont je venois d'orner l'idole de mon coeur" (440). This idyll at Eaubonne, like the naïve idyll at the Château de Toun, is founded on a proscription of eroticism. But here its stability arises from a sanction whose source is entirely inward—from moral law. This sanction, however, is voluntary; it does not arrive of its own accord. And though it has its external guarantee in St. Lambert, St. Lambert is absent. In the voluntary character of the restraint (supported, too, by the anti-sensual character of vehement imagination) there is an exaltation. A voluntary moral consciousness and an imagination that is no longer "cette molesse trop seduisante" but is, indeed, "dur et sévère" lend the nocturne at Eaubonne its sublimity. And indeed this is the correct word: we have to do here with an exact experience of the Kantian "dynamic" sublime. "[U]n soir [. . .] nous allames nous promener au jardin par un très beau clair de lune. Au fond de cet jardin étoit un assez grand taillis par où nous fumes chercher un joli bosquet orné d'une cascade dont je lui avois donné l'idée et qu'elle avoit fait éxécuter" (444). The manner in which the setting connotes intimacy is perfectly attuned to an idyll from which the naïve sensation has been banished. It is filled with things "dont je lui avois donné l'idée et qu'elle avoit fait éxécuter." The intimacy of the scene is not that of natural things with each other but of natural things with artifacts. The language which attunes scene and consciousness is, consequently, not the language which links two natural perceptions but the figurative language of a consciousness disjoined from nature. Rousseau declares: "Souvenir immortel d'innocence et de jouissance! Ce fut dans ce bosquet qu'assis avec elle sur un banc de gason sous un Acacia tout chargé de fleurs, je trouvai pour rendre les mouvements de mon coeur un langage vraiment digne d'eux. Ce fut le première et l'unique fois de ma vie [. . .]" (444). A language truly worthy of rendering the movements of his heart is a figurative language which reflects nature as a sign of nature's *dépassement* by the moral consciousness.

Now have we to do here with an authentic moment, a moment in which the mind makes contact with its own source, and preserves in its insight the entity through which it has taken its passage? We shall not think so if we require that this access be furnished by the immediate experience of the privileged entity so that passage is won by a genuine, a sorrowful, renunciation of the real. For it is not, properly speaking, the renunciation of the real Sophie d'Houdetot which provides Rousseau a language to render the movements of his heart; nor are those "movements" sentiments for Sophie d'Houdetot. These movements arise as the intent towards a reality which is from the start entirely mediated by imagination and reflection.

The lovers' setting has been fashioned by Rousseau's imagination of the romance; Sophie d'Houdetot is clothed in the virtues of the fictional Julie: Rousseau addresses his own imagination. And yet the real presence of Sophie d'Houdetot is not entirely eclipsed by the mediations of the imagination: she preserves just enough reality, in her function as the Other, to excite Rousseau's amour propre. It is as an Other that she determines this scene, exacting from Rousseau the typically inauthentic response, the need to justify himself. We have the embrace, and the words of Mme. d'Houdetot: "Non, jamais homme ne fut si aimable, et jamais amant n'aima comme vous!" at which moment the episode bares its apologetic intent: "mais votre ami St. Lambert nous écoute," says Mme. d'Houdetot, "et mon coeur ne sauroit aimer deux fois." "Je me tus," asserts Rousseau, gravely. The reader has no more than the injunction: "Lecteur! Pesez toutes ces circonstances; je n'ajoûterai rien de plus (445)." Rousseau will add no more lies.

That language worthy of the movements of the heart, which is here embedded in the language with which Rousseau imaginatively reconstructs its occasion, surpasses nature—only as a language of apologia. Swiftly the language of this episode has passed into the generalization of moral self-defense: the language of sentiment is inaudible. For the detail of a language genuinely worthy of his heart, a figurative language, we must look elsewhere —to *la Nouvelle Héloise*; this is the covert indication of the passage. Afterwards Rousseau will forget this "souvenir immortelle d'innocence et de jouissance;" it becomes (in the language of the Third Letter to M. Malesherbes) one of those pleasures "trop mêlés d'amertumes" he would rather remember the "promenades solitaires, [. . .] ces jours [. . .] que j'ai passés tout entiers avec moi seul [. . .]" (1139). The imagination that would enact a moment of happy intersubjectivity from which poetic language arises, founders —and testifies to a conflict where it suspected none.

For all the claimed perfection of its intimacy, the moment with Sophie d'Houdetot is at once foreshadowed, and eclipsed, by the central experience of Part I—that of Mme. de Warens. Mme. d'Houdetot is loved because she can be fused with an imagined object: "je vis ma Julie en Mad^e d'Houdetot." She is swept along in the ecstatic mood that flows from a hidden source and terminates in the fiction of Julie. "[I]l est certain," writes Rousseau, "que j'écrivis ce roman dans les plus brulantes extases; mais on se trompoit en pensant qu'il avoit fallu des objets réels pour les produire" (548). Her reality in the *Confessions*, is totally inferior, to her presence in Rousseau's imagination. The case with Mme. de Warens is different. The prophetic vision of her at Annecy is fulfilled—tragically—by a real moment at Les Charmettes. For the young Rousseau, the real Mme. de Warens is a constituent of the revery, close to its source, linked to its goal; the experience of Mme. d'Houdetot must be "ornamented" (*orné*) to connect to a source of pure vision. Mme. de Warens is experienced as herself near-origin and goal of the imagination, always prefiguring the next real experience of her that lies in the future. The immediate stimulus to the revery of Mme. de Warens is an intuition of the instability of the real present. The loss of the present matters. This intuition prompts the imagination itself to take over the burden of originating a new reality. Every experience of Mme. de Warens has this temporal structure.

[U]n jour de grand fête, [. . .] j'allai me promener hors le la ville, le coeur plein de son image et du desir ardent de passer mes jours auprès d'elle. J'avois assez de sens pour voir que quand à présent cela n'étoit pas possible, et qu'un bonheur que je goûtois si bien seroit court. Cela donnoit à ma rêverie une tristesse qui n'avoit pourtant rien de sombre et qu'un espoir flateur tempéroit. Le son des cloches qui m'a toujours singulierement affecté, le chant des oiseaux, la beauté lu jour,

> la douceur du paysage, les maisons éparses et champêtres dans lesquelles
> je plaçois en idée notre commune demeure [. . .] (107-08).

The passage contains the familiar emblems of an immanent imagination.
Its origin is a holiday; the day is fine: birds sing; human voices—bells—
respond to their music; the natural scene—"les maisons éparses et champêtres
—is full of an idea envisioned by Rousseau of "notre commune demeure;
tout cela me frappoit d'une impression vive, tendre, triste et touchante, que
je mis vis comme en extase transporté dans cet heureux tems et dans cet
heureux séjour, où mon coeur possédant toute la félicité qui pouvoit lui plaire
la goutoit dans des ravissemens inexprimables, sans songer même à la volupté
des sens. Je ne me souviens pas de m'être elancé jamais dans l'avenir avec plus
de force et d'illusion que je fis alors [. . .]" (108). And Rousseau the writer
adds: the dream was to be realized; but more important, he claims that the
vision was in itself prophetic. "Si jamais rêve d'un homme éveillé eut l'air
d'une vision prophétique, ce fut assurément celui-là."

The forcefulness and intensity of the dream is a sign the significance of
which can be revealed only by the future "accomplissement" of the dream;
hence it is a sign of prophecy. And since this peculiar vividness essentially
distinguishes the experience, the dream is transparent to itself as its prospective
character. This prophetic or prospective character, moreover, is not a merely
contingent predicate of the imagination. On the contrary, the imagination
arises as the intent to exist into the future: ". . . j'avois assez de sens pour
voir que quand à présent cela ['passer mes jours aupres d'elle'] n'etoit pas
possible." It originates by negating the present—first, the sensuous objects
around Rousseau, then, the visionary experience of a specific "tems . . . et
sejour;" it functions in its most fundamental sense as the power, temporally
ahead of itself, to disclose the sign as significance. In this instant the future is
present in a genuine present which discloses the thrust of the imagination. An
experience of temporality links dimensions of time that otherwise exist in
disjunction. For the necessity that the moment accomplish itself in the future
announces its own past. Yet the imagination that projects itself as prophecy
desires that the moment of presence to itself endure, and endure as the movement towards its own annihilation.

In remembering such a moment Rousseau aims to preserve the mood of a
future unfolding. This mood grasps the future as the sense of the imagination
that thrusts itself and for an instant sustains that thrust. The moment of
prophecy in Rousseau, like Kant's aesthetic judgment, reprojects in the
structured time of mood (*Stimmung*) the time which enables any consciousness whatsoever. The prefigurative imagination projects itself as a mood of
"ravissement."

It is illuminating that Rousseau's very words "ravissement" (Entrückung)
and "extase" ("Ekstase") denote for the philosopher Heidegger, too, the
active sense" of the phenomenon of the "Augenblick" or "moment-of-vision."
In this moment, man "is carried away to whatever possibilities and circumstances are encountered in the Situation as possible objects of concern;" this
rapture is "held in resoluteness." But "the moment-of-vision is a phenomenon
which *in principle* can *not* be clarified in terms of the 'now' . . . which belongs
to time as within-time-ness: the 'now' 'in which' something arises, passes

away, or is present-at-hand. In the moment of vision nothing can occur; but as an authentic Present, . . . the moment of vision permits us *to encounter for the first time* what can be 'in a time' as ready-to-hand or present-to-hand."[8] For Rousseau, too, the authentic present, in revealing the imagination, reveals that power which encounters natural objects in their correct temporal identity— i.e. as signs of their own *dépassement* through interpretative acts.

Otto von Bollnow further clarifies this moment, though Rousseau's term, "durée imaginaire," must be substituted for von Bollnow's "eternity."

> What is peculiar to this experience is that it is a liberation from temporal existence which itself occurs in the moment, that is, in temporal existence, and is not abolished because this moment is itself short-lived. This means then that this experience of eternity is independent of the duration of the experience; as a result the character of the eternity experienced here is something other than that of infinite temporal extension.[9]

This is precisely the distinction that Rousseau will make. No sooner does the revery end than he begins to distinguish between time, or "within-time-ness," and the authentic temporality of "Dasein's coming back to one's own-most Self:" "Je n'ai été déçu que dans sa durée imaginaire; car les jours et les ans et la vie entière s'y passoient dans une inaltérable tranquillité, au lieu qu'en effet tout cela n'a duré qu'un moment. Helas! mon plus constant bonheur fut en songe. Son accomplissement fut presque à l'instant suivi du revéil" (108).

The prophecy takes the reader to the future time in which it was fulfilled, the occasion of another walk—with Mme. de Warens, on St. Louis' day. The epoch has been propitious, one in which "je me félicitois de mourir à l'âge où l'on trouve assez de courage en soi pour envisager la mort [. . .] Je n'ai jamais été si près de la sagesse que durant cette heureuse époque. Sans grand remords sur le passé; délivré des soucis de l'avenir, le sentiment qui dominois constamment dans mon ame étoit jouir du présent" (243-44). And now the distinction becomes overt between an inauthentic indifference to the future, such as that which formed the backdrop to the Rhône nocturne: "Je n'avois pas le moindre souci sur l'avenir" (168); and an authentic indifference to the future, based on a comprehension of death. The anticipation of death— precisely in an act of envisagement which enables the correct encounter between Dasein and things—enables an authentic present. Moreover, "along with the sober anxiety," writes Heidegger, "which brings us face-to-face with our individualized potentiality for Being, i.e. Death, there goes an unshakeable *joy* in this possibility."

In this mood, "[n]ous partimes ensembles et seuls de bon matin;" Jean-Jacques and Madame de Warens depart for a country of the imagination, wholly prefigured by the earlier dream. "Tout sembloit conspirer au bonheur de cette journée. Il avait plu depuis peu; point de poussière, et des ruisseaux

---

[8]Martin Heidegger, *Being and Time*, a translation of *Sein und Zeit* by J. Macquarrie and E. Robinson (New York and Evanston, 1962), pp. 387-88.

[9]Otto von Bollnow, *Das Wesen der Stimmungen* (Frankfurt am Main, 1941), pp. 34-35.

bien courans. Un petit vent frais agitoit les feuilles, l'air étoit pur, l'horizon sans nuages; la sérénite regnoit au Ciel comme dans nos coeurs." The intimate lovers and a fresh and germinating nature configure the landscape of the "sentiment intime." The pulsing brooks announce the sentiment of the temporal Self. They wander at liberty: "Nous allions de colline en colline et de bois en bois, quelquefois au soleil et souvent à l'ombre; nous reposant de tems en tems, et nous oubliant des heures entières; causant de nous, de notre union, de la douceur de notre sort . . ." There sharply intrudes into the idyll a sign of the ultimate negation toward which the "élancement" of the Self goes out: "et faisant pour sa durée des voeux qui ne furent pas exaucés." Jean-Jacques absorbs himself in natural objects. Suddenly "une idée qui vint me frapper fit diversion aux fleurs et aux plantes. La situation d'ame où je me trouvois, tout ce qui nous avions dit et fait ce jour-là, tous les objets qui m'avoe int frappé me rappelerent l'espèce de rêve que tout éveillé j'avois fait à Annecy sept ou huit ans auparavant [. . .]" (245). In a transport he cries to Mme. de Warens, "Mon bonheur grace à vous est à son comble, puisse-t-il ne pas décliner desormais! puisse-t-il durer aussi longtems que j'en conserverai le gout! il ne finira qu'avec moi." But he knows it will decline. This moment, founded on the prefiguration of the "extase," is still further than that moment from the source: it remembers, it does not imagine. Because it is more real, it is more vulnerable as it were to the negativity of a temporal destiny. Whereas in the first moment Rousseau knew "une inaltérable tranquillité," now more pathetically he must solicit a duration. He knows the moment of vision will decline and that his life afterwards must aim again and again at projecting it anew—this movement of understanding towards its source; and at conserving this movement, in its essential finitude, through the mediations of the act of writing.

Princeton University

NOTES ON CONTRIBUTORS

EHRHARD BAHR is Associate Professor of German at the University of California in Los Angeles. Author of a book on irony in Goethe's later work and a biography of Georg Lukács, he has published articles on Goethe, Kafka and others and is now preparing a new edition of *Wilhelm Meisters Lehrjahre* and *Wanderjahre* for Reclam Publishers.

WILLIAM BUSH is Professor of Contemporary French Literature at the University of Western Ontario. He has published extensively on Bernanos.

S. B. CHANDLER, is Professor of Italian at the University of Toronto. In addition to editing, with J. A. Molinaro, *The World of Dante: Six Essays in Language and Thought*, he has contributed articles to American and Italian periodicals and is preparing a book on Alessandro Manzoni for Edinburgh University Press.

MARGARET CHURCH is Professor of English and Chairman of Comparative Literature at Purdue University. Among her publications are *Time and Reality: Studies in Contemporary Fiction* (1963); *Don Quixote: The Knight of La Mancha* (1971), and numerous articles on modern fiction. She is Co-Editor of *Modern Fiction Studies*.

STANLEY CORNGOLD received his Ph.D. in Comparative Literature from Cornell and is now teaching German classical literature at Princeton. He edited Max Frisch's *Ausgewahlte Prosa* (1968); and Bantam Books is publisher of his translation and critical bibliography of *The Metamorphosis of Kafka*.

KAREN O. CRENSHAW has studied and taught at San Diego State College, and is pursuing graduate studies in German at the University of Oregon.

WILLIAM GORDON CUNLIFFE, Associate Professor of German, University of Wisconsin (Madison), holds the doctorate from Hamburg University. In addition to many years as librarian, translator and interpreter, he has published numerous articles on modern British, American and German writers, including articles on Günter Grass, Max Frisch and Peter Weiss, as well as a monograph on Grass.

HORST DAEMMRICH is Professor of Germanic Languages and Literature at Wayne State University. Author of *The Challenge of German Literature* (Wayne State University Press, 1971) and a forthcoming book on E. T. A. Hoffman, *The Shattered Self*, he has published widely in such journals as *Journal of Aesthetics and Art Criticism*; *Germanic Review*; *Papers on Language and Literature*; *Modern Language Quarterly*; *Colloquia Germanica* and others.

LILIAN R. FURST holds a B.A. in Modern Languages of Manchester University and a Ph.D. of Girton College, Cambridge. She has published two books, *Romanticism in Perspective* and *Romanticism* and many articles on the Romantic Period, modern German Literature and other aspects of comparative literature. Until recently Senior Lecturer-in-Charge of Comparative Literary Studies at Manchester University, she is this year Visiting Professor at Dartmouth College, and will next year assume the directorship of Comparative Literature at the University of Oregon.

GRAHAM GOOD teaches English and Comparative Literature at the University of British Columbia. He holds degrees from Oxford and Princeton, and has published on Balzac; his current work is on Rilke and the theory of the novel.

STEVEN KELLMAN'S area of special interest is "The Self-Begetting Novel," the reflexive tradition in the French, British, and American novel from Proust to Beckett. He was formerly editor-in-chief of *Occident*, and is at present a contributor to *Abstracts of English Studies*. He teaches at the University of California, Berkeley.

RICHARD H. LAWSON, Professor of German at San Diego State College, has written on Kafka and Schnitzler, as well as on earlier Austrian and German authors. He has also published several articles on the literary connections between Edith Wharton and a number of German authors; he is currently writing a book on this relationship.

CLAUDE MAURIAC is son of François Mauriac. Secrétaire particulier du Général de Gaulle (1944-49), author of: *Un autre De Gaulle*, 1971, he has written many works of literary criticism: *Jean Cocteau ou la vérité du mensonge*; *Aimer Balzac*; *Malraux ou le mal du héros*; *André Breton*; *Marcel Proust par lui-même* (by marriage, Claude Mauriac is the grand-nephew of Marcel Proust); *L'Allitérature contemporaine*. A novelist, Claude Mauriac is known by *Toutes les femmes sont fatales*; *Le Dîner en ville*; *La marquise sortit à cinq heures*; *L'agrandissement*; *L'oubli*. He lives in Paris.

BRUCE C. MERRY is, at present, lecturer in Italian at the University of Kent, England. His chief research interest lies in the application of structuralist and formalist methods of criticism to modern Italian fiction; he has published analysis of this kind on Pavese, Fenoglio, the literature of the Resistance and Vittorini. He has translated articles by Moravia, Eco, Calvino and Avalle for English periodicals and brought to light two manuscripts by Fenoglio (1922-1963) which are discussed in *Transactions of the Bronte Society*, 1971 and *Strumenti Critici*, Vo. 16, 1971. His analysis of Fenoglio's unpublished Resistance novel in English is in *Italica*, Spring, 1972.

HENRI MITTERAND is Professor at the University of Paris VIII. Well known for his Zola scholarship, he has edited, with A. Lanoux, Zola's *Les Rougon-Macquart*, 5 volumes (Bibliothèque de la Pléiade, Paris, 1960-67). Editor of Zola's *Oeuvres complètes*, 15 vols. (Cercle du Livre Précieux, Paris, 1962-69), he is also the Editor of *Les Cahiers Naturalistes*. Professor Mitterand teaches frequently as a Visiting Professor at the University of Toronto.

ROGER RAMSEY teaches at Rockford College (Illinois) and has published articles on modern literature in *Modern Fiction Studies, Studies in the Novel* and other periodicals.

W. D. REDFERN who teaches French at the University of Reading, England, is author of *The Private World of Jean Giono* (1967) and *Paul Nizan: Committed Literature in a Conspiratorial World* (1972), as well as a new edition of Jules Vallès *Le Bachelier* (1972). He has contributed widely to scholarly reviews and collected essays on such figures as Camus, Stendhal, Louis Guilloux and others.

LEON S. ROUDIEZ is Chairman of the French Department at Columbia University. He has contributed articles and reviews to the *French Review, Romanic Review, Saturday Review, New York Times Book Review, Symposium, Yale French Studies*, and *Critique* (Paris). He is the author of *Michel Butor* (Columbia University Press, 1965); and his *French Fiction Today: A New Direction* is scheduled to be published this June by Rutgers University Press.

MENO SPANN, Professor Emeritus at Northwestern University, is currently teaching as Visiting Professor at Michigan State. He has published many articles on such figures as Heine, Thomas Mann, and Kafka. His book *Heine* in the series *Studies in Modern European Literature and Thought* appeared in 1966; a book on Kafka for Twayne Publishers is now in preparation. He is also author of various German grammars and other college texts.

RENATE USMIANI is an Associate Professor of Literature at Mount Saint Vincent University in Halifax, Nova Scotia, whose special area of interest is modern drama. Recent publications include articles in *Modern Drama, Seminar* and the *Canadian Humanities Association Bulletin*; Professor Usmiani contributed an article to MOSAIC special issue *New Views of Franz Kafka* (1970).

EUGENIA NOIK ZIMMERMAN of the French Department at Carleton University (Ottawa) received her Ph.D. from Wisconsin. Author or co-author (with Germaine Brée) of articles in *Comparative Literature Studies, Criticism*, etc. she is currently preparing a book on "Metaphysics and Technique in the Expository Prose of Sartre, 1936-60" for publication by Mouton (The Hague).

JACK D. ZIPES, who teaches at N.Y.U., is author of *The Great Refusal: Studies of the Romantic Hero in German and American Literature* (1970); translator of Hans Mayer's *Steppenwolf and Everyman* (1971), and a co-author of *Crowell's Handbook of Contemporary Drama* (1971); he has been published in a wide variety of scholarly periodicals in both North America and Germany.

Forthcoming Special Issues:

Fall 1972

Ulysses and
The Waste Land
Fifty Years After:
A Retrospective View

●

Winter 1972-73

The Eastern European Imagination
in Literature

●

Spring 1973

The Major Novels of
William Faulkner